❖ ANNIE'S GIRL ❖

Maureen Coppinger emigrated to Canada in 1955, where she married and raised three sons. She worked as a school secretary for 25 years before retiring in 1994 and now spends her leisure time as a volunteer for the Galway Association.

Michael J. Coppinger is a writer and musician from Toronto, Canada. He is currently working on his first novel and a memoir, and teaches literacy and guitar.

Annie's girl

How an Abandoned Orphan Finally Discovered the Truth About Her Mother

Maureen Coppinger
with Michael J. Coppinger

MAINSTREAM
PUBLISHING

EDINBURGH AND LONDON

For my mother, who gave me life, and for my late husband, Jim, who lives on in my heart. For my three sons, John, Michael and Patrick, my two daughter-in-laws, Julie and Emile, and my two beautiful granddaughters, Chrissy and Francesca. And, finally, from the deepest part of me, this book is for each and every individual who suffered in the Irish industrial school system. For those who made it out and for all those who did not, it is for you, with my love.

First published in Great Britain in 2009 by
MAINSTREAM PUBLISHING COMPANY
(EDINBURGH) LTD
7 Albany Street
Edinburgh EH1 3UG

ISBN 9781845964931

A catalogue record for this book is available
from the British Library

Typeset in Caslon and Requiem

Printed in Great Britain by
Clays Ltd, St Ives plc

▦ ACKNOWLEDGEMENTS ▦

I would first like to thank Bill Campbell at Mainstream Publishing for choosing to publish my story, a decision that made a dream a reality and rewarded many years of labour. Thank you, Bill. Also at Mainstream, thanks to Paul Murphy, Ailsa Bathgate and Graeme Blaikie for their consummate professionalism, guidance and expertise during the final editorial stages of the book. And thanks to Fiona Brownlee and Emily Bland for their wonderful energy and talent in moving the book forward.

A very warm, affectionate and special thanks to Emma Walsh, of Walsh Communications in Dublin. Once my editor, and now my agent and more importantly my friend, Emma's expertise, direction, ceaseless energy and encouragement helped keep me going through all the days of doubt and waiting. You've been so much a part of this book, Emma, and I thank you with all my heart.

A special thanks to Fionnuala Donaghy in Toronto, Canada, for her sharp editorial eye and critical feedback on an early draft of the manuscript. Thank you, Fionnuala. Your advice helped changed the direction of the book and made a major difference.

I would also like to thank Dr Andrew Smith of Sunnybrook Health Sciences Centre in Toronto, who saved my life in 2000 when cancer returned a second time. Thank you, Dr Smith. You have given me the precious years I needed to tell my story.

I would like to acknowledge in memory my late husband, Jim, who spent so many hours without me at the family cottage when I needed to write and whose quiet support for the book was always present and always with me. Although you will never read the book, Jim, I know how proud of me you would be, and I miss you.

Finally, I can thank no one more than my son Michael, without whose skill, love of writing and dogged determination this book would not have been possible. I thank you, Michael, for all you have done during the long and often lonely process of writing my story.

❧ PREFACE ❧

OUR LADY OF SUCCOUR INDUSTRIAL SCHOOL, NEWTOWNFORBES, COUNTY LONGFORD, IRISH FREE STATE, 1933

It must have been spring. I remember walking in a garden among the flowers and holding a nun's hand. I remember looking up at the nun. I recall clearly that I wore a black-and-white checked coat with a black collar that day. The nun was leading me away. I was sobbing terribly and crying for my mammy. My mammy was leaving me – I knew she was. Why was my mammy not coming with me? Where was she going? What was this place? Why was my mammy leaving me there?

This fragment of a scene was my only memory of the day I was taken to the orphanage in 1933. It was a glimpse, a haunting detail torn from an unknown past. It would remain with me as the only link backwards to a world and a life before the orphanage. No details of the face of the woman who left me with the nuns survived with the fragment. Only the knowledge that the woman was my mammy, that she had always been my mammy, and that she'd loved me and then taken me one day to a strange place and left me there.

I had no idea that day that the place with the nuns and the garden with its wildly blooming flowers was called Our Lady of Succour Industrial School or that it would become my home and whole world for the next thirteen years. Other than this one memory, with its faceless mammy, there was no other world – my conscious life began in the orphanage.

I would learn many years on that my mammy returned a few weeks later to see me. She didn't find the same child she'd left there such a short time before. My beautiful blonde curls were gone, as my head was completely shaved, and my entire body was covered in ringworm. When I was brought before her, I refused to speak a word to her or to smile – I knew she was not there to take me home with her. I had gone somewhere inside myself, a three-year-old girl, numbed to silence by what must have been an unthinkable betrayal. Her visit could only have increased my confusion as I sat there helpless and silent. She was my mammy, and she had left me in this place. She was so shocked and appalled by my altered state that she fled the orphanage never to return.

And so my young life had changed: Mammy was gone, family was gone, childhood as I might have known it was gone. My world was now strange and foreign, my existence anonymous. I had become an orphan, a ward of the industrial schools.

❖ PART I ❖

OUR LADY OF SUCCOUR
INDUSTRIAL SCHOOL, 1936–46

❖ ONE ❖

The school day is at an end, and I've been ordered up onto the project table with another girl. The rest of my classmates have been sent out, and we are being punished. One at a time, we are hit across the bare legs with a cane, first the other girl and then me. I hear the swish of the cane and the sound of it hitting her hard on her legs, again and again. Breda Logan whimpers as she's hit, and I look straight ahead, my legs trembling as I wait my turn. Six times each we are hit, and the tears start to rise in my eyes. I try to stop them from spilling down my face, but I can't help it. I cry from the terrible stinging of the cane. 'Stop your crying this instant, Harte!' Sister Carmel shouts at me. 'Stop that! And you as well, Logan. Stop it!'

The fear of more blows is worse than the pain, so I stop crying, but I can still feel the sobs trying to jump in my chest. I'm being punished now because I've not memorised my catechism properly. My last punishment was for giving a wrong answer to an arithmetic question. Usually it's only the three slaps on each open hand held out. I've never been made to stand on the table like this before. Sometimes I don't know why I'm being punished, and I always try hard to memorise my catechism to save myself a beating. I hate being singled out by Sister, to have to stand up and recite something perfect in front of the others. 'Stand up, Harte!' she says, and I try hard to think of the right answer as I get out of my seat, then I feel the eyes of the others on me and my mind goes blank. I might get a little of the right answer out, but then I stumble and the rest won't come. 'Now then, Harte, we went over this lesson so many times. I expect you to know it!' Sister Carmel gets angry with me then, and I freeze, knowing that I'll get the usual three on each open hand.

'I don't know, Sister,' is all I can say, and the terrible feeling of fear comes into me.

'Come up here, then!'

School makes us afraid, and we don't know why the nuns are so cruel to us. We are only little.

It's after bedtime, and I lie awake in the night thinking about being beaten on the project table today. Why did Sister make us stand there like that? Now I'll worry that she'll do it again for some mistake I make in class.

Along the rows of beds in our dormitory, I hear a girl crying somewhere close by. She moans quietly in the dark, because we're to be silent – no talking or whispering is allowed, not a sound. I try not to listen to these noises because they'll make me worry more and maybe I'll cry, too.

There's always someone crying at night, maybe from bad earache or something else hurting them, and the little bugs that get onto us bite and itch and keep us awake if they get into the bed. Maybe the wet-the-beds lie awake worrying that as soon as they sleep they'll wet themselves and then be punished first thing in the morning for it.

There are only younger girls in our dormitory, and during the night we're left alone and no one bothers about us. Sometimes one of the girls will have a bad nightmare and scream out in the dark, and when it's quiet we can hear the scurry of a rat running along the pipes or under our beds.

The orphanage is the only place I know, and I've been here since I was very young. The sisters have never told me why I am here or anything about where I came from before the orphanage. I know someone brought me to the nuns, my mammy, but I can't remember her face or anything else about her. I remember one of the sisters bringing me away by the hand through the garden, by the flowers where the nuns sometimes walk.

I know there are other places outside the orphanage because of the externs, the children from the village who come to school with us each day. The village is Newtownforbes, I know that much, and I know about the Holy Family and Baby Jesus as well. He has a family and a mammy and a daddy, just as the externs do. But we're different from the externs, us orphans. I know because of the way we're treated by the nuns each day. The village children are never treated like us. Why am I so different? Why do the nuns treat us so terribly? And why am I in this place?

The externs are never punished like we are, but then it's true that they always get the answers right. Sister Carmel always calls us by our last names, while the externs are called by their first names. This always makes me feel less important than the village children, because I want to be called Maureen, and only a couple of the nuns do this. Most of us orphans have welts across our legs and back; some are new and others are old and healing a little. The externs sometimes look at the marks left on us. They don't think we know they're looking, but we do, and I'm sure they feel bad for us, but they can do nothing.

Nellie O'Brien is an extern in my class, and she's very nice. She has lovely clothes and wears different coloured ribbons in her hair and pretty ankle socks. I'm always dressed the same in my plaid dress and old black socks and everyday boots. I'm sure the little bugs that bite us don't bother Nellie – we never see the externs itch – and Sister doesn't beat Nellie and the externs or even slap them like she does us. I wish I was like Nellie, able to talk up to Sister and able to go home each day to a mammy and a daddy, and to have another dress and ankle socks. Sometimes I hear Sister say to Nellie, 'Take this note home to your mammy, Nellie,' and she smiles at Nellie when she says this. How nice it would be to get a smile from Sister Carmel and to be spoken to so kindly like that.

When I see how Sister is with the externs, I imagine being treated the way they are by the nuns. Maybe if I could please Sister Carmel more, it would be a little different and there might be less punishment. I try to, but she doesn't notice. Every day, it's always the same thing, being hungry and afraid of punishments, which stops me from learning my sums. Sister doesn't seem to care about us orphans, and this only confuses me about why I don't have a mammy and daddy. Where are they and why did they leave me here in this place with the nuns?

I see Sister Carmel and the other nuns every day, but I still have questions with no answers, like why they're called nuns and why they dress like they do. On the way to the chapel every morning, we walk past the convent where they live, but because I've not been inside there I don't know if they share a dormitory like we do. From the outside as we pass it, the convent looks very different from where we live. The walls aren't dark grey like ours, but a pale yellow stone made up of all different shapes, and they've long windows that reach almost to the ground. I told my friends the top of one of those windows looks like the moon when only half of it's showing. And they've a summerhouse, the nuns, with white benches and so many beautiful flowers round it, and little stone paths going here and there for them to walk on. They live in so beautiful a place, the nuns do, so why are so many of them so cross with us?

The orphans' lives are very hard here, but there are some good things, too, like my friends and Baby Jesus and God. My friends are Katy, Maggie, Colleen and Lucy. They're all in my class, and they've no mammy and daddy and don't know why they're here, either. Katy Fallon is my best friend, and she's short with dark hair and two lovely rosy cheeks like apples. Katy isn't timid like Colleen: she loves to talk and speak up in class, and she's very good at her lessons as well, which Sister Carmel likes. Outside at playtime, Katy will teach me the written subtraction when I'm finding it hard. 'Look, Maureen,' she says, writing on a big stone with a bit of chalk she sneaked out of our classroom. 'This is how it's to be done.' It's different as I watch Katy teach me, because she's a friend, and we care for each other.

Maggie O'Rourke is short and has straight brown hair and is always smiling, but she's more quiet and serious than the rest of us. Maggie is good in arithmetic as well, and she helps me with my sums, too, when we're in school. She watches everything and listens closely to what the older girls say, learning things from them that she can share with us.

Lucy Nolan has blonde hair and blue eyes, and gets very excited and fidgety. She'd talk and play all the time if she could, and her mind is always on her belly. She makes us giggle at our table, always wishing there were three of everything on her plate. We tell her that it will never be, but she still says it, and we laugh at her for dreaming of her belly again. Lucy is very curious like me. She likes to ask questions, and sometimes we share our thoughts with each other. 'I don't like this place, do you, Maureen?' she'll say to me, and I always say that I don't like it here, either.

Of my four best friends, Colleen Carey is the quietest. She's tall and skinny, and she has red hair and freckles. Colleen wets the bed at night and is punished in the mornings for it. That's what makes her so timid and unhappy, because she's one of the wet-the-beds. Colleen is the only one of my friends who wets her bed, and we can't understand why it happens to her every night. I pray hard to God to help her stop wetting her bed, and I thank him that I don't wet my bed as well.

I usually wake to the sound of hands clapping in the early morning. 'Time to get up, up!' calls the voice. 'Time to get up, children. Move now – move!' It's Sister Anthony, and we're terrified of her. She's young and very tall, with wire glasses and a little smile always on her face that frightens me.

There are close to thirty girls in our lower dormitory, with our beds set out in rows of three. The moment we hear the hands clapping, we're up and on our feet and making our beds as fast as we can without a word or looking at the next girl. Our mattresses are striped and have ticking covers filled with some kind of horsehair, and where buttons are missing the horsehair sticks out through the hole. A few of the springs on my bed are broken and part of it goes down in a hollow, but I don't mind because it makes me feel cosy. Most nights I sleep sound in my bed, but sometimes the horsehair sticks into me and I wake up, or the hollow in the bed makes me turn over. I don't like it when that happens, because then I'm awake in the night with all the frightening sounds around me, like the rats running along the pipes or the girls having nightmares. There are no nice smells here, only the stink of wet-the-bed all round the dormitory in the mornings. The heavy white sheets must hold the smell.

Sister Anthony stands in her usual spot with the ash-plant stick in her hand. It must be three feet long, and it's thick, the dark wood of it shiny. She watches us until we're finished making our beds. 'Those who wet the bed come up here,' she calls out, and five girls walk from their beds to one end of the dormitory with their heads down. Colleen is among them, and the rest of us must stand by our beds and watch. Each morning, I hope my prayers work and that Colleen won't be one of the wet-the-beds, but today we'll have to watch again while Sister Anthony beats her and the other four. When Sister raises the stick to hit the first girl, she has a smile on her face, and most of us move our eyes down to the floor. We don't want to see the miserable faces of the wet-the-beds, but we hear the blow of the cane on their bottoms and the whimpers that get louder on the fourth and fifth lashes. It's terrible to hear, and my legs shake from fright. I look up again to see Colleen with her head down and off to one side and her rough calico night shift pulled up. Sister Anthony is hitting her across the bare bottom with the cane, and I look away again, down at the floor. I want to cry every morning when I see this, but if I'm seen with tears in my eyes, I'll be punished as well.

Colleen's only in first class, and she might stop wetting her bed soon. She tells us that she's trying to stop, and we believe her. Maybe if Sister Anthony stopped punishing her the way she does, it would be different. Why is Sister Anthony so cruel to Colleen and the wet-the-beds? Please, Baby Jesus, I pray to myself. Please help Colleen to stop wetting her bed, then Sister will stop beating her . . .

Colleen has been our best friend since we were very little. We've stayed together like four sisters, and we care for each other the best we can, but we can never do a thing about Colleen's bed-wetting. She was just like us before Sister Anthony started punishing her every morning for wetting the bed. She would run and skip at playtime, and at the end of the day when she had the look of worry in her eyes, one of us would say, 'Maybe tonight, Colleen, you'll not wet the bed!' and she'd say, 'I know,' or, 'I know, but I try not to.' Now, little by little, we've noticed a change in Colleen at playtime. We're all seeing how far away she is from us and how she sits off on her own in a corner of the playground and just stares at nothing. We take turns going to her, trying to drag her out of it. Sometimes she'll just turn away like she doesn't notice us, and when she does join in our play, it's not long before she goes away again into her corner.

After the five are punished, we go to the wash basins to brush our teeth and comb our hair. Our bathroom has one big square tub in the corner, but we're allowed to bathe only once a week, supervised by the nuns. Beside the tub is one closed-off toilet that flushes with a long pull-chain, and the cistern is high up above the toilet. There are three sinks in the dormitory, where we line up at night to wash our faces before bed. The carbolic soap we use is in a big red bar at the sinks, and there's an even bigger one in the bathtub for our bodies.

It's always very quiet in the bathroom in the morning, with only the sound of girls dressing and sometimes 'Hurry now' and 'Move now, girls' from Sister as she stands watching. When the last of the girls finishes at the basins, we hear, 'Line up now, children,' and we jump to her command. In two long rows behind Sister Anthony, we leave our dormitory for the chapel and morning mass. Never is the order of the morning broken; so much as a whisper might get a girl punished, and outside when we're walking from place to place it's six slaps instead of three. 'Who whispered now?' Sister Anthony will say, stopping and coming back down the line. The girl who opened her mouth will then be pulled from the line by the shoulder. 'Hold out your hand!' she'll be ordered, and the ash-plant stick comes up and down six times. Sister Anthony is the only sister who has a big stick; the other nuns have canes. Maggie heard them called 'sally rods' by the older girls.

Down the wide stairs and out through a big wooden door we go, along past the cloisters to the long footpath that leads to the chapel. On the way, we pass by the nuns' garden and the old stone building where the laundry is, but we're not allowed near there. Even if I was allowed to walk up to the laundry, I never would because I'd be too frightened.

As we go past, we can hear the grinding of the machines and the awful rough voices of the workers shouting back and forth to one another behind the steamed-up windows. The older girls say the nuns send orphans to the laundry if they are bad and won't learn their lessons at school – laundry girls they're called. They weren't allowed to leave the orphanage when they turned sixteen, and now they're old women. They don't know anything other than the laundry, and we think that's why they're so mean looking, because they work so hard and still have to obey the rules like we do. These laundry workers follow behind us into the chapel for mass, where they sit in their own special pew in the side chapel across from us. I try not to stare at them during mass. They seem so mean and old; they'd as soon slap me in the face as look at me. And they look so unhappy. I don't want to look like that. How terrible it would be to end up in the laundry and never see the outside world. As we pass by the laundry building along the footpath, I often pray to Baby Jesus to keep me from going there when I'm sixteen.

❖ Two ❖

During mass, Sister Anthony sits behind us in our side chapel off the altar. The older orphans sit here, too, but they've their own dormitory upstairs from us. The nuns come into the chapel through their own door as we sing one of our hymns, 'The Bells of the Angeles' or 'Immaculate Mary, Our Hearts Are On Fire', walking in procession to their special stalls, two rows of them facing each other. Each one is a big chair made of lovely wood, with beautiful red cushions covering the seat part and carved crosses on the top with pretty designs on them. The reverend mother's stall is at the front, closest to the altar, and that's because she's the most important nun.

The chapel is my favourite place in the orphanage, and morning mass is my favourite part of the day. For a little while I can feel good inside as we sing our hymns and say our usual prayers, with my thoughts on God and Baby Jesus instead of worrying if Sister Carmel will be nicer today or if I'll be punished later. Father McClure is our curate, and he says mass in Latin, standing with his back to us as he faces the big crucifix behind the altar. The altar is so pretty, with lots of shiny white stone and lovely red carpets and two altar rails, one for us and one for the nuns. Father McClure is a very nice man, and sometimes after mass he comes over to our side chapel to talk to us. 'Good morning, children,' he says, smiling, and we always hope he'll ask one of us a question, anything at all to hear him speak in his kind voice and see him smile as if he cares about us. I know Father McClure is an important person, because Sister Carmel acts differently when he is around, and she smiles more. I never feel afraid of Father McClure, and I think he maybe knows what it's like for us to live in the orphanage.

After mass, we walk in line, back along the footpath to our dining hall by the nuns' vegetable garden. During mass, I think of food and eating a lot. I know it isn't right, as I'm to pray and think of God in the chapel, but it's very hard to pay attention at mass because we're always hungry.

Clap, clap, go Sister Anthony's hands once we're all in the dining hall and standing silently in front of our plates with our hands joined. 'Children, we will now say grace. In the name of the Father and of the Son and of the Holy Ghost, amen.'

'Bless us, oh Lord, and these thy gifts which of thy bounty we are about to receive through Christ our Lord, amen.'

We finish with the sign of the cross, and then there's a great noise as the benches are pulled out from the tables and the chattering starts. The older girls sit at long tables each side of us, but they must line up for their food, while we younger orphans have our own table in the middle of our big dining hall, with its bright-red brick floor and high windows. Finally, we can talk to each other without the nuns watching over us and listening to every word we say. But with the great clattering about us, we have to speak up loud. The tin plates and porringers (tin cups) on the table make an awful noise, with everyone eating and talking. Sister Michael and her helpers, the two old ones we call them, serve our food to us from a big wooden table. As Sister Michael gets close to us this morning, we give her big smiles in the hope she'll talk to us, and it works. 'Well, children, are you all eating enough, now?'

'Yes, Sister Michael,' we answer together.

'And what are all your names?' She knows we love to be asked our first names, because almost all the nuns call us by our last names only, and being called Maureen makes me feel more special. We all talk up, each after the last.

'I'm Katy.'

'I'm Maureen.'

'I'm Maggie.'

'Well, now, children, you all enjoy your porridge.'

'Yes, Sister,' we say together.

'And God bless you, children, you are very good children indeed.' And away she goes, back to her big table.

'I really like Sister Michael, don't you, Maggie?'

'I do, yes, she is always so kind to us.'

'Me, too,' says Katy, with her mouth full. 'But why are her cheeks always so red?'

'It must be from cooking our meals on the big stove,' I tell Katy. 'She's a big stove she cooks on.'

'I'd love to see this big stove,' Maggie says, looking over at Sister Michael, 'and I think Sister Michael likes little children.'

It's a little cold this time of the year, so after breakfast we're told to play in the recreation hall for a while before school. If we had warm clothes, we wouldn't feel the damp and cold, but we've only our usual light plaid dresses, underneath which we wear a homespun petticoat, which feels very rough on the skin, and striped underwear that comes down to our knees – our drawers, we call them. The sisters give us a clean pair of drawers when we have our weekly bath, but our petticoats are never changed. We'll wear them until we grow out of them, and the little bugs that bite and make us scratch get into the thick petticoats under the arms. We have to crack the bugs with our fingernails to get rid of them – that's the only way. Our clothes are never warm enough for the mornings when the frost is lying across everything outside, and in the evenings we're happy to be in the recreation hall, where we huddle in little groups by the radiators trying to stay warm.

The hall has plain grey walls and high windows like our dining hall, and a stage as well. We play here until the whistle goes for line-up, with two of the sisters walking about, checking on us. It's the same thing all through the day: hands clapping, then a whistle, or sometimes a bell, then lining up. 'Line up for school, children!' Sister Anthony calls out. If one of us isn't quick enough, we get a blow across the arm. I try to get in line as quick as I can, but those who dawdle at all will get a good blow with the stick for being too slow. 'You heard the whistle. Move along with the others, now.'

There are about twenty of us orphans in first class, and we wait silently in our line-up outside Sister Carmel's classroom until she comes to open the door and let us in. Today, I'm at the front of the line, and I peek through the blurry glass of the big square window in the classroom door. Things look odd and shadowy through the glass, and I watch closely until I see Sister Carmel stand up. I can hear her beads rattling as her dark shape moves quickly toward us. The fear comes into me then as I wonder whether she'll be nice today or not, then the door swings open and she looks down at us with a stern face. 'Good morning, children.'

'Good morning, Sister,' we answer together.

'Come in and stand by your desks.'

I sniff as I go by Sister Carmel to get the lovely smell from her. I can notice it when I'm close to her, and I always wonder what makes her smell so nice. We hang up our coats at the back then stand by our desks with our arms straight down at our sides, with no talking. Sister goes to the other door to let in the nine or ten externs, who go quietly to their desks and stand with the rest of us after they have hung up their coats. There are some boys among the externs, but they're very rough, the way they play and box each other in the yard outside, and I keep away from them.

Sister Carmel's look changes when the externs come in. She smiles at them and speaks to them in a gentler voice. We stare at them when they arrive in the morning, at their bright faces and their nice clothes with the earthy smoky smell on them. It must be from their houses in the village, and I smell it on Nellie O'Brien when she sits in front of me or when I breathe it in from her coat when she's hung it up next to mine. My friends and I love to look at the girls from the village to see what colour ribbons and socks they're wearing. How we must stand out alongside them in our drab plaid dresses. I worry that I smell because I'm wearing the same dirty drawers every day. I hope Nellie O'Brien and the other externs don't notice me that way. And most of all I wish I could leave at the end of the day and go home to a mammy and daddy.

Sister starts a Hail Mary to begin our school day. I love everything in Sister Carmel's classroom, like the pretend shop with a real counter in the front and shelves at the back full of pretend goods, and the paper money we use to learn to shop with. Going to the pretend shop helps me remember my arithmetic, as we take turns giving change back after we buy something. On the other side of the classroom is a small model of our real chapel where we go to mass every morning, and I know Mr Foley the carpenter from the village made it and the pretend shop, too. It's so beautiful, just like the real chapel, with the front left open so we can stand and look in at the tiny nuns' stalls along the sides. There's coloured windows as well inside it, and a lovely little altar with a red carpet and two little wooden kneelers. Mr Foley must be a great man to make something like this.

In another corner of our classroom is a table full of coloured wool and thick knitting needles, where we sit in a circle learning to knit. 'Bring the wool forward, now,' says Sister Carmel as she walks behind us, teaching us how to tie a knot and fix the wool to the needle before we start knitting. The needles feel thick and slippery in my hands. We must hold them a certain way, with Sister checking our work before we go on to the next step. I want to learn and please Sister Carmel, and I like knitting because I can do it a little better than some other things, and I feel relaxed at it. Not like when I make a mistake on my sums, which I get slaps for. That's what all the charts and numbers that cover the walls are for: learning and counting and sometimes reading from.

By the glass door that leads to Sister Brendan's classroom there's a beautiful piano that Sister Carmel plays on to teach us singing and dancing. I like the singing and dancing lessons best of all. Just like the knitting, I forget about being afraid, and I don't hear my tummy rumbling. There are some fun things in our first class, but because of the punishments when I do wrong in arithmetic and religion it's hard to learn my lessons. I get so scared when Sister asks me a question that I can't remember the right answer to. All I have left is to pray hard each day to Baby Jesus, to help me learn and not be so afraid.

When the bell sounds out in the halls, it's time to break for our midday meal, so we tidy up whatever we're doing and get into line. The cold porridge and the bread and dripping we get for breakfast never hold

us for long, and we're always hungry by the middle of the day. This is
our one big meal, and we get a potato, a small portion of vegetables
from Sister Michael's garden and maybe cabbage one day and turnip
or green peas the next. Another time we'll get a piece of beef or baked
fish, and I love to chew on the crispy part of the fish's tail. Never do
we leave a single crumb on our plates.

After we eat, if it's warm enough outside, we go to the little field
behind the recreation hall where we do all our playing. There's a long
cloister there as well, and we take shelter beneath it when it rains or
when bad storms come in the summer. In the field where we play,
there are three thick grey cement lavatories with rusty old metal roofs
on them. They're awful filthy things, with no paper for us to clean
ourselves. The lavatories are dirty and ugly, but the high grey wall
at the end of our playing field is worse. We hate this wall because
it keeps us locked in this place. There are cracks in it, and we peep
through them toward the green fields beyond and the outside world.
There's the green as well, where the older girls play special sports like
field hockey, and Father McClure comes now and then to stand at
the railings, looking down on their games. He'll smile and wave to
the girls, and they love this attention and will give him a big wave
back and call out, 'Hello, Father McClure!'

On the field where we play, there are girls of all different ages
together, sitting alone talking in their little groups or looking for
a spot of their own to play games. The older girls like the cloister,
where they can skip and bounce balls, or sometimes they sit close
and whisper, and we know they're telling secrets. There are bad fights
outside, and it's awful to see. Girls around the age of fifteen, they are,
and they fight by pulling each other's hair and using terrible words
like 'You aul scut' and 'I'll kill you. You're an aul tinker!' They keep
in little groups, these ones, and we stay away from them, because
they're awful bullies if you get in their path. We'll stay in our own
spot, my friends and I, but when the fights start we stand round like
the other girls and watch them pulling each other's hair until they're
almost to the ground and still screaming out the bad names at one
another. We'll look on at them until the sister in charge breaks it

up. Then it's inside for the two fighters, where they're certain to get a terrible beating as punishment.

Today, my four friends and I play tig, which we love. We like to be free to run about the place with no one to bother us for a time. 'Eeny, meeny, miny, moe . . .' we cry, our fists stacking one on top of the other to see who'll be 'it'.

'I'll be it today, I will. I'm it today!' Maggie says.

'No, me, I'm to be it,' says Katy.

Maggie is it first, and the rest of us run round the little area, in and out of the long cloister where the older girls sit. Katy, Lucy and I fly in little circles, here and there, running as fast as we can from Maggie and laughing as she gets close to us. The green and the cloisters seem so big to us, and there are many places to run. Maggie chases one of us then another until she catches Katy, then Lucy chases us, and we run and run, not wanting the great fun to end.

We get so tired after a while we have to slow down, our faces smiling in the fresh air and all of us breathing hard. It's then that I notice poor Colleen. Again she didn't want to play with us today, sitting off on her own and looking so sad and far away. She has her head down, just like in the mornings when Sister Anthony punishes the wet-the-beds. 'You might not wet the bed tonight, Colleen,' I say when I walk over to her.

'Think so?' she responds. 'I can't help it. I try . . .'

'I know you do, Colleen. Will you come and play with us? We want you to play with us the way you always did before.'

She looks up at me. 'Oh, all right, Maureen.'

We spend a little more time at tig and then it's on to playing family – it's one of our favourite games, and we don't want to waste a second of our playtime together. 'Maggie, Katy!' I cry out. 'Hurry or we'll not get the corner for ourselves.'

'I'm waiting for Colleen,' Katy shouts across to us. 'She's awful slow, she is!'

Maggie and I tear on ahead, along past the cloister to our favourite corner at the bottom of the yard. It's right in front of the high cement wall that hides us from the village and the world outside. I peek through the cracks in the wall as we wait, in the hope I'll see a cow grazing or maybe a donkey in the lovely green fields.

Colleen and Katy run up to where we're sitting, smiling with excitement, and the four of us make aprons of our dresses to collect the little stones along the bottom of the wall. These are our dolls, and we need different shapes to play family.

'Maureen, I've a large shiny one for the daddy,' Colleen calls to me.

Katy comes back with a smaller one for the mammy, and Maggie and I find little stones for the children. Lucy's caught up with us now, and the five of us sit in a circle, with Katy, Lucy and me taking turns drawing faces on the stones with a bit of chalk that Lucy sneaked from the classroom. Maggie looks at me, smiling as she and Colleen tear off little pieces of rag they have ready to wrap our dolls in. Soon we're done dressing the dolls and giving them little faces, and our pretend family is at last together. This is the best time of all for my friends and me, and it's so short a time when we're not afraid and playing at what we like. Colleen's the mammy first – it's special being mammy, so we take turns. She picks up the baby and hugs it close to her. 'Don't cry, baby, don't cry,' she says, looking down at the baby, rocking it back and forth.

We take turns acting like the different people in a family: washing the children, lining them up for school and putting them to bed when it's bedtime. When one of the children has an earache or a tummy ache, we always hug them to make it better.

'Don't wet the bed tonight,' Colleen whispers, hugging the stone baby doll close to her. We always tell the children not to wet the bed at night, and we try to be nice and to love them. We don't know how to play the daddy very well, but we always put him close by, sitting off to the side and watching over the family. We can think of nothing else in the world but our game by the wall, and when the sharp whistle sounds across the yard we look up, knowing now that playtime is all over and that we'll have to go back to life beneath the rules again.

'Ring a ring o' roses, a pocketful of posies. Atishoo! Atishoo! We all fall down.' The group of small girls across from us are just finishing in answer to the whistle. They fall about each other and down to the ground laughing, then roll over onto their knees to get up. Then I see one of the younger children standing up and crying. As I look at her, I see why she's so upset. A huge white worm thing is creeping down her leg and onto the ground. 'Oh!' I cry, running fast to Sister Elisabeth, Katy and the others right behind me. 'Sister! Sister Elisabeth, come quickly! Come quickly!'

She hurries over to me. 'What is it, Maureen?'

'There's a worm thing, Sister! On her leg! Oh, it's white and long and keeps coming down! What is it, Sister?' I'm really so scared now. As the little girl watches the thing slowly coming down her leg, her eyes pop open with the fright of it, and she starts screaming and crying. All the other children are gathered round now and pointing, saying, 'Look, Sister, look. What is it that worm thing?'

'Quiet, now, children. It's nothing at all! Hurry, now, all of you and get into your lines!'

Sister Elisabeth looks at the girl quickly and then takes her away by the hand, inside somewhere, maybe to the sickroom. My friends and I hurry off to get into line, all of us nervously looking down and feeling our legs beneath our dresses. I'm afraid now because I know the worm thing came from inside the little girl. All of us saw what happened, and we're terribly worried now that it will happen to one of us as we play.

❖ THREE ❖

I awoke to Sister Anthony's clapping hands as usual this morning, but I feel important and grown up, so I'm in a good mood today. My friends and I are seven now, the age when we make our First Confession. We know that these special days tell us how old we are by what the older girls say. First Confession is to prepare us for the most important day of all: my First Holy Communion, only two weeks away.

My classmates and I sit in the chapel waiting to confess our sins to Father McClure. I've heard all kinds of things about what confession will be like, so I look closely at the face of each girl ahead of me as she comes out of the little cubicle. I want to see if they've changed in any way from having to admit their sins, but they seem all right, even happy, so it can't be that bad. I've practised hard to know exactly what sins to tell Father McClure, but I don't know what my penance will be. I've talked in line-up, quarrelled with other girls, told some lies and sometimes I've had bad thoughts about Sister Anthony, wishing she would go away from here and never come back.

When my turn comes, I walk very slowly into the dark cubicle, kneel down, join my hands and wait for Father McClure to slide the little square window across. It opens, and I can see him dimly, behind another caged window. 'Tell me your sins, my child,' he says to me.

'Bless me, Father, for I have sinned,' I begin, saying all the words Sister Carmel taught us. I know Father McClure is listening closely, and I tell him all my sins like I'm supposed to. But I stop talking before I get out the bad thoughts about Sister Anthony.

'Is there something else, my child?'

'Yes, Father.'

'Well, tell me then. It's all right.'

His voice makes me feel safe to say it. 'I've bad thoughts sometimes, Father . . .'

'Yes, my child? Bad thoughts about what?'

'I've bad thoughts about . . .'

'Go on.'

'Bad thoughts about Sister Anthony, Father!'

Father McClure is quiet for a time, and I'm not sure if he's heard what I said. Is he trying to guess who I am by my voice? But then, only a moment later, he says, 'Practise obedience, my child, and for your penance say three Hail Marys.' He stops for a moment and then says, 'And pray for Sister Anthony.'

'I will, Father.' I make the sign of the cross, then I stand up and walk out of the cubicle back to my pew.

I say my Hail Marys right away and pray hard for Sister Anthony, whispering with my head lowered into my closed hands. 'Please, God, make me not be angry with Sister Anthony and help her to be kinder and to stop beating Colleen and the others who wet their bed.' I feel good now that I can tell God my sins, and it might help me when I get afraid or whenever the nuns punish me.

All day long I've been thinking about my penance, and I'm aching to learn what penance Father McClure gave my friends. They'll want to know what I got as well. As soon as we get to the recreation hall, we rush to find a quiet corner. 'I only got one Hail Mary,' Katy tells me.

'Me too,' Lucy says. 'One Hail Mary.'

'And you, Maggie?' I ask. 'What did you get?'

'The same – one Hail Mary.'

'You'll not believe it,' I say to them. 'Father McClure gave me three Hail Marys for my penance.'

'What?' Lucy cries. 'You must've a load of sins, Maureen.' I don't say anything, but I think it must be the bad thoughts about Sister Anthony that got me the bigger penance.

Outside, we play a game of tig on the grass, and I'm it. As we run about, I chase the others toward the old iron fence along one end of our playing field. Suddenly, I catch sight of Sister Michael through the fence as she stands up among the rows of vegetables, tending her garden. 'Hello, Sister Michael. Hello!' I call out to her, running up to the fence and forgetting all about tig. Maggie, Lucy and Katy rush up to join me. The four of us hold the rails with both hands, smiling through the wide gaps and hoping Sister Michael will come to us.

'Hello, Sister Michael,' we call together, and as she looks over with a big smile we call out again. 'Hello, Sister Michael!'

'Here she comes,' I whisper to the others. 'She's coming.' How we love it when this happens: Sister Michael bringing food over and being so kind to us! We don't take our eyes off her as she walks over.

'Hello, children,' she says as she takes little bits of vegetables from her apron and passes them through the railings to us: stumps from the cabbage, lumps of raw turnip and sticks of rhubarb, all grown in her lovely garden. 'Here you are, Maureen, Maggie,' she says. Her smile is nice, so warm. 'Enjoy it, now, children. Katy and Lucy, you must be hungry as well, I know. God bless you all, now. God bless you, children.'

'Thank you, Sister. Thanks so much, Sister,' we say, the four of us already chewing away on the cabbage stumps as we watch her go off along the rows of vegetables. Sister Michael uses our first names when she talks to us, and it makes me feel that I'm a separate person and not just another orphan.

'Isn't she kind?' Katy says. 'Isn't Sister Michael so kind?'

'Let's find Colleen,' I say. 'You know she won't talk up, but she'll be hungry, too, so let's share our treats with her.'

Colleen is off on her own, over in one of the corners, so I call out to her to come over and share the bits from Sister Michael's garden. She runs over, and the five of us devour the treats. We hardly ever have extra food like this, and I love to share with my best friends. 'Isn't that good, Colleen?' I say, in the hope she'll join in our chat while we eat. 'Isn't Sister Michael nice to us?'

'Ah, yes, Maureen, she's very good to us.' Colleen still has her head down as she eats, and it doesn't seem to matter what I say. She's so far away even when she's sitting right here beside us.

I hear the birds singing outside the dormitory window and the rows of beds are totally quiet. I lie awake, feeling terribly excited about the day ahead. Today will be so different, with no harsh punishments and not much lining up, just special activities, which means the nuns will be in better form. And our white dresses, they'll be so lovely. Oh, I feel so happy today, Baby Jesus. Thank you for making me feel so special inside.

I sit up a little in bed, and looking round I see other communicants wide awake and just as excited as I am. That's what we are on this special day: communicants.

At seven o'clock, Sister Anthony arrives, and as we get out of our beds she says, 'All children who're to make their First Communion will wait aside for Sister Carmel. All those who wet the bed come up here.'

Colleen Carey comes over to stand with us, and because she's a communicant, she'll not be beaten today. She's smiling already, and I know it's because the morning has started so differently for her.

Sister Carmel comes up to collect us. We go down to her classroom, and she has us stand in a little circle while she goes over the ceremony again. 'You are to live up to your First Holy Communion day and be on your best behaviour for Father McClure,' she says. 'Now, let's get you all dressed and prepared.'

In the little room off the classroom, we get into the special white dresses, to be ready for when the externs arrive. As we dress, I exchange looks and smiles with my friends, and I can see they're as excited as I am. How different it is to be wearing my long white gown, white socks and the soft veil with a bow on each side.

We go to the chapel and stand at one end, ready to walk slowly along the aisle to the altar. Nellie O'Brien, an extern, is walking ahead of me with her partner, and today I know that I look as good as she does, dressed nice and feeling clean. Colleen Carey is actually smiling over at me, and she's lined up with another quiet boy named Patrick Murphy.

My mind is wandering with excitement when the ceremony begins to the sound of the organ and the choir of older orphans singing 'Hail Queen of Heaven'. As I walk in procession with my partner Ralph, I see the faces of the parents from the village looking so proud of their children as we pass them in the pews. When the children before me reach Father McClure, they stop to receive the Body of Christ. With only three pairs ahead of me, I feel nervous as I stand waiting with Ralph. Then we're in front of Father McClure: 'Body of Christ,' he says as I stare at the Sacred Host in his hand.

'Amen,' I answer, and he places the dry wafer on my tongue. I close my mouth tight as I walk back to our pew, for fear the wafer will drop out. I kneel down with the others, thinking serious thoughts about the Body of Christ. I try to think of nothing else, and, as curious as I am, I don't look over at the families until the ceremony is finished.

When all the children have had their turn and the ceremony at the altar ends, Father McClure blesses us then shakes hands with Sister Carmel and the parents, whom he knows very well. Ralph and I stay together as we leave the chapel, but as soon as we're outside the externs go off ahead of us with their parents towards the convent while we wait for Sister Carmel to come out and take us over separately. For once, we can do anything we want: call back and forth, and skip, run and jump without anyone bothering us.

'Come along now, girls!' Sister Carmel calls to us as she hurries out of the side chapel.

'Now we'll see,' Katy says to us as we walk back towards the dining hall, 'if what we've heard is the truth or if it's just made up by the older girls.'

'I tell you, it will be. There'll be loads of food! It's true!' Lucy won't hear of it not being true.

'Sure, we won't know until we see for ourselves!' That's Maggie. She likes to think about things carefully and see for herself.

Sister Carmel stops us before we enter the convent and gets our attention by clapping her hands lightly. 'Now, children, this is your special day, and Reverend Mother is waiting to see you in her parlour when you're finished eating. You all look lovely, so go in and enjoy yourselves.' Sister's smiling a lot at us today, as if she really cares and is happy to see us enjoying our special day so much.

We go inside, and I see a big hallway with long windows on one

side: these are the ones that we can see from the path we take every
day to the chapel. How different it looks from the inside: the floors
are so shiny and everything is so clean and proper. There are holy
pictures hanging on both sides of the hall, and the smell of cooking
coming from the nuns' kitchen fills the air. We can hear the voices
of the parents gone on ahead into the refectory with their children,
and all of this makes us lose our tongues because we don't think it
can be happening to us. Sister Carmel tells us to have a good look
around, and I go right over to stand in one of the windows where
I can see the path we take every day. Maybe one of the sisters has
stood here, right where I stand now, watching us as we pass on our
way to mass in the mornings.

After we've all walked about and had a good look around, Sister
Carmel calls us. 'Come along now, girls. It's time for your breakfast,'
she says, and we move on, all of us looking with big eyes at this
world so different from ours.

In the refectory, I sit with my friends and the other orphans at
a round table, gaping over my shoulder to see what will be brought
to us. The externs sit with their parents and the nuns at a different
table. When I see the food being carried over by some young novice,
I know that what the older girls said was true. We can only gawk;
none of us has seen food like this before. There's bacon and eggs,
sausages, pots of jam, fried potatoes and fresh milk to drink. None
of us is able to get the words out to talk about it, so rather than
bother we devour everything in front of us without stopping, for
fear the food will disappear if we wait. The sausages, jam and fried
potatoes aren't the end of it, either, because after this the novice
brings out a tray of cakes. We eat and eat, loving each second of
it until, finally, Sister Carmel claps her hands quietly to get our
attention. She announces we're to have a visit to the parlour to see
the Reverend Mother Xavier, and right away there are whispers as
we try to guess what it will be like to see her parlour and what she
does in there.

We follow Sister Carmel out of the refectory and further down
the long hallway through the lovely convent with its shiny floors,

listening to all the sounds that echo and bounce about in the quiet. We come to a door where Sister Carmel stops, puts a finger to her lips to hush us and then knocks lightly. 'Come in,' a voice calls out, and we know that it must be the Reverend Mother Xavier. 'Welcome, children, to the nuns' convent,' she says with a smile as we go in and stand in a circle before her. 'Don't you look so lovely today – just lovely in your beautiful white gowns.'

'Good morning, Reverend Mother,' we answer together. I've not seen Reverend Mother Xavier so close up before, and she looks older, but her face seems kind behind her glasses.

How lovely the parlour is, with the beautiful furniture and the chairs with high backs on them, and a long table with candleholders and sofas with legs of shiny wood. The wooden floors are very clean and they smell of polish, and there's some sort of stuffed bird by the looks of it, resting up high on a ledge. I catch Katy's eye and then flick my own eyes back up at the bird. That'll be a thing to talk about: where that bird came from and why the Reverend Mother keeps it up there like that.

We don't stay long in the parlour, but before we leave the Reverend Mother invites us to play outside. 'I want you all, on this special day of your First Holy Communion, to feel free to roam the garden now that you've had your breakfast. Enjoy yourselves, now, children.'

Off we go outside, along the paths of the garden in amongst the different flowers, and I feel I'm in another world altogether. There are pansies and daisies and buttercups and even some rose bushes – the nuns have taught us all the different names of flowers. I feel like a butterfly as we play among the many bright colours, and I wish I could feel like this every day. On to the summerhouse we run, stopping there to talk to some older nuns who are sitting reading there. 'Look, the older sisters are sitting meditating,' I whisper to the others before we're close.

'Meditating, Maureen?' Katy laughs at my word. 'Sure, they're reading not meditating.'

Lucy looks over at the sisters then says to us, 'And why can't they be doing both?'

'Will you be quiet,' Maggie whispers. 'They're sure to hear you!'

'Ah, now,' says one of them to us, 'you do look lovely today, girls. Very lovely indeed.'

'Thank you, Sister!' We love to hear this said to us; it feels so nice.

Some of the externs' parents have come out after breakfast to sit on the summer benches along the path while the externs run among the flowers as well. We play by ourselves, me and my four special friends. Even Colleen is smiling today, and she has a bounce in her step like the rest of us. We don't want this to end, but, like when we play family with our stone dolls, the whistle will blow and we'll have to go back to the orphanage and back to the way it always is. When the whistle sounds for us to line up, we'll know it's time to go back and get out of our First Holy Communion dresses. They'll be put in the press until the next year's communicants use them on their own special day.

Our summer holidays, which began in July, are over, and it's the first day of school. The nuns have kept us busy with ball games and skipping ropes, and regular walks through the village or along the Sligo road in the other direction. The older girls have played hockey, and they went on a lovely picnic to the River Shannon. I'll be able to do these things with my friends when I'm old enough, and I can't wait, especially for the picnic day.

We've already been given our new boots, which we get at the beginning of each school year in September. By this time each year, our boots are always so full of leaks and our socks so full of holes that as soon as we get the new ones we throw out the old ones. The new leather has a lovely smell, and all the girls like to sniff their new boots before they put them on.

All my closest friends are with me in Sister Elisabeth's second class. It's obvious straight away that she really is a nice teacher. She praises our work and calls us by our first names, just like Sister Michael does, and this year I'll learn my lessons better because I won't be afraid like I was with Sister Carmel. It'll be like a load is lifted from off me. 'You've done well, Maureen,' she'll say. 'And you, too, Maggie. That's good work indeed.' Her classroom is very plain, not like Sister Carmel's, but I'll learn to read better, and I'm sure my arithmetic will be a little better, too.

At the end of class, Sister Elisabeth tells us a surprise. 'Now, children, today I'm allowing a little time for your questions. I'm sure some of you must have something you'd like to ask, something that's been on your mind for a time. Anyone?' I've long wanted to know how I came to the orphanage, and I don't think she'll tell me that my question is silly. There are looks round the room to see who'll ask first, then still more gawking at one another. When no one moves, I throw up my hand, hoping Sister Elisabeth will pick me. 'Yes, Maureen, what is your question?' she asks, and her smile makes me feel safe.

'How did I get here, Sister?' I ask.

This is quite a bold question that I've asked, and there's much stirring and settling in seats as the children, especially the other orphans, wait to hear the answer. All eyes are fixed on Sister Elisabeth. 'Well, Maureen, yes, I can answer that for you,' she says. 'You were only three years old, the day you came here. I was in charge of the pre-school children that day, and you were given to me, and, well, you were crying for your mammy very badly, and I couldn't get you to stop crying. "I want my mammy, I want my mammy," you cried again and again. I held you and rocked you for a long time, and finally you stopped crying and fell asleep in my arms. So that's how you came here, Maureen. That was your very first day here at the orphanage.'

'Thank you, Sister, for telling me that.'

'All right, Maureen, is there another question? Speak up while you have a chance.'

One of the externs throws up a hand to ask a question, but while Sister Elisabeth answers I'm in another world altogether. I only asked her one single question, but now I've so many more, all coming from what she told me. Please! Please! Sister Elisabeth, tell me more about my mammy! Where did she go? Who is she?

I feel very different inside now and closer to Sister Elisabeth, knowing it was she who held me in her arms the day I came here. I feel important, and I can feel the eyes of my best friends on me, looking at me as if I'm special and different now. Maybe my mammy will come back for me one day and tell me why she left me in this place. Sister Elisabeth's story has given me a new kind of hope. I feel it building up inside me. I sit lost in a dream, thanking God. I feel so grateful to finally hear more and add to the one little memory I have about my first day at the orphanage. It is so much more than I've ever hoped for.

When I'm in bed, I think about what Sister Elisabeth said so many times that I can't sleep. I must've loved my mammy if I was crying that way for her. Oh, how I wish I remembered her face. But why did she leave me in this place? Was it something very bad that caused it to happen? I think that's what I really wanted to ask Sister. But I could tell, after she answered me, that it was all I would get, and I felt too afraid to ask more.

The next day, I notice that the bug things are back and all over me. I turn to Katy. 'Katy, do you have the bugs on you?' I ask.

'I do, Maureen, I think, and I saw something crawling, I did. Did you?'

'I did, and they bite terribly.'

We ask the others, and all of us seem to have the bugs, biting us and driving us mad. They're on my clothes and under my arms and around my neck. The nuns must have seen us all scratching like the devil, because, just as we're talking about it, in walks Sister Brigid with a helper. 'Line up now, children, at the washroom, and you'll be done one at a time.' Wearing a big white sheet, gloves and a white apron, she pours out a grey liquid from a big drum into the bowl. I watch from the line as the other girls are done by Sister Brigid. She takes a fine comb, dips it into the liquid and then combs it through the girls' hair. 'This will get the nits out. They're the eggs, the babies of the lice, the little pests on your scalp,' I hear Sister Brigid say, and I think that's what they must be called, what we have on us: lice. Another girl behind heard the name, too. 'That's what we've got:

lice,' she whispers to another behind her, and the whisper goes back along the line to all the others waiting.

As each one gets to Sister Brigid, I feel afraid because they're crying from the sting of the grey fluid on their heads. I see the nits on the comb and watch them fall into the bowl as she dips the comb again. My turn comes, and I feel like running away, but then I'll still have the lice things. Sister Brigid, her hands seeming big in the rubber gloves, pulls sections of my hair apart as she checks my scalp. 'You're not quite as bad as the others,' she says. Then I feel wet and then burning. I squeeze my eyes shut and make tight fists as it burns, the comb sliding roughly across my head and through my hair.

Finally, Sister Brigid finishes dousing us all in the awful grey liquid and sends us outside. We chat about which one of us still burns the most from the lice treatment. I hear an older girl say how the lice are still in our beds and that they'll only come back again, and she's right about that, because that's what always happens. Before long, they will come back, and the scratching and itching will start all over again.

✦ FOUR ✦

I t's winter now, and getting close to a very special time of year for us: Christmas, when we celebrate the birth of Jesus. As the weather gets worse, the wind howls through the yard and the cloisters, and at night we hear it blow through the cracks in the windows of our dormitory. The bitter frost lies across our playing field like a white sheet, and Lucy always says that it's a ghost and it fell during the night. We're not able to go outside and play our favourite games, so instead it's off to the recreation hall to play inside. The externs have lovely gloves and scarves to keep them warm, but we've nothing like that of our own.

Long before Christmas arrives, we begin to feel the excitement build, because we know how exciting everything will be, especially on Christmas Eve and Christmas Day. The first big thing to happen is our Christmas play. Each year, the younger orphans perform for the villagers and Father McClure. Katy, Maggie and I will be performing with some of the older orphans in a play with two parts, and the younger children will do a dance called 'The Gypsy Dance'. They'll be dressed as gypsies in bright skirts and scarves that Sister Elisabeth made. Rehearsing for the big Christmas play is so exciting, and this will be our first time to act in a real play in front of Father McClure and the villagers. I'm to play the character of a nurse. Acting in a play makes me completely forget where I am for a little while. We're so excited that Katy, Maggie and I can't help whispering about our play during line-up, but we must be careful not to be caught by Sister Anthony.

Each year, a life-size manger is put up in one of the side chapels, with Baby Jesus lying in his cradle while Mary and Joseph stand watching over him. There are three wise men and two shepherds as well, with a lamb and a donkey lying down. The manger calms my heart, and I remember what we've been taught about Christmas: that Christ was born to help the world with all of its sins. With thoughts like these, I'll worry less, but I still think constantly about someone coming to visit me.

I know why I'm lonelier inside at Christmas: it's the Christmas parcels and visitors that many of the girls get at this time of year. The parcels are full of beautiful treats sent from families in the outside world, or just from someone who is being kind to one of the girls at Christmas. For weeks before Christmas, I pray hard that maybe this year I too will get a parcel. I dream that it might be my mammy remembering me, and this year it's been bothering me more because of what Sister Elisabeth told me about the day I came here.

On Christmas Eve morning, we wake to Sister Anthony's clapping as usual, but she doesn't call the wet-the-beds up to be beaten, because it's a special day. After we wash and brush our hair, it's off to the dining hall with big hopes of a day filled with excitement and thinking of the freedom we'll enjoy. The dining hall looks beautiful, and there's a lovely smell from the plum puddings hanging on the ceiling. Sister Michael mixes plums, raisins and currants in a big cloth and hangs about six of them on the ceiling to ripen them for our Christmas Day dinner. And it is Sister Michael herself who serves our breakfast today from the big wooden table. This is such a treat and a change from the two old ladies who always serve us. I look up at Sister Michael's smiling face as I stand in front of her; it's all red from cooking over the big black stove in the kitchen. I don't take my eyes from what she's doing as she puts two slices of bacon on my plate as well as the usual bread and dripping. It's a real treat to have two slices of bacon on our plates.

At dinnertime, Lucy is just in front of us as we line up to be served. She strains hard to look up ahead, trying to find out what the treat is. 'Sister Michael's serving us again,' she says, looking round excitedly.

Finally, we reach the big wooden table at the front and are served roast beef, green peas from the garden and roast potatoes with gravy. Our surprise is a large baked apple with custard. We've tried to guess what it would be all day long. 'Thank you, Sister, thank you,' is all that can be heard.

We walk back to our table, and Lucy is already going on about tasting the lovely treat. 'Look at the size of them, will you? The apples!' she cries.

We sit down and devour our special meal, chatting away and enjoying our Christmas Eve as much as we can.

In the recreation hall after dinner, I call Colleen over for a game of see-saw, Marjory Daw, a game we made up ourselves, where one girl sits on a bench facing out to the hall and links arms together at the elbows with another girl sitting the opposite way, facing the wall. Then, back to back, we pull hard, rocking back and forth and singing, 'See-saw, Marjory Daw, Johnny shall have a new master. He shall earn but a penny a day, because he can't work any faster!'

Colleen loves this game, and she joins in with us. 'Look at Colleen, Maureen. She's smiling,' Katy says to me quietly. 'Maybe she's coming out of what's wrong with her.'

We go on having a wonderful time playing see-saw and then a little game of tig as well, until the loud clapping of hands stops all of us in the middle of what we're doing. It's time for the parcels. Sister Carmel waits until all the girls are quiet and listening. 'All of you know that this time each Christmas Eve the gift parcels sent from outside are given out. One at a time, I'll be calling out the names of those girls who have received something. Listen for your name if you're expecting a parcel, and the rest of you go on playing quietly until I have finished.'

The hall quietens down a little as the parcels are given out, but only those fortunate ones will be called up to the stage by Sister Carmel and handed a parcel. I sit with my friends on a bench off to the side, watching as one at a time each lucky girl walks up to get her parcel. It's so easy to spot the ones expecting something: they're all crowded round near the stage and are barely able to hold in the joy they feel. They dance on the spot and wring their hands, so excited are they to be getting something. We look on, trying to imagine what it would be like to be them now, but as the pile of parcels on the stage gets smaller and smaller, none of our names are called. 'There's still a little hope, Maureen,' Katy says quietly to me. 'Maybe your mammy who left you here with Sister Elisabeth will send something this year.'

'Oh, I really don't care, Katy, who the parcel would be from. Any parcel at all would be so nice, don't you think?'

'Yes, it would, Maureen, getting anything at all,' Lucy answers, but with sadness in her voice now, because we all know that there's little chance we'll get anything. No parcels and no visitors again this Christmas.

We've never had sweets, and we try to guess what treats might be in a parcel and what else a family might send to an orphan. As the final parcel is handed out, we turn away, watching the girl skip off with it to a little group of her waiting friends; they'll devour them later in the dormitory when we're allowed to sit up and talk before midnight mass.

After the parcels are handed out, we gather round for the Rosary, and then we line up to go back to our dormitory to rest up for midnight mass. Sister Anthony watches while we line up in front of our wash basins, and when we've cleaned our teeth and brushed our hair, we go to stand beside our beds to undress under our large white calico shifts. The shifts are big and wide and very rough on the skin. We undress beneath them because of the modesty the sisters are always talking about.

Finally, Sister Anthony leaves the dormitory, and we can chatter away without worry about anything we want. 'Are you sleepy now, Katy, or are you still awake and excited?' I call to her from my bed.

'I am, Maureen,' she says, and we burst out giggling, rolling around on our beds because Katy's mucked up the answer.

'Maureen asked you if you were awake or sleepy, and you said, "I am, Maureen!"' Lucy says, teasing Katy, and we can't stop giggling. Katy blushes red but still she laughs at herself.

'Maureen,' Lucy calls out when we quieten down a little, 'I'm not going to be able to close my eyes, I just know it!'

'You will, Lucy,' I say. 'We need to be rested to sing all the hymns.'

Lucy only gets more excited by this, tossing around on her bed to face me with her big blue eyes. 'Maureen, I can't wait for the feast tomorrow morning and again at lunchtime,' she says, with her chin on her two folded arms as she chats to me. 'And tonight after midnight mass we've the big currant bun to look forward to. I hope my bun is a huge one!' I hear the noise of her bedsprings squeaking as she settles down, thinking only of her currant bun, I'm sure.

'I can't wait to sing "Silent Night" at midnight,' Maggie calls out before flopping over the other way to say something to Katy.

Slowly, it gets quiet in our lower dormitory. I lie awake with my eyes open for a little while longer, listening to the voices at the far end of the dormitory and the rustling of paper from the girls sharing treats from their gift parcels. Finally, I drift off to sleep, thinking of the special ceremony ahead.

When Sister Anthony's clapping hands wake us again, we're up in a moment. Full of excitement, we wash and change into our dress uniforms, and walk over to the chapel for midnight mass. The younger children are all seated in the front rows of the chapel, and the beautiful manger is in full view off to the side of us. I try my hardest not to think about the currant bun during mass. I know my friends are thinking of it as well. Father McClure will be here soon, and maybe he will come over after mass and talk to us.

The organ comes to life and begins to play 'Adeste Fideles', the opening hymn, and we begin to sing. All through the mass, we sing our hearts out in Latin, and finally, right at midnight, we sing 'Silent Night' as the nuns walk in twos towards the manger. I feel my voice blending with the other girls as the nuns move in their solemn procession by the manger through the soft lighting of the chapel. I feel part of something so beautiful, and my heart is lifted up, and I get lost in the moment. How I wish it was like this all the time.

As we walk back to the dormitory after midnight mass, each of us has a currant bun in our hands. We try to make them last, because we'll not see another one now until next Christmas. Lucy keeps licking the icing off the top of hers and saving the rest of it. 'Ah, look,' I say to her. 'You've got a big fat one like you wished for!'

In the morning, mass is very short and without the singing, but we don't mind this. We still have one more day where we can ignore the rules. We chatter away to one another about the same things we did yesterday, and what we'll get for each meal. Our last special breakfast comes and goes so fast, and the taste of the sausages and bacon will have to last us all for another year.

All the plum puddings are gone from the ceiling. Sister Michael has taken them down to be cut up for today's Christmas Day dinner. Though they're gone, a little is left in the air of their beautiful scent.

Colleen Carey sits across the table from us, and I don't think she's as happy as she was yesterday. She's back to staring into the air at nothing again. 'Colleen,' I say to her, 'we're going to play see-saw again in the hall, your favourite game.'

But she only nods to me. 'All right, Maureen.'

We run about the recreation hall, playing and skipping until we finally see an empty bench where we can play see-saw. As the others run to claim the bench, I go and get Colleen as I promised I would. I find her off in a corner, sitting alone. 'Come on, Colleen,' I say gently to her. 'Come on for see-saw. We've a bench like I promised. Come on.'

Colleen comes out of herself a little as we play, but tomorrow she knows that if she wets the bed, she'll be beaten again – that's what she's worried about. How much more of these beatings can she take, I wonder? Her bottom must be black and blue with welts from Sister Anthony's stick. At night, I can often hear Colleen tossing and turning in her bed, crying out as she tries to find a good spot to lie on. I often whisper to God before I fall asleep, 'Sister Anthony has a lot to account to you for, God.' Then my bad thoughts come, the ones I'm not supposed to have that get me the extra penance now that we go to confession once each week.

When we're called to the dining hall for the last of our special meals on Christmas Day, I know that all my friends feel the way I do, but we say nothing to each other about it. We don't want this special time of the year to pass us by, and tomorrow it will seem to us as if it was never here at all. We'll hear, 'All those who wet the bed, come up here!' again, and the rules and line-ups will all be on top of us again.

Spring has arrived. I don't miss the damp and the frost of winter, and it's nice to run free outside in the warmer weather.

As we play in the sun today, a long shrill whistle sounds. It's Sister Carmel, calling all the orphans inside to the recreation hall. We stop playing as we notice a group of older girls huddled together and talking excitedly, some of them pointing and gesturing. Something unusual must be going on. As we hurry inside, Lucy runs off to find out what's going on, then flies back, breathless with her news. 'Two of the older girls tried to escape from here. They went over the walls, and the Gardai has just brought them back. They're to be punished for it!'

We know that all the walls have shards of glass fixed into the top. I wonder if they've been cut trying to climb over. All the girls stream inside, some of the older ones still whispering. 'Sure, they didn't get far at all,' I hear someone say.

'Silence in line!' Sister Carmel shouts at us. 'Hurry along now, all of you! Inside, move!'

Inside, the two girls stand in the centre of the recreation hall; they look so terrified, standing defeated with their chins on their chests as they wait for Sister Anthony to finish speaking to us. One, I see, does have a gash of blood above one of her hands, and some of it is dripping off onto her dress. With the awful stick in the other hand, Sister Anthony points her arm at the two senior girls as she looks at us. 'These two foolish girls are to be an example, an example of what will happen to any of you who try to escape from this institution.' She pauses only for a moment, the arm still pointing as the strange smile appears on her face. 'And did they get far, you're all wondering? I'm sure that's what all of you are thinking at this moment. The answer to that is no, they did not get far! Just down the road, in a foolish, desperate attempt to leave. None of you will get far from here should you be as foolish as these two! There are consequences for being foolish. Now then!'

She turns to the girls, one of them trembling at the knees as the tears stream down her face, shouting at them to lie across a large wooden bench. She begins beating them across the arms, legs and back. She keeps on beating them until finally one of the girls cries out, 'Please, Sister! I'll never run away again. Please, Sister Anthony, I'll not do it, never again, never . . .'

'I don't think you will!' she screams at them, and then she turns to all of us watching. 'I don't think they will do it again!' She then beats them both harder with the big ash-plant stick, across the bare legs now.

I watch, terrified, hating to hear the awful sound of their screams as they plead for her to stop. I hold back the tears that want to burst from my eyes. Please, Baby Jesus, make her stop, make her stop. Maggie and the others are terrified as well, but the older girls have a different look in their eyes. They don't seem afraid like us; they seem bold and look as if they hate Sister Anthony. Maybe I'll be like them when I'm older.

I've felt sick and afraid all day in school, and none of us have been able to talk about what we saw until now that we're outside sitting together on the grass with none of the sisters around. 'I will never try to escape from here,' Katy says.

We nod our heads, agreeing, and after a while Maggie says quietly, 'I think Sister Anthony liked to beat those two older girls.' Again, we agree by nodding our heads. But none of us can find a way to say how terrified we are, how afraid all the girls will be in our dormitory at bedtime tonight when Sister Anthony comes in. We sit quietly for a little longer then Katy suggests we play our wishing game. The dandelions, round balls of grey fluff, stick up through the grass in the yard at this time of year, and we like to blow on them and make wishes. After running off in different directions to find a good wish dandelion, we stand in a small circle. Katy goes first, closing her eyes with the dandelion held up and ready. 'I wish for someone to come and take me from this awful place!' she cries out and then opens her eyes and blows hard on the top of her dandelion. We watch as the little pieces of grey fluff fly off, drifting up into the sky like tiny little birds across the fields, taking our hopes and our dreams to the outside world. These are our precious wishes, hundreds of them, and we follow the little pieces as they disappear, praying that our wishes will come true. My wish is always the same: to hear one of the nuns say, 'Maureen Harte, please come to the parlour. There's a visitor to see you.'

Five

My friends and I are now nine, and we've moved to the dormitory upstairs. We've been given beds among the rows of younger girls in our own section at one end of the dormitory. I feel very grown up living with the older girls there, but what I like best is that my bed is near a window that faces the village, while the windows on the other side face the cloisters and the green. As soon as I get a chance, I'm going to stand at that window and look out over the rooftops and the fields below. From there I'll be able to look out as far as my eyes can see, and dream and try to imagine what it's like in the outside world.

It's summer, and the nights are pleasant. As I fall asleep, I can hear braying donkeys and barking dogs through the open windows. I listen to these sounds from outside, rather than the sobbing of the orphans or girls having nightmares. When I get a chance, I look down on the village from the window near my bed, where I can see far across the green shades of the fields and into the distance. I look out at the mounds of hay and at the cows grazing and moving slowly about. I daydream and let my thoughts run free. The smoke from the village chimneys swirls up in grey wisps that disappear into the sky. It isn't often I get a chance to stand at the window, and I must be quick about it. Not even my best friends know about my special window, and I'll tell no one – it will be my very own secret place. It will help me have hope that one day I'll get out of here.

It's my third night in the new dormitory, and something has disturbed me in my sleep. Am I dreaming, I wonder? Then I hear whispered voices next to my bed, even though it's well after lights out. 'Maureen, wake up. Ssh, now . . .'

'What! Who is it? What do you want?' I mumble, still half asleep.

It's no dream, only Rita Duffy and one of her friends. 'Ssh, it's just me, Rita. Come on,' she says to me. 'Come to the window and you'll see now what I've told you, about the dead ones standing there.'

For days now, Rita has been telling me about the nuns who've died here and are buried below in the cemetery. They've been seen walking about round the cloister below our dormitory. As frightened as I am, I cannot help myself. I slide out of bed and put my hand in Rita's, letting her pull me along towards the window. The three of us are like little ghosts in our loose calico shifts, padding silently across the wooden floors in our bare feet. 'They stand looking up at us, the dead nuns,' Rita whispers to me. 'Didn't I tell you? But it isn't every night they appear, Maureen. Isn't that right, Eileen?'

'It is,' Eileen Quinn whispers back. ''Tis the moonlight that brings them out.' In the quiet I can hear the wheeze in little Eileen's breathing. That's what everyone calls her: little Eileen Quinn. She suffers from a bad chest, and when she gets frightened or excited, she starts to wheeze.

My heart knocks with excitement and dread as I wonder if I will see one of the walking dead tonight. There is, I notice, a high round moon flooding the dormitory with pale light, as if looking in at the sleeping girls. 'Go on, Maureen, have a look,' Rita whispers to me at the window.

She and Eileen take a step or two backward as they glance around. On the tips of my toes, I stretch up, trying to get my balance on the little ledge to see properly. I look down into the shadows, my eyes moving slowly along the length of bench beneath the rippled iron roof of the cloister. Then my heart leaps! I do see! There's a nun standing there looking up at me! I can't see her face, only the white gap at the front of her habit. 'She's there. I saw her. I did!' I hiss under my breath as the three of us fly across the moonlit dormitory, back to the safety of our beds.

We have been in our new dormitory for a week, and it's time for our baths. At one end of the bathroom, I stand in line, according to my age, waiting with the others to bathe. Sister Benedict is a stern nun with the same expression always on her face, and she never smiles at us. She is very strict about cleanliness and modesty. She'll inspect us when we get out, sitting on her chair at one end.

When it's my turn, I undress behind a big white sheet held by two girls so my body won't be seen. Then I get into the big bathtub, where seven or eight girls have been before me in the same water. My foot splashes through the grey scum floating on the top as I step in, and I try not to look at it as I scrub myself hard with the red bar of disinfectant carbolic soap. Meanwhile, the two girls holding the sheet look obediently towards Sister Benedict, their eyes averted from my unclothed body. They wrap the dry sheet around me when I step out. Then, behind a curtain, I dry off and put on my large calico nightdress. When I'm sure no part of my body is exposed, I get into line to be inspected. Suddenly, Sister Benedict's hand flies up in a blur as she slaps the face of the girl ahead of me. 'Get back in the water, Duggan. Your ears are filthy!' she shouts. The unlucky girl has a look of shame on her face as she passes me, and she's trying to hold back the sobs as she gets back into the dirty water. 'Next!' calls Sister Benedict loudly.

Terrified that I'll be slapped for not cleaning myself well enough, I move forward towards where she sits to place my foot up onto the white apron that covers her lap. She checks between my toes then roughly pulls my head down to look at my ears and neck, grunting occasionally to herself as she inspects me. I pray silently that I've cleaned myself properly, dreading a return to the cold and dirty water. 'What's this? What are these on your hand, Harte?' she says, accusingly.

'I don't know, Sister,' I answer truthfully. I'd hoped she wouldn't notice the little lumps that have been growing on my hand for a while now.

'Warts they are, child,' she says as she squeezes one of them. I wince a little, trying not to show that it hurts. 'What? Do they hurt you? Go on now, they're nothing!' She throws my hand aside and calls for the next girl in line. I shuffle away, happy at least that I passed inspection.

I show my friends the warts growing on the pointing finger of my right hand, below my fingernail. I explain that I've had them for some time now and that they're getting bigger. Katy peers closely at my finger. 'They must hurt you, Maureen. They look awful.' They examine the finger with the warts and agree that I should go to Sister Brigid to have them checked out.

Last Wednesday, I went to see Sister Brigid, who sees to things like this. When I showed her the warts, she said that they'd have to be removed and that I was to return today.

Before I left for the infirmary, Katy asked me how the warts were to be removed. I had to admit that I'd no idea at all, but surely Sister Brigid would know how to take care of the problem. But now that I've arrived at the infirmary, I don't like at all what I've been told. A strong thread, like a twine, is to be tied tightly round the warts. The other end of the thread will go round the door handle, the door will be slammed shut and this will pull the warts out, roots and all. 'Yes, Sister,' I answer, shaking inside as she ties the strong-looking thread around the warts and then the other end around the door handle. I feel the thread begin to cut sharply into the warts.

'Are you ready now, Maureen?'

'Yes, Sis . . .' Before I can answer fully, the door is slammed. I feel the sudden jerk, and it's done. My finger goes numb, and my whole hand tingles. Black reddish blood oozes thickly out of the holes in my finger where the warts had been. I'm in too much shock to cry out and too afraid to say anything at all. A few moments later, in place of the numbness is a terrible pain. I cry quietly, holding my finger tightly. 'Now, that wasn't too bad, was it?' Sister Brigid says as she wraps a piece of sheet around the bleeding holes in my finger. I nod my head without answering. 'I'll look at the finger again in a week. You may leave now, Maureen.'

I walk from the infirmary, holding my right wrist in my left hand, crying from the pain. Already the blood is soaking the piece of sheet red. My friends are shocked when I tell them how the warts were pulled out, but, as always, they can do or say nothing to make it better for me. They try, though, by joking or saying something to get my mind off the pain in my finger. It bleeds all day and all through the night. I pray for the pain to stop, or even lessen a little bit, still holding my hand at the wrist to relieve the pain and help me sleep. Tonight, I'm one of the girls crying because something is wrong. Will one of the others hear my sobs, I wonder, and try to shut it out with her pillow like I do?

The next morning, Katy whispers to me on our way to the chapel. 'Maureen, your bandage, it's full of blood. That's not going to last a week. You'll have to get a clean one before next Wednesday.'

'I know, Katy. It's hurting me very much.'

'That's awful, Maureen. You poor thing. What a cruel way to remove warts. I pray I never get them.'

Sister Anthony looks back, and we can say nothing more about it. It'll be weeks before my finger heals. It's very tender to the touch, and I'll have to try not to use it. I hope I never have to experience this again. I shouldn't have said a word about the warts in the first place.

Today is going to be a very special day, for both the nuns and the orphans. A young novice is to be professed into the order by the bishop, and she will receive her white veil and begin a long life of devotion to Jesus Christ. As I'm nine now, I can take part in this special ceremony as a choir member. I can't wait to see the bishop. I've never seen a bishop before, and he's a very important person: more important than Father McClure and Canon Dolan from the village. A bishop is closer to the Pope. The nuns have told us we should feel honoured to be taking part in a ceremony where the bishop will be present, and we've all been so excited awaiting this special day. We don't have to go to school, which means no strict routine, but what I love most of all is that most of the nuns will be in good form, so we probably won't get beaten or shouted at today.

After breakfast, we get into our good uniforms used only for special occasions. Even mean old Sister Anthony smiles at our excitement. Maggie seems to know a lot about what's going to happen during the ceremony. She tells me, quietly and in spurts when she gets a chance, how the young nun will be dressed as a bride and how she'll lie face down on the chapel floor in front of the bishop to get her

white veil, and that the bishop will be wearing a big hat just like
the Pope does.

'Who told you that?' I ask.

'Rita Duffy. She's seen this ceremony before.'

'What else did she say?'

'She said,' continues Maggie, 'that the novice's parents, sisters and
brothers will be there watching from the side chapel.'

Sister Anthony's clapping hands announce that it's time to walk
over to the chapel, and there's a low buzz of excited whispering
along the line. The nuns also look alert and proper with the bishop
here.

'No whispering, children,' says Sister Carmel, looking back in
my direction as we walk into the chapel. I stand with the choir
of younger girls in the front row of our side chapel. Everything
is ready, and we're well practised in the Latin hymns that we're to
sing for the ceremony. A red-cushioned chair with a high back sits
in the nuns' section, while a smaller chair of the same sort sits to
the right of the bigger one. The smaller of the two must be for the
reverend mother.

Reverend Mother Xavier comes out and stands by her smaller chair,
waiting for the bishop to enter. We've been told a little about the
ceremony, and I know she's to attend to him throughout it. The organ
starts to play, and the bishop comes out, walking slowly to his red
plush chair. His gold-and-green vestments remind me right away of
the statue of Saint Patrick that rests in the hall outside the parlour in
the nuns' convent. With our cue from Sister Carmel, we begin singing
to full organ accompaniment, and the procession begins.

Because my view is blocked, I watch the turning heads of the family
members, which must mean that the postulant Bride of Christ is
now walking slowly up the aisle toward the bishop and the reverend
mother. When she comes into view, I almost catch my breath while
singing. With her face covered behind a plain white veil, she moves
slowly. She looks like an angel, with the beautiful white bridal dress
flowing out behind her in a long train. Two young attendant novices,
one on each side, follow behind her, protecting the train.

She looks so beautiful, so pure and innocent, like a statue of Our Lady of the Blessed Mother, only without the blue cloak. I think to myself as I sing that I might one day become a nun and walk up the aisle in a lovely white dress like that with the two attendant novices and have a special blessing from the bishop. If this ever happens to me, I will be very kind and never walk around with a stick or a cane in my hand. I will help the children to learn in school without being afraid. Yes, one day I might be a nun with God's help.

I hear a whisper beside me that brings me out of my thoughts. 'Maureen, you're daydreaming again,' Maggie says, smiling at me because she too is so happy today.

When the postulant stands before the bishop, he places his hands out above her head in a blessing. Next is the part I've been waiting for, though I'm not sure if what Maggie told me was true. But it is! The young bride lies face down on the floor, humbly waiting for the bishop to pray over her and continue with the rest of the ceremony. He sprinkles holy water on her while saying more prayers. My eyes stay fixed on each part of the ceremony as it passes. I really want to remember all of it. I sing my heart out with the choir, cherishing every moment of this special day and the feeling of being part of something so important.

At the end of the ceremony, the bishop comes over to our side chapel and addresses us kindly. 'Children,' he says, 'I want to thank you for your special part in this ceremony today. You've been wonderful.' To Sister Carmel, he says, 'You have an excellent choir, Sister Carmel, excellent. They sing like angels.'

I stare at the bishop, so close to us, only a few feet away in front of our altar rail. He seems so kind, and I feel truly blessed to be in his presence. As I look across at the other girls in our choir, I can see by their smiles that they too are very moved by his words. We are being singled out by the bishop himself and praised by him for our special part in the ceremony. It feels so nice to hear this from the bishop, especially after our long hours of practising the hymns, and I can tell by Sister Carmel's smile that she's pleased with us as well. Before the bishop leaves, he asks us all to kneel for a special blessing. He raises his hands and sprinkles holy water on us, and I know his blessing will bring me happiness in the future.

At bedtime, I kneel beside my bed, undressing modestly as Sister Anthony walks from the dormitory. Thinking her out of hearing, I whisper to Katy about how wonderful the day was, her bed being right next to mine. 'Who whispered just now?' Sister Anthony snaps, turning back to glare at us. 'Who was it?'

I swallow hard as the dormitory goes deathly silent. Each girl stops, frozen and terrified. We don't dare look at one another. All eyes are on Sister Anthony as that terrible smile of hers twists up one side of her face. Her eyes are cold and pitiless as they search our faces from behind her thin wire-rimmed spectacles. Her words are clipped and quiet, her steps slow, one after the other, as she moves toward my row. 'I will cane all of you if the guilty one doesn't own up. All of you! Do you hear me? Who was it that whispered?' Her eyes find mine and seem to bore right into them. I swallow again, my throat dry and my legs trembling. 'I know it came from this corner!' she roars.

'It was me, Sister.' I've no choice but to own up.

'You, Harte, was it?' She rushes across the two rows of beds, never taking her eyes off me. A look of terrible hate has banished the twisted smile. The rosary beads around her waist rattle, and the thick, harsh stick is already raised. I fumble as I try to get my hands out from under my loose calico nightdress, but I'm not quick enough. Only at the last moment do I realise that I'm not to get the usual six on the hands. While I'm still kneeling, she reaches me, my arms still inside my nightdress. She hits me all over: down across my back, my arms and my backside. I hear the stick cut the air wickedly. Nothing protects me from her cruel beating. 'This will teach you to obey me, Harte!' she screams as another blow hits me. 'When I say no talking or whispering, I mean it!'

I'm numb already and too afraid to cry. My friends watch in silence, terrified, knowing it could have easily been them. She stops beating me, her breathing heavy from the effort. The pain is already starting to take hold of my whole body. She begins shouting at me as I try to undress under my large shift. I want to disappear, crawl away anywhere but here. 'Hurry up, Harte, and get undressed. You've kept the whole dormitory up with your foolish whispering. You'll not do that again in a hurry, I don't think!'

She watches me as I get into bed, her eyes burning into me. I feel ashamed and humiliated. The other girls are already in their beds, silent. I pull the covers up over myself, listening, shaking with pain and fear as the rattling beads and clipped footsteps move across the floor to the door. The lights go off. The heavy door opens and slams shut behind her, then the sound of the long black bolt being pulled across for the night is heard, then the lock, then silence.

There isn't a sound or a whisper along the rows of beds in the darkness. I sob into my pillow as I wait. Every girl waits, afraid to move or breathe. There are no footsteps fading away outside the door. She's waiting for another whisper or the sound of another voice. She isn't finished yet. I see her out there, tall, with her arms folded, the stick in one hand, the cold dead eyes staring through the door as she listens. Ten minutes pass until the sound of her footsteps is heard. The dormitory is dead still, and it will stay like this until the morning comes and she wakes us with her clapping hands.

My friends gather round me in the playground the next morning. 'We feel so bad for you,' Katy says. 'I've never seen you take such a beating, Maureen. Your back must be badly marked.'

'I'm very sore,' I answer. 'I was barely able to bend over and get on my boots this morning.'

They stare, wide-eyed and pitiful, at the welts on my arms. 'She's a lot to account to God for,' Maggie says.

She always says that about Sister Anthony, and she's right. 'I know, Maggie. I wish she would go away and never come back.'

We don't dwell on this. It doesn't matter that I was the one that got it this time. Sister Anthony is a wicked woman; we know this. There is no way to predict what she'll do next. We've no power or defence against her, so we just go on and spend each day trying to survive. By the time this day is out, all of us will be thinking more about our empty stomachs than about the terrible beating the night before.

❈ SIX ❈

The class has been dismissed for recess, but Sister Edna has picked out ten of us and told us to stay behind. Are we to be punished for something? Katy, Maggie and Lucy have all been asked to stay back, as well as six others and me. 'What do you think we've done?' I ask the others.

Katy shrugs at my question as she joins us in the circle. 'There are ten of us,' she says. 'It mightn't be a punishment at all. Maybe we're to be picked for a play or something.'

When the classroom is empty and only the ten of us are left behind standing in our circle, Sister Edna stands looking at us, waiting until she has our full attention. 'In a few minutes, children, a couple, a man and his wife, both teachers in Cloonfad in County Roscommon, will be coming into the classroom. They are to choose one of you for adoption.'

None of us speak, so shocked are we by this news. I quickly exchange looks with Katy, then Maggie and Lucy. Each girl in the circle knows what the other nine are thinking at this moment: it might be me. None of us raises a hand to ask what's going to happen or how. Sister Edna says nothing more, allowing us a few more moments to let her words sink in. Then she walks to the door of the classroom and steps out into the hallway.

Alone in the circle with our thoughts, we stand stunned, terribly anxious as we wait for the door to open. I start to pray silently, as hard as I can, to be the one picked. Then I hear a man's voice and a different woman's voice, muted, through the closed door of the classroom. The man and wife are speaking to Sister Edna. I sneak a look at Katy to my left. She looks calm, but Maggie and Lucy seem nervous like me. I know they must be praying hard, too.

Two or three painfully slow minutes pass before Sister Edna comes back into the classroom with the couple. 'Children,' Sister says, 'this is Mr and Mrs McCann. They're going to decide now which one of you will be chosen for adoption.'

Sister Edna has us turn outward in the circle, facing away from each other. The man and wife are well dressed, and they must be clever if they teach school. I imagine it's not an orphanage where they teach. They begin to walk along our circle, stopping in front of each orphan, looking us up and down, smiling gently at each girl, saying nothing. It reminds me of inspection time when the doctor comes each year. There isn't a sound in the room. Why are they taking so long? I think. What are they looking for? They stop in front of me, and I pray even harder that they will pick me, afraid to blink an eye. I try to make them want me. Will it be me? Oh please, dear God! What if I am adopted out of this awful place? I will then have a mother and father who will care about me. I will go to school like an extern and have beautiful shiny hair with different coloured ribbons in it. I will even smell like they do, and maybe the teacher will smile at me, as I'll no longer be an orphan. They move on. The last girl in the circle is being examined. It won't be long now. Who will it be?

After the inspection, the couple walk with Sister Edna towards the door. Just before they go out, Sister stops suddenly, turning round to us. 'I want you all to remain in the circle and in complete silence until I return.'

I can hear a lot of talking outside in the hall, and I'm certain that they know now which one of us is to be adopted. Will it be me? Will it be me?

Sister Edna returns to the classroom alone this time. She walks to the rostrum where she teaches. All eyes are on her, waiting. 'Well, children, Mr and Mrs McCann have chosen Katy Fallon for adoption.' Nine faces turn to stare at Katy. She doesn't seem to have heard; she only stares ahead. 'Yes, you, Katy,' Sister repeats. 'They've chosen you, and you will be leaving immediately. The McCanns are waiting outside to take you with them to County Roscommon to live with them.'

Katy turns slowly and looks at me, her face deeply flushed as if she were embarrassed. She says nothing, but her expression seems to say:

why me, Maureen? I can't tell if she's happy to have been chosen. I wish I were Katy Fallon this minute. She must have been praying a lot harder than the rest of us to be picked.

Before I can think about anything further, Katy is leaving. 'Katy,' Sister Edna says. 'Come with me now. Mr and Mrs McCann are waiting.' Katy hasn't spoken a word since she was picked. 'Remain where you are until I return, girls,' Sister tells us, 'and stay quiet.'

Just before Katy follows her out the door, she turns and looks right at me. I notice that her cheeks are still red. Then she's gone, through the door and into the hall behind Sister Edna. Only now, at this moment, does it begin to sink in. Still in our circle, we look at one another for a moment. Then we begin to cry, silently almost, and without words because we've been told to be quiet. Why can't we say goodbye to her? Surely Sister Edna will bring Katy back to the classroom before she leaves so we can say goodbye to her? But because of the way she was rushed out of the door, I don't think we'll ever see her again. How very cruel, to snatch her away from us in this way. The three of us who were her best friends cry harder, wiping away our helpless tears, still not speaking a word. We hear footsteps, and Sister Edna comes into the classroom alone. She looks at us in silence for a moment then says, 'You may leave now, children.'

We go outside for the remainder of recess, still shocked by what has just happened. The sudden fresh air and the voices of the playing girls seem to wake me a little from my daze. Colleen Carey looks over at us as we walk out, smiling in her vacant way. No one speaks as we take a spot on the grass. Colleen seems puzzled by our odd silence, and then she notices Katy isn't among us. She's slowly growing worse as the daily beatings go on, but she's looking for Katy, whom she has known since we were all very little. 'Why is Katy not coming to play?' Colleen asks, looking round at each of us for an answer.

'Katy's gone, Colleen,' I say. 'She's been adopted by a family.'

'What?'

I don't think she understands, so I try to explain. 'Yes, she's been taken away to a real family in County Roscommon, a long way from here. That's why we were kept back.'

She looks away sadly, pulling at the grass with one hand, but there are no tears. She still doesn't seem to understand, but she'll know soon enough that Katy's gone and that she'll not be coming back to us. 'What d'you mean, Maureen?' she mumbles, looking down at the grass still. 'What d'you mean Katy's gone? Where?' Colleen and Katy were very fond of one another.

What are we going to do without Katy? She was my best friend, the one who was brightest in school and always knew the right answers. I loved her two rosy cheeks and her jet-black hair and green eyes that seemed to smile at you. She was like our sister, and now she has gone to live in a real home with a mammy and a daddy. Imagine how she must feel going all the way to a place called Cloonfad in County Roscommon. I don't know where that is, but it's a long way away, surely, far away from this awful place.

Katy must have something about her to be picked for adoption by a mammy and daddy. Maybe Sister Edna told them Katy was clever in school and that's why she was chosen over us. I wonder, am I good enough to be adopted? Will this miracle happen again, and will I be picked the next time? Imagine being wanted like that, being chosen to leave here and to suddenly have a family to go to.

Our little circle of friends is down to three, four including Colleen Carey, but she spends more time sitting on her own, and her mind seems to be going a little more. We care so much, and it hurts us to see her like this, but we can do nothing. We're slowly losing Colleen, that's the truth of it, and now with Katy gone she'll surely only get worse and go inside to that place where none of us can reach her. She can't even express her feelings any more, and she won't look us in the eye. She seems so alone. If only she would show some life or cry or get angry.

Sometimes I wonder why God allows things like this to happen, and I try to imagine what goes on in Colleen's mind. Maybe shutting everything out helps her to deal with it, but then how terribly alone she must be because of that. How can the nuns just watch this, day after day, and have no concern at all for her? They're supposed to be Sisters of Mercy, yet they care nothing about what's happening to her. I feel like we're being punished because we are orphans, because we have no families.

A week has gone by since Katy was adopted, and I miss my best friend terribly. We've been together every day and done everything together ever since we were in high infants. I stare at her empty chair in the dining hall, and I walk past her empty locker in the linen room with the large number eight on it. Her bed is empty in the dormitory.

Today, down by the wall in our corner, our stone dolls lie neglected at our feet, dressed in little bits of rag in the place of clothes. For the first time, we talk to one another about Katy. We talk about how she'll have real dolls to play with in her new home. That's the first thing they'll do for her, we agree: buy her a real doll with pretty clothes. We don't know exactly what a real doll looks like; we've heard about them from the externs but never seen one. Katy will have her own room and a soft bed, I'm sure, and lovely meals to eat any time she wants to, and she'll be free to walk with her mammy and daddy to the shops to buy sweets, and I know she'll be dressed up in pretty dresses and will have new friends who will like her as much as we do. We talk about all the things she'll not have to bother with any more: line-ups and Sister Anthony and always being hungry and being told to be quiet. Maggie says Katy will look so lovely in the new clothes they'll get for her. 'I'd love to be Katy now,' I say quietly.

'So would I,' Lucy agrees, looking away with tears in her eyes. She turns back to me. 'Did you pray, Maureen? Did you pray to be adopted by the McCanns?'

'I never stopped praying. I . . .'

'Did you, Maggie?' Lucy goes on.

'I couldn't stop praying, the whole time, but . . . the way Katy was taken, it was so cruel, and I'll never forget it. She must miss us awfully.'

Our precious playtime will soon be over, and we make an effort to play our family game, but the stones lying in their bits of rag only remind us of our sadness. We don't want to think about our deep loss.

We try to help each other as best we can. Each one of us wonders if we will ever get to leave this awful place and what will happen to us if no one wants us in the outside world. Rita Duffy told us that many of the senior girls, on their leaving day, go into what's called service. That means a family takes them in, and they do some sort of work for the family, like chores.

'Maybe someone will want to adopt more children from here,' Maggie says to us after a long silence.

'Do you think that might happen?' I ask her, feeling a glimmer of hope. 'We can pray even harder next time someone comes.' Maggie always makes me feel so much better when she talks likes this.

'It won't happen again!' Lucy almost shouts. 'No one else will come here to adopt any of us again!' I've never seen Lucy like this. Her big blue eyes are so hurt and lonely looking, and her lip trembles as she pulls at a piece of grass. 'I know. Rita Duffy said that it's so rare that it happens, adoption. Katy's gone, and we'll not be adopted. We're all to go into service when we turn sixteen. Rita told me all about it.' Lucy turns away from us, silent.

We all go quiet as we think about what she's said. It's true: maybe there's not a soul in the outside world who cares that we're here. My thoughts drift back to the day Katy was adopted. I feel very different now about Sister Edna. I thought she was one of the kinder nuns, but now I feel angry with her, and I'm not supposed to think bad thoughts about the nuns. It's a sin to be angry all the time at Sister Edna. I'll have to tell Father McClure this week in confession about my anger. He'll just tell me to pray for Sister Edna and for Katy. I know he will, and I'll get three Hail Marys instead of just the one.

Three new girls have arrived at the orphanage: Emma, Molly, and Alice Casey, all redheads from Dublin. There are six children in the Casey family, but their mammy died and their daddy couldn't take care of all the children. Alice is my age and in my class, and instead of seeing Katy Fallon's empty bed each day beside mine, I see Alice there. She's not been here long, but already she hates the orphanage, especially Sister Anthony.

Today, Alice gets into an awful fight with another girl in the recreation hall. We all stop to watch as the two girls pull one another's hair, clawing and scratching and screaming out bad words. 'I'll kill ya, ya feckin' bitch, I will!' Alice howls at the other girl, who's a little older and bigger. When Alice is finally dragged off by the nun in charge, she screams out her anger. 'I hate you! I hate this place! I hate all of you. I'll not stay here!'

As furious as she is, Alice is crying terribly, too. It's awful to see because I like her. Some of the words Alice used in the fight, towards the other girl, I'd never heard them before. I decide that I'm going to ask Rita Duffy about it but not in the yard when her friends are with her because I don't want to sound foolish.

A couple of days pass when, after bedtime, I run into Rita going to the lavatory late at night. 'Rita,' I whisper. 'Do you know what "feckin" means and "bitch"?'

She screws up her eyebrows and looks into my face, then she claps her hand over her mouth and pulls me back into the lavatory as she tries not to burst out laughing. I watch as she bends over at the waist trying not to laugh. 'Ah, Maureen,' she says finally. 'You're a funny one. I don't know where those words came from, only that they're very bad words. There's no end to your curiosity! Sure, where did you hear them?'

'One of the Casey sisters, the new girls. Alice, she's in my class, she used them during a fight in the hall.'

'Ah, yes, that little one. Do you know Anthony's got her eye on that one, has her marked out as trouble, she does, and Alice will play right into it, you watch.'

Today is a breezy day in September, and Alice and I sit chatting in a grassy corner of the green. 'What's it like in Dublin, Alice?' I ask, wanting to hear it all again. She's already told me how she could walk, all alone, from where her family lives to the shops if she had a bit of money. I can't imagine it – sweets any time you want them – but it's nice to hear about it.

'Ah,' she says, looking around the yard, 'it's ten times better than living in this terrible place. It's nothing but a jail here.' She stops for a moment, looking down. 'I really hate it here, especially that Anthony, the aul rip, always beating us, the aul skinny bean!'

'Skinny Bean' is what the orphans call Sister Anthony, but we're careful that she never hears us. I look round nervously as I listen to Alice speak so boldly, but she goes on. 'I want out of here, Maureen, I do. I want to go to the shops again and live in my house. I miss me daddy and brothers, and I hate lookin' at the walls here, every day like this. I miss Mammy . . .'

Alice always gets upset when she talks about her mammy, so I say, 'At least you've your older sisters. They'll stick up for you if you're bullied in the playground.'

'I know,' she says, 'but they're feeling worse than me. They hate it here as well, and they're missing Daddy something awful, they are . . . and Mammy.' She looks like she wants to cry, but she's too angry, staring down and pulling at the grass. Poor Alice. It shows in her eyes how terrible she feels – there's such a hard look to them, but inside she's nice, too. 'If only Mammy hadn't died,' she says quietly. 'If only she didn't get the TB. I thought she'd get better, I really did . . . then they took her to the hospital and she died there.'

'That's a terrible thing, Alice. I wish it hadn't happened to you. I've never had a mammy, but I think I know how you feel a little bit.' She looks at me, then back at the ground, saying nothing. 'One of my best friends was taken from here, about two months ago. I miss her awfully, too. She was like my sister.'

Suddenly, Alice goes into a fit of temper, using those same words she brought to the orphanage with her. 'Feck, I hate this feckin' place! How am I going to stick it out? Feck! I hate it here! And that aul skinny bean, she's so mean. I hate her!'

I try to comfort her. I don't want her to be in trouble with the nuns. I tell her that they know exactly who the angry girls are, and they try to beat it from them. I tell her that it will be better for her to try to fool them and go along with what they say. I tell her about the two senior girls who tried to escape over the walls and were brought back by the Gardai and beaten by Sister Anthony.

Alice almost spits at her name, tearing out bits of grass and shaking her head.

'What is it about the laundry?' she asks, jerking her head in the direction of the old stone building off one side of the square.

'Oh no,' I say, 'you don't want to land there. They say you never get out again if they put you there. It's true! Just look at those women in the morning in the side chapel. They've to sit by themselves, away from all of us. Just look at them and you'll not want to end up like them, you won't!'

'But, Maureen,' she says to me, 'they can't do that. I've a daddy, and he'll take me out of here when I'm sixteen.'

'Oh, that's right you do,' I say. 'And you know what that means? You'll be allowed out to see him in the summer.'

'Really? Do you think so?'

'Yes, because you've a daddy you'll be allowed out, and your daddy can come here to see you. Visitors go to the nuns' parlour, and then the girl is brought there to see the visitor.'

'How do you know, Maureen? Have you had a visitor?'

'Me? Oh no, not me. Nothing so far.' This makes me feel very lonely, and I look away with a lump in my throat.

Alice looks at me steadily. 'Have you no mammy at all then, Maureen?'

'No, I don't know what happened to my mammy and daddy.'

'I've a daddy left at least,' Alice says. 'He brought us sweets every week, on a Friday, when he got his pay from his job . . . but I miss me mammy something awful . . .' She goes very quiet again, staring at the ground with a dark brooding look in her hard eyes. Then I think about showing her our dandelion wishing game. Maybe she'll like it and she'll feel better, and she can tell her sisters about it if she wants to.

Though there aren't any with the grey fluffy heads right now, we decide to use the lovely yellow ones that grow along the edge of the grass. As we run off to search for good dandelions, Alice shouts out to me that she's going to make a big wish for her daddy and for her mammy, who she's sure is in heaven.

✿ ✿ ✿

Sister Brendan has chosen me for the special chore of cleaning her classroom after breakfast each day. I feel very important and special, and she must think me a good worker as well. It will mean missing our half-hour play period before school at nine, but I don't mind that too much because Maggie is to clean Sister Carmel's room at the same time, and the two classrooms are joined by a short passageway and glass doors, so I will have some company. I like my chore. It gives me a good feeling, like I'm doing something important and helpful.

Sister Brendan is tall and a few years older than most of the teaching nuns. She has a very kind oval face and a gentle smile, and she smells so lovely. When I was very little, I saw Sister Brendan a lot because her classroom was so close to Sister Carmel's room. She would come in to talk to Sister Carmel, and she'd smile at us and call us by our first names.

Sister Brendan's classroom is a big room, with desks in separate rows nearer the front and long benches with built-in desks that students must share at the back. A blackboard covers most of one wall, and holy pictures hang in between each window. Her room feels warm and friendly, and I'll be in here when I'm a senior, with Maggie and Lucy. And Colleen, too, but she's so behind in school, and the nuns might keep her back.

A big part of my chore is dusting and polishing the wooden frames of the beautiful fancy glass doors dividing the two classrooms and the glass and wooden door where the students enter from the back stairs. The long windows in the room open and close with cords, and I have to stand on a stepladder to reach the windowsills to dust and polish them.

Sister Brendan is extremely particular about the piano and her rostrum. Each morning she inspects my work, going round with her finger along the windowsills and doors to see if I've done my work properly.

This morning, halfway through my cleaning chore, I hear the familiar footsteps of one of the nuns approaching. When I turn to see Sister Brendan come into the room, I hope that I haven't done anything wrong, and I wonder why she's coming to see me. 'Well, Maureen, you're doing a very good job at cleaning,' she says, one of her fingers sliding along a windowsill. 'Go now, will you, next door and ask Sister Carmel if I may have Maggie O'Rourke here for a few minutes.'

'Yes, Sister.'

'Why does she want to see me?' Maggie whispers as we walk back between the two classrooms.

'Don't worry, she's in good form,' I say, knocking gently on Sister Brendan's classroom door before walking in.

Sister Brendan smiles at us as we walk in, telling us to sit down in front of her. Then she reaches into her loose wide sleeve and brings out two thick slices of bread. 'I've brought you some bread and jam from the nuns' kitchen. Enjoy this treat now, girls. You must be hungry.'

She doesn't stay to watch us eat, and the two of us are too shocked as we hold the fresh warm bread to get out our thanks as she leaves the room. This kindness is so unusual for a nun. In between bites of the delicious fresh bread, I turn to Maggie and say, 'Sister Brendan is a true Sister of Mercy.' She nods her head in agreement with this.

'Why would she hide it up her sleeve?' Maggie asks. 'Do you think she sneaked the bread from the nuns' kitchen?'

'She must have a lot of power over the other nuns,' I answer. This is all I can come up with. The lovely bread is all that matters at the moment. Sister Brendan knows we will keep her kindness to ourselves.

On the way to confession, Colleen Carey walks just ahead of me, but she's so slow today. 'Come on, Colleen, you can walk a little faster,' I say to her, smiling. She doesn't answer or look at me; her mind is off again, in whatever place she goes to escape. Maybe if I pray harder for her, something will change for Colleen. I often wonder if sometimes God hears our prayers or if sometimes they don't reach him. I don't understand why Colleen must suffer like this, but tomorrow at mass I'll say an extra prayer for her — it might help.

We walk on into the chapel in our pairs and sit in our usual rows to wait for confession. Father McClure is already there, speaking quietly to Sister Carmel. He'll give us a little time to prepare before beginning.

Half of the girls have finished with their confessions and are kneeling in the pews doing their penance when there's a sudden commotion behind me. I turn to see Colleen Carey laughing aloud and mumbling to herself. She's been behaving like this more often lately but never in the chapel. Such a thing is unthinkable. Now the mumbling becomes loud, and a strange giggle echoes terribly around the empty pews. We can only stare as she continues. I can't take my eyes from her vacant stare. Surely she doesn't know where she is.

Sister Carmel reacts right away, her beads rattling and echoing as she walks up the aisle quickly from the back. We stare silently as she takes Colleen roughly by the arm. 'Come along now. That's quite enough!' she says, her voice low and menacing. Colleen scarcely seems to notice or care as she allows herself to be dragged along limply. Sister Carmel glances quickly at the confessional, where Father McClure is, as she takes Colleen out of the chapel. She doesn't want him to see this. If he hears, he'll come out to see what the fuss is. They'll be very careful about allowing Colleen back into the chapel again, if indeed they ever do.

After confession, we line up as usual for our walk back to the orphanage, but there's no sign of Colleen. We wonder where they've taken her. Has she been brought to the infirmary, the little building off the laundry that's every girl's nightmare? None of my friends or I have been in the infirmary sickroom, but it's said there are always a handful of sickly orphans kept there for long periods. Poor Colleen, I think. I'll have to pray harder for her to come back to us.

❖ SEVEN ❖

The nuns from the Dominican Order have come today for their yearly visit to the orphanage. As you must be ten to be allowed to see the movies they show, Maggie, Lucy and I are going to go and watch for the first time. These nuns, I hear, wear all white habits because they are from Africa, where it's always hot. They are missionaries. They go to Africa to teach all the poor pagan black babies that are starving there, and then they come back to Ireland to find money for their missions.

'What's pagan?' I heard one of the other young girls ask a senior girl last night as they whispered about the Dominicans coming today.

'They've no God. 'Tis awful,' the older girl answered.

'Why?' the younger one wanted to know, but she was shoved away rudely.

'Ah, go away will you. They've no God or Jesus is all there is to it!'

We've been allowed half the day off from school, and a big screen has been set up at the front of the recreation hall. The two Dominican missionary nuns stand dressed all in white, and they seem very young to me. What excitement they must feel going off to Africa to help those poor people!

The blinds are drawn and the still movie begins. There's no sound, only pictures of naked black babies sitting with their mammies. The nun standing beside the screen explains what they're doing in Africa on their mission. She uses a yardstick to point out certain things, to make sure we understand. 'These poor children, they live in a world of poverty, a benighted place, a place without the word of God. Think, you young children, here today with your own chapel so close and God so close, what that would be like.'

I don't know what poverty means, but it's not good because she said the pagan babies are often sick. I look at the pictures of the babies with their mammies, thinking it would be terrible to be starved all the time. We're always hungry in the orphanage, especially at night, but to be totally starved is hard for me to imagine. The poor pagan babies must get so weak that they find it hard to walk about and play. I don't know what I would do without Baby Jesus. He helps me through each day.

I feel so bad for these poor children, and I start to cry. I can see many of the other girls and my friends are all crying quietly. The pictures on the big screen keep changing. There are hundreds of pictures, of the children and their mammies mostly, and many of the missionary nuns helping them in Africa. The nun points to awful-looking little huts, half fallen apart, where the poor people and the black babies must sleep. Where are all the daddies, I wonder? The Dominican Order, the nun tells us, are in need of more nuns like themselves to go and teach the pagan Africans about the word of God.

After an hour or so, the lights come on and a chatter of voices rises in the hall. All of us feel terribly sad for these families in Africa. I turn to whisper to Maggie and Lucy, 'I'm going to be a missionary nun when I grow up.'

'Me too!' says Lucy, while Maggie nods her head.

Sister Carmel claps her hands for our attention, and the hall becomes silent. 'Children,' she says. 'Sister Therese has something more to tell you. Listen attentively, now.'

Sister Therese puts her yardstick down and takes a couple of steps towards where we sit. Most of the younger girls are nearer the front, looking up at her with eager waiting faces. 'Children, you have just seen the work we are trying to do for these pagan children,' she says, looking round at us. 'We of the Dominican Order need you to pray daily to help us with this great task. Hands up now those who wish to become a missionary nun like myself.'

There's a sudden shooting up of arms and wiggling fingers, mostly from the younger ones, and chattering voices. 'Me, Sister. Me, Sister, me! I do!'

We're fine, each of us, calling out as a group, but I think the nun wants one of us to tell her what we think about the pictures. I won't talk up – I'm far too shy – but Katy would have stood up and talked if she were here with us today.

'Children,' Sister Therese goes on, 'you will have to work very hard in school if you wish to become one of us. You would have to devote your life to Christ, and this is very different from anything else. It is a very special job, children.'

I look over my shoulder at the older girls. They don't seem to be interested, and they haven't raised their hands to ask questions. Do they not want to help the starving black babies? The nun tells us more about Africa, and we listen closely, but none of us asks a question. We are so used to being silent, and none of us has the nerve to stand up in front of so many other girls and say how we feel. The older ones might scoff at us. I want to tell this special Dominican nun, Sister Therese, that one day I would love to be a missionary nun like her. I want to tell her how I feel about the pagan babies not knowing who Jesus is, or God, and I want to tell her that I love the silent pictures and that her coming today made me happy. I have so many strong feelings about what I've seen, and it would be lovely to be able to just speak out about it – about how exciting and different it is that these nuns have come here to our orphanage today. I really do want to be a nun just like them, but now I'll have to choose between being a Sister of Mercy nun or a nun of the Dominican Order.

Today is one of our special days when we're to be inspected by a doctor. Anything that gets us out of the same old routine is very exciting for us – we don't care what it is. The doctor comes once a year, and we get the whole morning off from school. Dressed in our best uniforms of yellow blouses and black gym tunics, we stand in the recreation hall in rows. I feel proud when I wear this uniform. It's such a nice change from the old plaid dress.

The doctor walks along very slowly, looking at each of us without touching us or examining us closely. Sister Carmel walks beside the doctor, and if he sees someone looking sickly, he immediately tells her and the girl is pulled from the line. The doctors are different each year, but they all look so kind, and they smile at us. I've never been pulled from the line before, but when the doctor gets to me he looks at me and then picks me out as being sickly. This delights me. I don't care what's wrong with me; now I'll be given some sort of special attention.

The inspection ends with six other girls and me being pulled from the rows. I stand with the others before Sister Carmel calls us into her classroom. She turns to me first. 'Maureen, Dr O'Loughlin thinks you look pale and a little delicate. How do you feel?'

'Fine, Sister.'

'Do you feel more tired lately than you normally would?'

'No, Sister.' Why is she asking me these questions? I feel the same as I always do. How can a doctor just look at a person and tell what's wrong with them? I feel that I've not answered her the right way and wonder what I should have said.

'Now, Maureen, you're to go every morning to Sister Michael. She'll give you a drink, an egg flip, to help you become stronger. Start tomorrow morning for one month straight. Is that clear?'

'Yes, Sister.'

While Sister Carmel talks to each of the other girls about their sores or scabs, I think about going to Sister Michael's kitchen. How fortunate am I? I've no idea what an egg flip is, but I'll not be afraid to ask Sister Michael.

Of course, the others can't wait to hear what's wrong with me, and as soon as we're together they're full of questions. I tell them how the doctor thought me delicate and that I'm to go to Sister Michael every morning for a whole month to have this drink called an egg flip. 'Egg flip?' they both say together. 'What's an egg flip?'

I tell them I haven't a clue what it is, but the big question for us is this being delicate thing. The three of us ponder what it could possibly mean. Maggie, after thinking deeply about it, seems to have an answer. 'Maureen,' she says, 'your cheeks aren't red like Lucy's and mine . . . Maybe that's what being delicate means?'

'That's it!' cries Lucy in agreement. 'Turn towards us so we can see. Yes, ours have more colour!'

'I think that's why Katy was adopted,' says Maggie, 'because the McCanns thought she wasn't delicate looking.'

But whatever delicate means, I know I'll be fine. I don't think I look so very different from them. 'Sure, how can a doctor tell anything by walking by and just looking me up and down once?' Maggie says doctors know a lot about these things. They look after sick people in hospitals, she explains patiently, and they can tell.

This worries me a little more, but I shrug it off. 'Well, I can't be too bad, and I don't have to go to the hospital in Longford. I'm glad I'm delicate, and whatever this egg flip is, I'm going to enjoy every drop of it!'

At eleven-thirty in the morning, I'm excused from Sister Edna's class to go for my first egg flip. With great excitement and curiosity, I walk quickly to the big wooden door by the cloister entrance. This door is always kept locked, although we've often hoped to see it open as we go by so that we can have a peek inside. I knock on the hard wood and stand back to wait. Moments later, Sister Michael opens the door. 'Ah, Maureen, I thought it might be you. Are you here for your egg flip?'

'I am, Sister.'

'Come in then and get that stool out of the corner so you can sit beside the stove. It's warm there, and I'll make your egg flip for you now.'

I go over to get the little stool and place it next to the big stove. While Sister Michael takes down a large ceramic mug, I sit by the warmth of the big stove, looking around the kitchen and taking everything in. There are holy pictures on the wall, and a beautiful Sacred Heart lamp is burning in the corner. The stove has big pots and pans hanging above it and a big black kettle sitting on top. In a huge open press, there are containers labelled 'flour', 'sugar' and 'oatmeal'. Another press is full of wooden bowls, spoons, clay bowls of different colours, white enamel mugs, and milk and tea jugs. On the far wall there are two large white sinks and a window facing out to Sister Michael's vegetable garden. How I'd love to go to Sister Michael's garden. I could see where we play from there.

'What's an egg flip, Sister?' I ask quietly.

'Oh, it's just raw eggs and milk,' she answers, breaking the eggs into a bowl and beating them with milk for my drink. After pouring it into the big mug, she hands it to me. 'Now, you must drink every drop like a good girl,' she says in her kind way. 'It will help you feel better and give you a little more energy and colour, Maureen.'

'Yes, Sister,' I answer. 'I'll finish it slowly so as to get it all in me.' I'm going to make this last, I think, as I sip the egg flip. It doesn't taste very nice, but I'll drink anything she gives me if I can sit in her kitchen for a while.

How special it feels to get attention like this on my own. I watch Sister Michael bustle about the kitchen wearing her large white apron. She looks over and smiles at me to see how I'm doing. Sister knows how I feel being here, and her smile seems to say to me, 'Everything will be all right, Maureen. You enjoy this special attention while it lasts.' Maybe being here with Sister Michael is what it's like to have a mammy, with someone to do things just for you and to smile at you and make you feel special.

I am still daydreaming, lost in my contentment and the warm glow of the big black stove, when Sister Michael's voice brings me round. 'You must be all finished with your egg flip by now, Maureen. Are you?'

'Yes, Sister, it's all gone,' I answer, standing to leave the kitchen.

Before I leave, Sister Michael reminds me to come each day at the same time for my special drink.

During our midday meal, I tell my friends about sitting beside the big stove and all about the kitchen and where everything is kept and what it looks like. We've been wondering for so long what her kitchen was like, and all the other girls are so excited to hear all about it. 'I actually asked Sister Michael what an egg flip was,' I say proudly, 'and I wasn't a bit afraid to speak to her.'

'Tell us what an egg flip is!' Lucy cries excitedly.

'It's raw eggs and milk, but I didn't see how many eggs.'

Lucy makes a sour face. 'Oh, did you really drink that stuff, Maureen?'

'I didn't mind a bit, and I took my time drinking it down. Sister Michael smiled at me a lot, and I think she knew I was trying to make the egg flip last. She didn't shout at me and say, "Hurry up, Harte, and drink that down." She called me Maureen, just as she calls us by our first names when she gives us bits from her garden. I can't wait to go back to her each day.'

As we finish our meal, Maggie turns to me and says, 'You're so lucky to be delicate, Maureen.'

I know my month of mornings in Sister Michael's kitchen will go by too quickly, and I'll feel awful when it ends. I wonder why Sister Michael is so different, and why she treats us so kindly, while the other nuns don't seem to care about us. If I ever find my mammy, I hope she'll be like Sister Michael.

❖ EIGHT ❖

Sister Carmel finds me while I'm doing my cleaning chores in the classroom. I stop working when she enters, standing respectfully as I wait for her to speak. She tells me that I will be turning eleven years old this month. I can only respond by saying, 'Yes, Sister,' because I'd no idea when my birthday was. Sister Carmel doesn't tell me what day I was born, only the month – April. I feel good knowing my proper age at last and at least the month. 'Do you know what being a milker is, Maureen?'

'Yes, Sister,' I answer. 'I hear Sister Joseph calling the milkers every morning.'

'That's right,' she says, 'and you will be going to the farm at five in the evening as well. The cows need milking then, too. Did you know that?'

'Yes, Sister,' I answer. 'I know because Rita Duffy told me.'

'Good, very good.' She looks at me silently for a moment, then remarks, 'You look much healthier now, Maureen. Are you feeling stronger these days?'

'Yes, Sister, I'm feeling fine,' I reply.

'I think Sister Michael's egg flips have helped you. You're much more robust looking now, and you should be strong enough for this new chore.'

'Yes, Sister, I am.'

'Very well. Sister Joseph will call on you on the Monday morning you're to start. Carry on with your work.'

I wake long before five-thirty, to be ready to get out of bed when I hear Sister Joseph's loud knocking on the dormitory door for my first day as a milker. Rita Duffy has told me a few things about being a milker and that I'm starting at a good time of year, as I won't have

76

to clean out my cow's stall until wintertime. She's said that by the time the winter settles in, I'll know more about cows and the farm. The winters are fierce cold and damp, she's explained. The frost goes right through you, and you only have a light cape to protect yourself against it. You're given a pair of woollen socks, wooden clogs and a grey flannel cape with a hood, but you're not dressed warm enough for the winter months.

I close my eyes and try not to worry about what today will be like, but just as I am drifting off to sleep again I hear the familiar rattling of keys and then the great hammering on the dormitory door. It's her, Sister Joseph. 'Up now, up!' she roars as she enters the dormitory, coming straight to my row. 'Come on, Harte!' she shouts, moving down the rows and shouting in her raspy voice at all the milkers to wake. 'Up now, up, move!'

I jump up out of bed, moving as fast as I can to dress, fold my white calico shift up, put it under my pillow, make my bed and then pull up the blanket. When the morning routine at the basins and the brushing of hair is finished, I rush back out to the main dormitory, trying my best to stay invisible from the eyes of Sister Joseph. I'll stand beside Rita Duffy, I think, but it's no good. I'm spotted, like a thief trying to get away. 'Harte! Is that you?' booms the rough voice. 'Over here, Harte, to the front of the line. You're a new milker. Stay with me!'

I move to the front, very close to Sister Joseph. I flick my eyes up at her for a quick look. She's not at all like the nuns who teach us. Her black habit is soiled and worn from working hard on the farm. It looks almost green to me. As she barks at the slow ones in her rough voice, her buckteeth stick out in front. I feel terrified of her as I wait to go to the farm for my first day as a milker, but I'm glad to see that she doesn't have a stick in her hand.

We walk quickly, out of the dormitory and along the cloister, past the dining hall, then the laundry, through the nuns' garden and across the main Sligo road to a long narrow lane that leads to the farm. The lane is a good few feet across with wild green hedges either side, and it looks well travelled. A patchwork of old gravel fights with the hearty spring grass that forces its way up.

With Sister Joseph well out of hearing now, I trot faster to catch up with Rita Duffy walking just ahead with her milker friends. I want to ask her some questions before we get to the farm. 'How many cows are there that need milking, Rita?'

'Fourteen.'

'Is it easy to learn to milk?'

'Yes, you'll get used to it, and your cow will soon learn to know you. Buttercup knows my voice well now, and I stroke her, too, when I'm with her, to calm her.'

'Buttercup?'

'My cow's name.'

'That's a lovely name, Buttercup. I wonder what my cow's name will be.'

'They're all called after wild flowers by the nuns. Two older girls have just left the orphanage, and their cows will need to be milked: Primrose and Cowslip they're called. Maybe you'll be given one of those cows.'

I like the sound of the cows' names, but this news about stroking them surprises me. 'And she'll not kick you?' I ask worriedly.

'She won't. She's never kicked me. They're ready when they get to the stall to be milked and don't mind it at all.'

The lane ends, and just ahead is the farm. On the right, Rita points out the cow byre with its corrugated-steel roof. 'That's where the milking stalls are, in there,' she says as we walk quickly over the last stretch of field. 'You'll be fine, Maureen. Just watch carefully when Farmer Giles shows you how to milk the first time, that way you'll keep out of her way.'

'I will, Rita. Thanks.'

Sister Joseph stands aside as we file by into the farm. 'Harte!' she cries out as I reach her.

'Yes, Sister.'

'Miss Giles will show you how to milk your cow when the cows are brought from the paddock and how to chain her for the milking.'

'Yes, Sister.'

She walks off, and I stand waiting in the big cement square by the cow byre. I pray quietly while I watch for Miss Giles. My eyes roam about nervously across the details of the farm. Out of a shed in the far corner among some smaller cement buildings walks a tall woman with a pail in her hand. As she gets closer, I recognise her from mass. It could be no one else. I stand waiting with my head down, already trembling. I'll wait until she speaks to me first. She stops and looks down at me. The moment seems to last an eternity before she speaks. 'Well, what's your name, then?' she demands.

'Harte, Maureen Harte, Miss Giles.'

'Well, Harte, I'll show you a couple of mornings and evenings how to chain and milk the cow, and then you're on your own.' She stops talking suddenly, staring at me for a moment. 'And you'll do exactly as I tell you, Harte, d'you hear me?'

'Yes, Miss Giles, I will.' I try not to stare at the hair on her face or her wild grey hair, parted in the middle and hanging down her shoulders, or her huge hands with warts, one still clutching the heavy galvanised bucket. She's so ugly and frightening that I hope I learn quickly so she won't shout at me.

From behind me suddenly comes the loud mooing of cows. 'Out of the way, Harte!' Miss Giles shouts roughly. 'Move over to the side and let the cows in!' I get out of the way so I won't get trampled on. The cows seem to be moving quickly into their stalls.

In the byre, Sister Joseph and Miss Giles walk up and down, making sure all the cows are chained properly for milking. 'Harte, this is your cow, Primrose,' Sister Joseph says, finally calling me. 'Now watch Miss Giles closely,' she tells me before going off again. I stare at the huge cow named Primrose. Her great head turns a little, and with one big dark watery eye she takes a good look at me as if she knows I'm a new milker. How, I wonder, will I ever manage to get my arms up around her neck? What if she kicks me? I'm not tall like some of the eleven-year-old girls are.

'Look, Harte, are ye followin'?' asks Miss Giles. 'Take the chain from the ring on the wall and throw it round her neck and hook it in to the chain link on her neck.' I watch closely as Miss Giles shows me how to milk. 'Now, Harte,' she says, 'ye sit close to the cow's udder and pull her teats, opening and closing your fingers until ye feel the milk pouring into the pail, and when her teats are soft ye're finished.'

'Yes, Miss Giles,' I answer as I watch her milk Primrose. Her rough, wart-covered hands pull on the teats, and there's a steady sound of the milk streaming into the pail. I hear the same sounds from the other stalls, where the rest of the girls are milking away. I watch every detail, dreading missing some little thing that will force me to seek out Miss Giles for help.

At the evening milking later that day, Miss Giles showed me again how to milk Primrose, and again the following day. Today, my third day, I know I have to milk Primrose myself. I pray hard on my way to the farm that she'll be quiet for me and that I'll please Sister Joseph and Miss Giles. I don't want to be shouted at and beaten for doing it wrong. On the way down to the paddock with the rest of the milkers, Rita calls me up to walk with her and her friends. Bridie, one of Rita's friends, tries to encourage me. 'Ah sure, don't let old Farmer Giles worry you, Maureen.'

'I'll try Bridie, but she scares me.'

'Oh sure, don't we well know about that one?' Bridie says. 'Didn't we all start at your age? You'll toughen up like we have.'

'That's right,' Rita adds. 'Don't let Farmer Giles scare you. Do you know what we do to her? We squirt her sometimes with the cow's teat when she's her back to us.' They all laugh loudly at this. 'And she never feels a thing, she doesn't,' she goes on, 'with all those clothes.'

'You don't really do that to her, do you?' I ask, wondering where they get the nerve to be so bold.

'Oh, we do!' Rita promises me. 'It's the only way to get back at her sometimes, and it's loads of fun.'

Walking with thirteen- and fourteen-year-old girls makes me feel more grown up. They're not afraid of anything, and I'll soon be grown up like them. By the time we all reach the paddock, I feel more settled, convinced now that I can accept what's in store for me, good or bad.

I help to bring the cows in, finding Primrose in amongst them, and I am surprised to see that she knows to go right to her own stall. When she's standing still, I throw the chain over her neck, bringing it under her again to hook her up as I was shown. I surprise myself by doing it well and sit down for the milking. With my hands under Primrose, I take the teat like Miss Giles showed me, squeeze while pulling down and relax my grip a little, then again. It works! I can hear the echo of the warm milk falling into the empty pail. I milk Primrose, feeling very good about my first day as a milker on my own.

'Move in closer, Harte. Closer to her. That's right.' It's Sister Joseph checking on me, and I do as she says. I feel such relief knowing now that Rita is right: that it's easy to milk a cow and that I'll be fine as a milker.

Three weeks have passed for me, milking twice a day, without any trouble at all, but today, for whatever reason, Primrose is acting up, and I can't get her to settle down at all to chain her into the stall. Miss Giles must've heard all the fuss, and she comes rushing into my stall straight at me. 'Give me that chain, Harte!' she shouts, and I'm instantly terrified. 'What's wrong with ye?' she screams, pinning me back against the wall with one hand, the chain swinging wildly in the other.

I start to cry, suddenly terrified she's going to hit me with the chain. 'I'm sorry, Miss Giles, honestly! I'm trying hard to do it . . .'

She looks right into my eyes, her wild grey hair falling forward as she gives the chain in her hand a quick shake. 'Look, Harte,' she says, pushing me back against the wall. 'This is how ye chain a cow!'

I cry even harder, convinced by now she'll knock me out with the heavy chain any moment. 'I'm sorry, Miss Giles. I'll try again, I'll do it right this time!'

'You'd better, Harte. From now on you'd better do it right!'

'I will.'

'That's good, because you'll answer to me if you don't! D'you hear me?'

'Yes, Miss Giles.'

I cry through the whole milking, remembering what the older girls told me about toughening up. From now on I'll not ask for Miss Giles's help no matter what I've done or what I've to do to fix it. Then I'll know enough after a time not to need help from old Farmer Giles. No matter what happens, I'm going to be a good milker.

Each morning, I go with the others to the paddock along the narrow cow path. Farmer Giles is always about, and she sometimes follows us down if we dawdle at all. This morning, Rita Duffy and her friends are full of whispers ahead of me on the path. I wonder what they are up to and move closer to them to hear. I see one of them look back over our heads as we get to the paddock gate. 'Maureen, come on!' Rita says to me. 'We'll play on the hill for a few moments: king of the castle!'

Rita tears up the little hill, then Bridie goes on up after her. Bridie tries to throw her arms round Rita's waist to pull her off the hill, but Rita shoves her away. 'I'm the king of the castle, get down ya dirty rascal!' Bridie lets herself tumble and roll down the side of the hill like a sack. I hesitate then follow them and begin rolling down, taking turns at being the king of the castle. Soon, six or seven of us are playing the game, fighting, rolling, crying out 'I'm the king of the castle' and not even thinking about being caught. What freedom there is sometimes in being a milker.

When we finish, the older girls rush to the gate, still looking and whispering. 'Maureen!' Rita calls out to me, her face flushed with excitement and mischief. 'We'll have a bit of fun with Bluebell, wait till you see it! We're going to get her all worked up! Farmer Giles is busy in one of the sheds, so she'll not be down for a while if we hurry.'

Rita heads off toward the paddock with two older girls, while I stand off to the side with the other younger milkers. As Rita opens the gate, it gives out its usual long, dry squawk. We're told to wait outside the paddock beyond the gate and watch for Miss Giles. As the cows begin to file out, two of Rita's friends keep Bluebell from leaving. Of all the cows, old Bluebell is the wildest. Seeing the other cows going ahead of her and being held back makes Bluebell angrier and angrier. Her dark eyes seem to flash at the girls in her way, and her hoofs stamp on the straw beneath her in an effort to escape and catch up with the other cows. The two girls begin to laugh loudly as they try to avoid her and hold her back at the same time. I cannot believe their boldness! I grow very nervous thinking that I'll see Miss Giles charging down the path in her heavy farm clothes, shaking her wild grey head in anger at us.

All the cows are now out except for Bluebell, who the older girls leave behind the closed gate so that she'll get into a worse state, thinking she's going to be left back at the paddock. The other cows are bothered by Bluebell's angry behaviour. They fuss and moo more than normal as they hurry along the path towards the farm and the milking stalls. Bluebell by now is in an awful state at being left behind. All of us are howling with laughter at her antics. How funny and strange it is to see a cow having a fit of temper! 'Oh, Rita,' I call out, 'sure, she'll knock the gate apart, she will!'

'A minute longer, Maureen, a minute longer,' Rita says. 'She's a crazy aul thing, this one is!'

Meanwhile, the other cows and some of the girls are on their way to the stalls, just ahead on the path. Some look back at what is going on, waiting for something big to happen. 'Now, stand back, and I'll let her out,' shouts Rita excitedly. She swings open the squeaky gate, and Bluebell charges on up the cow path racing like a bull. There are screams coming from the other milkers as Bluebell gets closer, rushing her way up the path through the other cows as if to take her proper place. We laugh hysterically at the sight. What a great bit of fun and a great distraction from the dull routines of our day.

Then, out of nowhere, through all the laughter, commotion and screaming girls, comes the dreaded voice of Farmer Giles. 'What in the name of God is going on down here? What is this? These cows are to be brought up and milked!' I turn to see the form of Miss Giles charging down the cow path like an angry scarecrow, her stick raised and her wild grey head jerking and bobbing as she looks around for someone to blame. Just then, the still-charging Bluebell collides with

Miss Giles, knocking her off her feet right into a huge briar bush. Rita Duffy is bending over at the waist trying not to burst with laughter. 'Ah, Maureen, let's go before I wet myself! Did you see that?'

From down amongst the briar comes another frightful roar. 'What in the name of Christ! Well, by God, I'll have the life of one of them, I will, so help me God!' There are suddenly fourteen very serious-looking girls walking as innocently as possible beside the cows to the byres. When old Farmer Giles gets herself untangled from the briar bush, she'll catch up to us, and there'll be an awful price to pay for her little accident. But it will be worth it, I think, as we'll have something to laugh at now for a long time to come.

Maggie and Lucy have become milkers, too: Maggie three months after me at the beginning of August, and Lucy in November. The three of us now walk each morning to the farm with the other girls, and I'm so happy that we are together.

Maggie's cow's name is Cowslip, and her stall is just two down from mine. Maggie has taken her new chores in her stride without getting worried or upset. She'll never let Miss Giles frighten her, I'm sure, and the same goes for Sister Joseph.

This winter has been the first on the farm for all three of us, and we often shiver in the bitter frost and wind as we've hurried to the farm in the dark mornings. Our light capes aren't warm enough, and we're not given any mittens to warm our hands in. Because of this, we get chilblains on our hands, feet and legs: the small red lumps that itch terribly and sometimes break out into festering sores.

Lucy takes her new chore seriously. She too is determined not to annoy Miss Giles or Sister Joseph. She copes well, but her complaining voice is heard often as we walk along the lane towards the farm in the mist and bitter cold. Yet, as the winter has passed by, so too has some of her complaining, and when she has forgotten about the dung and other hardships she has actually begun to enjoy milking Daisy. We've cheered her up with stories of the coming springtime and games of king of the castle on the hill beside the paddock. In the summer months, we'll distract her by taking her to pick berries along the cow path, stuffing them into pouches pinned secretly beneath our petticoats so we're not caught and punished. And when, once in a rare while, one of the older girls dares, we'll hold back old Bluebell until she's all fired up and then let her go!

I've been a milker for seven months in total, and I've avoided Farmer Giles since the day I couldn't chain Primrose up properly and she was so mean to me. I love Primrose; she knows me so well now. I sing to her when I milk her, and she often gently rubs her head against my shoulder when I do this. I never dreamed a cow could show such affection. Maggie and Lucy love their cows just as much as I love Primrose. Twice a day, the three of us go to the farm: morning and evening, always hoping the winter months will pass quickly, so we won't have to hurt as much in the awful cold.

❖ NINE ❖

Only Christmas is more exciting for us than our once-a-year summer picnic to the River Shannon. We stand in line in the square, paired in twos waiting for the big grey doors to open, and then it's off down the Sligo road. We always pray hard for weeks for good weather, and this year we are again rewarded with a beautiful day. God never fails us on our picnic outing.

Lucy looks about impatiently. 'Sure, it must be ten o'clock by now!' Just as she says this, we hear the van doors shut, and Frank drives slowly through the doors to the road. He's the nuns' laundry driver, and every year he loads his van with bread and jam in hampers for the picnic and drives on ahead of us to the same spot beside the river.

I watch the line of orphans move towards the doors out onto the road and to a day of total freedom. This is the only day each year we get away from the orphanage. The trip is a three-mile walk along the busy Sligo road to the river, and along the way we see cars and buses, asses and carts, ponies and traps, bikes and motorbikes, and many beautiful little cottages as well.

I'm paired with Lucy, and right behind us are Maggie and Eileen. As we walk, facing the oncoming traffic, I can hear shouts of happiness and delight from all around me, up and down the procession of orphans. But poor Colleen's been left behind again. She's too slow, we were told by the nuns, and they've kept her back at the orphanage with the younger children. It's a terrible thing to see her failing like this, slowly, in front of our eyes. She should be with us on such a special day. She should be included and not kept back; that will only make her worse. We all notice her absence and feel sorry that she can't be with us.

As we turn round the next bend, it comes into full view, as lovely as ever: the little cottage with the half-door. 'Look at that door, the half-door. It's so different, don't you think?' I say to the others. 'How the top half is open wide and the bottom half is shut?' I look at the lovely door again. Nellie O'Brien told me about this. She said that these doors are called half-doors. I asked her after I first saw the one at this same cottage. In the country, Nellie told me, the half-doors can let in the fresh air and sunshine while the bottom stays closed to keep the animals out.

As we get a little closer, three or four children hurry out to the garden gate to watch us pass. We must look so strange to them, I think, all of us holding hands and in the same plaid dresses and black boots, with two nuns at the top of the line and two at the bottom. It's always the same – people staring. The villagers do the same thing from their doorways when the nuns take us out on walks through Newtownforbes. The children stand there at the gate, looking as if they feel sorry for us. They know we're orphans, and they know we're different. I don't like always being different and being made to feel it and to know it. There's a sudden hush along our line as we pass, them staring at us and us at them, each from our different worlds.

Continuing our walk, I hear the sound of a pony and trap passing on the road, and it shakes me out of my deeper thoughts. 'Maggie!' I call out. 'Don't you just love the trotting sound of the ponies?'

'Yes,' she answers back. 'Look at the carriage. It's so pretty!'

All the people passing in the traps wave to us, and we shout our hellos back at them, eager to be recognised and have a friendly word. The next thing to get our attention is an old donkey and cart with a farmer sitting in front, going along in a slow, lazy way. The farmer lifts his hat to acknowledge our waves and shouts of hello, smiling at us and amused by how excited we are.

I hear Eileen ask how much farther it is, and someone tells her another half a mile. Eileen's wheezing a lot because of her asthma. It must be all the walking today that is making her short of breath. She hasn't said much, and it's because she's suffering. 'Are you feeling all right, Eileen?' I ask, looking back at her.

'I'll be fine,' she answers. 'I'll be able to rest by the water when we get there. I love being near water. Don't you, Maureen?'

'Ah, yes. I can't wait to paddle my feet after this long walk.' I know she doesn't want to think about her bad breathing too much. Just like the rest of us, she wants to enjoy this beautiful day by the river as much as she can while it lasts.

At the front of the procession, the girls begin to turn down the lane that leads to the river: the last leg of our long walk. The nuns allow us to run the remaining distance once we're at the lane. I turn back to Eileen, telling her to walk down and to pay no attention to the rest of us running. 'I'll see you by the water, then,' she answers.

As my section of the line turns into the lane, I can see the River Shannon in the lower distance, a sparkling ribbon of blue with speckles of sunlight dancing on it. 'Look! It's beautiful!' I shout. 'Let's run and see who'll be first in the water! Are you ready? All right. Go!'

I scarcely feel my feet under me, lost in these seconds of joy and the freedom of the wind blowing my hair from my face. I want to run and run and always feel like this. We get to the river at the same time, tearing off our boots and socks and wading into the cold water without a second thought. 'Oh, it's much colder than it was last year!' Lucy cries out, a big smile stretching across her face, her blue eyes twinkling and alive.

I sit on a large rock soaking my feet while watching for Eileen. The air is full of lovely smells and so alive with the feel of summer. Sounds of laughter carry on the air from the girls already in the river, squealing with delight as they paddle their feet in the water. Eileen arrives at the water's edge, her chest rising and falling rapidly after the long walk. She joins me sitting on the rock, and the two of us look out at the slow current, listening to its gurgling sounds. The river has its own voice, its own song, and I feel so peaceful here. There are no walls or dormitories here, and the wide-open spaces and soft breeze are gentle and soothing.

Lucy looks over towards us, waving wildly as she runs down to tell us about the apples, jam sandwiches and big enamel jugs of fresh milk that Frank has brought for our lunch. Maggie joins us at the edge of the river, and the four of us sit with our feet in the cool water. Most of the younger girls paddle about at the river's edge, while the senior girls brave the deeper parts, where they can sit on the rocks, talking in small groups while the River Shannon flows lazily on either side of them. Now and then one of the nuns walks down to keep an eye on us.

Lucy and Eileen wander off to explore the bulrushes while Maggie and I stay gazing at the scenery. 'I never want this day to end, do you?' I ask her.

'No,' she replies sadly, 'but it has to, doesn't it?' We say nothing more, content to listen to the secret song of the river. 'What're you thinking about?' she asks after a time.

'About what's across this river . . .'

'Across the river? What d'you mean?'

'I mean, what it's like in the outside world.' I point across the river. 'Look, Maggie, away across the fields is the whole outside world, full of people who aren't orphans, with families and real lives . . . and sometimes . . . I wonder . . . will we be as good as those people out there?'

'We will, surely we will. Why not? Just let things happen.'

'Sometimes I wish I were like you. You worry much less than I do, and you know more things, too.' She doesn't say anything, only smiles the smile I know so well.

Lucy runs back over, entirely out of breath. 'You two,' she says, 'so serious! Why so serious? Today is a great day! I've been watching, and it looks like we'll be eating very soon now!'

As if they've heard Lucy, Sister Edna and Sister Brigid blow their whistles, calling us to sit for our picnic. Lucy's gone like a shot, and we follow her to the folding tables where the sandwiches are set up with the jugs of milk beside them. We move into line and each of us takes a sandwich, a porringer of milk and an apple. Today we can eat anywhere we want to, and we agree to go back by the bulrushes where it'll be quieter. There, we gobble everything up fast, saving our conversation until we return to the river, where we can talk and paddle about in the water.

We sit, trying to forget about time as the Shannon moves slowly by us. Each one of us, I know, is trying not to think of going back, wanting it to go on like this without stopping. Eventually, we hear the whistle and see the nuns calling to some of the girls still in the water to get out and get their boots on. 'I don't want to go back,' I say, to no one in particular. 'What a great day it's been.' We stand and walk away from the riverbank, towards the line that is already forming between Sister Edna and Sister Brigid.

I hear the sound of Sister Joseph knocking on the dormitory door to wake us for milking the same as any other morning, but when I move to get out of bed the room spins and my whole body burns like fire. I can only lie back down, terrified already by the sight of Sister Joseph rushing up the row of beds to thump me out of mine. 'Come on, Harte! Out of bed now, up!' she shouts.

'I . . . can't, Sister. I don't know what's wrong with me. I can't move . . .'

'What! There's not a thing wrong with you, Harte. Move now, move!'

'Please, Sister, I can't move. I feel dizzy,' I say, scarcely able to talk.

'Let me feel your head,' she says, laying her rough hand across my brow. 'Ah, yes, you're warm. You've a fever, you do, so stay where you are, then, Harte.' She stands back from my bed and looks about the dormitory. 'O'Rourke, where are you?'

'Here, Sister,' I hear Maggie answer.

'You milk Harte's cow until she's better, O'Rourke, d'you hear?'

'Yes, Sister.'

An hour and a half passes before the younger girls are woken by Sister Anthony. I hear the drab morning routine, and then they shuffle away for mass. The dormitory is silent and empty now. For the next three hours or so, I lie in bed burning up with fever, alone and scared, until finally Sister Brigid appears by the side of my bed. 'I hear you're not feeling well today, Maureen,' she says, standing over me and holding a glass of water. 'Can you raise your head for me?'

'My head hurts, Sister. I feel hot.'

She lays her hand on my forehead: it's soft and white, very different from Sister Joseph's hand. 'Are you dizzy?'

'I am.'

'You're very warm, very warm indeed. Swallow these tablets. They're to get the fever down.' She helps me sit up to swallow the tablets, but even this little movement causes the room to whirl about me. 'You may need to stay in bed for a couple of days, Maureen. I'll be along later in the day to check on you.'

I listen as the swish of her robe and her footsteps on the wooden floor fade away, then the door opens and closes and all is still and quiet around me. It's awful being alone and unwell in the empty dormitory. I've never been sick enough before to have to stay in bed away from my friends and our daily routine. 'Please, God, make me better soon,' I mumble, my head rolling round the pillow, but in moments I slip into a deep sleep.

The hours pass in a fog of fever, and some time later I wake to see Sister Brigid standing beside my bed again, looking down at me. She seems far away as I try to focus my eyes and turn my head to look at her. 'Are you feeling a little better now?' she asks, placing her palm on my forehead.

'A little, Sister,' I reply weakly, my words sounding cracked in my dry throat. 'My headache's better, but I'm very thirsty.' She helps me up, allowing me a little water. The room spins again as I swallow more tablets. She says something to me as I lie back down, but I don't hear her. I only want the room to stop spinning and to be able to sleep. Dimly, I hear the retreating footsteps, then the door. The rest of the day is a blur of waking and sleeping and the vague sense that Sister Brigid has been back once or twice to look in on me.

Maggie, Lucy and the others come into the dormitory at nine o'clock as usual. I hear the familiar shuffling sounds of the bedtime routine then Sister Anthony turns off the lights and leaves the dormitory, locking the bolt of the heavy door behind her. A short silence follows before the sound of her footsteps fade away. A minute later, I hear Maggie's voice whisper across the darkness. 'Maureen? Can you hear me? Are you awake?'

'Yes,' I whisper back.

'Are you all right? We missed you today.'

'I'm so sick,' I tell her, my voice still weak and dry. 'It's awful here alone in the dormitory during the daytime . . .'

'Will you be at school tomorrow, Maureen?' whispers Lucy, off to my right.

'I don't think so.'

'Shut up!' demands another voice from a far row, in an angry whisper. 'Leave her alone so we can sleep!' The voice belongs to one of the tougher senior girls. Not wanting trouble with the likes of her, our whispering ends for the night.

I lie in the dark feeling very ill, thinking about tomorrow and feeling scared about being alone in the dormitory again. Whether from too much sleep today or the fever, I find myself waking to all the sounds of the dormitory during the dark hours. Hearing the rats scurrying and the nightmares of the other girls is dreadful. It was worse before I became a milker, but with the long days and the hard work I sleep through the worst of it these days. Now, though, as the fever comes and goes and the long hours creep slowly by, I hear moaning and then a sudden muffled scream, and later another girl talking in her sleep. I try to block out these sounds as I pray for the morning to come quickly and for God to help me get better soon.

During the daytime, the tablets cool the fever, and I doze on and off, always waking with a thirst, the bedclothes damp from my sweating. I drink from the water left for me and pour some of it on a cloth to lay across my head.

How I miss my friends and the dreary routine. I'd rather be with them than lying here among the rows of beds in the empty dormitory. No one is allowed near me for fear I'll infect another girl with whatever it is I have. I feel so lonely. I use the changing slant of the light coming through the windows to follow the passing time. Sister Brigid comes in occasionally to fold sheets at the far end of the dormitory. I feel better knowing someone is near me, and I look forward to her coming even though she doesn't speak to me. I yearn to be better and back with the other girls.

It is now Saturday, and I'm allowed up out of my bed for the first time since I started to feel ill on Wednesday. I stand, sore from lying in bed, on weak and shaky legs. Sister Brigid watches to see how I make out as I hold Maggie's arm to steady myself. She tells me to go out for some fresh air with my friends, asking Maggie to stay with me while I get used to being up and walking again. Later, I'm able to keep some soup down. But I won't be going back to my milking chores or to school until Monday.

I'll soon be back to my old self again, I'm sure, but I now feel differently about all the sickness I see about me. I know now that I'm fortunate not to have been sick more often. And I pray hard, of course, that I will stay healthy and robust, because it is awful to be so helpless and alone.

It is the end of October, and now that we are twelve our Confirmation day has arrived. We're very well prepared. Dressed for the sacrament in our lovely white dresses, we wait in line outside the little chapel. My mind is consumed with thoughts of Colleen Carey and her absence from us on this important day. I think of our First Holy Communion five years ago and how different this day feels compared to it. Colleen should be here making her Confirmation with us, but she isn't, and we're convinced that the nuns have locked her away in the infirmary sickroom so she'll not be an embarrassment in front of the bishop. We can't imagine any other reason why she wouldn't be allowed to take part in the Confirmation ceremony.

I look down at my lovely white dress and at Maggie and Lucy in theirs, and I think about this religious day and about the nuns. Why can't Colleen be here to get this sacrament? She deserves it as much as anyone. Our Confirmation is supposed to make us closer to Christ and to make us soldiers for God and Jesus, and when I think of Colleen and how she has been treated, I feel very confused and very angry, especially with Sister Anthony.

After we're confirmed, we go through the same routine as we did

five years ago on the day of our First Holy Communion. We are
brought up to the nuns' refectory for a lunch, including the externs
and their parents, and again the young novice nuns serve us at our
own table. They smile kindly as they bring us chicken, roast potatoes,
home-made bread and rice pudding. Again we feel special being
served such a feast by the young nuns, delighted to be receiving this
wonderful food.

We repeat our walk among the nuns' garden, but it's almost
November, and the beautiful flowers that line the winding paths are
not in bloom now. A cool damp breeze comes up, and we walk slowly
this time, not like we did when we ran and played here as young girls.
'I wish I was more excited about this day,' I say quietly as we turn
onto one of the winding little paths in the garden.

'We're older, Maureen, and we know more things now.' Lucy sounds
so much more serious than she usually does.

'I know. It's different now, isn't it?' I reply. 'We've been through so
much, and we feel so terrible about Colleen and what has happened
to her. I was thinking of her all through the ceremony.'

Lucy stops walking and looks at Maggie and me. She lowers her
voice. 'You know, the nuns put on a big show for the bishop, not for
us. It's all done to impress him, not to celebrate us and our special
day. It reminds me of when we were little and the doctor came once
a year and we were all lined up and dressed nicely. It's only a show.
They don't care about us, they don't.'

Suddenly, I don't want to talk about any of this. It frightens me,
and I feel so empty. I cannot get poor Colleen off my mind. 'I'm
going into the chapel to say a prayer for Colleen,' I say to the others,
walking slowly off without waiting for an answer.

They follow along after me into the chapel, kneeling silently
beside me in one of the empty pews of our side chapel. After a
time, Sister Carmel finds us in there together, praying for Colleen,
who's had so terrible a life and whom no one knows or cares about.
'There you are, you three,' she says to us in the quiet way the nuns
speak when they're in the chapel. 'Come on now. You're to take
off your dresses and change back into your day clothes.' We stand

obediently, turning to see her beaming proudly at us. 'I'm glad to see that you're all better soldiers of Christ already. That's very good to see, girls. Come along now.'

We nod dutifully and follow her out of the chapel towards the dreary grey buildings of the main institution. I look at my two best friends. I can see in their faces that they're thinking the same thing I am. What would Sister Carmel and the other nuns think if they knew how angry we felt towards them? As the three of us gloomily make our way back to the linen room to change, there is an unspoken understanding between us that things will be different from now on. Slowly the truth of our world is becoming clearer to us.

❖ TEN ❖

Colleen is getting no better. She seems to have gone to a place in her head where no one can reach her. She roams the dormitory almost every night now, and it is getting worse very quickly. She'll often try to get into one of our beds in the middle of the night and can always be found laughing aloud and mumbling. I don't know how long she can go on this way. Each night she tries to get out of the dormitory by screaming and pounding on the locked wooden door. But the nuns are far away, and no one hears her screams but the other girls. 'Shut up will you!' a voice will shout out. 'Someone put lunatic Carey back into her bed!' Maggie helps me to get her back into her own bed, but then she'll just get up again later. She sits on her bed, laughing and waving her arms about. Oh, dear God, what's going to happen to her? I ask myself. Something will happen soon – we can feel it. The nuns don't allow such things to continue. How terribly lonely she must be in her inner world, up in the night all alone like that, and no one in the world to help her or make it better for her.

Tonight, five minutes after Sister Anthony has left the dormitory, Colleen is at the side of my bed. She still knows enough to wait until the nun is gone before getting out of her bed. 'Colleen, this isn't your bed,' I say gently to her. 'Let me take you back to your own bed.' She looks right through me.

'Fine, fine, Maureen! I'll go back.' She giggles quietly and then she sighs and looks at the floor, her arms hanging by her sides.

'Come along, Colleen.'

I take her across to her bed. She hesitates, staring at her bed as if frightened by it, a place she doesn't want to go. My heart breaks as I watch her. What nightmares she must have in that bed, the bed she's wet almost every single night for so many years. I recall the years below in the lower dormitory: the heavy odour of urine that filled the air each morning. The nuns put plastic sheets down on the beds. I'm sure there's one on this bed now. I wonder if she hears any more the taunts out in the yard: 'Wet-the-bed, you're a wet-the-bed!'

'Go on, Colleen, get into your bed. It's fine. Go on.'

'Fine, yes, it's fine, Maureen, fine,' she says, followed by that awful little giggle again.

After tucking her in, I go back to my own bed with tears in my eyes. It's sometimes hard to believe that this has happened to her, that she is this way after the years of beatings and torment she suffered.

The hours pass in the darkened dormitory. Some time in the middle of the night, I feel someone pulling at me, then a voice. 'Let me in beside you.' It's Colleen again, but much later, in the wee hours of the morning. 'Let me in beside you. I'll not wet the bed. Let me in beside you.'

Dear God, what a look in her eyes. Does she know me, I wonder? I swing my legs out and sit on the edge of my bed. All is quiet as I look around the dormitory and see that she's disturbed no one yet. I look into her vacant eyes and then glance down at her thin droopy frame and stick-like arms, all lost under a large white calico shift. 'It's all right, Colleen. I'll walk you back to your own bed now,' I say, trying to soothe her.

But as I walk her back, she suddenly starts laughing, then louder, before I can shush her quiet again. 'Get lunatic Carey back to bed and shut her up!' a sleepy voice calls out. Some of the girls seem to have no feelings at all; that's what this place has done to them.

I remain beside her bed for a while until I feel she'll stay put. I feel so helpless that I can't reach her. The two of us sit on the edge of her bed while I hold her hand tightly. She stares up at me now and then, with the look of a lost child, as if she could sit here with me for ever and never face the morning or life again. I try very hard not to cry. Never have I felt so helpless before. What will happen to her? God only knows. I've a bad feeling about it. The minutes pass as Colleen rocks beside me on the bed, squeezing my hand tighter now and then.

Through the windows, I see the smallest paling of greyish light. I've been sitting with her for over an hour now. 'We should go back to our beds, Colleen. It will soon be morning, and the dormitory will be opened.'

She looks over at the little wash of grey coming through the windows. Taking my hand in both of hers, she squeezes it, making a sound like 'Ahh, umm, noo'. Then she giggles again and says, 'Fine, fine, Maureen.' She lets go of my hand and lies quietly down on the bed.

As I walk away, I turn to look a final time and see her curled into a tight ball, staring at the ceiling. I slump onto my bed hopelessly. Something inside me wants to scream out against all of this. But I cannot scream out any more than I can help Colleen to come back. She's gone. With a helpless feeling of anger I can do nothing about, I bury my face in my pillow as silent sobs come for Colleen, whom the nuns have beaten into madness. The dormitory is pale with the first light and still and quiet.

Last night, as we lined up to wash at bedtime, Colleen wasn't among us. I couldn't speak up and ask Sister Anthony where she was, as we're not allowed to open our mouths while we wash before bed. I went to sleep thinking that she must be in the infirmary sickroom and that Sister Anthony would bring her in later. I expected her to be up roaming the dormitory again. I was so tired from sitting with her the night before that as soon as I was in bed I fell into a deep sleep. But when we woke early for our milking chores this morning, there was no sign of Colleen.

My head spins as I try to figure out what could have happened. I wait until we're in the lane to talk to Maggie and Lucy about it. 'Colleen's missing,' I tell them in a quiet voice. 'You must've noticed last night as we went to bed she wasn't there.'

They only look ahead, silent until Maggie simply says, 'I know, I noticed. Is she in the sickroom, then?'

'Lucy?' Lucy says nothing, her face twisted grimly as she stares ahead. 'Lucy, what do . . .'

'I don't know!' she almost snaps the words at me. 'God, Maureen. I don't know! I don't know what they've done with her, she's been so bad . . .'

'I'm worried, I really am this time, with the way she's been. Yes, maybe the sickroom for a rest.'

The days have come and gone, and still there's no sign of Colleen in our dormitory, in class, in the dining hall, anywhere. She's just gone, nowhere to be seen. There's been rushed talk with Maggie in the lane on the way to the farm, but Lucy won't speak about it. I asked Maggie what we should do about it and that I was going to speak to Sister Brendan because I'm so worried. She said that I should but warned that the sister might not tell me anything.

This morning, therefore, before school starts and before leaving Sister Brendan's class after my chores, I pluck up the courage to ask. 'Sister Brendan?'

'Yes, Maureen, what is it?'

'My friends and I, Sister, ah, we've, well, it's just that we've not seen Colleen Carey around. We've not seen her anywhere at all. Is she in the sickroom at the infirmary, Sister? Is that where she is?'

She stops and looks at me very seriously, folding her hands together on her rostrum. A slight tremor of fear shoots through me. Am I being too bold, speaking out like this? Will I be punished? As if reaching a decision, Sister Brendan's expression changes, and she moves a small stack of paper on her rostrum, following the movement with her eyes before looking back at me. 'Well, Maureen, you know how Colleen's behaviour has been. We simply cannot take care of her here any more. She's been placed in the asylum in County Longford.'

'What's an asylum, Sister?'

'It's a special hospital for those who are very sick like Colleen is.'

'Will she get better and come back here, Sister?'

'I'm afraid not, Maureen. She's too far gone with her illness.'

I listen to this, shocked, as I stand in front of Sister Brendan. I fight for something, some words to say or to hear. There must be more to say about it than this. Her voice seems to come from far off. 'You may go now, Maureen.'

✻ ✻ ✻

Rita Duffy dances from one foot to the other in the cold outside in the cloister during morning break. 'What? An asylum? Oh, she'll never get out of that place,' she says straight away when I tell her what Sister Brendan said. 'An asylum is for crazy people. They send all the maddies there.'

'She wasn't crazy!' I cry out at Rita, but she only shrugs her shoulders at this. 'Oh, God help poor Colleen! That Anthony, she'll have to account to God she will, for all her cruelty,' I say, my voice shaking with raw emotion. I can feel the sting of the tears in my eyes, but I'll not start crying in front of everyone. Instead, I look away from my friends, full of helpless anger.

'Yes, she will pay for it one day,' Lucy says, almost in tears herself.

After this day, I will never again look at Sister Anthony without feeling a strong hatred for her. I know this isn't right – it's not how God wants it – but I can't help it. I'll never give her an excuse to beat me badly, the way she did before. I'll not give her the satisfaction. I'll do it for Colleen. I'll not whisper in the dormitory; I won't ever speak out loud in front of her. I'll give her no excuse. I will never forget you, Colleen. Please, God, help me survive these last two years of Sister Anthony and this terrible institution.

❖ ELEVEN ❖

At the age of thirteen, we've finally reached our senior years in the orphanage, and Maggie, Lucy and I have become well used to the place and the nuns who run it. We're very happy to finally have Sister Brendan teach us this year. We feel we know her a little better than the other students in our class because of our special chore of cleaning the two classrooms, hers and Sister Carmel's. She's maybe a few years older than most of the teaching nuns, and we have noticed how the younger nuns seem to look up to her.

There are nearly forty-five students in Sister Brendan's class. There are at least six girls from the village as well, girls I've known since low infants class. These next two years are important for us because we're to do our preparation for our primary certificate, and eventually our final examinations will come at the age of fourteen in eighth class down the road. Our formal education will end then, according to the rules of the Irish government.

Sister Brendan begins our first day in her class by saying a special prayer to the Sacred Heart, getting us to memorise it by copying it on the blackboard. This will be our opening prayer each day. 'This year, girls,' she announces, 'we have a large number of seventh-class students, and I think it will be a busy year for us, but a good year as well. Are you listening?'

'Yes, Sister Brendan,' we answer. I can see that it's true what the older girls have said. Sister Brendan is different from the other nuns, and I feel that she does care about us. I wouldn't want to let her down or get into trouble with her. We know from the older students that she's fair and rewards girls if they try hard. Also, I've heard that she doesn't use the cane as freely as the other nuns.

The class immediately seems to fall into an easy routine with Sister Brendan. She has a way of keeping all the girls enthusiastic and alert, understanding their different levels and needs. This is very different from anything I've known before with the other teaching nuns, and I find myself enjoying the lessons much more, and I'm less scared this time.

In the early morning hours of a bitter Christmas Eve, it is barely light and the sky is streaked with cold yellows and greys. Fourteen of us walk or run lightly through the frost and mist toward the milking byres, treading clumsily in our wooden clogs, our capes swinging out behind us. Neither the capes nor the clogs protect us from the cold, but it's a special day for us, and we ignore the chill in our bones. We've thoughts only of the hours ahead and being allowed to talk freely in the dormitory again.

In the evening, we gather in the recreation hall while Sister Carmel sits on the stage handing out Christmas parcels and gifts from family and relatives. I stand chatting with Maggie and Lucy at the back, the three of us paying little attention to the goings on. All the girls expecting something sit in small groups, their eyes on the stage, watchful as they wait to be called. This goes on for a time when suddenly I hear Sister call out my name. We stop what we're doing and look toward the stage. 'She's called your name!' Lucy says, pulling my sleeve.

'No, it can't be me. I've no mammy, Sister!' I call out.

Sister Carmel leans aside in her chair, looking past a group of girls until she finds me with her eyes. 'Come up here, Maureen. You do have a parcel, and it is from your mammy.'

I walk toward the stage still thinking it a mistake. 'Yes, you have a mammy, Maureen,' she says again with a big smile as she hands me a parcel. 'Now go and enjoy this lovely gift from her.'

I take the parcel, holding it and staring at it. It must be true, then: I have a mother! My mammy is alive! I walk away stunned, full of different feelings, all of them rushing up at once. I don't hear the excited questions pouring out of Maggie and Lucy when I reach them. 'Maureen!' A voice brings me round. It's Lucy. 'You've a mammy, Maureen. How can this be? Did you expect this? How?'

'Oh, Maureen,' says Maggie. 'Do you know what this means, to have your mammy send you a parcel?'

I feel shocked, smiling as I stare back at them, unable to fully believe it yet. Having a mammy means I'll be claimed by her when I'm sixteen. For a moment, all the other strange feelings seem to fade, and I can think only that someone will be there to claim me when I leave this orphanage. I come out of my shock to see both Maggie and Lucy looking down at the parcel in my hands. They look back up at me, all of us thinking the same thing: oh, the treats that must be in it. 'Come on. We've a little time,' I say to them. We go off to find a corner to ourselves while the parcels are still being handed out.

'What do you think is in it?' Lucy says, almost skipping off the ground with excitement.

'Sweets, I'd say, and maybe biscuits, too!' Maggie suggests.

'Shake it a little, Maureen,' Lucy says. 'Give it a shake and let's listen!'

'But wait,' says Maggie. 'What if there's something in it that'll break? Don't shake it, just smell it a little. Smell it to see what's in it.'

Before we can shake it or smell it or guess what's in the parcel, Sister Carmel's clapping ends the assembly, and we line up to go back to the dormitory. Before we leave the recreation hall, I ask Rita and little Eileen Quinn to share the treats from this wonderful unexpected parcel.

The moment we're left to ourselves in the dormitory, I sit proudly on my bed while the others gather around, chattering away, a happy little band of orphans about to open a rare treasure. I look at Maggie, and I can tell she feels only happiness for me; I see it on her face. 'Hurry up!' the others say. 'Hurry up, Maureen, and open it!'

I tear at the parcel without fuss, and when the last paper wrapping is thrown off, there are great gasps of delight from us all as we stare at treats the likes of which we've only ever dreamed of: chocolate bars and Rolos, candies and biscuits, even oranges, which are rare! 'Look at it!' Lucy cries out. 'Look at all the treats!'

'Oh, Maureen,' Maggie says. 'Look at that. You're so lucky!'

This can't be happening to me, I think, as I pass round the treats, feeling so special to be sharing this parcel from my mammy with my good friends. We gorge ourselves with the lovely goodies until we're almost sick to our stomachs, not used to the rich chocolate bars and oranges but so happy and contented. This is something we've dreamed of doing together for years. It will be a Christmas and a feast to remember.

Our little banquet of sweets slowly breaks up, and we go to our beds. Other little groups lie awake, talking quietly. I listen to the odd crinkle of a sweet wrapper and the sound of low laughter, thinking how different these sounds at Christmas are from what we normally hear in the dormitory. For a few minutes, as we drift off to sleep, we lie awake in the half-dark, calling softly to one another across the rows of beds.

'Did you hear that, Maggie?'

'What?' asks the sleepy voice.

'Was that a rat?'

'I dunno . . .'

'Are you still awake, Lucy?'

'Goodnight, Maureen . . .'

'Goodnight.'

Alone with my thoughts, I lie awake and restless in the still hours before midnight mass. I just can't believe it, my mammy sending me a parcel? My whole world is suddenly so different. Where has she come from? Where has she been for all these years? Why is she only contacting me now? I don't know what to think about it all. I try to listen only to the muted country sounds outside the building. They sound so far away they make me feel lonelier still. I try to imagine what my mammy looks like and what it would be like to meet her. What would I say to her? What would she want to say to me?

I calm my mind enough to go over what happened in the recreation hall – Sister Carmel telling me I've a mammy and the parcel of treats – but no one explained it to me, and there wasn't even a letter inside the parcel. I imagine what a note might have said had I found one. 'Dear Maureen, you must be wondering . . .' But there

wasn't any note. How confusing it is. I want to believe what I've
been told, and yet something inside me tells me not to hope for
too much. Has Sister Carmel told me everything? Has she received
some letter from my mammy that's being kept from me? I mustn't
imagine things that haven't happened yet. Oh, but I want to hope. I
want this miracle to be real. I've a mammy now, and she'll claim me
when I turn sixteen, which means I'll not go into service as a maid.
I let go and hope with all my heart. I finally belong to someone!
What a feeling!

It's springtime now, and the cold damp winter months have passed
by. I sit daydreaming in class, thinking of my mammy and the parcel.
There's been no mention of her since Christmas, no letters from her,
but still I hope. I've been walking about in a trance, and it's as if I'm
not the same person now.

Still lost in my thoughts, the class ends. As I stand to leave,
Sister Brendan calls me. 'Maureen, please remain. I wish to speak
with you.'

'Yes, Sister.' I walk to the rostrum and stand obediently before her.

She folds her hands on the top of the rostrum and looks directly
at me. 'I have very good news for you, Maureen.' I nod my head,
waiting as she picks up a sheet of paper. 'I have a letter here, Maureen,
from your mammy. She has requested permission for you to leave the
orphanage for three weeks of holidays this summer. Reverend Mother
Xavier has granted the permission for you to visit with her. Your
mammy is living in Mullingar, so that's where you'll be going.'

I stand before her stunned and speechless, my mind beginning to
spin with excitement and a thousand questions. Can this really be
true? My mouth moves silently, but I can find no words. I feel I could
both laugh and cry. Sister Brendan stops talking for a moment and
looks at me, watching my reaction before going on. 'I am very happy
indeed for you, Maureen. This is wonderful news, to know you have
a mammy after all these years and to be going to see her soon. You
will call your mammy Mrs Hughes, Maureen.'

Why 'Hughes', I wonder, feeling almost giddy now. It's a different name altogether from mine, but I don't care, and I brush the thought aside, thinking only of the sheer joy I feel at the thought of meeting my mother. Wait until I tell the others! This is more than I've ever dreamed about. Sister Brendan gathers up the papers, and, after making sure I understand what she's told me, she allows me to leave.

I walk away stunned and half afraid this is all a dream. Why, I wonder, are these wonderful and exciting things happening in my life now, after so many years of accepting that I had no one in the world? This can't be happening to me, and yet it is – Sister Brendan just told me so.

But as I hurry to find Maggie and Lucy, I feel a little frightened inside, too. Will she like me, my mother? Will I like her? Will she tell me why she put me in this awful place? Oh, I have so many questions rattling round in my head. But it doesn't really matter. The only thing that matters is that I will be leaving the orphanage for the first time ever to stay in a real home with my very own mother. I don't care where she's living or what her life is like; that doesn't matter to me. I just want to be loved by her. I'm sure any home will be like a palace in comparison to this ugly place.

I rush to find my friends, knowing they'll be waiting to see why I was kept behind. 'I'm going to Mullingar to meet my mammy in July for three weeks!' I blurt out before they can say a word. They're speechless for a moment, looking at one another, knowing how incredible this is and what it means. But as the three of us move off to find a quiet place in the yard to talk, they're full of questions. 'Who is she, Maureen?' Lucy asks. 'Why Mullingar?'

'Sister said her name is Mrs Hughes and that's what I'm to call her.'

'I wonder if that's her married name?' Maggie asks.

'I don't know, but I can't believe I'm leaving here this summer,' I say. 'As to Mullingar, Lucy, I think I must have been born there or somewhere close to it.'

'You must bring us back something, Maureen,' Maggie pleads. 'Like chocolates and sweets!'

'Or biscuits, or apples or oranges!' Lucy adds to the list.

As we walk on, I realise how happy they are for me. I feel sad for Maggie and Lucy, though. I want a miracle to happen to them as well. How I'd love to take them with me on this holiday, especially Maggie, as she and I have become very close since Katy was adopted and taken from us.

How very different my life feels to me since this wonderful news. Everything around me shines a little brighter: the sun, the fields, even my milking chores seem easier to me. I sing to Primrose, stopping now and then to share with her, in words under my breath, secret feelings about my big adventure. I stand at my window each night looking out over the grey wall, wondering at the different possibilities that float through my thoughts. She is out there, miles distant, in a little town called Mullingar. Is she thinking of me now, my mother, waiting to meet me? Each morning when I wake, my first thoughts are of my holiday in July. For the first time in my life, I feel truly blessed, knowing I'll soon come to see the world outside the walls of the orphanage. Three precious weeks I'll have away from this place and the dank dirty dormitory. I'll not truly believe it until I'm on the train, so I pray and hope and wait for the day to arrive.

❖ TWELVE ❖

The day, the fourteenth of July, has finally arrived, and I stand with six other orphans, all of us proudly dressed in our best uniforms of black serge gym tunics and deep yellow blouses, waiting to be collected. I cannot describe how excited I am this morning. This is more than anything I've known or felt before. I'm leaving the orphanage for the first time in my life at the age of fourteen. It feels amazing.

Frank waits for us beside the old laundry van to take us to the train station in Newtownforbes, but first the Reverend Mother must formally see us off on our holiday. 'Now, children,' she says, 'God bless you all, and come back to us safely, do you hear? And don't forget your prayers each day, now.'

'Yes, Reverend Mother,' we all answer in unison.

'In you get now, into the van with Frank, children.'

Eager to get going, we pack into the van while Reverend Mother goes on talking through the windows at us. 'Be good now, children,' she says. 'Are you listening to me?'

'Yes, Reverend Mother.'

'Frank,' she says, 'see each child safely onto the train, will you, please?'

'I will, Reverend Mother.'

He drives off through the high gates while we wave a final time to Reverend Mother Xavier. Moments later, as we round the little bend that seems to hide the old grey buildings from the world, none of us think to look back.

Frank smiles as he listens to our chatter. I think he knows how happy and free we feel right now. In less than ten minutes, we're out of the van and following him into the little waiting room of the train station. Our feet echo on the old wooden floor as we walk across to a window. Frank talks to a man at the window for a moment, and one of the other girls, Celine, turns to me and says, 'That's the station master, Maureen, that man there in the window.' I nod my head.

'Come on, girls,' Frank says, fussing round us. 'Out to the platform now, and ye's can talk there while you wait.'

On the platform, we huddle close in a group, each of us holding our belongings in a brown-paper parcel tied with twine. The other people on the platform look over at us, thinking we don't notice their curious glances. It's easy to see that we're from the orphanage, and it's nothing new to us, being stared at. This time, though, we don't mind. I know we look smart in our dress uniforms. I'm glad I'll not have to meet my mammy for the first time in my plain old day dress: that would've shamed me.

The six girls I'm travelling with have all been out before, more than once. They want to show off to me and tell me all that they know about the train route. 'Oh, Maureen,' one says, 'you'll love the train ride, you will. The little towns we pass, and the lovely green fields . . .'

'And people waving,' cries another, 'on the platforms, when the train's stopped for passengers. Did you tell Maureen about that?'

They go on like this, explaining how Mullingar is a larger station where one line connects with another and travellers often change trains there. I nod my head listening, pleased I won't be alone for my first trip to the outside world. I can't imagine how nervous I'd be. 'Don't worry, Maureen,' one says. 'You're to get off long before we do, so we'll tell you. We've another fifty miles to go after that, all the way to Dublin.'

I look about the little station, with its trimmed hedges along the tracks and the wild red and white roses and other colourful flowers blossoming all around the grounds. The little building with the creaking old floors is covered on the outside in a blanket of ivy. The whole station looks so peaceful, so full of colour and so different from the drab orphanage. For the first time in my life I feel freedom bursting inside me, enjoying just standing here in this beautiful quiet place. We're only minutes from the orphanage, yet it feels like a world apart. How strange to be leaving it, waiting for a train and not standing in a line. No nuns, no Sister Anthony, none of the routine I've been used to for so many years. It feels wonderful.

I come out of my thoughts and join the others, chattering away about everything, our eyes constantly darting in the direction the train will come. Suddenly, a long high-pitched whistle seems to cut the air above us. 'The train!' one of the girls cries out. 'Listen, it's coming!'

My heart leaps as I hear another blast of the whistle and then another. I lean out daringly to get a look. The train speeds toward us with steam spouting from the engine like a great kettle boiling. Frank fusses round us as the train approaches. 'Careful, girls. Not too close, now. Stand back till it's gone by, d'you hear me?'

Then a great roar erupts as the engine rumbles past us louder than I could have imagined, drowning out the sound of our girlish voices and covering us in a wash of steam. The train grinds to a stop, and a moment later the seven of us are shouting, waving to Frank and boarding the train.

One of the more confident girls leads us to a man in uniform, and she finds us a compartment where we can stay together. The seats in our compartment are beautiful, all plush and finished in green and red velvet. They remind me of the nuns' parlour furniture.

Celine, Nora and Margaret are three of the girls travelling with me today. They are very kind to me and say I should sit next to the window because it's my first time and I'll be able to see the scenes outside better from the window seat. I do as they suggest, sliding over as we move slowly away from Newtownforbes. I feel giddy with joy and adventure. The motion of the train fascinates me, being inside something so big and powerful. I look out of the window as if into a dream as the train picks up speed. Fields and farms come into view, places I've never seen or known. It feels like a new world, and I watch it all as the others talk away behind me about all the things they'll do on their holiday. 'I'd like to go to the pictures again like I did last time,' one is saying. 'And to the seaside. My aunt took me there last time.'

'Are there shops nearby where you're staying?' asks a different voice. 'I love to visit shops . . .'

But as I listen and watch the incredible things passing outside, my mind drifts back to Maggie and Lucy. I almost expect to turn round and start talking to them, but I've left them behind. I wonder if they're thinking about me out here, wishing they could be with me.

Someone tugs at my sleeve. It's Celine. 'Maureen, what're you thinking so deeply about there? Come on. We're going to go exploring, out in the corridors. C'mon!'

I follow Celine into the long corridor that runs outside our compartment. She looks back at me smiling, happy to be leading me on this adventure. 'We stand here, Maureen, to watch all the scenes speed by. It's lovely, isn't it?'

''Tis, Celine. It's lovely indeed.'

With our skinny arms leaning on the polished brass handrails, we watch the passing countryside. The little villages appear and disappear in the blink of an eye, each one bringing me nearer to Mullingar and closer to my mammy. The train's route takes us along beside a lovely lake: Lough Ennell, Celine explains. We pass so close to the edge of the lake that for stretches it seems the train is gliding on the water itself. We stand for most of the trip, walking up and down the narrow corridors, pointing at the passing sights, waving to people on the station platforms when we stop and again when we pull away. I lose myself in the scenes, in the joy and peace of being free, not noticing the minutes pass, enjoying this experience that's so different and fascinating.

A little later, one of the girls calls out over the noise of the train. 'Just another twenty minutes, Maureen, and we'll be in Mullingar! You should get ready!'

These last minutes seem to rush by. I pass the time saying goodbyes, wishing my companions a great holiday and praying silently to calm myself as I stand waiting. The train slows as we near Mullingar, stopping finally in a grinding of wheels accompanied by a musical greeting of the whistle. Passengers pour out of the train while the girls gather round near the door to see me off.

'Goodbye, Celine. Thanks for showing me round the train.'

'Goodbye, Maureen. I'm happy for you, and I hope you enjoy your first time out.'

❖ THIRTEEN ❖

After some final goodbyes, I step off the train, clutching my brown-paper parcel and immediately looking quickly about me, not sure from which direction my mother will come. The nuns didn't tell me what she looks like, so I have no idea what to expect other than what my imagination has built up.

The train is already pulling out of the station, and I turn back to see my friends standing at an open window waving, six smiling faces looking at me. 'Have a great time with your mammy!' calls a fading voice. I manage a big smile and a quick wave but suddenly feel very afraid as I watch them go. They're the only connection to everything I know, and in a moment they'll be gone. I don't take my eyes from them until the waving arms and yellow of the uniform sleeves fade from sight around a bend. I feel very alone.

Moving back near a wall, I stand searching the length of platform as the crowds thin out. No one seems to be watching for me. Surely I must stand out in my uniform and my mammy will know me, I think. A family passes by, and I look at them with great curiosity. The young children seem so happy, jumping and skipping alongside their parents. A minute passes and then another, and still no one has come near me. I begin to fret. What if something's gone wrong?

It's been ten minutes, maybe, since I got off the train, and the platform is without a soul. I stand, scared, a lone figure in the empty station.

A few minutes later, I see a stooped elderly lady moving slowly along the deserted platform in my direction. She doesn't look towards me or wave as she gets closer. Surely this can't be her. She stops in front of me and says, 'You must be Maureen.' I nod my head, managing a shy smile as she reaches out to take the parcel from me. She doesn't embrace me. 'Come with me now, Maureen,' she says in a gentle voice. 'I've a hired car waiting to take us home.'

112

Home. Oh, what a word! I follow her along the platform for about a good fifty yards, walking just behind her and neither of us saying a word. I look at her. She must be in her late sixties, with a thin build and a narrow pleasant face. Her curly hair is going white, pulled back and tied and capped in a brown beret. She has on a long skirt and a long, loose-fitting tweed coat. I keep looking at her and feel I'm in some sort of dream or something. This is my mammy; this is my mammy: the phrase repeats in my head, again and again. Ahead of us, near a narrow street, a man waits, leaning against a car. He holds out his hand to greet me as we arrive. 'Oh, here she is,' he says, in a friendly way. 'And how was your trip? All right, was it?'

Too shy to answer him, I manage a smile and a quick glance. Everything around me, every detail, is new and strange and different. I've never been in a car before, and I sit in the back with my mammy as we leave the station. The seats are like those on the train – plush and comfortable – and there's room enough for two or three more people besides us.

As we move through the busy town, I sneak sidelong glances at my mammy. She seems kind and gentle, judging from these first few minutes, but I think in my mind I'd imagined that she would be a little younger. Though she's quiet so far, I sense that my mother likes me, and her warm smiles suggest she's as excited as I am about our reunion. My eyes are constantly drawn back to the car window to see the exciting world outside. I've never seen such sights as this: so many cars and shops, bicycles, people standing talking to one another, and buses coming and going. Then, as we turn a corner, I see a beautiful cathedral in the distance, with two high pointed steeples at one end. Everything around me seems so full of life. It's an incredible change from the ordered, quiet routine I'm used to, and it frightens me and excites me at the same time.

The car turns into a street of low two-storey houses in a quieter area. I notice that the shops and houses are very close to the pavements, with no front lawns or gardens. 'We're here now, Maureen,' my mammy says. I look one way and the other, trying to guess which of the little houses is hers. So many restless nights in the dormitory as I waited for my holiday I imagined a hundred different houses where she might live, all special and beautiful. 'It's this one,' she says, pointing. 'The last one there.'

I step out of the car, looking up and down the street while my mammy pays the hired driver. A woman appears in the doorway of the house next door. 'Maureen,' my mammy says, walking up slowly. 'This is my neighbour, Mrs Burke.' I can only smile with my head down. I haven't a clue what to say or how to behave in this situation.

'How are you, Maureen?' Mrs Burke asks. 'You're very welcome. Your mammy told me you were coming to visit.'

'I'm fine,' is all I can get out.

Mrs Burke is a tall, neat-looking woman, well dressed and with an upright posture. She must be younger than my mammy by a good ten years. She has a pleasant smile and for some reason reminds me of Sister Brendan. I wait while the two of them have a quick chat, terribly anxious to see inside the house. Then I discover that Mammy's door is a half-door. Oh, wait until I tell Maggie and Lucy.

Mammy finishes her word with the neighbour, and I follow her in through the half-door and through a second inner door. When I'm standing inside, I stop and thank God for this miracle in my life. 'Come on upstairs, Maureen. I'll show you where you'll be sleeping.'

I follow her through a large kitchen then up a short, narrow wooden stairway. Upstairs are two bedrooms: a large one and a much smaller one. 'This is Mr Hughes' room,' she says, pointing to the smaller of the two. 'You and I will share the large bedroom.'

Her words take a moment to sink in: Mr Hughes. She's married, then? I've not thought about her being married. The nuns told me nothing about her circumstances. So, it won't be just my mammy and me here. I hope Mr Hughes is nice to me and wants me here. I wonder if he's my father? There are too many things happening in my head to think straight. With all that's been going on, am I now going to have to think I might have a daddy as well? It's too much. I'm not used to seeing a man about. How will I handle it if it's true? I'll have to calm down and try not to worry about it. He must have agreed with Mrs Hughes to take me out of the orphanage, otherwise I would not be allowed here.

'Where is Mr Hughes?' I ask, very curious now. When she doesn't answer me, I speak a little louder. She notices me talking to her and says, 'Ah, Maureen, I'm a little hard of hearing. You'll have to speak up, dear.'

'All right. I'll remember.'

She goes on to answer my question. 'He's at work. He'll be in later in the day. You'll meet him then. Now, Maureen, go on and change out of your good clothes and wash up. There's a basin on the little table and water in the jug beside it. Come on down when you're ready.'

She leaves me to change, and I tear open the brown-paper parcel. Inside is my plain plaid dress, a pair of clean socks and a change of underwear that the nuns sent me off with: all my worldly possessions. I'll save my uniform for mass or special outings with my mammy.

Dying to explore the house, I'm dressed in a minute and back down in the kitchen and sitting by the fireplace. My mammy looks up at me with a warm smile as she sets out cups and saucers for tea. I've never had tea before. Maybe I'll get a treat with it: a cake or some biscuits. 'Well, Maureen,' she begins, 'how does it feel to be here?'

I struggle for an answer: 'Oh, I love it, but it's so different. Everything's new to me . . .' I let my words trail off.

'Don't worry about a thing, Maureen. I know it's new to you, but just relax now and enjoy your holiday, d'you hear me?'

'Yes, I will. I know I will.'

I look around the kitchen with a deep sense of contentment. Beneath the single window facing onto the street is a big scrubbed wooden table with an oil lamp in the centre. How beautiful it must look at night when it's lit. On the far wall is a high wooden dresser, with different plates made of china on top and food in the bottom. On the kitchen walls hang a couple of holy pictures: one of the Pope and another of the Sacred Heart, over in the corner by the stairs. Behind the image, a Sacred Heart lamp burns softly.

As I sit staring at the low turf fire, the smell of it right away reminds me of mornings in high infants and first class with Sister Carmel when we were five and six years old. And now I'm in Mammy's kitchen, with the smell of turf smoke, and it feels good. 'The fire has gone down, Maureen. I'll get some turf now,' she says, going out of the back door. 'Go on now and have a good look around the house.'

I wait until she comes back in with a couple of sods of turf for the fire and then I'm up. Out back, I find a small cemented area with a pump for water and a lavatory, the same flush toilet we use in the orphanage with a chain handle. I see the pail with the sods of turf in it for the fire inside. There's no electricity in the house. The big black kettle hanging on a crane over the fire in the kitchen must be for the hot water. I go back inside, walking slowly around and running my fingers lightly over the wood of the old table. I want to touch all this, to feel everything and remember it. I want to know how people live in the outside world: how they cook, where they put the food, everything that makes this world so different from mine. I want to store it all up in my head so I can tell Maggie and Lucy about these things when I have to go back.

Of all the lovely things in the little terraced house, I save the half-door for last. I stand looking out at the street where my mammy lives with great curiosity. They're all small old houses attached to one another, each door close to the one beside it. To the right are more houses. The Dublin road, here outside of Mammy's place, isn't as busy as the streets in the town were. There's just a few shoppers returning with bikes or on foot, and they all say hello to me. I smile but avoid their eyes, not knowing how to answer them.

Finished with my exploring, I sit by the fireplace, watching my mother cook. She hasn't said much so far, and I feel too shy to begin, though I'd love to talk to her. She has her back to me, quietly tending the cooking, and is so close I can almost touch her. I feel so content here. She is old and stooped, but she is mine.

I hear the latch of the door being lifted, and a moment later Mrs Burke walks in. 'Well, Maureen, are you settling in a little after your train ride?' she asks with a big smile.

I smile shyly while Mammy, who mustn't have heard the door open, finally greets her. 'Ah, Mrs Burke, hello. Will you stay for a cup of tea, now?'

'Indeed I will, thanks.'

I wait, feeling awkward, sure that Mrs Burke will talk to me and fearful because I won't know how to reply or what to say. What will I do? 'Are you happy to be here, Maureen?' she asks. 'Sure you must be, and your mammy couldn't wait to see you. This is your first time out of the orphanage, isn't it?'

'Yes,' I answer, but my head stays down on my chest, and I'm unable to look at her. She glances quickly at my mammy, then back at me. 'Why don't you hold your head up, Maureen, and look at me?'

I do as I'm told out of habit, as if answering the command of one of the nuns. 'Now, that's better, Maureen.' Mrs Burke looks over and nods at my mammy, who sits smiling at this. 'Don't be shy with us, your mammy and all her friends. We're happy you're here with us.'

That seems to be all the questions for the time being, so I sit back and try not to bring attention to myself. Mammy and Mrs Burke talk about different things as they sip their drinks, and I'm happy to just sit and listen to them. I've not touched my own tea yet. I look at the cup with its delicate little handle on the side. If I dropped it, it would shatter into a million pieces on the hard cement floor, not like the old tin porringers I'm used to. I sneak a look at how Mammy and Mrs Burke hold their cups, how they drink the tea in little sips while they chat. Imitating them carefully, I sip the black tea, surprised by the strength of it. Seeing the milk and sugar, I add a little of both, thinking I'll like the taste when I get used to it.

They continue to chat while I think of what Mrs Burke has said, about holding my head up. I'll try to remember to do it, but it isn't easy. I'm used to keeping my head down in the orphanage, and it's hard to remember not to do that. Mrs Burke's words about how they're happy I'm here ring in my head, and I feel warm and special. That's what I want to say if I could: how happy I am to be here with them. But how can I explain my life before today to them? How can I say all the words that are always trapped inside me? My thoughts drift on like this until, after a time, Mrs Burke stands up to leave. 'Sure, himself'll be in shortly for his dinner, so I'll be off now,' she says to my mammy in a loud voice. 'Remember now what I've said, Maureen, and I'll see you soon. Sure, I'm right next door and always in for tea with your mammy.'

When Mrs Burke leaves, I go back to sit by the fire again; it's already one of my favourite spots. I let my mind drift slowly as I gaze into the hearth, soothed by the calming effect of the flames as they flicker low off the burning turf. The time passes easily like this, with me sitting peacefully before the small glowing halo of the fire and Mammy moving about the kitchen quietly, looking at me occasionally with her warm smile. Then I hear the half-door opening, and I'm sure it must be Mr Hughes in from work. I stand to greet him as he steps into the kitchen in his brown work coveralls. 'Ah, there she is! Sure, you must be Maureen!' He reaches out to shake my hand. 'Pleasure to meet you, Maureen,' he says, taking my small hand in his big rough one. I feel terribly shy as I shake his hand, my face looking down at the cement floor. I have no idea what to say to him.

Mr Hughes is short and balding with a stocky build and a moustache, but he's softly spoken and seems kind enough. Mammy stands off to the side with her hands on her hips smiling at us. 'How was your trip?' he asks.

'It was great,' I answer quietly.

'Ah that's lovely, lovely. Well, make yourself at home, Maureen,' he says. 'I'll wash for tea now.'

Later, we sit down to dinner at the wooden table, where I'll be able to see everything go by outside as we eat. How I've dreamed about and waited for a day like this: being part of a family meal with people I belong to. It's peaceful here, without the clatter and banging of tin plates and porringers in our dining hall that I'm used to. My mammy offers me cheese and home-made bread with fresh milk. 'Now, Maureen, eat up. There's lots more food.' I've never tasted cheese before, but it's lovely. I let it sit slowly in my mouth, savouring the taste while I sneak looks at Mammy and Mr Hughes. He eats in silence, which makes me a little uneasy at first. Then I realise he's just a quiet man by nature, because he smiles at me now and then when he sees me enjoy the food. Seeing this table full of food makes me think of all the times we've gone hungry. I can't believe that I'm sitting here, a part of this. It's like a dream.

After tea, I go back out to stand at the half-door. With my arms resting on the closed section, I stand watching everyone and everything going by on the street. For the first time in my life, I am free. I can feel it all around me, and I'm only beginning to understand what it means. The quiet is what I notice the most: a peace I've never known.

The street outside the terraced house is almost dark now. Only the odd motor car passes by on the busy road. I can feel the soft summer night gather around me, the welcoming stillness of it feeling almost familiar. Before going back inside, I close my eyes to experience once more the quiet and peace, this beautiful new feeling in my life. I breathe in deeply the happy new smells and whisper a soft prayer. 'Thank you, God, for letting me be here. Thank you for your goodness.'

Inside, I find Mammy lighting the oil lamp and Mr Hughes already gone to bed. She asks me to sit down a while by the fire before it's time for bed. The old kitchen looks so different at night: warm and cosy with the light of the oil lamp thrown softly across the ceiling and walls. The fire is small, with a warm red glow and the odd spark popping dully in the grate. My mammy moves silently about the kitchen putting things away in the press. Her gentle smile when she looks over at me makes me feel special. These are family things, these little chores she does probably every evening. At last everything is in its place and the table is set for Mr Hughes' breakfast. 'Well, Maureen,' she says, 'you must be very tired from your trip. We'll go on up to bed now.'

I nod my head, yes, with a smile, looking a final time at the dying embers as I realise that tonight will be the first time in my life, that I can remember, sleeping anywhere but in the dormitory. It's sure to feel strange. My mammy holds the oil lamp as I follow her up the stairs, the light flickering silently round the tiny hall that leads to the bedrooms. In the room, she sets the lamp down on the small table, and the two of us change without a word. We kneel to say our prayers together before getting into the bed we'll share. I try to pray properly, but this is too exciting and mysterious for me to concentrate. It's so different from lining up with fifty other children and Sister Anthony looking on. Then the light is out and I'm beneath the soft, clean-smelling sheets in the quiet darkness.

I lie awake beside my mammy, listening to her slow, steady breathing. She's asleep already. How still it is in the room – only the occasional sound of a motor car passing and the voices of people going by on the street below. On the bedroom ceiling, beams from the motor cars' headlights flash into the room, as if spying on us. I watch the light change shape above me as one car passes, falling away again until the next one. I think of the sounds I won't hear tonight, for the first time in my life: the rats and the fretful nightmares of the other girls. As I count the passing cars and listen to the sound of steady breathing beside me, I slowly slip off into sleep this first night in the little terraced house in the town of Mullingar, where I was born.

❖ FOURTEEN ❖

The next morning, after a good night's sleep, I wake to the sounds of the heavy morning traffic on the road outside. I look around the bedroom sleepily, puzzled until I hear my mammy below in the kitchen. Yes, it's still real. I lie thinking a while in the cosy bed, enjoying the smell and sensation of the clean, fresh sheets. Finally, I get up and shuffle over to the bedroom window to gaze at the scenes below, still so new to my eyes. When I hear slow steady footsteps coming up the stairs, I jump back into bed like a flash, pulling the covers up over me. 'So, you're awake now, are you, Maureen?' Mammy says, coming into the room.

'Yes, I've been awake awhile now,' I answer from beneath the cosy sheets.

'Well, when you're washed and dressed, come down for your breakfast, dear.'

I use the hand basin and jug of water on the table to wash, and then rush to get into my plain plaid dress. I've thoughts only of the breakfast I'm about to eat. It'll not be cold porridge and cocoa like at the orphanage, and I'm looking forward to it. Judging by the lovely smell and the sizzling sounds, it'll be bacon, or a sausage maybe, and home-made brown bread as well, like I had yesterday with my tea.

I'm right. On the table downstairs is a breakfast I've not seen the likes of since my Confirmation. I get both bacon and sausages on my plate. A loaf of brown bread sits on a wooden board waiting to be cut beside a pot of raspberry jam, and there's milk and sugar for the tea. Mammy sits down, and we say grace before I tuck into the food. I try not to devour the food too greedily as she watches me, but she seems pleased to see me eat so well.

After breakfast, I go out to relax at the half-door. I wonder what will happen today and if I should be inside helping my mammy. But it isn't long until she tells me that she needs to go into town for a few things. I'm happy to go along with her, but walking along the busy road scares me a little, with the traffic rushing past me so close. On the way into town, we meet one of the neighbours, Mrs Lynch, who lives two doors down. She's a heavy-set woman with greying hair, and she works as a nurse in the county hospital. Mammy smiles as she introduces me. 'This is Maureen. She's with me for three weeks' holiday.'

'Well, how are you, Maureen? It's a pleasure to meet you.'

I stand with my head down not saying a word until Mammy says, 'Ah, she's shy, so she is. Very shy indeed.'

'Did you know that was my son Michael who collected you at the train in the hired car?'

I smile back as best I can at this pleasant jolly neighbour of Mammy's. As we walk on, Mammy speaks to me. 'Now, Maureen, you're not to be so shy. Most of the people you'll be seeing while you're here are my neighbours. They're lovely people, and you shouldn't worry yourself, d'you hear me, now?'

'Yes, I'll try,' is all I can offer for an answer. But I dread meeting anyone else. As nice as they are, I'll blush as soon as they look at me. I haven't a clue what to say, and I'm sure they'll notice it.

The man behind the counter in the butcher's shop knows Mammy, too, and I have to say hello to him. He smiles at me, and I pray he won't want to talk to me. Am I going to meet every neighbour and shopkeeper in one morning?

It's been a couple of days since I arrived. I'm getting my dress uniform on to go to Sunday mass when I hear Mammy's footsteps coming up the stairs. 'Here's something for you to wear,' she says, coming into the room and smiling as she hands me a small bag. I open it excitedly, finding a pink hair clip and a pair of ankle socks inside. 'They'll go with your hair, I think, Maureen.'

'Oh, thank you so much. I'll wear them right now to mass!'

'That's fine, dear. We'll be leaving in half an hour.'

'All right, I'll be ready.'

A few minutes later, I'm in my dress uniform with my white ankle socks on and the new clip in my hair. With a quick look in the mirror, I decide Mammy is right: the clip does go with my hair.

Before we leave for mass, I stand at the front of the house watching the pony and traps trot by our house on the way to the cathedral, listening to the high step of the ponies and the musical clip-clop of their hooves on the road. Farmers clatter along in old carts with donkeys leading them. What a beautiful sight it is, this steady march of families passing in fine colourful clothes, the men in their Sunday best and the women in hats and nice dresses. The streets are black with people as they come out of houses, closing doors behind them, everyone walking in the same direction towards Christ the King Cathedral, the church I saw from the hired car the day I arrived.

Mr Hughes and my mammy appear behind me, and the three of us step through the half-door to join the crowds going to mass. Mr Hughes walks on ahead while I walk along beside Mammy. This puzzles me for a while until I see that most of the men are walking together in groups or a little way ahead of their wives and children. We get closer to town, where all the shops are closed for the day, and there are many families with children. I look at them, especially the girls with their long shiny hair and their lovely clothes. Do I look as nice as these girls do, I wonder, as I glance down at my new ankle socks. But, for today at least, I feel like I belong, that I look just like these other children, walking with my mammy and Mr Hughes like a family.

Closer to the cathedral, I can see its two great high steeples, one of them with a clock set into it. Christ the King Cathedral has lovely grounds all around it, with high wrought-iron railings that remind me of the convent section of the orphanage. There are people strolling in from all directions – alone, in couples or in families – and some arrive on bikes that they leave resting along the railings. 'What do you think, Maureen?' Mammy asks, leaning close to me. 'Isn't it grand?'

'Oh yes, it's so lovely. It's just beautiful.'

We walk up the wide steps to the front of the cathedral and through carved wooden doors that stand open between two high pillars. I follow Mammy to one of the pews close to the middle, where we'll have a good view of everything. Again, Mr Hughes has slipped away to sit with a group of men, greeting one or two of them as he approaches.

The cathedral is beautiful inside, with a high ceiling and many rows of pews and a long wide centre aisle covered in red carpet ending in front of the altar. I stare round, looking up one side of the pews and down the other. Something in the colours of the clothes catches my eye. As I look round again, I realise that most of the men are on one side of the church and the women on the other. But why is this? I don't have the nerve to ask, but it does seem odd.

The priest begins saying mass in Latin. His voice echoes in the large space while I secretly watch all the families and the children, fascinated by all the people around me. An image of the orphanage suddenly intrudes, and I keep seeing the faces of my friends in little flashes. I try to push the thoughts away, wanting only to enjoy mass in this beautiful cathedral with my mammy and Mr Hughes, but I cannot help but see us in our little chapel at the orphanage. I cannot help but think about us orphans arriving there every morning after milking, in the wintertime walking in with our capes over our shoulders, rubbing our hands to warm them, always cold and hungry. I think of little Eileen Quinn having trouble breathing, and the old ones from the laundry off in their own side chapel, and the very young orphans looking sleepy and hungry. I can see Father McClure saying mass in Latin with his back to us and Sister Anthony sitting behind the young ones. I see poor Colleen talking nonsense in the chapel and being taken away by the nuns . . .

Mammy is nudging me back to attention; it is time to receive Holy Communion. I smile at her and walk from our pew to the altar. Doing this with her makes me feel very special. Being here in this lovely cathedral in the outside world with all these families is wonderful. For the first time, I am part of it all and not just watching from the outside and wishing. I must try harder not to think of the orphanage so much and just enjoy where I am while I am here, but I see now, so clearly, how very different the real world actually is.

'Maureen,' Mammy says to me outside after mass, 'I want to bring you for a little visit to meet a good friend of mine, Mrs Donovan. They're a little way from here, a good fifteen-minute walk, so we'll start now.'

'Where's Mr Hughes?' I ask, looking around for him.

'He's gone on ahead.'

I'm excited at the thought of seeing inside another real house. We walk along for a while into a different part of town to the Donovans' house, which is situated on a little street off a busy main road. They don't have a half-door, I see, as we walk in through a little hall to a small kitchen at the back of the house. A woman in a flowered dress greets us, and Mr Hughes, I see, is already sitting down chatting with another man. 'This is Maureen,' Mammy says, and the Donovans stand to say hello.

'Hello, Maureen. Come in, now. 'Tis a grand day,' Mrs Donovan says to me, while Mr Donovan comes forward to say hello and shake my hand. He too is in his Sunday best, wearing a white shirt buttoned to the collar and dark trousers with a large shiny belt around his waist. Mrs Donovan, her hair black and greying like Mammy's, has on a flowered dress and black boots laced up to the ankle. I sit away from the fire by the back door, still very shy.

I listen quietly while the older people chat, curious to learn all I can from their conversation and so delighted to be here and part of it. While the women sip tea, Mr Hughes and Mr Donovan drink pints of Guinness, a thick black drink with a cream-coloured foamy top. The men admire it greatly after they drink it, a little of the foam ringing their mouths as they smack their lips. The adults talk of prices of certain items, people they know and the weather, but when they begin speaking of the old days I'm lost. There are quiet moments when the talking stops and the four of them gaze into the fire as if meditating. Their faces glowing in the red-orange firelight remind me of statues.

After a time, more tea is made, another pint taken and the conversation starts again. Mrs Donovan gets up to prepare a tray with some food, bringing it over to offer me something. 'Here, Maureen, enjoy this bit of lunch, now.'

'Thank you,' I answer, taking a plate of buttered bread and cheese.

'Go on, eat up, now!' she commands pleasantly.

We've been at the Donovans' for gone two hours when Mammy finally makes a move to leave. The men are already out the front and doffing their hats goodbye when I walk out with Mammy and Mrs Donovan. 'Now, Maureen, you enjoy your holiday, and we'll be seeing you on Sundays, sure we will!'

I thank her as best I can before walking back to the terraced house with Mammy, Mr Hughes having gone off ahead of us, already on his way home.

My first week with my mammy has gone very well, even though I'm nervous and awkward much of the time. I won't venture far or go to the shops alone, not even to the ones close by. Mammy tries to encourage me. 'Go on,' she says. 'Sure, it's just round the corner.' I smile at her and nod my head, but I never actually go, and she doesn't keep on about it. I'd be content to simply stand in the half-door all day long and dream away as I watch the world go by. When I'm at the half-door, I can soak up the joy of being here, moment to moment, like warm sunshine smiling down on me. No words can explain what it is like to have someone care about me, to look at me, to smile at me and take notice of me. Any girl who's been an orphan with no one else in the world would feel the way I do. Nothing could be more different or opposite than the two worlds I'm now able to compare. This little terraced house is so full of life and kindness. It's more beautiful than anything I have known in my fourteen years.

The hardest part of my visit is trying to talk to Mrs Burke and the neighbours, and when I walk to town with Mammy. Mrs Burke is always dropping by for tea with my mammy, and I'm slowly feeling a little more comfortable with her. She often reminds me to hold my head up and pushes me to be less shy and nervous. 'Look at people,' she tells me. 'They won't hurt you.' Or she'll bring up the subject of the orphanage, asking me about schoolwork or outings we might've been on. I'm nervous, though, about being asked how the nuns treat us. I'm dreading that question from her. Of course, I won't say a word about what it is really like. Anything might happen if I did that. Maybe my mammy would write a letter back to the nuns about it, and they wouldn't let me out again. But Mrs Burke seems to keep her questions simple, and I sometimes forget my terrible shyness a little as I tell her about our picnics on the Shannon or what we study in school. Other than this one worry, I really like when Mrs Burke visits my mammy, and I enjoy listening to them as they talk with one another.

I often stand in the half-door, dreamily watching the scenes on the road or the faces of passing strangers and some of the neighbours I've met from across the way. I think about the shame I feel, the shame that's been reflected in so many ways back at me here in Mullingar. I wish with all my heart that I could stay here, feeling special and wanted. Mammy seems happy to have me here at least and shows me off to her friends, looking proud in front of them or when we walk into town together. No one has ever been proud of me before.

I'm full of questions about the past, of course, but I'm far too afraid to ask them. I'm scared of upsetting things and disrupting all the peaceful feelings I have inside. I do wonder, though, why she hasn't said anything of the past.

❖ FIFTEEN ❖

It's the last weekend of my vacation, and two young neighbours of my mammy's, Noreen and Olivia, have invited me to a travelling fair on the green at the top of town. I've agreed to go along, although I'm very nervous about meeting them.

We walk together to the green while their mammies follow behind us. They tell me all about the fair and what amusement rides are there. They sound like wild and dangerous things. I've never heard about them before, and I'm both scared and excited about seeing them.

'What rides have you been on before?' Olivia asks me.

'I haven't seen any before,' I answer.

'Really!' they both say together, and then Olivia explains. 'Oh, they come to town every year, the fairs . . .'

'Oh, wait until you see them, Maureen,' Noreen butts in.

'And it's not raining this evening, which makes it even better!' Olivia adds.

I turn my head from one to the other feeling their excitement and trying to keep up with their fast-paced conversation.

After walking for fifteen minutes, the sound of music, children's voices and general commotion floats across the air towards us. Ahead, spread out on a large, flat grassy area, are some huge coloured tents. As the noise gets louder, I feel caught up in the excitement and happy confusion about the place. 'What's that?' I ask, seeing a gypsy-looking lady in a booth and people lined up alongside it.

'That's a fortune teller,' Olivia explains. 'She'll tell your future by reading your palm. There's always a fortune teller at these fairs.'

'But where does she come from, the fortune teller?'

'Oh, I dunno. She goes round to all the towns charging money to tell fortunes, I suppose. There's always a great line for it.'

The girls are getting excited about something ahead, forgetting all about the fortune teller, and their squeals of delight tell me it's one of the amusement rides they've been going on about. 'Oh no,' I say, seeing it up close. 'I'll not get on that, I won't!'

'Ah, Maureen,' says Noreen, 'look at those little ones, younger than you and they're loving it. Come on, give it a try!'

'Ah, no thanks, Noreen. I'll watch for a little while. You go on,' I tell her, standing back near a bright-coloured tent and taking in all the excitement of the fair. I can't help but feel caught up in it: the people and the laughter. Across the way, near another huge tent, children are getting rides on ponies. There are clowns with balloons, and more children eating ice cream and running and skipping around asking their mammies for this or that. Olivia and Noreen are right: it's wonderful! How will I get the nerve up to try the ride?

Finally, Olivia comes running over to me after another go on the roundabout chairs. 'Come on, Maureen. Will you give it a try now?' As afraid as I am, I have to try it. Seeing me slowly give in, she takes me by the hand towards the carousel of chairs. 'Just stay next to me, and I'll show you what to do.'

I allow myself to be led to the amusement ride, my stomach fluttering wildly. An attendant is helping some other young people into the seats, pulling up a bar and then placing it down in front of them again once they're seated.

'Oh, I don't know,' I say, feeling a sudden case of nerves.

'Ah, now, Maureen, you're almost on your way,' Olivia says, smiling at me from one of the other chairs, waiting to go again. Ahead of her I see Noreen waving back at me, a big smile on her face and her eyes laughing with excitement.

Before I can lose my nerve I'm in the seat, and the bar is clanked down in front of me. My knuckles are white as I grip the two lengths of chain attached to the chair. The ride begins turning slowly round as I smile at Olivia and Noreen. This isn't too bad at all. The chairs start to turn faster, and then faster still, and I don't know whether to scream or laugh. So I do both as the chairs fly around, swinging out wider and higher as they spin faster and faster. My fear falls away like the ground below me, and I feel like a bird flying in the air. I find

Noreen's chair and her eyes, and then I look for Olivia, the three of us making a game of trying to find one another with our eyes.

The ride stops, and we line up again, then again, and once more before running on to get into line for the next ride. I've never had such a wonderful time in my life – it's such pure exhilarating fun. I'm the same as these other young people: a fourteen-year-old girl enjoying a day at the fair, and the world of the orphanage is far away. It feels incredible.

After at least four hours, one of the mothers comes to say it's time to leave, but I think my two friends and I could stay all day.

'Did you like it, Maureen?' Mammy asks when I arrive home.

'I did. We had loads of fun, and there was a fortune teller, and the amusement rides were wonderful, and Olivia and Noreen were so kind to me!'

'Oh, that's wonderful, Maureen. Now, didn't I say you could enjoy yourself while you're here?'

'You did. It was so much fun. Thanks for letting me go.'

'Not at all, Maureen, not at all.'

I go on telling Mammy about all we did at the fair, and she stands listening intently, her two hands on her hips and a warm smile on her face. She seems so happy for me that I enjoyed myself so much. Before bed, we sip our tea by the low turf fire, and Mammy sits up with me a little later than usual, knowing that I'm far too excited to go to bed.

It's finally arrived, the day I've dreaded when I must return to the orphanage. I sit quietly on the bed thinking while Mammy stands at the edge, folding my clothes for the trip back. Some of the neighbours will be dropping in soon to see me off, just before we drive back to the train station in the hired car. 'We mustn't send you back to the nuns with dirty clothes, Maureen,' Mammy says in her gentle voice as she turns towards me. Her words fill my heart with dread at the thought of returning to the sisters. 'You'll look good in your new white socks and the hair clip, Maureen,' she continues.

'I love them,' I tell her, raising a leg to admire my socks again.

She looks at me proudly, touching the pink clip in my hair. 'Well, come along downstairs when you're ready. The neighbours will be by shortly to say goodbye.'

With my parcel in her hand, she turns to go. I listen to the sound of her slow, familiar steps fading down the stairs. This little terraced house is so familiar after three short weeks, as if I've always known it. I feel very sad about leaving, so afraid and uncertain of what will follow. What will I do with these incredible new feelings? They seem to fill me like trapped birds, fluttering and wanting to burst out of me and fly somewhere, say something, find a place to share how I feel. There'll be no talking about this when I get back to the orphanage. I'm dying to tell Maggie and Lucy about it and bring them the sweets I promised, but there isn't any point trying to tell them what it really feels like. They'd have to live through it, just as I have.

I stand and walk about the room looking at everything for a final time. I'll try to remember every detail, as I don't know for certain if I'll be back. My mammy's old and a little stooped, and I wonder if the nuns will let me out again next summer. It all seems so far away, with nothing but the same old drudgery, beatings and hunger to expect in between. Suddenly, my eyes brim with tears, and I kneel quickly beside the bed.

Oh, I'm so sorry, God. I'm so ungrateful. Please help me. I feel shocked by these feelings. The outside world is so beautiful, what you've shown me . . . and people can be nice, and people do care. Thank you so much for showing me this. I'll not forget. I've never had to leave anyone like this before, and I don't know how to think about it. I'm afraid, God, so afraid. Please keep my mammy safe . . . and please help me to come back here again . . . Please, God!

I dry my eyes and, after making sure I haven't forgotten anything, walk downstairs after one last look at the tiny upstairs of this special place.

Downstairs, Mammy cleans her kitchen and tidies up while I sit by the fire. How I long to tell her what I'm feeling inside: how this has changed me and what it means now to leave and go back. They've no idea at all what it's like, to never in my whole life have seen the outside world. I begin to cry quietly to myself, unable to keep it all in. When Mammy sees me crying, she stops and looks over at me for a moment. 'Now, don't be crying like that. You will be back,' she says.

But this only makes me worse, and all I can say is, 'I can't stop. I can't help it!'

'Maureen, listen to me. I'll have Mrs Burke write to the nuns next spring for me, and I'll ask them to let you out again. I don't think there'll be a problem with it.'

'Do you think so?' I ask, wiping the tears away before the neighbours show up.

'I do. There's a good chance of it. Now, you're not to worry, all right?'

'Yes, all right,' I answer, but her words do little to convince me. I'll not believe it until I hear it from the nuns themselves.

Mrs Burke is the first neighbour to come in to say goodbye. She looks at my eyes, swollen from tears, and then at Mammy. 'Now, Maureen,' she says, 'you'll be out again, sure you will. And if you try to hold your head up more often, by the time you're back with us next year you'll not be so shy. Promise us, now.'

'I'll try to, Mrs Burke,' I say, attempting to hold my head up and look her in the face, but at the same time trying to hide this deep sadness. I don't want to leave here. I don't want to go and leave these nice people and all the beautiful things I've seen.

Mr Hughes and Mrs Lynch are in the kitchen now. 'You'll be out again, please God, next year, Maureen. You will. You'll be out again, surely.' They keep saying this to me, trying to comfort me.

I move to the door with my brown-paper parcel under my arm. Through my tears, I look at this little street where all Mammy's neighbours live so close to one another. They seem far away, waiting to see me off. My dream is slipping away. I can feel the orphanage reaching out as if trying to claim me back. Never did I suspect how like prisoners we are in that place, not until I came here. Lynch's hire car stops in front of the house. Michael Lynch waves and smiles at me, but I barely notice. Then Mammy's words again echo behind me. 'Now, Maureen, you'll be fine. You will be back next year!'

It is time to leave. I look back at the old kitchen before walking to the waiting car with Mammy, waving a final time to the others. In ten minutes, we're standing on the platform of the train station. I'm too upset to talk, and Mammy seems unsure of what to say. The whistle of the train breaks our silence. 'The train is here,' I say to her.

Through the din and grind of the slowing train, I hear the sound of girlish voices. 'Maureen, Maureen. Over here. Here!' I turn to see my friends waving from a window, their big smiles welcoming me back. I give them a quick wave and then turn back to Mammy. She leans forward to embrace me, taking one of my hands in hers. 'You will be back, Maureen. You just think of that now and pray, do you hear me?'

I nod my head and sob as I look at her. 'Yes . . . but . . . I don't really want to go back. I love it here.'

'Now listen, Maureen. You'll soon be out of that place. Just be strong, now, and hurry before you miss the train.' She squeezes my hand a final time, giving it a little shake as she smiles at me in her gentle way.

'All right. Goodbye . . . Mammy.' There, I did it. I called her 'Mammy'. It's taken me the whole holiday to work up the courage to do it. I almost feel that I don't have the right, and it feels both strange and beautiful to call her Mammy. Well, she is my mammy, and that's what I'll call her from now on.

She turns and walks slowly away along the platform, just as she had the day I came. I follow her with my eyes, crying harder and feeling so sad. I'm now alone again. I watch her until she is out of sight, fighting the sudden empty feeling and the near panic that fills me. Please, God, give me another chance to see her. Please let me come back here . . .

Suddenly, the calling voices bring me back to myself. The girls are farther down the platform now and still waving. Wiping my eyes, I rush along to the car they're in and board the train. Celine is the first to greet me, taking me along to the compartment where the others wait, excited to share all their holiday stories. 'How was it, with your mammy?' Celine asks. 'Did you have a good holiday?'

'Oh, I'd a lovely time, so I did.'

'What did you do there?'

'Oh, I went visiting with her mostly and to the rides at the fair. It was great!'

'Oh, I've seen those,' she says, 'but not so much in the city as in the small towns.'

'I just love your new socks, Maureen, and is that a new hair clip, too?' Nora says.

'It is,' I say, delighted they've noticed. 'My mammy got me it.'

The train pulls out of the station with the whistle sounding again, and we begin showing off the new things we've been given. Nora has new striped socks, Margaret two new blue clips to put in her lovely blonde hair, while the other girls have mostly sweets and chocolate bars. Like me, they'll share them with their close friends when they get back to the orphanage. We start talking about our different holiday stories, but when I try to share my own adventures the words won't come, and I suddenly begin to cry and can't stop. 'Oh, what's the matter, Maureen? Are you feeling all right?' Celine asks, her voice soft and caring.

'I don't know, Celine. I just feel terrible about going back.'

'But, Maureen, you'll be let out again next year, surely.' Margaret, Nora and the others all say the same: 'Stop crying. You'll be out again next summer.'

Why are they not crying like me? All of them have been out before. Maybe this is what keeps them going. I'll toughen up like them soon. I'll have to.

The passing scenes outside the window of the train are the same as the ones I saw on the outward journey – the little villages and people going about their day so freely – yet how changed I am now after what I've seen. It will be very hard returning to the old routine and just waiting out the sixteen months or so until my leaving day. I feel angry and restless, so very restless. In a couple of hours' time, we'll all be back in the orphanage under the authority of the nuns and their cruelty and injustice. I look across at the other girls, who seem to accept this. But as the train rolls along towards Newtownforbes, I know in my heart that so much has changed and that I'll never be the same again. I'm not the same person I was three weeks ago now that I've been in the outside world and seen how free and easy people live, especially children. I feel a rage inside me. How dare they call themselves Sisters of Mercy? Only Sister Brendan and one or two of the others are anything of the sort.

By the time the whistle sounds on entering the little station at Newtownforbes, the other girls are quiet and sombre. All their chatty energy seems to fade as the train rolls closer to our destination. Frank stands waiting on the platform when we step off the train. 'Well, there ye's are now, back safe and sound. That's lovely,' he says, greeting us cheerfully. 'Into the van now, girls. Sister Carmel will be waiting.'

Nothing is said during the short ride to the orphanage. I glance at the others – each girl's face is a mask hiding her thoughts. We turn round the little bend in the road and the grey buildings come into view, standing coldly there before us like a prison about to swallow us. The van passes through the gates, and the tall doors close behind us, ending our freedom. In the little square, we step quietly out of the van, where the Reverend Mother stands waiting to greet us. 'Well, girls,' she says, 'here you all are now, safe and sound. Did you have a good holiday?'

'Yes, Reverend Mother,' we answer quietly together, watching Sister Carmel approach from the cloister. She asks the same question, and we reply again with the same response.

'Ah, that's good, very good,' she says. Then, with a clap of her hands, Sister Carmel continues. 'Now, girls, go and change out of your good uniforms and head straight down to the playground.'

'Yes, Sister.'

In the linen room off the upper dormitory where our lockers are, I put on my plain dress, feeling very much an orphan again. My heart is heavy and everything round me feels different: grey and lifeless. When the other six girls are changed, we walk together, sweets in hand, towards the play area to find our friends. I spot Maggie and

Lucy in a corner and wave to them, knowing they've been expecting us back. 'They're here!' Lucy shouts as she looks up, part of a general commotion as the different friends round the yard rush to greet us, all with one eye on the sweets.

I feel a twinge of guilt at my mood when I see the bright smiles of my two best friends. How I've missed them. 'Maureen!' Maggie comes running up with Lucy. 'We're so glad you're back!'

Both of them are excited to see me: Maggie in her quiet way and Lucy in the only way she knows, as if she'll burst at any moment. 'Oh, I know! I've missed you both, too, and I kept my promise and brought you back the sweets!'

By now Lucy's jumping up and down and can't wait to reach our favourite corner in the cloister. When I see Rita Duffy and little Eileen Quinn looking on hopefully, I ask them to join us. With eyes fixed hungrily on the sweets, they welcome me back. A sudden deep affection for these girls rushes up in me. I feel the tears start to come but force them back, thinking only of the pleasure in their faces. 'This reminds me of the parcel you got last Christmas Eve, Maureen,' Lucy is saying in her excitement. 'Will you get another one this year?'

'I hope so.'

Without fuss, we begin to devour the treats, with thoughts of nothing else in the world. For a couple of minutes, there's only the sound of wrappers, crunching and the moans of rare enjoyment. I give Rita and Eileen a handful of sweets to take away with them, knowing they'll want to take some back to their own little circle of friends. 'I'm happy about your mammy, Maureen,' Eileen says, before leaving with Rita. 'Thanks so much for the sweets!'

Maggie, curious no doubt, begins to ask me about my holiday. 'What was it like living in a real house with your mammy? Did you like her right away?'

'What does she look like?' Lucy wants to know, taking a moment between finishing one sweet and beginning another.

'Well, she's older than I imagined her.'

'Really?' Lucy's surprised by this.

'Yes, and very stooped over and close to stone deaf in both ears, I think. But she's the kindest lady, and she seems to care a lot about me. I could tell from the first day at the train station.'

'How could you tell so soon?' Maggie asks.

'Oh, the way she smiled at me all the time. The way she took me round to visit her friends like she was proud of me. I just know. I feel it inside that she loves me and wants me back again.' My friends listen to every word, trying to imagine what is so new to them: the idea of being loved. 'There's a Mr Hughes living there, too.'

'Is he your father, Maureen?' Maggie asks.

'I don't know,' I say with a shrug. 'I don't think so. Something tells me he isn't.'

'Were you afraid of the outside world?' Lucy's curious to know.

'Oh yes. It was so strange but exciting, too. There's so much to tell you, but it'll take me for ever to get through it all.'

'Did it feel very strange to you at first?'

'It did,' I reply to Maggie's question. 'Being free to do what I want and not having to line up at mealtimes was very odd. I kept expecting to be spoken to by the people I met, you know, the way the nuns do, and . . .'

'And did they?' they both ask, almost together.

'Not once, not at all. It's so different you wouldn't believe it! I thought of you both, many times, and wished I could share it all with you.' I can tell that Maggie and Lucy see me differently now, the way they're hanging on every word and looking at me differently.

'Where did you sleep?'

'With my mammy, in a lovely bedroom upstairs that had a small window facing the street. I could hear the motor cars going by at night and people talking on the footpath outside the house.'

'What's Mullingar like?' Maggie asks.

'A lot bigger than Newtownforbes. It has buses coming and going from Dublin every day. I actually walked past one in the town. It was so close I could touch it.' Reliving all of it is making me sadder by the moment, and I feel like crying. How I miss it already.

'Did your mammy take you on a bus, Maureen?' Lucy asks.

'No, but I was in a motor car! Mammy hired one to take us home from the railway station the first day that I arrived.'

'What's hired mean?'

'You give money to the person who owns the car, Lucy, and they pick you up from the train or bus station and take you where you want to go. Very few people own a car there.'

Maggie starts to ask me something else, but then I suddenly begin to cry. 'Oh, Maureen, I'm so sorry. Honestly. I know you must miss her terribly,' she says, probably feeling bad for asking so many questions.

They know I'm not normally weepy, and they try to comfort me. But how can I tell them what it was like? How I wish they could have seen what I've seen, then they'd know. But we still have each other, and we still have to survive this place and our chores and the rest of it.

Later in the day, the evening sun is still warm and a light breeze drifts across the yard and along the cloisters. I sit off on my own, waiting for Maggie to return from the evening milking. As she walks up to me, I say to her, 'At least you'll have only Cowslip to milk tomorrow,' knowing she's carried my chore and milked Primrose for me while I've been away.

'Yes, and she knew only too well that it wasn't you milking her. I think she missed you singing to her.'

'Ah, I can't wait to see her tomorrow morning, but I could do without seeing old Farmer Giles. How's she been? And Sister Joseph?'

Maggie shakes her head. 'Oh, Maureen, they're both as cantankerous as ever in the mornings, barking away at us as usual!'

The two of us sit on the hard bench at one end of the open cloister, quiet for the moment as the day fades. Behind a line of cloud just above the horizon the whole sky glows deep orange as the early August sun sinks slowly. 'Do you know what I loved most of all, Maggie? It was sitting by the fire watching my mammy. Just watching her while she moved about the kitchen. And I loved sharing meals with her and Mr Hughes, eating off the china plates and never feeling hungry going to bed. And most of all just being there with them, with my family.'

Maggie looks away. 'That must have been great for you, Maureen.'

After a little silence, I decide to change the subject, asking Maggie more questions about what has happened while I was away. Our talk is light and sincere, but the understanding that I've seen something Maggie hasn't, something she cannot truly imagine, is now between us. I look around the old yard and across at the grey buildings, now more like a prison to me than ever before. Nothing about this place is any different. The change has happened to me, inside of me. I glance over at Maggie, her face glowing almost orange in the late evening light. I wonder why a miracle can't happen for her as well. Our conversation slows, and I think ahead to the coming school year and the start of classes when the same routine will begin again as it always has.

❖ SIXTEEN ❖

It is the second day of the new school year, and Sister Brendan has us stand in a circle in front of her rostrum. Usually, when she does this, she chooses one of us to stand apart and talk on a topic, a religious one sometimes or maybe a poem. 'Maureen Harte, come up here, please.' I'm surprised to hear her choose me, and I step forward to stand next to the rostrum with curiosity. 'Maureen, I would like you to tell the class about the three weeks you spent in Mullingar, visiting your mammy.'

I'm taken completely by surprise. It never occurred to me that she'd ask me this. Sister Brendan looks happy as she waits to hear me share my holiday stories with my classmates. They stand waiting as well, expressions of curiosity on their faces. When I see this, it does something to me. All the worries and feelings I've kept to myself choose this moment to come to the surface. I open my mouth to speak, but I cannot. My chin starts to tremble, and I lower my head, seeing flashes of my mammy and images of being with her. I start sobbing, and I cannot talk. I feel terrible for my classmates, who'd love to hear my stories about the outside world and instead just watch open-mouthed as I cry and cry and cry.

'What's wrong, Maureen?' Sister Brendan seems truly shocked by my reaction.

'I don't know, Sister, I don't know.'

'Well, try to stop crying now. I'm sure you'll be allowed out again next year. Go back to the circle with the others.'

I look up at Sister Brendan. She just said that I'll be allowed out next year. This will give me hope. She wouldn't have said it otherwise. I walk back to the circle where the others stand silently watching me. They seem to understand what's wrong with me, Maggie and Lucy even more so.

❖❖❖

I stand outside with my friends looking for Maura Nolan, one of the senior girls a year ahead of us. I've not seen her in some time, and she's nowhere in sight today, either. Maura's very tall and easy to spot in the playground, usually knocking about with Rita and Eileen. This isn't a good sign. None of the orphans go anywhere for very long, and it's easy to see when someone's missing. I've noticed a huge yellow scab on the right side of Maura's nose. All of us are used to seeing orphans walking about with different sores, and mostly they're left untreated, like Maura's. What frightens me, though, is that when a girl disappears they almost never come back. We never see or hear of them again, and the nuns tell us nothing.

'Where's Maura Nolan, Rita's friend?' I say to the others, still looking round.

'I'll run over and ask Rita, Maureen,' Maggie says, hurrying off across the yard.

I watch silently with Lucy as Maggie talks with Rita, shaking her head at what she's hearing. I know something's wrong, something bad. Maggie walks back to us with a shocked look on her face. 'What is it?' I ask impatiently.

'Maura's been taken to the county hospital in Longford, and Sister Brigid told one of the girls that the thing on her face is something called cancer.'

'That's what that big ugly sore was?' I say. 'Poor Maura. Why didn't the nuns take care of her?'

Maura Nolan will never come back. None of us will ever see her again. We know you're not taken to Longford unless it's very bad. When they send you to the hospital in Longford, it's like an early leaving day. But why is it left so long, until it gets so bad, I hear the angry voice in me crying out. And I know the answer, too. I saw Maura Nolan walking about with the huge sore on her nose for months. I remember the yellow pus coming from it and half of her nose eaten away by it. Maggie again says that the nuns have a lot to account for, but these days, the way I feel now, I can see that the nuns are not accountable to anyone at all.

❊ ❊ ❊

Only days after Maura's disappearance, Kitty Joyce takes another one of her fits, this time in the dining hall. She has them at least three times a week, and we feel so terrible and helpless. We've seen it so many times.

Maggie and I run over to the other side of the table and bend to help Kitty. She's frothing at the mouth while her limbs flay about and her heels bang on the floor. Maggie kneels beside me with a spoon, hesitating. 'Give it to me. Quick, Maggie, before she swallows her tongue or bites through it again.'

I snatch the spoon from Maggie and try to get it into Kitty's mouth, but her head is still jerking all over and smashing on the floor. By the time I get the spoon in her mouth, the fit is ending, and I slowly pull it out. I glance up at Sister Anthony. She never moves an inch to help, never! She just stands there with the ash-plant stick, her arms folded and looking on with a face of stone. God forgive me, I say to myself, but how I hate you, Sister Anthony! How I hate you!

Maggie and I wait until Kitty comes to. Still lying there, limp now, her eyes seem to focus a little. 'What . . . where am I?' she moans. 'Who . . . I've had another fit, haven't I?'

'You have, Kitty,' I tell her. 'Let's get you up and back to your chair. You've got to finish eating.'

The hall always goes quiet when Kitty has a fit. Many of the girls just ignore it. Some look on with dull curiosity – just Kitty having one of her fits. Now that it's over, the buzz of chatter in the hall picks up again, as if nothing had happened.

We try to get Kitty to finish her meal, to get some energy back into her. 'Go on, Kitty,' Maggie begs her. 'Try to finish your meal. You can do it.'

Suddenly, Kitty flings her plate off to the side, throws her head down on the table and begins to cry like a baby. 'I can't take it any more . . . Maureen . . . Maggie,' she says between heaving sobs. 'I'm so sick . . . and . . . I just don't care any more . . .'

The tears want to burst from me, but I'll not give Anthony the satisfaction. God help poor Kitty. I wish with all my heart that I could do something about it, but I can't. None of us can.

✳ ✳ ✳

A few days after her fit, Kitty was gone. Just like Colleen, she'd become too much for the nuns, too sick, and that's why Kitty didn't make it to her leaving day. We don't know exactly what happens to the sick ones taken away to Longford, but they surely must go from one bad place to another. For a girl here to make it to her leaving day, she must be strong enough to get there, and I feel very lucky that I've not had such terrible illnesses thus far.

And then, as if God were taking them from us one at a time, Peggy Murphy is also taken away to the hospital in Longford. Peggy suffers from St Vitus's Dance – that's what Sister Brigid told one of the other girls it was. St Vitus is the patron saint of fits, the illness Kitty Joyce suffers with. What Peggy Murphy has causes her to have no control over her arms and legs. We often saw her trying to balance herself as we stood in line, hopping from one foot to the other and her arms always moving. Now Peggy is gone. She's so pretty with blonde curly hair and a friendly smile, and we've never treated her any differently because of her illness. We've lived with this every day of our lives, for as long as we can remember. I thank God again that I don't have such terrible things wrong with me. If I did, I don't know how I'd survive. I'd just be gone one day, like Maura and Kitty and Peggy, taken away and never seen again.

It is the end of May, and I have finally been given confirmation of my three-week holiday to see my mammy in July. I have to fight back the pure joy I feel. I wasn't sure the nuns would let me go, and hearing that they will fills me with relief and joy. This time I'm determined that I'll talk to people and try to hold my head up high when someone is speaking to me. Mostly, I think about returning to that other world, where everything is so different and where I'm free and special and loved.

The spring days are lovely, and the sound of the country at night through the open window is like a gentle lullaby. In just two months, I'll be on that train and on my way to Mullingar. Mammy will be there with Michael Lynch's hired car, and she will show me her gentle smile, and I will be free again.

❋ ❋ ❋

June has come quickly, and our two years with Sister Brendan as our teacher are almost over. Today we'll be taking our compulsory final examinations. All month long, Sister Brendan has worked patiently to help us get through them, constantly reminding us how important it is that we receive our certificates. She has pushed us, encouraging us each day to work a little harder, making us feel that we can do it and treating the orphans and externs in the same way. I've managed to advance in all my subjects, even in mathematics, which I didn't expect to do well in. We also have to learn things in Irish, such as poetry, reading, history and geography – we've been studying our Irish since we were in high infants.

Right after morning prayers, Sister Brendan stands at her rostrum. We hear the rapid tap, tap, tap of her cane on the desk nearest her. This is her way of getting our attention. 'Girls, pay attention now! Mr Whelan, the inspector, will be along shortly. Just remember what I told you, and you will be just fine. Good luck to all of you, now.'

Ten minutes later, there is a knock on the door and in comes Mr Whelan. 'Girls,' Sister Brendan says, 'this is Mr Whelan, the inspector. He will be spending most of today with you here, overseeing your final exams.' She nods to Mr Whelan, who steps to the front to speak to us.

'Thank you, Sister,' he says. 'Well, there's little more to do now other than get on with it. It will be a long day, but I'm sure Sister Brendan has prepared you well for these exams, so we'll get started. English, history and geography exams, in that order, before we break.'

The pens, ink and lined copy paper are handed out, and we begin. The inspector walks up and down the rows, watching our every move, while Sister Brendan remains sitting at her rostrum. As I go through the exams, I try to relax, knowing I have been prepared well for the questions in front of me.

Back in the classroom after the break, during the arithmetic exam, I hold tight to my medal of the Virgin Mary, my lips moving slightly as I read over the problems in front of me. I feel good so far about these questions. I think I can do them. The mathematics exam ends, and we go on to the next subject.

A little before three o'clock, we have almost finished the lot. When the day finally ends and Sister Brendan collects all the papers to give to Mr Whelan, I slump with relief, still holding onto my medal. I look around the classroom, and the other girls seem exhausted but pleased it's all over as well. Mr Whelan speaks to us. 'Your final exams are now complete, and I'm sure you've all tried very hard to pass them. It's been a long day, but you've done well. Goodbye, girls.'

What a relief it is that these final examinations are over and done with. Now, no matter what happens, I feel I am one step closer to avoiding the laundry. It's an enormous weight lifted off my mind, and I thank God again for his help.

❈ SEVENTEEN ❈

The day for my holiday has arrived, and, other than one missing girl who's left the orphanage, my travelling companions are the same as last summer. Though I know what to expect this time, I'm no less excited, and before long we're on the train and on our way. I'm filled with a happy warm feeling inside, a real contentment, and I feel a strong sense that I'm going home. As the train rolls along beside Lough Ennell towards Mullingar, I think of Mammy's lovely cooking and what we might have for dinner when I get there.

I step off the train, turning to wave fond goodbyes to the others. 'Goodbye, Maureen. See you on the way back!' call out the girls in response. As the train moves off slowly, I watch the waving arms in their yellow blouses until they've faded from sight.

I stand aside to wait, and in less than a minute I spot Mammy in the distance and walk quickly towards her. Embracing me, she says, 'Ah, Maureen, it's lovely to see you again. Look how tall you are. Now didn't I tell you last time that you'd be back again?'

'I know, Mammy! You did! I'm so glad to be here.' I called her Mammy, something I promised myself I'd try to do on this visit. It feels good, and it makes me feel closer to her.

'Well, now, I've Michael Lynch with the hired car again. Come along now.'

As we move off through Mullingar, I close my eyes and picture the little house and the half-door only minutes away now. Thank you, God. Thank you for your kindness.

I feel so different this time with Mammy. I'm surer of myself, and I'm not worrying if she will like me. All those past worries are behind me now, and I'm certain Mrs Burke will see a change in the way I'm holding my head up and looking at people. When we stop in front of the house, Mammy tells me to go on ahead while she pays Mr

146

Lynch. I take my brown-paper parcel and run to the house, stopping at the half-door for a moment to admire it. When I step into the kitchen, a beautiful smell greets me. There on the old wooden table is a loaf of Mammy's freshly baked bread. I stand and breathe in the lovely smell. 'I couldn't wait to see this kitchen again and smell your lovely bread,' I say to Mammy as she comes in behind me.

'I made it just for you, Maureen. Now, go up and change while I put on the tea, and we'll have some of the bread with it.'

I go upstairs to change quickly before hurrying back down to sit on the stool in front of the turf fire. I've made it back and nothing has changed since I sat here sobbing and dreading the return to the orphanage a whole year ago. It's all still here: the quiet and the peace, the smell of the bread in the air, the warmth and comfort of the surroundings. The cast-iron kettle is boiling on the fire, and Mammy is moving round her kitchen. 'We'll have our tea and bread now,' she says.

'Thanks, Mammy.'

We sit together at the table enjoying our tea and bread, saying little, but with the same closeness between us. I'm not surprised when Mrs Burke drops by to welcome me. 'Well, now, Maureen, aren't you looking grand,' she exclaims. 'And you've grown so tall! Let me have another look at you . . . ah, that's the girl, and you're looking at me and holding up your head. That's grand, Maureen!'

I feel so proud, like a real person here in Mammy's house close to the kind neighbours who know me. The kettle's boiled again, and while Mammy and Mrs Burke chat by the fire I sit watching to see what passes on the street outside the window. I sit for some minutes, letting the orphanage fade away and enjoying the dreamy peace of the terraced house. Eventually, I begin to listen to their conversation. 'You know I've a nephew in London,' Mrs Burke says. 'O'Neill, Patrick O'Neill, married to an English woman, Claire, a Londoner. They've just the one girl, young Julia, only nine years old. Well, don't you know Patrick's passed away. Very sudden it was. So sad, especially for little Julia.'

'Ah, that's terrible news altogether. 'Tis an awful shame,' Mammy says. 'And he wasn't old at all. He was young, sure.'

'Thirty-five he was,' says Mrs Burke, holding her cup of tea to her mouth. 'Thirty-five, and gone just like that.'

When I hear this, so unprepared at this moment for talk of dying, I feel shocked and so sorry for this nine-year-old girl who has lost her daddy so quickly and so young. Oh, how terrible it must feel. I know nothing of death, and it doesn't fit into what I'm feeling now, here at Mammy's house in the outside world.

I begin to listen more closely to what they're saying. Mrs Burke talks some more about these people from England. It seems she's invited Mrs O'Neill, the young widow, and her daughter to Mullingar for a two-week holiday. 'It will do them well to get away from London,' she's saying. 'It's been very hard on Claire, with the war not long over and England in the state it's in now.'

'And when will they be here?' asks Mammy.

'They'll be arriving in a week,' answers Mrs Burke.

It occurs to me, as I listen, that I've never met a person from another country. I wonder what they're like. I'm sure to meet them if they're to stay with Mrs Burke. I'm looking forward to meeting the little girl, Julia, though she's only nine. Most of the people I've met in Mullingar are older, except for Olivia and Noreen, who took me to the fair on the green last summer.

Yesterday, just two days into my holiday, another neighbour, Mrs Flynn, dropped in for tea with Mammy. She mentioned that her daughter, Sarah, would be home for a visit from London, where she works as a nurse. 'I'll introduce you to her, Maureen. She'll be here tomorrow, and maybe the two of you can do something together.'

'Thank you, Mrs Flynn. That'd be nice.'

Since then, I have been wondering what Sarah Flynn will be like and if she'll like me. I'm sure that she'll be lovely, and I shouldn't worry about meeting her, although I had better look up at her when she talks to me.

This afternoon, Mrs Flynn brings her daughter over to say hello to Mammy and to meet me. Sarah is a few years older than I am, twenty or so, and looks very beautiful in her modern stylish clothes, the likes of which I've never seen before. 'Hello, Maureen. Pleased to meet you. You're here for three weeks are you?' she asks, reaching out to take my hand.

'I am. Pleased to meet you, too,' I answer as we shake hands. How confident she is: the way she smiles; the way she talks. How glamorous she appears. I can't take my eyes off her.

'Have you been to the pictures here in Mullingar, Maureen?'

'I haven't.'

'You haven't! Would you like to go?'

'Yes, I'd love to!'

'I'd love to take you, since you've not been to the cinema here in town.'

'Oh, I haven't been to the pictures ever!'

'You haven't been at all?' She seems a little surprised. 'Well, then, that's more reason to go. How's tomorrow, then?'

'That's fine. Tomorrow's great.'

I've decided to wear my best uniform for this special occasion with Sarah. I fix the pink clip in my hair and check everything twice. I feel so curious about her, and I wonder how she has such a sense of glamour and how she is so confident.

I hear someone come in below. It must be her come to get me. 'Well, Maureen, don't you look lovely today,' she says when I come down the stairs. 'Is that a dress uniform you're wearing?'

'Yes, it's only for special occasions in the orphanage.'

'Well, I like the colour of the blouse. It's a lovely yellow and looks good with your dark hair.'

I look down at my outfit, feeling so proud in it and loving this attention from someone so interesting and sophisticated. I must look good if she notices it. I'm so glad she's talking to me, for I'd be lost if she hadn't said a word. Sarah herself is dressed beautifully in a light-blue suit with a white-lace blouse and high-heeled shoes. How can she walk in those heels? Then I notice the make-up she has on. It makes her more beautiful still. I've never been in the company of anyone so beautiful. Mammy stands watching us, smiling with her hands on her hips the way she does when she's proud, though I doubt she can hear a word.

The two of us set off walking through town to the pictures, and all I can think of is how nice it feels to walk beside Sarah. 'Do you see that brown-and-yellow building up there on the right, Maureen, just beyond those two buses?'

'Yes.'

'Well, that's where the picture house is, and the picture we're going to see is a musical called *Little Nellie Kelly*. Do you think you'll like it?'

'I'm sure I will,' I answer.

'Here we are, Maureen,' Sarah announces, walking up to a little window outside the picture house, where she pays for our tickets. 'Just follow me when we get inside. It's very dark in there. I'll try to find us a pair of seats close enough so we can see the screen well, but you don't want to be too close because it's bad for the eyes and you end up staring straight up into the air!'

I follow her down a long, dark red-carpeted aisle and into a row of seats. The cinema isn't full because it is the afternoon, and only a few people are scattered here and there. 'These two look fine – almost in the centre. Are you all right, Maureen?'

'I'm fine, thank you, Sarah,' I answer in a whisper. I feel afraid in the dark as I peek about at the shadowy outlines of people, aware of their hushed talking. At the front is a huge stage with heavy dark-green velvet curtains drawn closed.

'Do you see the stage there, Maureen?' Sarah asks, pointing to it.

'Yes.'

'Well, when it's time for the picture to start, the curtains will open and you'll see a big screen.' Sarah hands me a small bag of sweets. 'Here's a little treat, Maureen. Now enjoy yourself. The film will be starting any minute now.'

'Oh, thank you!' I answer, delighted at this unexpected treat, sweets still very much a novelty to me.

Suddenly, the dim orange lights along the side blink out and the theatre darkens. Loud music thunders out, filling the whole place as the heavy curtains part in the middle and swing back smoothly.

The picture starts, but I find it hard to follow the story. I do like it, though, when the young woman in the film sings a song called 'Nellie Kelly I Love You'. That'll be something new that I can sing to Primrose when I go back. I concentrate on the words of the song and the melody, trying to memorise it.

An hour and a half later, when I walk out into the street with Sarah, the afternoon sun almost blinds me. 'Well, what did you think, Maureen? Wasn't that great! Did you enjoy your very first picture?'

'Oh, Sarah, I loved it so much, honestly I did. Thanks again for taking me.'

'Ah, don't mention it!'

The two of us walk home together while Sarah tells me a little about the places that we pass, saying that she grew up here and knows it all very well. I listen contentedly while she speaks, so happy to have experienced another new thing.

Mrs Burke's guests arrived from England a couple of days after my visit to the cinema. With my curiosity growing all day, I was finally able to meet them that same evening when Mrs Burke brought them over. Mrs O'Neill said hello and shook my hand, while her daughter Julia greeted me in a bubbly confident manner that seemed so different to me, especially for a child of nine.

Julia is a lovely girl, with light-brown hair and the bluest eyes. She is very smart looking and appears full of life. Mrs O'Neill is beautiful, quite tall with dark hair, an oval face and deep green eyes, and she dresses very nicely, like Sarah Flynn. Their English accents fascinate me. They are so different from anything I've heard before. As I listen to her speak, I'm in awe and try my best to understand the different words she is saying – they sound so odd! Wait until I tell my friends about this when I return to the orphanage.

'Hello, Maureen,' Julia says in her lovely English accent, bounding into Mammy's house. 'Mummy said to ask if you might come and play with me. I've got my dollies in the pram, and I haven't anyone to play with. We can go along the walk here in front!'

'I'd love to, Julia. Where are your dolls?'

'Wait and I'll run and get them. Mummy said I was to ask first!'

Mammy has been standing watching us, and with a smile she says, 'That's nice, Maureen. Sure, there's no one her own age round here. Just be careful on the road.'

I wait for her, fascinated that I'm about to see a real doll. A minute later, Julia is back and leading me out by the hand. 'Come on, Maureen, let's go. The pram's in front. Come on!'

The pram is a dark-blue colour with shiny metal parts around the frame and big narrow wheels. 'I have two dolls, Maureen, and right now they're sleeping, but they might need us and wake up as we walk them.'

'What a beautiful carriage, Julia.'

'It's a pram, Maureen, a pram. Do you want to see inside?'

'Oh, I'd love to!'

She goes to her pram to untie a white lace top covering the inside. 'Look, Maureen, they're sleeping,' she says as she pulls back the white-lace window. My breath stops and my heart leaps. Lying back, just like real babies, on matching pillowcases, are two of the most beautiful things I've ever seen. The dolls have small delicate china faces. The dark-haired one has rosy cheeks and eyes that open and close. Right away, she reminds me of Katy Fallon. The other one has soft fair plaited hair and a chequered dress that's very pretty. I stare at the detail of the dolls: the dresses and carefully tended hair. They're so far from the stones covered in rags we knew as dolls. We couldn't have dreamed of toys such as these before me now.

'Oh, they're very beautiful, Julia,' I say finally, still staring into the pram. 'I've never seen a doll before.'

'Never seen a doll!' she says, looking at me oddly for a moment before taking my hand. 'Come on, Maureen!' And so we begin our walk along the road in front of Mammy's house.

I understand now! We're going to walk the dolls and play at being mothers. As I push Julia's pram along the sidewalk, she chats like a mammy to her dolls in her pretty accent. 'Stop, Maureen. I think I hear crying. I'll fix them up now.' She picks up one of the dolls, the dark-haired one that reminds me of Katy, and rocks the doll like a mammy might a baby. 'That's right, now. Don't you cry, now, baby,' she croons to the doll. She seems to know just what to do to play the part of a mother, and I watch her carefully, wondering if my mammy ever rocked me in the same way when I was a baby.

Julia straightens the hair and dress of the doll and carefully puts her back in the pram, just like a sleeping baby. These dolls are so beautiful to me, like precious little angels. I must hold one to know what it feels like. 'Can I fix the dolls up, too, Julia?' I ask.

'Right, Maureen,' she instructs. 'You pick her up now. Ssh, the other one might wake up, so be careful not to disturb her.'

I pick up the dark-haired doll with both hands, examining every detail of the delicate china face, the perfect red lips, the beautifully stitched clothes, the eyes that open and close. 'That's all right, now. That's all right,' I say to the doll, comforting it like I've just seen Julia do.

As I cradle the doll in my arms, I wish I had a fraction of the confidence that this little girl has. Listening to Julia comforting the dolls, I realise that her own mammy has probably taught her all this since she was little. She isn't a bit afraid to talk to me and appears older than me in many ways.

'Oh, I think the other one is crying now. Pick her up, Maureen. Tend to the baby!'

I pick up the other doll as we walk back and forth along the narrow footpath in front of the house, continuing our game. Very curious to know about her life in England, I decide to ask Julia so I can find out more. Between tending to the babies, she chats about a London that seems incredible to me. The flat where she lives with her mammy is in a place called Kilburn. 'A busy, busy place,' she says, with long streets of terraced houses but much bigger than here in Mullingar. I'm shocked by her description of the 'tube' trains that run underground and the double-decker buses and motor cars that she explains are in London.

A train that runs underground seems so strange and a bit frightening to me. 'I can't imagine living in such a big place,' I say.

'Oh, I'm used to it. I was born there.'

'Was the war there in London, near you?'

'Oh, yes! It was right on top of us. My mummy told me a little bit about it, but I was too little to remember much myself.'

'Would I like it there, Julia?' I ask her, trying to imagine living with all the busyness and noise that she describes.

'Oh, I think you would. What about where you live, Maureen?'

'It's called an orphanage, where I live.'

'A what? What's an orphinish?'

'An orphanage,' I say, already fond of this affectionate, open-hearted girl. 'It's a place where girls live when they've no mammy and daddy. The nuns raise us, and we sleep in dormitories where . . .'

'I've no daddy now,' Julia says suddenly, gazing remotely into the face of one of the dolls she's picked up. 'My daddy died, and Mummy says he's gone to heaven. Do you like where you live? What's it like there?'

I hadn't expected this. I hadn't been thinking when I'd said I'd no mother and father. A big lump forms in my throat, and I turn away to hide my face, but I quickly force the feelings down. 'Well, we live together in a big open room called a dormitory, forty-five girls between your age and fifteen.'

'Really? Do tell me about that!'

Julia listens as I explain to her how we sleep in rows of beds and how my two best friends' beds are near mine. She stops me and has me explain exactly where Maggie and Lucy's beds are in relation to mine. I tell her about our noisy meals in the dining hall, about the play area, and about the cloisters and chapel. I tell her about the farm and about milking Primrose, and she giggles delightedly at Primrose's name. It's a lovely name, she thinks, and she wants to know if she moos back at me when I sing to her. She's fascinated by my descriptions of the farm and listens to every word with great attention. But of everything I've said about the orphanage, she's most taken with the idea of the dormitory. She returns to it with great curiosity, as if it's something she's never imagined before. 'What's that like, Maureen, being in the room with all those other girls?'

'Well, it's like having many sisters, and there's always someone to play with.'

'That would be wonderful!' she cries, seemingly taken with the idea. But of course I haven't mentioned a word about the other side of life in the orphanage.

While we walk and chat, keeping up our pretend game, I touch and handle the dolls as often as I can. Look at me, I think, fifteen years old and playing with dolls for the first time in my life, seeing the world through her eyes, a nine-year-old child from England! This girl, so full of life and enthusiastic about everything, even though she has just lost her father, really makes me wonder about my future and my past, what could've been and what still might be to come.

As the days have gone by, Julia and I have become good friends, and our walks with her dolls in the pram have been a daily thing. I've often gone with her and her mammy for picnics or for long walks along the canal that runs a little way behind our house. On such trips, Mrs O'Neill has packed an open wicker basket with biscuits, brown bread and jam, and lemonade, and off the three of us have gone, down the quiet narrow street that leads to the canal. Julia has pushed the pram with her dolls in it, never leaving them behind. Most days, she has brought along a pail and a little net to catch minnows along the edge of the water. Down on the sloped grassy banks of the canal, we've laid a rug out for our picnics. It's a peaceful spot to watch the people fishing and the odd little boat move lazily by. Julia, with her boundless energy, has run back and forth with her net, trying to net the tiny minnows, never giving up hope that she would catch them. On one occasion, Mrs O'Neill explained this hobby of Julia's by telling me that the parks in London with natural ponds are full of minnows. 'A proper little expert at it, she is,' she assured me proudly as she followed her daughter with her eyes.

Though I've loved being with Mammy and doing all the things we did on my first holiday a year ago, the arrival of the O'Neills from London has made a huge difference this time. Each day, I've had someone to talk and walk with instead of standing alone at the half-door. Even with the difference in age between me and Julia, I've been content to have a little friend, and I've felt like a big sister to her. I've watched how loving and caring Mrs O'Neill is, something I've never witnessed before, and it has made me realise deeply what I've missed in my own life. Julia's mammy seems to love her very much. She's always looking at her, hugging her and worrying over her. Yes, that's it: her mammy loves Julia, all the time, and that is why she's such a happy child.

As we sit here before the fire, I know my mammy loves me, but she loves me in a different way from the way that Mrs O'Neill loves Julia. Mammy is a lot older, and maybe hugging is not the Irish way, because I haven't seen much of it here during my time in Mullingar. I think Mammy shows her love by looking after me and smiling at me a lot and taking me with her on visits and proudly introducing me to the neighbours.

Tomorrow, I return to the orphanage. With a warm smile on her face, Mammy turns to me and begins to speak. 'Maureen, listen to me, now. I want to tell you that I will be officially claiming you when you leave the orphanage. I want you to know this so that you'll not worry yourself, d'you hear me?'

This is wonderful news, for I surely would have worried, right up until my leaving day. I search for words to answer her. 'I'm so happy to hear that, Mammy, but what about the nuns? Do they know this?'

'Oh, yes, I discussed it with them through letters, so you're not to worry yourself, all right?'

'I'll try my best, and thanks so much for telling me.'

'Not at all, Maureen. Before you know it, you'll be back here and out of the orphanage.'

I gaze into the fire contentedly, so pleased that I'll have one less thing to fret about until my leaving day arrives.

It's no easier for me to face going back this time. In a sense, it's worse. I get that same sense of a precious dream ending, of crossing back into a different world.

While Mammy gets my clothes ready upstairs, I sit by the fire meditating on how different this holiday has been from the first one. I've been having too much fun to think of the orphanage, spending my time playing with Julia or having picnics with her and her mammy, and, of course, doing many of the same things as last summer: mass at the cathedral on Sundays and a visit to the Donovans.

I rouse myself from my thoughts as I hear the first of the neighbours arrive to say goodbye to me. I've been dreading this all day, thinking it'd be easier if there were some way to slip away quietly and get the leaving part over with quickly.

I stand when Mrs Lynch comes in followed by Sarah Flynn. 'Well, Maureen, are you ready to go now? I hear it's your last trip back to the orphanage,' Mrs Lynch says warmly.

'Yes, Mrs Lynch, it will be.'

'Ah, now, that's grand news, grand indeed. Then you'll be back for good in April, Maureen.'

Sarah Flynn takes my hand. 'Well, Maureen, I'll say goodbye to you now. I'll not be here much longer myself, as I'm due back in London at the hospital in less than a week. It was lovely to meet you and to be able to take you to the pictures for the first time. Do take good care, d'you hear?' I manage to say thank you to Sarah, speaking through my tears, wondering if I'll ever look as glamorous as she does.

Mrs Burke is the last of the neighbours to drop by, and she arrives with Julia and her mammy. I only get worse when little Julia hugs me so affectionately and then Mrs O'Neill does the same. The kitchen then empties of people, and Mammy rushes to get ready for Michael Lynch, who'll be along soon with the hired car. I concentrate on storing up the precious memories. They're all I can take with me.

As we stand waiting for the train, I lean close to Mammy's ear. 'This will be my last trip back to the orphanage. I'll be seeing you for good next year in April, please God.'

'Now, Maureen, don't worry. You'll be fine,' she says just as the whistle sounds. We stand watching the train coming slowly into the station, and I look for my travelling companions. There they are, standing watching for me at an open window. We exchange waves and smiles as they pass. 'Don't worry now, d'you hear?' Mammy says, turning to embrace me warmly.

I hug her and then look a final time at her warm kindly face. 'I will be back next April, I will!' Feeling the tears well up and the lump in my throat, I turn to rush along the platform to my friends and another journey back to Newtownforbes.

❖ EIGHTEEN ❖

It's easier to talk about my holiday with Maggie and Lucy this time, and I don't cry as much. After a good ten minutes of crunching sweets and scrunching wrappers, Lucy says a typical thing as she reaches for another sweet. 'I'm going to miss these treats when you leave us in April, Maureen. And sure don't some of these have toffee in them this time?'

At this, Maggie smiles affectionately and shakes her head. 'How was it this time with your mammy?' she asks.

'Even better than before.'

'Did your mammy get more stooped over?' Lucy wants to know, adding another wrapper to the growing pile in her lap.

'No, not really. The same.'

I tell them about Julia and her mammy from England and their strangely different accents and about our walks and picnics, and when I mention the beautiful dolls, they're all ears. 'Julia has real dolls she brought from England and a little pram she pushes them in, and we went walking, the two of us, with the dolls in the pram,' I reveal, breathless with the excitement of recounting this part of my experience. 'And one was dark-haired and had red cheeks, just like Katy Fallon, and its eyes opened and shut like a real child!'

'Really?'

The shrill sound of the whistle across the yard puts a sudden end to our conversation for the time being. 'I've more to tell you both later. Come on, we'd better run!'

All is back to the usual routine for me as I walk through the grass and gravel lane, dawdling a little with Maggie and Lucy on the way to the farm for the first time since arriving back at the orphanage yesterday. Sister Joseph charges on ahead of us, as always, the twelve or thirteen milkers a ragged train following in her wake. It's not yet six in the morning, and the sky on the horizon is awash with colours: inky blue with shades of pink and green colouring the thin clouds. While Maggie reminds us we'll be late if we don't hurry up, I begin to hum my new tune for Primrose, 'Nellie Kelly I Love You', that I heard at the pictures with Sarah. 'What's that you're humming to yourself?' Lucy wants to know as we quicken our pace, out of the lane now, the cow byres and outbuildings of the farm dark familiar shapes in the distance.

'Ssh, shush, or I'll not remember it.' That's the only answer she'll get for now, and I can see she's not satisfied with it. Off we go beneath the pretty sky, past the boarding school for the girls from well-to-do families, quiet this time of year, shuffling along the ground in our heavy wooden clogs.

As soon as I get Primrose into her stall and secure the heavy chain up and over her neck, she turns to rub my shoulder with her head. I'm delighted she hasn't forgotten me this time, either. 'Primrose, I'm going to give you a new song today,' I announce as I begin milking. After a quick listen for old Farmer Giles, and one more silent reminder of the melody, I begin to sing 'Nellie Kelly I Love You'.

'Ah, you like it, do you?' I say to Primrose as she rubs me again. 'That song's called "Nellie Kelly I Love You", from the picture I saw with Sarah Flynn.' Singing to Primrose and knowing that this creature has affection for me always makes me feel peaceful. She's like a special friend. I go on singing.

One evening during recreation, I spot Maggie sitting alone down in a corner of the yard, trying to hide something by the looks of it. As I get closer, I see she's at work sewing something. 'Why are you sewing rags together?' I say, laughing and thinking she's gone mad. 'And why here?'

She stops what she's doing, then looks round suspiciously. 'I didn't think you'd started yet, Maureen,' she says. 'I suppose I was right.'

'Started what? Right about what? What are you going on about?'

'It's for the bleeding,' she answers, searching my face for a hint of understanding. Seeing only puzzlement, she goes on. 'Ah, sit down and I'll tell you. You'll have to know. The nuns won't say a word.'

I sit down, still not sure whether my dear friend has lost her wits somewhere. 'Well, Maureen,' she begins, stuffing the white rags into her petticoat, 'at a certain age we bleed, down there. You know.' She nods her head ever so slightly downward, with a quick flash of her eyes.

'Down there? Oh yes, down there.' I understand her now.

'It happens once each month, or it's supposed to,' Maggie explains. 'I bleed from down there once a month, and I'm making a pad with some rags, a couple of them, so I can rinse them out each night and hang on the radiators to dry. Then I'm able to use the two of them, going back and forth.'

'Who taught you how to make these rags?' I ask her.

'Pads, Maureen, they're pads. Rita Duffy did. She showed me just before she left, a few months back.'

'Ah, now I know what those were. I saw them, rags like those, behind her bed, but I was afraid to ask about them, and no one's ever said a word to me about this.'

'This is my second month bleeding, Maureen, and Lucy's first,' Maggie confides. 'I showed her how to make them, the pads.'

'I haven't seen Lucy sewing anything,' I say, and she nods her head in understanding.

'She hides in one of the outdoor lavatories during playtime and sews them together there then stuffs the pads inside her petticoat until she gets back upstairs.'

I sit with Maggie, silently watching her as she finishes her sewing, anxious now about this change to my body that is coming. After a nervous few minutes of wondering, then worrying and then almost panicking at the thought, I ask Maggie how: how will I know when I'm to start this thing? In her practical way, with a quick look and a maddening shake of her head, she tells me I won't know when, not exactly, until it happens. But not to worry, she'll sew an extra pad before we have to go in. When we do walk from the corner, both of us have the pads hidden, tucked out of sight beneath our petticoats.

* * *

Lucy finds me sitting alone in the cloister. She scurries up and sits beside me. 'Maggie told me you know about her and me bleeding once every month,' she says, her blue eyes staring into mine.

'Yes, I saw her stitching the rags, and I wanted to know why. Is it always the same day each month?'

'Oh, yes . . . well, sometimes. I've only had the bleeding once, so I can't tell you for sure.'

'I've not seen any bleeding yet myself,' I confess to Lucy.

'Oh, you will, and now you'll know what to do about it.'

'But why haven't the nuns ever told us about these changes?'

She sighs. 'I've no idea, Maureen, honestly I don't, but all the girls are learning like we are, probably from an older girl. That's how Maggie found out what to do. She was frightened when her bleeding started, so she asked Rita Duffy, and Rita taught her about making her own pads from bits of old sheets.'

'Well, I hope I don't see my bleeding too soon, Lucy,' I say, deeply puzzled as to the reason why the nuns don't tell us about these changes coming to our bodies. They're nuns, yes, but . . . surely they must also know?

On our first day of school in September, my final year in the orphanage, Maggie, Lucy and I are asked, by way of an excited junior messenger, to report to Sister Brendan's classroom to receive our placements for the year. This is a day we've worried about probably since we first heard of it as younger girls. All the years of fearing the laundry have made us nervous about our placements. And though I've passed my final exams, I still fear the worst. 'Please, God, please not the laundry,' I whisper on the way to get the news.

There are some other girls leaving the room after getting their assignments, and they don't look as if they're off to the laundry. We hear Sister Brendan's voice, 'Maureen Harte, Maggie O'Rourke and Lucy Nolan. Come in now, girls, for your assignments.'

We file in and stand before her, obediently awaiting her judgement. She looks up at us seriously. 'Well, girls, it has been decided that the three of you will be continuing in my class. You'll receive advanced studies in all subjects and each of you will be assigned an individual chore outside the classroom three mornings a week.'

She stops, looking each of us in the face as she goes on. 'I want none of you to end up in the laundry. Trust me when I tell you that you do not ever want to see the inside of that building as a worker. It is not a place to better yourselves.' I'm filled with relief at hearing this. No laundry, not now and not ever! For the first time, without doubt, I know I'll make it out of the orphanage.

Sister Brendan is still talking to us. 'I want you all to learn more this final year with me. I want to see results from all of you in the advanced learning programme that I will set up. Any learning, girls, is a good thing, and it will help you always in your futures.' She pauses for a moment, searching our faces before continuing. 'Now, the actual assignments. Maureen, I'll start with you. You will be sent to work with Miss Brady, Canon Dolan's housekeeper, in the village, three mornings a week, as I said. You should feel honoured to be selected for this assignment. You're to go to the side door, not the front door. That is for special people like priests and the bishop, so the side door, please, for you.'

'Yes, Sister.'

'Maggie, you'll be assigned to Sister Carmel's infants and high infants to help her with those children who are slow learners, and Lucy, you will help in Sister Sacred Heart's second class, doing the same, helping some of the children to read. Now is that clear, girls?'

'Yes, Sister,' we answer in the usual chorus.

'You may leave now, girls.'

Outside, I wait for what I know is coming. 'Well, aren't you the lucky one, Maureen, to be allowed out three mornings a week.'

'I know! I'm just as surprised as you are. Honestly!' I say, fighting to hide the joy. 'I thought I'd be sent to help out in a classroom as well.' They say nothing.

It is the first morning of my new assignment. I wrap my cape closer round me as I walk slowly through the village along the main street, fighting to keep out the October wind. It feels strange to be walking

for the first time alone through the village. Sister Brendan called this
assignment at the canon's an honour, meaning the nuns think me
trustworthy. They wouldn't give an assignment like this to a rebellious
orphan for fear she might think of escaping.

What will this Miss Brady, the canon's housekeeper, be like, and
will I see the canon himself? I feel a little anxious, especially about
meeting Miss Brady, as she's the one who'll supervise me.

The canon's house, where the bishop must stay when he visits to
give sacraments at the orphanage, is a two-storey brick building with
wrought-iron railings surrounding the tidy grounds. Next to it is the
church where I occasionally sing in the choir at evening Benediction.
I walk nervously up the path to the right of the house and knock,
remembering to avoid the front entrance. A thin middle-aged lady
with black-rimmed glasses opens the door – without doubt, it's Miss
Brady. 'So, you're Maureen, sent to us by the nuns,' she says, looking
me over once and then again. 'Well, you might as well come in now
and get started.'

'Yes, Miss Brady,' I answer as she steps aside to allow me into her
kitchen. I feel the weight of her stare as she watches me, appraising
and judging. I'm instantly self-conscious as I stand waiting for her to
say something, uncertain where to look or what to do with myself.
She watches me for a long moment before saying, a little roughly,
'Well, take your coat off then, Maureen, and leave it on the chair
there by the fire.'

I do as she says and stand again in front of her, waiting out the
long stares, feeling I'm being tested or something. Mrs Burke's words
about holding my head up suddenly come to mind, but I'm not in
Mammy's kitchen. It's very different here in the village, and though
I'm nervous I want to do well for Sister Brendan and for myself.

Finally, Miss Brady begins to talk about my duties here at the
canon's. 'Now, Maureen, pay attention. The first thing you're to do is
go along to the village pump and bring me in two buckets of water
– two buckets – and you're to do this each morning. I'm sure you
must've passed the pump on your way here?' The slightest raise of
eyebrows behind the black rims tells me she's waiting for an answer.

'Yes, Miss Brady, I did,' I get out quickly.

'Good! There'll be this chore to start with and some others I'll explain when you get back with the water.'

She turns and goes into a closet off the kitchen, and I take a quick look round at the big square kitchen with its black range, open fireplace, press and large wooden table. 'Well, here you are, and try not to spill too much of it, now, Maureen.' She holds out two galvanised buckets like the ones that are used on the nuns' farm.

'I will, Miss Brady. Ah, no, Miss Brady, I won't spill it,' I answer, stumbling over my words, trying to say the right thing.

I take the pails and head off to do my first chore as best as I can. The village is still quiet as I make my way back to the pump with the empty buckets; only a mother pushing a pram and some people coming out of the church beside the canon's house are about. The two buckets, full to the brim, make the walk back take longer, as I go slowly, spilling very little. When I get back with the water, I'm sent to do my next job, which is to gather a few armfuls of turf to stack beside the large stove. I'm to keep the area around the outdoor store of turf tidy and sweep the yard and the side path to the kitchen door as well. I begin sweeping outside, trying to do a good job of it but letting my mind wander at the same time. The minutes pass when suddenly a voice from nowhere intrudes on my daydreams. 'Over there in the corner, Maureen!' the voice commands.

'Yes, Miss Brady,' I answer, turning in the direction of the voice. Seeing no one there, I go ahead and do as I'm told. The voice has eyes as well, and they're watching me.

'That's right. Don't be missing the corners, now.'

Where is she? I sweep myself into a position where I can search for her. With little flicks of my eyes, I finally spot her in the shadows of one of the windows. Oh my! How long has she been standing there? I'd better do a good job and keep my mind on things.

The rest of the morning goes by quickly, and when I'm finished for the day and expecting to leave, I'm surprised when Miss Brady invites me to remain for something to eat. I'm a little uneasy as I sit down with her in the kitchen to lovely home-made bread and jam that I last had at Mammy's table. 'You'll not get the likes of this from the nuns, Maureen, sure you won't,' Miss Brady says as she pours tea and serves me the bread sliced and covered in delicious-looking raspberry jam. I nod my head in agreement as I enjoy her beautiful bread; indeed, we never do get this. She watches me eat and drink my tea, the framed eyes not missing a thing. I mustn't be seen to devour my food; it wouldn't look right. Then, still looking at me the same way, she says, 'I hear the nuns are not too kind to the orphans, Maureen.'

I almost choke on my bread. 'Oh no, Miss Brady, they're fine, really,' I answer respectfully. 'They treat us fine.'

'Oh, do they now, well . . .' she says, leaving the rest unsaid, turning to look out the window with a small smile, as if to say, 'I know better than that.' I realise that she must do this with all the girls who come to work with her: search for bits of gossip – the price of bread and tea, I suppose. Still, it was delicious, and she'll not get a thing out of me.

After finishing, I thank Miss Brady politely, and she sees me to the side door. I feel satisfied with my first day at Canon Dolan's as I walk back through the village. Miss Brady just wants me to respect her authority; she wants to see what kind of girl the nuns sent her. She's very particular and a bit rough in manner, but I sense something kind in her as well.

Each day after my chores, Miss Brady gives me tea with bread and jam, or sometimes a sweet-tasting cake, and she continues with her questions about how the nuns treat us. It's always the same, after allowing me time to enjoy my treat and tea she'll start with something like, 'Ah, now, sure it can't be that good for you down there, Maureen.' To this, I shake my head in a vague sort of way, avoiding her look or trying to change the subject somehow. But she'll go right to the bone. 'Ah, we hear things, we do, in the village,' or 'I've heard such and such, from so and so,' or sometimes 'Ah, now, no, that's not what I've heard, not at all. They're hard on you. Cruel to you, surely.'

Sometimes, when I'm fed up with this questioning, I wish my

leaving day was closer, and I answer Miss Brady silently in my head. 'Maybe if you saw one of the bad beatings that you know goes on in there, you wouldn't ask any more. Because it's terrible when it isn't village gossip but real!' I say nothing, of course, and I get through it, and I always look forward to my mornings away from the orphanage to work for Miss Brady, never thinking it a burden. The walk through the village is a great break from the regular drudgery of my days.

❋ Nineteen ❋

My final Christmas in the orphanage has come and gone, and this winter is a very bad one. The January mornings on the farm are bitterly cold, and the frost, as we move hurriedly across the fields like shadows to the byres, is a pale shroud covering the land.

Sister Brendan had me remain behind after class the other day to tell me that my birthday was the twenty-first of April. She gave me this news so casually, as if it were nothing to her. But it's so special for me to finally know the exact day I was born. I try to imagine that spring day, the twenty-first of April, the day I came into the world. It fills me with a longing to know more. Sister Brendan also tells me that I'm to start making my leaving outfit with Sister Elisabeth. All the girls must do this for their leaving day. How strange that Sister Elisabeth should be the one to help me with my leaving outfit when it was she who rocked me to sleep in her arms the day I arrived in the orphanage, some thirteen years ago.

When I report to Sister Elisabeth to begin making my leaving outfit, there are three other girls working on their own outfits. One is leaving in February, and the other two in March. I know the girls to see around, and one of them, Breda Logan, is a milker. The other girls say hello, but they don't open up beyond mentioning their leaving day. Breda, though, starts up a conversation with me while I wait for Sister Elisabeth to gather the proper material. 'So, you can't wait to leave this place, I'm sure, Maureen.'

'Indeed I can't, Breda.'

'But you have someone to claim you, do you not?'

'Yes, I've my mammy in Mullingar. I was born there.'

'Ah, that's lovely. You're very fortunate.'

Though I've never said anything to Breda about my mammy, the word has gone round quickly enough in the small circles of the orphanage. Breda nods, smiling as she runs a length of material beneath the up-and-down blur of the treadle machine's needle, her foot operating it in short bursts. She keeps her eyes on her work as she talks. 'Well, I've no one to claim me. I'm to be placed in service somewhere.' Her machine goes quiet as she stops for a moment, turning to me. 'And d'you know, Maureen, I don't care where, as long as I'm out of this place.' Breda runs another length of garment beneath the whirring needle before stopping and turning again to me, this time with her voice lowered and a bitter look on her face. 'Tell me, Maureen, do you remember that day you and I were beaten by Sister Carmel on the project table? First class it must've been. We couldn't have been more than six years old. D'you remember that?'

'I've never forgotten it, Breda. How terrified we both were, standing up there waiting for the next lash. What had we done wrong? Forgotten half a line of something, wasn't it?'

'It was something like that, Maureen. Some small little thing we did or didn't do,' she answers. Breda pauses again, and then a heartbreakingly sad look appears in her eyes. 'Do you know that when I leave here those memories will come with me, and I don't think I'll ever forget what I've been through in this place. Never.'

'Nor I, Breda,' I answer, thinking back to the day we were so savagely punished by Sister Carmel. I feel upset for Breda as well as myself. We all know, deep down, that we'll never forget these experiences, but to hear her say she'll take those memories with her wherever she goes makes me realise that even when we leave we'll never be entirely gone from this place.

Sister Elisabeth comes back to show me the material for each garment that I'll be making, and my conversation with Breda ends. While Breda returns to working silently, Sister Elisabeth patiently explains the various steps I'll go through. We're given no choice in the design or colour of our outfits, and I'm to begin with the undergarments and work outwards to the hat and coat. The undergarments will be made of black-and-yellow-striped material – awful colours. The style is even worse, with the legs extending below the knees and elastic sewn into each one. Next will be a petticoat cut from a thick homespun grey material, with buttons to go down the front, and then a finer grey material for the dress, which will have a Peter Pan collar and a row of lovely red buttons halfway down the front. Finally, a mustard-coloured coarse homespun material will be used for the coat, with a matching beret to top it all off.

As I begin my leaving outfit at the machine next to Breda's, with Sister Elisabeth always nearby to see that everything is done properly, I know I'll look forward to my one afternoon each week working on it here. I like Sister Elisabeth as much as Sister Brendan and Sister Michael, and every stitch that goes into this outfit will bring my leaving day so much closer.

The winter has continued, worse than ever. The biting cold and frost have shown no sign of lifting, and the sheer drudgery of it has seemed to affect us that much more. In the mornings, on the way to the farm, our mood has been sullen, each of us silent and cloaked in our own misery. How different the summers are down this same stretch of lane, when we can skip along between the hedges, so high and green that time of year, or chat openly on the cow path on our way to the fields to bring in the cows, playing king of the castle or teasing old Bluebell. Even Lucy has very little to say this morning until we're almost at the byres. 'I hate this job more and more.'

We say nothing to this, keeping an eye open for old Farmer Giles. She's always waiting and ready to lash out at any one of us for the littlest thing. But I've toughened up some since I was eleven years old, and she rarely gets a chance to go off at me these days.

As I milk Primrose, I rub my left hand on the outside of my leg, feeling the fingers of that hand going a little numb. I sing constantly to Primrose this morning, to keep my mind off the cold and my low spirits, while continually moving the fingers of my left hand to keep them from getting worse. Suddenly, I hear a bit of a fuss in one of the other stalls and the rough voice of Miss Giles, raised as she gives out to one of the milkers. I stop singing, realising that she's in bad form and will come along sticking her head into each of the stalls. I don't look up when I hear her behind me, concentrating on getting the timing of it right. I feel bold this morning. Just when I know Miss Giles is leaving from the swish of her heavy clothes, I make my move. In one quick practised motion, I pull down on my cow's teat, bend it sideways and follow with my eyes as the long stream of warm milk finds its way to Farmer Giles's backside. I watch with my head turned ever so slightly as the milk dribbles unnoticed down her clothes. 'Got her, Primrose,' I whisper triumphantly beneath my breath, and then I start singing 'Nellie Kelly I Love You' again.

On the way to mass after milking, we rub our bare hands to keep them from going numb. The sudden warmth of the chapel is such a relief, but it isn't until we reach the dining hall that we're able to properly warm our hands on the radiators. We huddle there before sitting to eat, rubbing and rubbing to get the circulation back, starved by now for our bread and dripping and porringers of cocoa. We know that this is a bad thing to attempt, this sudden heat after extreme exposure to the cold, but all we can think about is getting the blood flowing again in our numb fingers. With the winter so bad, we worry about chilblains, and now, as I warm my hands, I see the fingers of my left hand come out in big red blotches, and the awful itching starts that goes with it. We never go on about such things, and I keep my worry to myself as we sit to eat our breakfast.

As I was going to bed one night, a few days after the red blotches on my hand had first appeared, I noticed that the middle finger of my left hand had got very bad. It looked like a chilblain, and the pain was quickly getting worse. Not wanting to have it looked at, I tied some old rags around it and hoped it would heal a little. Treating our own hurts and illnesses is normal, and over the years I've rarely had to go see Sister Brigid. After what happened with the warts, I've not been back except once when stricken down with the fever, and even then I managed to avoid the infirmary.

But now, a week later, the red lump on the middle finger of my left hand is a huge sore and terribly painful. The other girls say that it will heal and that I should keep tying it up in a piece of rag and not let on about it to Sister Joseph. It's a chilblain, but it will heal. But on the farm, one morning soon after, Sister Joseph sees me favouring my left hand as I work. 'What's wrong with your hand, Harte?'

'I've a bad chilblain, Sister, but I'm sure it will go away.'

'Well, move along then, and don't be all morning cleaning that stall. D'you hear me, Harte? Move!'

'Yes, Sister.'

Every shovelful of cow manure I lift is agony. The raw pain shoots through my hand right up to the elbow. I want to scream or cut the finger off just to end this! I toss down the shovel and lean against the wall for a moment, breathing heavily as tears of pain and frustration stream down my face. I know I can't go on taking care of this wound myself. I've no choice but to report it to Sister Brigid.

I stand before Sister Brigid in the infirmary, trembling to keep my emotions from showing through as she holds the bad hand up, looking with much concern at the finger. 'Why on earth didn't you come to me before this?' she says, angry with me for hiding such a terrible sore.

'I thought it would get better on its own, Sister! But it hasn't, that one finger. I was wrapping it with . . .' But I cannot finish. Suddenly, all my feelings rush up at the same time, but not because she's angry with me for keeping this from her. I don't know why I feel this way, but I begin to sob openly with my head down.

'You know, Maureen, you may lose this finger, or a part of it,' she says, ignoring my tears as she examines the finger under a light. 'It's ulcerated, that's certain. It's very serious. I'm going to treat this with bluestone, Maureen, and we'll keep an eye on it and hope for the best.'

Sister Brigid treats the finger with the bluestone and bandages it afterwards. The bluestone is stone, crushed to a rough powder and made into a kind of paste. I've to come back regularly so she can treat the finger with more bluestone and change the dressing.

Being right-handed, I've continued with my chores without missing a day. My one worry, as the days passed into March, has been that my finger would not heal before my leaving day. But slowly it has.

The time has passed quickly, and my leaving outfit has taken shape, my excitement growing with each passing week. Then, some twelve weeks after I began my outfit with Sister Elisabeth, I finished the mustard-coloured double-breasted coat and the beret-like hat. With the bad chilblain and my chores here at the canon's as well, I've had no time at all to think about leaving. Now, suddenly, my sixteenth birthday seems to be rushing up on me, and I start to worry deep inside. For no matter what I think about the final day that's steadily approaching, I haven't the slightest idea what to expect.

In front of the turf fire in Miss Brady's kitchen, I stand warming myself, my chores finished on the last day of my assignment at the canon's house. We've had our final tea and treat together, and I wait to thank her and say goodbye. I've done a good job for Miss Brady. She's been firm but fair with me, and kind, though fed up, surely, with my unwavering answer of 'We're treated fine, Miss Brady' to her constant questions about the nuns.

With my two hands held out towards the red glow of heat, I notice a little crook in the chilblain finger, a barely noticeable bend. I was lucky I didn't lose the whole finger or a part of it and that it healed before my leaving day, which is less than a week away.

I turn when I hear Miss Brady come into the kitchen. 'Now, Maureen, I'm taking you over to the parlour soon to see Canon Dolan,' she says to me with a smile. 'He's offered to give you his blessing before you start your new life. Would you like that? To see the canon?' That the canon would give me his blessing shocks me, and I can only gawk at Miss Brady, waiting for her to rescue me. 'Well, come along,' she says. 'We'll go in now.'

I follow her through a beautiful hall, and then another, as we go towards the front of the house where the parlour is. I think of what Sister Brendan said about only important people being allowed into the canon's front parlour. Miss Brady knocks gently on the closed door and waits. 'Please come in,' I hear him say. I go in behind her, peeking at the canon as he gets up from a large black leather chair in front of a window. He walks towards us, but I stay hiding behind

Miss Brady, using her as a shield from the canon's presence. I'm in complete awe at having been allowed into his parlour. 'Good morning, Canon Dolan,' Miss Brady says. 'I've brought Maureen Harte to receive your blessing. This is her last day here with us.'

I stare at the canon: he has snow-white hair and a kind face and looks to be in his sixties. A large cross with a gold chain hangs down over the front of his black robe. When he turns to me, I meet his eyes only for an instant. 'Miss Brady tells me you've been with us almost a year now, Maureen,' he says, smiling at me, 'and that you're a fine worker.'

This is all too much for me. I just stand before the canon unable to say a word, but he goes right on. 'Come over and kneel so I may give you my full blessing. Don't be afraid now. Yes, that's a good girl, kneel right there.' Miss Brady watches all this, seemingly a little proud of me. The canon drapes a long white-and-gold stole over his black tunic and picks up a prayer book. While reading a prayer, he shakes holy water over my head, and when he finishes he says to me, 'You may rise now.'

I stand as he continues. His words are warm and easy, not rushed, as he speaks them. I listen as if nothing else exists. 'You will go through some difficult times, Maureen, when you leave the safety of the orphanage where you've been sheltered. I want you to say the Rosary daily. It will help you through the trying times and the trials that lie ahead for you out in the world, and always remember to remain pure and keep your love for God.'

'Yes, Canon Dolan, I will.'

'Now here is a gift of money for you, in appreciation for all your hard work here with Miss Brady.' He hands me an envelope and then says, 'May God protect you always, Maureen.'

I leave the parlour and walk back with Miss Brady to her kitchen, just about able to hold back the tears. 'Wasn't that a kind thing for the canon to do?' she says as we go through the lovely quiet halls. 'And you should listen to him and remember what he's said. It will be very different for you outside the orphanage.'

'I know, Miss Brady. I know it will.'

Miss Brady sees me out and thanks me again for all my hard work. 'I wish you all the best now,' she says finally, 'and God bless you again.'

'Goodbye, Miss Brady. Thank you.'

At the road, I stop to look a final time at the big house with the tidy grounds and wrought-iron fence. I walk on through the village along the quiet road. Absently, I take the unopened envelope from my pocket and open it. Inside it is a ten-shilling note, and it occurs to me that I've never been given money before.

I look at all the familiar buildings, the homes and shops of this sleepy village of Newtownforbes. It hasn't changed much over the years, the little houses close to the road where we walked so many times when we were little. Ahead of me, the orphanage comes into view and I stop, fingering the envelope with the ten-shilling note tucked safely in my pocket. You've come a long way, Maureen, I say to myself as I walk on towards the orphanage.

The words of the canon's blessing come back to me, like a mysterious echo in my head. 'You will go through some difficult times, Maureen, when you leave the safety of the orphanage where you've been sheltered.' I wonder, as I walk toward the grey buildings, just what the canon means by difficult times. The thought frightens me.

❧ TWENTY ❧

With heavy thuds on the dormitory door, we are roused from
our sleep. Without thinking and from pure habit, I'm out of
bed in a moment and reaching for my clothes, but when I see Sister
Joseph walking calmly towards me I realise that today is different:
it's the twentieth of April, my leaving day. 'You're leaving here today,
Harte,' she says. 'Stay there, and I wish you well in your new life.'

Sister Joseph turns away to thump any milkers slow getting out
of bed. By now, the last of them are quickly and silently walking
from the dormitory on their way to the farm. I follow Maggie until
I catch her eye before she goes out of the door. She gives me a sad
smile and a little nod of her head. I lie down in my bed, fighting
back the urge to throw on my clothes and follow them to the byres.
The dormitory is so still and quiet with the younger girls asleep, the
way it must look each morning after the milkers file out for chores.
Not at all sleepy and with nothing to do until mass after chores, I
sit up in my bed with my legs stretched out. Maybe one of the nuns
will come to tell me something I need to know about my leaving
day, about the train ride, maybe. No one comes. I begin to think
about what today means. 'I'm sixteen tomorrow, sixteen,' I whisper.
Tomorrow is my birthday, and I will be in Mullingar with Mammy
and no longer an orphan. Butterflies fill my stomach as I have these
thoughts, so strange does it feel to actually be leaving.

Wide awake, restless and with nothing to do, I sneak quietly over to
stand at my window for the last time. Below me, silent and still, are the
fields I know so well and the roofs and chimneys of Newtownforbes.
As the sky pales with the first light, I close my eyes to listen. This
is when a single bird can be heard chirping, and then another and
another after that, until they're all singing good morning to the
sun as it comes along to wake the sleeping village. I think about

the world that I'll be leaving behind me today, and my dear friends whom I'll miss terribly, and this window, with its special meaning that I've shared only with God. All that I have ever known will be left behind after today.

And what of my cow, Primrose? Maggie will milk her today. Twice a day for five years I've milked Primrose, singing to her while she rubs my shoulder with her big head. How that simple affection and love calmed me. It made my life bearable on days when old Farmer Giles was in bad form or when my hand ached with a chilblain in the bitter cold of a winter morning. Primrose knew my little moods and habits. I'll miss her dearly.

I hear Sister Anthony draw the bolt of the dormitory door, and I move away from the window. Unsure what to do with myself, I sit back on the edge of my bed. She knows it's my leaving day today, so she'll not bother me. But the morning routine carries on, and I'm forced to witness, for a final time, a scene I've been spared since becoming a milker. 'All those who wet the bed come up here,' the cold familiar voice commands. Sitting still on my bed, I look back towards the window, averting my eyes. But I've no escape from the sounds of the calico nightdresses being raised and the ash-plant stick falling on bare behinds. I do not watch, but I cannot help but hear. I will always see this scene in my mind till the end of my days: the wet-the-beds called to lie across the large wooden bench to be beaten. It has been burned into my memory. I feel every blow this morning as if I was lying there being hit, and I'm struck suddenly by the routine of it. I force thoughts of Colleen Carey away, gone three years now to the asylum, another face I know I will never forget.

When it ends with the wet-the-beds, I line up with the others to wash before moving on to the little chapel where I'll see my friends and pray with them for the last time. Sister Anthony's eyes find me for a moment, but she doesn't say a word. I'm grateful for this, though, because I honestly think her incapable of uttering a kind word to anyone. As I leave the dormitory for the last time, I get a sudden image of my First Confession day: just a flash of me and my friends in our white dresses. The line moves like any other morning, by the laundry with its steamed-up windows, past the nuns' convent and all the other dreary familiar sights. Today, though, it all seems to be happening as though in a dream, as if I've left already. What an odd feeling.

I join Maggie and Lucy in our section of the side chapel, where we've sat for years. As mass starts, I notice a few faces look my way, including one or two of the nuns, and I'm sure the curious old laundry workers know I'm leaving today, too. I smile at my two special friends, and they smile back sadly. The memories flow through me as I look around at the familiar details of our chapel: the special ceremonies I've been a part of and the sacraments I received, First Holy Communion being the happiest, and our Confirmation when we were terribly miserable about the nuns locking Colleen away to hide her from the bishop; and the Christmas Eve procession of the nuns at midnight when we sang our hearts out to full organ accompaniment. This morning in the chapel is the last time I will pray together with my friends, and I pray hard for all of them, for my future and theirs. I ask God to guide me through my new beginnings and them through theirs.

We leave the chapel, walking in silence to the dining hall, where I have my last breakfast of porridge, bread and dripping. This will be the only time we can share our true feelings before I go, but we don't know how; we won't even look at one another. Suddenly, I feel a tight, almost panicky feeling creep over me, and the fact that I'm leaving seems so real to me now. I want to say something to my two dear friends. Surely there must be things for us to say now while we have the chance. Why are there never any words for us to express our feelings? 'You will write, won't you, Maureen?' Maggie says, looking down at her plate. 'When you're settled in Mullingar with your mammy?'

'I will,' I say, almost in a whisper as a terrible desperation hangs over the three of us. Even the racket of tin plates and porringers seems far away to me. Lucy's blue eyes are downcast and clouded over with misery. She won't even look at her food. She won't look at either one of us, and she says nothing.

Sister Michael walks over to wish me goodbye, and we look up. She's been so kind to us over the years. Again, I see a sudden flash in my mind, more like a sharp picture than a memory: her standing up from among the rows of vegetables in her garden in answer to our calls from the fence as little children. She reaches out to shake my hand. 'You're leaving today, Maureen, I know. I wanted to say goodbye to you.' She looks over for a moment at Maggie and Lucy. 'I do remember the three of you, sure, always together. Well, now, God bless you always, Maureen, and keep you safe. I will pray for you.'

Her warm smile and kindness does something to us, breaks down all the knotted feelings inside, and soon the three of us are crying openly. 'Now, girls, Maureen will be back to see us again. Won't you, Maureen?' she says, holding my two hands in hers.

'Yes, Sister.'

She releases my hands to return to her table and the business of feeding the many girls. These few minutes in the dining hall with my two dear friends will be our only time alone together today and although we are crying we still cannot speak or find words to express our sadness. I explain that I must leave to go round to each classroom and say goodbye to the nuns before leaving for the train station. 'We know,' is all they can say through their tears. 'We're going to miss you something awful.'

We've never hugged. We don't know how to hug one another or express feelings – it isn't allowed here. Is this how I'm to leave my two dear friends that I've grown up with? It's them, I suddenly realise, whom I've drawn strength from to survive these past thirteen years. I can only turn away and leave the dining hall, walking alone to the linen room to change into my leaving outfit.

I take off my plain plaid dress and heavy petticoat, throwing them on the bench and staring at them for a moment: an orphan's clothing. The leaving outfit I made with Sister Elisabeth looks good on me, and everything seems to fit well. With a final look back at my locker, I head straight to her classroom to show off the outfit. But I only break down crying again as soon as I'm standing in front of her. 'Now,

now, Maureen,' Sister Elisabeth says, trying to soothe me. 'You must stop getting yourself upset like this . . .'

'I know, Sister, but I can't stop. I don't know why . . . I'm going to miss my friends!'

'Yes, you will miss them indeed, and that's normal, but you're going to make yourself sick now, so just try to calm down a little.'

I try, but it's no good. I just keep sobbing though Sister Elisabeth tries to make me feel better. 'You are looking great in your leaving outfit, Maureen. Let me have a good look at you. Yes, I do like the colours on you, especially the grey and red in the dress.'

'Thank you, Sister. I love it, too, I do,' I answer through my tears.

She takes my two hands in her own and tells me she will pray that God will always bless me in the outside world. 'Maureen, you will come back to see us,' she goes on. 'You must write and let us know how you're getting along.'

It's now time to say goodbye to the rest of the nuns; every girl must do this on her leaving day. Each classroom, each different nun, brings both happy and sad memories back. I cry and cry as I go about this chore, reminded one last time of those nuns who so abused me in the past and who'll go on being cruel toward the young orphans just starting out. I force back terrible feelings and thoughts as I look at the faces of the young ones; they've so much to go through yet. Will they all make it out? Is there another Colleen Carey in this room, terrified of wetting her bed tonight? God, please look after them . . .

The worst is still to come, and I tremble with the effort of controlling my feelings as I approach Sister Anthony's classroom. I stop just outside, seeing her shadowy figure moving through the mottled glass of the door. God, I want to get this one goodbye over with quickly. I don't want to show her how weak I am at this moment. But as I knock, the tears are already pouring down my cheeks, and my heart is pounding.

She steps out of her classroom and closes the door quickly behind her, standing in front of me with her stick in her hand. When I see the stick in her cruel hand, it's more than I can handle. All the horrors and abuses of the past rush up in me like a sudden black storm. Terrible pictures whirl past in my mind: the face of Colleen Carey, so downcast without hope and lost; the daily beatings; the expressions of the wet-the-beds. All the welts, the moans and nightmares in the dark dormitory are right here. I feel suffocated, like a huge fist is closing round me, and I want to run . . .

Sister Anthony speaks first. 'So, it's your leaving day, Maureen, and you've come to say goodbye.' I cannot meet the eyes of this woman. I stand before her with my head down.

'Yes, Sister, I'm leaving on the 12.30 train.'

She reaches out to shake my hand. 'Well, goodbye, then, Maureen. We will pray for you.' With this she turns and walks back into the classroom, the door closing behind her with a click. There was no feeling or life in her words. As I walk quickly on, I think of those orphans in her class and what horrors they've ahead of them beneath her cruel power.

The very last classroom I visit is Sister Brendan's. I try to find courage as I walk in, knowing this is it: the last time I'll see Maggie, Lucy and the others before leaving for the train station. I walk towards Sister Brendan, keeping my eyes on her. She turns and smiles at me. This will be a wordless goodbye with my friends. But I must look at them. I must try for their sake.

I raise my head, and I turn to meet their faces, my friends and the externs I'd come to know and care for. My eyes meet Maggie's, then Lucy's. Something in their look, in their eyes, reaches out and hits me like a hammer blow. I sob. My heart is breaking as I look round at the helpless expressions. Everything good I know is in the faces of these dear friends, these beautiful orphan girls whom no one wanted. We were all thrown away here. I will never forget their faces – never.

Sister Carmel enters the room from her adjoining classroom. 'You will get along very well now, Maureen,' she says, trying to comfort me. 'You will write to us now, won't you?'

Sister Brendan touches my shoulder ever so lightly. 'Come along now, Maureen.' Through my tears and heaving sobs, I look back a final time at the faces of my friends before leaving the room with her.

Out in the square, Frank waits with the old van. One or two of the laundry workers who know me come out of their old building off the square. How that place haunted us as little girls. Some of the other nuns also come out to see me off, although I don't know all of them that well.

As I stand here in the square, saying these last goodbyes, I feel like the loneliest person in the world. I've no brown-paper parcel to hold onto this time, only what I stand in: the lovely outfit I made with Sister Elisabeth and the ten-shilling note from Canon Dolan still in the envelope and tucked safely in my pocket.

Sister Brendan reaches out to shake my hand. 'Well, Maureen, I will say goodbye now. God go with you. You will write to us and let us know how you're doing with your mother in Mullingar. We will never stop praying for you. Be strong, now!'

Sister Carmel, who'd followed us out, shakes my hand next, wishing me the best. Reverend Mother Xavier waits by the van, the last nun to formally see me off. 'Now, Maureen, you'll make yourself sick if you keep up this crying,' she says fussily, taking hold of my hand. 'We will always pray for you, and you must keep your faith always.'

'Yes, Reverend Mother, I will,' I manage to say, still sobbing as I get into the van. I turn to wave a final goodbye to Sister Brendan through the rear window as the van moves through the big grey gates. Moments later, I hear them slam shut behind me. I will never forget her. I will return some day, and when I do I will stand before her, and she will be proud of me.

Frank waits with me on the platform, busying himself looking for the train as I stare ahead trying not to think or feel. He doesn't know what to say to me. 'Ah, well, it won't be long now,' he says. 'These trains are usually on time, so they are, so not to worry.'

And sure enough the train bustles into the station right on schedule, steaming and whistling its arrival. 'Now, there you are, Maureen. The best of luck to you, now. God bless!' Frank waits to see me safely aboard. He's always been such a kind man. I'll always see him and that old van whenever I remember our summer picnics on the Shannon.

I avoid the eyes of the three other people in my compartment, feeling nervous about travelling alone and not wanting to speak with anyone. Through the window I watch the familiar scenes go by, the villages and fields, the old telegraph poles. I pray the whole time, wanting only to get to Mammy's terraced house and be with her. I try to close my eyes and listen to the rhythm of the wheels below me, hoping the sound will put me to sleep, but I see only the faces of Maggie and Lucy and the others I've left behind. The train rolls along, over Lough Ennell now. Then the flashes begin again, just like the two I had earlier of First Confession and Sister Michael standing up in her garden. My whole life begins to flicker past me in pictures: faces, days, smiles, tears, as if a part of me has been thrown open on this, my leaving day.

I push the images away, trying to master them. I wonder where my friends will be placed in service when they leave the orphanage. Will I see any of them again? I think of Katy Fallon, the lucky one who was adopted at the age of ten. How is she doing now? And Colleen, thrown into an asylum and forgotten. I hope she isn't suffering. Oh, Colleen, I'm so sorry for what happened to you. Why couldn't we help you? Why did that . . . that one . . . why did she do that to you? I mustn't cry. I wouldn't know what to do, and it'd only make me worse if these other passengers saw me sobbing. I just want the train ride to end so I can be alone . . . I'll hold on and pray the journey will soon be done.

Finally we arrive, but when I stand to leave the train in Mullingar my legs are like jelly. I feel strange and heavy, separated from my body. On the platform, Mammy waits in her usual spot. She's pleased to see me, I think, as I walk to her. 'Well, here you are,' she says, hugging me gently. 'Back again, Maureen. And how was the trip this time? Are there no other girls with you?'

'No, they're only allowed out in the summer for holidays,' I say, raising my voice above the noise of the standing train.

'Ah, sure, of course. And look at that outfit. Don't you look smart? Did they give you that to leave in?'

'I made it, with Sister Elisabeth.'

We walk together to the car. All this feels like a strange dream to me. I should be so pleased to be here on my leaving day with Mammy. I am, but it isn't the same as our other greetings. Everything's disconnected and far away. I smile and answer her little questions as we drive to the terraced house, my own voice sounding odd and distant to me, as if it were someone else's. Why don't I feel good here with Mammy? Why don't I feel safe? Why do I feel so alone now? But how can she help me? She wasn't there! I feel my emotions filling inside me like a giant balloon, filling and wanting to escape out of me. I want to be alone, to be by myself somewhere and rest.

The little house looks so warm, and I can smell the bread Mammy's baked for me. 'I smell your lovely bread, and it's so good to be home again,' I say.

'Yes, we'll have a nice cup of tea with a slice of it.'

I hold on as we have our tea, going upstairs as soon as I'm able to make an excuse. With my two arms held out before me, I stand trembling and trying to breathe deeply and slowly. Maybe if I can just rest for a little while, I'll settle down some. But the memories keep coming and coming, and I'm helpless to stop them: every moment of the thirteen years, all I witnessed and lived through behind those walls, the cruelty and sadness that no one saw or cared about . . . the old grey buildings . . . faces . . .

The thing wanting out of me rushes up, bursting free as a flood of sobs, and convulsions take over my body. I throw myself onto the bed, my stomach heaving and twisting. The convulsions become vomiting, and I throw up all over the floor, as if my body were ridding itself of demons and poison. It goes on and on, I've no idea for how long, before Mammy comes upstairs. 'Maureen, my God, what's the matter? What's wrong? Are you sick? What is it?'

'I miss my friends. I'm afraid. Oh, I'm so happy to be here. It's not that. It's my friends. It's my friends and Colleen. I'm sorry I'm like this . . .'

'Now, Maureen, why don't you lie down? You need some sleep, dear. Here's a cloth. Now clean up a little, and we'll get you into bed. My goodness, what's the matter?'

I keep saying to her that I miss my friends but that I'm happy and grateful to be here with her. I don't want her to think me ungrateful. I'm so afraid of what will happen if I don't behave well. 'Now, dear, that's all right now, ssh, ssh. You'll be better tomorrow, if I know you. Now try not to worry.' She helps me to clean myself up and to get undressed and into bed, staying with me until I calm down, rubbing my head and stroking my hair. The tone of her voice is soft and soothing. I hear that now and nothing else. 'Things will look better to you tomorrow, I'm sure of it. I know you're going to miss your friends for a while. That's only to be expected. But it will pass. Sleep now.'

Only dimly aware of her comforting words and then her movement as she leaves the room, I pull myself under the covers. My cheek sinks into the soft pillow. The familiar smell of the sheets protects me. Nothing remains of my leaving day, only a quick merciful fall into deep sleep, then stillness and peace.

❖ TWENTY-ONE ❖

I wake up unsure of where I am. Only after a long moment of confused staring around the bedroom does the reality start to trickle back to me. My whole body is stiff and sore, as if I've taken an awful beating. I must have slept deeply. I remember hurrying upstairs after tea, and then . . . nothing. I lie on my side staring at the April daylight streaming in through the window. Today is my sixteenth birthday, and I wonder if Mammy will mention it. I try to relive the hours and minutes of yesterday, but they're vague and cloudy and a great distance away now. Was it only yesterday I left the orphanage?

I smile when I hear Mammy's shuffling steps on the stairs. She seems to have the knack of knowing when I wake up. 'I've been up to see you a few times this morning. You were sleeping so soundly. How are you feeling now?'

'I'm fine,' I answer, a small lie. I don't know what to feel, other than this empty hollow feeling inside me, as if I've lost everything. I'm released from the orphanage finally. How strange it seems.

'Well, I'll leave you to get dressed, Maureen. Sure you must be ready for some breakfast now.'

I get out of bed and gaze at my reflection in the old hand-held mirror on the table beside the bed. I see a stranger there with a puffy pale face and a far-away look in her eyes. I splash water on my face, towel it off and then stand to look around the tiny room. I dress, then walk to the window that faces the Dublin road. I try to clear my head as best I can before shuffling downstairs for breakfast.

Mammy waits with a big smile, and a lovely breakfast is spread out on the table, along with some of her home-made bread and jam. She greets me with a warm welcome, knowing how I feel after the ordeal of yesterday. We eat quietly, and after helping her tidy up I go out to stand at the half-door. There I let my thoughts drift as the scenes pass before me on the Dublin road. This is home now, I think; there will be no return to the orphanage this time. I am no longer an orphan; in fact, today not only am I no longer an orphan, but I am sixteen years old – today is my birthday. I don't know what a birthday is supposed to feel like, as I have never celebrated one, but today feels like a new start for me.

From the half-door, I look up and down the street at the familiar houses and shops of the immediate neighbourhood. I try to think of Maggie and Lucy, but it only fills my eyes with tears and my heart with a heavy weight. I know exactly what they're doing now, and it must seem awfully strange that I'm not there with them. What a terrible goodbye it was yesterday, already a lifetime ago to me.

My birthday came and went without being mentioned, and, although I wondered why, I felt too numb to care much about it. For the next few days, I just drifted without any purpose, going through the hours filled with a dull ache in my heart.

Although I'm out of the orphanage and living with my mother, it doesn't feel as I thought it would. I ask myself what's wrong. Why do I feel this way? I'd be in service now if Mammy hadn't come forward to claim me. But everything I've ever known and done is gone, all at once. I've left it back at the orphanage with my friends, and now there's a hole inside where all of that was, and I don't have the slightest idea what I'm supposed to put in its place. I don't know how to adjust to this new-found freedom. I pine for my friends and for Primrose and for the life I had. When I was visiting here on my summer holidays, I was free for a time, knowing I had to return to the orphanage. It was easy for me to enjoy my new freedom. It was controlled for me, and I was still being told what to do. But now I'm in the real world. It's no dream, and so much more strange and frightening than I imagined.

But it isn't all bad. I'm happy here with Mammy and Mr Hughes, going through the hours and days as they come and trying not to dwell on the past too much. I've also thought, during these first days of freedom, about the many bad things that I'll no longer have to do or see. That too was suddenly gone on my leaving day, all of it – both the good and the bad left behind. The world must be such a very big place. I can't imagine how big it is.

The days have passed quietly during May, and I've slowly recovered from the ordeal of my leaving day, gradually getting a little of my spirit back. I've done the same things with Mammy and Mr Hughes as I did while on my holidays. They're so kind, and I feel safe and watched over when I'm with them, expecting nothing beyond this. I wonder if they know how much they've changed my life.

Julia O'Neill and her mammy are coming to Mullingar later in the summer for three weeks. I'd been hoping for another chance to see them. Mrs Burke tells me through the letters Mrs O'Neill sends that Julia talks about me and is anxious to visit again.

It isn't until now, in late May, that Mammy brings up the subject of me working. 'Maureen, do you think you'd like to work for the Walls, just a few doors away? You've not met Mrs Wall, but she's in need of a maid to help out with the housework.'

'I'd love to.' I agree right away, eager to do something and to be helpful.

'Ah, that's grand, Maureen. We'll walk over there now and speak to Mrs Wall about it.'

As I walk the short distance to the Walls' house with Mammy, I look down at my dress, feeling backward and worried I won't meet with Mrs Wall's approval, but when she comes to the door her open smile puts me at ease. A tall lady, she towers over Mammy in her brown tweed suit with a glittery brooch on the right lapel of her jacket. I can't be sure of her age, but she looks and acts a lot younger than Mammy. Mrs Wall leaves us in the parlour to prepare some tea. 'Now, Maureen, you'll be fine,' Mammy says to me while Mrs Wall is in the kitchen. 'Don't worry.'

I observe the lovely parlour, enjoying the comfort of the soft chair around me. The afternoon sun streams into the room through a large picture window, the full-length curtains pulled back. A small fireplace sits cold beneath a mantle, with family pictures hung on the walls above it. The Walls must be very rich. Mr Wall is a professor and has a lot of education, so education must have a lot to do with money,

I think. Mrs Wall speaks differently from Mammy and Mr Hughes, bringing out every word clearly, just as Sister Brendan does.

Mrs Wall returns to the parlour carrying a silver tray with beautiful cups and saucers and a fancy silver teapot. 'Now, have some tea and biscuits, both of you,' she says, pouring out tea for us. 'Go on, Maureen, try one of the biscuits.'

I take one of the pink biscuits, feeling a little out of place having tea served to me, but Mrs Wall seems fond of Mammy. While we have tea, Mrs Wall sits back and begins to talk about the position, her manner very direct and firm. 'I would like you to begin right away with us, and you know by now, I'm sure, that we have three children and this large house to keep tidy, inside and out. When can you begin, Maureen?'

'Right away, Mrs Wall.'

'Good. I will pay you ten shillings a week and your day will run from 8.30 in the morning until 8.30 in the evening, with Sundays off.'

I pay close attention to her as she speaks, nodding my head as she explains things for me. It seems I'll be kept busy cleaning the inside of the house, the four bedrooms and a bathroom upstairs, as well as setting up for the children's lunch at 12.30, then cleaning that up and again preparing another meal in the evening. There are other things to be done as well. The outside paths are to be swept, and the brass in different areas of the house cleaned and polished. I feel completely overwhelmed with thoughts of my orphanage chores returning to play on my nerves. I'm to be paid now, and there are people to please. I must earn it. I must do a good job.

While we're in the parlour, Mr Wall comes in with the children, and I'm introduced to them. Brendan, the oldest, is dressed in his schoolboy short pants and jacket with knee socks. The two younger girls are Fionnuala and Ciara. Mr Wall looks to me what must be typical for a professor: quiet, polite and tall with a thick head of ginger hair and serious-looking dark-rimmed glasses. He doesn't linger in the parlour, but the children wait for their mother to finish with my interview. The boy, Brendan, has a head of red hair like his father. I can feel his eyes on me, taking in everything about me while Mrs

Wall explains a few final things. Something tells me he'll be one to watch, this Brendan. I pray to God to help me over yet another hurdle in the outside world.

I reported for my first day at the Walls' after sleeping poorly, worried that I'd fail in my duties and Mrs Wall wouldn't be pleased with me. All the bad memories of the nuns and the people I'd worked for haunted me. But Mrs Wall treated me kindly as she took me through my duties. I was told that I was to drop what I was doing at meal times to have the kitchen table set when the children come in from school for lunch and again for the family's evening meal. I was shown where the scullery is and the closet, where the broom, pail, carpet sweeper and such things I'll need are stored. Though I didn't show it in front of Mrs Wall, I was shocked when I saw the children's bedrooms. So many toys fill each of their rooms: stuffed bears, a wooden horse, children's storybooks, toy tea sets, coloured balls, skipping ropes and much more besides.

Today, the Monday of my second week, Mrs Wall gives me a new black maid's dress with a white apron; surely this means they must be pleased with me and want me to stay. Having this new outfit to work in means I can save my leaving outfit for special occasions and going places with Mammy. I know nothing of the value of money, never thinking to buy anything myself. I'd be happy to give all my earnings to my mammy. She'll have none of this, though, and says, 'Now save some for yourself, Maureen. You're going to need it.' It makes me happy, though, that I can help with my earnings.

As nice as the Walls are, the boy Brendan is turning out to be a little brat. I just knew he would, the moment I laid eyes on him. He'll purposely slop some mess about, then stand smirking at me while I clean it up, or he'll make a proper mess of his many toys while he's home for lunch so I'll have to straighten them up again in the afternoon. He seems to enjoy this, knowing I'll not say anything. He's sneaky, letting me know he's looking down on me with his proud way. I ignore him. I don't want to get in trouble with Mrs Wall. He's trying to get under my skin. I know it, and I'm not going to let him get the better of me. I'll not give him the satisfaction of humiliating me just because that's what he wants.

As I sweep the path in front today, a warm summer's Saturday afternoon, Brendan sticks his head out through the parlour window. I look up to find him smirking at me while he enjoys an ice-cream cone. He's in his element, with a brazen, bold look on his face. He watches me for a couple of minutes and then says, 'There, you've missed that bit there. Why don't you sweep that better?'

I move to do his bidding, saying nothing but clutching the broom tighter in my hands, angered and humiliated. Why doesn't he leave me alone, the little brat? How I'd like to slap his bold face. I continue my chore, pretending he's not even there. But less than a minute later, he does it again. 'What about that little spot there near the road? You missed it. I saw.'

Again, I do as he asks, knowing how much he enjoys this. But I'll not give him the satisfaction of even looking at him. Why won't he just go away?

I begin to dust the window ledge he's leaning on. I stand and face him. 'Can you put your head in, Brendan, please? I've got to clean this window now.'

He ignores me, looking down at his ice cream thoughtfully. 'You're from an industrial school, aren't you?' he says in the proud, superior tone he puts on with me.

'I am!' I say, surprised by the anger that flares up in me. 'Now will you please move so I can clean!'

This gets his attention. 'Who are you to tell me? You're just our maid. You're an orphan! If I want to stay . . .'

This is more than I can take. In an instant I lash out and knock the top of his ice-cream cone off with the back of my hand. The two of us watch as it falls out toward me, splattering onto the ground and leaving him holding the empty cone. I look right into his brash little face. 'There! And don't you ever say that to me again! D'you hear me?'

He just gawks at me with wide eyes and his mouth hanging open, too shocked to find his tongue. I feel great satisfaction that I've stood up for myself. Now let him report me! I don't care if he does. He didn't think me up to it, sure he didn't! That was so insulting and hurtful to me. Besides, I'm not an orphan. I've a mammy just as he does.

To save face, Brendan stands silently in the window for another couple of minutes before disappearing into the house. I go on with my cleaning, sweeping the dirty white lump of ice cream into the gutter to melt. I hope he's learned his lesson and will leave me be from now on.

On the following Saturday, Julia and her mother arrive from London, and I'm able to see them in the evening in our kitchen. 'It's lovely to see you again, Maureen,' Julia says. Not much for fussing, she's straight to talking with me as though we were together the day before.

'Look at yourself, Julia! You've grown up so much since last year!'

'Only a teeny-weeny bit, Maureen,' she says, holding up her thumb and forefinger and laughing.

'How was your trip?' I ask her.

'Oh, too long! The train takes so long from London to, ah . . . Mummy, what's the name of the place where we get on the big ferry?'

'Holyhead, love.'

'Oh, right, Holyhead, Maureen. Well, the train ride is very long indeed . . .' Once again, Julia looks to her mother for help.

'Eight hours, it is, Maureen,' Mrs O'Neill says, expecting these questions and smiling at her daughter affectionately. 'It's a long ride, and I for one am exhausted by it. We are glad to be here and settled.'

'Will we walk the dollies again, Maureen, and go to the canal with Mummy for picnics? I brought my pram and dollies!'

'We will, but I live here now, Julia. I'm out of the orphanage, and I have to work long hours in my new job, but I'll have the evenings with you and Sundays.'

'Oh, that's lovely, Maureen. I can't wait!'

❊ ❊ ❊

After mass, I walk with Julia and her mammy down to the canal for a picnic, Julia pushing her doll's pram and chatting away with me. Mrs O'Neill has brought her open wicker basket, full of the usual goodies. As Julia plays by the water, hunting for minnows, her mother talks to me casually about my plans for the future. Have I given any thought to what I might want to do with my life, she wants to know. I can only tell her how happy I am to be out of the orphanage and earning a living, and that beyond this I haven't really thought of my future at all. 'But your job, Maureen, you can't be making very much money there.'

'I make ten shillings a week, and I'm able to help Mammy with half of that.' To me, it seems I'm doing very well working for Mrs Wall. I wonder why Mrs O'Neill's asking me all these questions.

'And you're happy here in Mullingar?' she goes on.

'I'm happy enough. There hasn't been enough time for me to think about much else.' I can say little more than this.

After a few more similar questions, she says, 'Would you like to come and live with us, Maureen, with Julia and me in London?'

'I'd love to,' I answer, thinking that she's only asking out of curiosity.

But then Mrs O'Neill begins to tell me how England is rebuilding after the war and that many young Irish people are streaming over there in the hope of a better life. She says that all the opportunities to get ahead will be over there and that at my age I should be thinking of my future. But I don't think Mrs O'Neill realises what it's like for me right now. I'm only learning to cope with everyday things, like looking at people in the face when I talk to them without blushing and stumbling over my words.

My mind starts working, trying to figure out what's going on. Is her offer to take me to England real? There can't be anything to it, can there? I do like the sound of it, though. What an adventure living in London would be! Maybe I could be like Sarah Flynn and get a wonderful job and better myself. Also, Mrs O'Neill is young and beautiful and so kind, and Julia would be like a little sister. We'd be like a family. This would be the chance of a lifetime. Maybe Mrs

O'Neill feels sorry for me because of my long hours and how I've not much of a life here.

Weeks have passed since Mrs O'Neill's offer, and I've given it little more serious thought since she and Julia returned to London. Mammy and I sit quietly with our tea before going to bed, the fire now a warm red glow beneath a bed of ashes. 'Maureen,' she begins, touching me lightly on the arm, 'listen to me now. Tell me honestly, would you really like to go and live with the O'Neills in England?'

'I'd love it!' I say, although this was the last thing I'd expected to hear. I wait anxiously as she stares into the fire, choosing her words.

'Now, I know Mrs O'Neill spoke to you, asking if you'd like to live in London. Do you recall that?'

'I do. She asked me at the canal.' And what, and what? Tell me! What?

'Ah, well now, Mrs Burke's received a letter from Claire O'Neill. She's offering you the chance to go, Maureen.'

'Do you mean for real? She's asking for me to go there and live with them?'

'That's right. Do you want to go?'

'Oh, yes, I'd love it! I'd love to go!' I'm so happy and thrilled that Mrs O'Neill is that interested in me. 'How, though?' I go on, terribly excited by now. 'I mean, London is far away. What's involved for a girl like me to move there?'

Mammy raises a hand with a knowing nod of her head, one of her little gestures. 'Mrs Burke said that if you definitely want to go, she'll help out with all of that, so don't worry. She's very helpful that way, she is. Now, are you sure? Do you want to think it over?'

'No! I'd love to go. It won't be right away, will it?'

'No, sure, not for a couple of months at least, but I'll talk to Mrs Burke tomorrow.'

'All right, but are you sure you don't mind my wanting to go? I mean, Mrs O'Neill, when she spoke to me, said that England is where all the opportunities are for the future, and I didn't know if she'd spoken to you already. I only want to go if that's what you think I should do, only if you think it best for me.'

'Maureen, listen to me. I know how you feel. You're not long out of the orphanage, and you're unsure of yourself and what to do with your life. Mrs Burke and I have spoken a lot about this, about what would be best for you. Mr Hughes wants only what's best for you also. He and I have already talked it over. We didn't say anything right away, because you needed some time to settle down after coming here from the nuns. You're working in service now with the Walls, and that's fine. But you're young, Maureen. You've your whole life before you. The truth of it is that all the young Irish people are going off to England now, after the war. It would be better for you over there, I think. Look at young Sarah Flynn. She left here to make a go of it in England, and she's done well. We feel you deserve the same chance, Maureen.' Rarely has Mammy said as much to me in one go. She seems so concerned about my future.

As we sit quietly before going to bed, I think about what it will be like to leave Mullingar after only such a short time living here with Mammy. There is another truth to all of this that I keep very much to myself, for it would do no good to speak of it to anyone else. It is the fact that I feel no strong emotional connection to anyone, not even to my mammy who came forward to claim me from the orphanage. Only Maggie and Lucy or another orphan who has spent years living the way we did would understand it. I feel a deep affection for my mother, it's true, and I'm so appreciative to her for what she has done for me, but so much has been left unspoken. I still have so many unanswered questions, so now that I have a chance to go out into the world I'm going to take it.

It is the middle of October, and the Irish frost has begun to creep over the land like a newly awakened ghost. It rains more often, and the dampness I know so well gets into my bones. The evenings come quickly to the little terraced house, and Mammy and I sit watching the dying glow of the turf, quietly sipping our tea as the darkness falls.

Mrs Burke has helped Mammy with all the arrangements and details of my move. In fact, with Mammy's bad hearing and poor writing, Mrs Burke has ended up taking over, and I have learned that my departure date for England will be the twenty-eighth of November. This makes me more excited about the journey ahead, and more afraid.

It's odd, but I know that no matter how afraid I become I'll not change my mind. I worry about everything: about the actual journey and about leaving Mammy. I wonder how I'll make out. If I fail, will it mean coming back and going into service?

It's only just over a year since little Julia and I walked for the first time on the busy Dublin road and I asked her about London. Now I'm actually leaving to go there to live and begin a new life, to a different country far away across the sea. And so I pray hard that it will all work out.

❄ TWENTY-TWO ❄

With the damp and frost of October outside the door, I feel safe and warm before the low turf fire, not long in from my job at the Walls'. The dying embers glow, and the oil lamp burning on the table throws its dancing shadows on the walls. Mammy knows how much I like this time with her. She looks at me, smiling as if she has something on her mind. Maybe she's beginning to miss me already. 'Are you looking forward to this, Maureen?' she asks. 'Moving to London with Mrs O'Neill?'

'I am.'

She turns back to the fire, and I hear a low sigh escape from her before she speaks. 'I've something to tell you, Maureen, before you go off to England. It's very important.' Mammy lets out another long sigh, her eyes downcast, before turning to me again. 'What I've got to tell you, Maureen, is . . . is that I am not your real mammy – not your real mother.'

For a moment I wonder if I've heard right, but a glance at her tells me that I have. My stomach knots, and numbness begins to crawl over my body. 'What? What do you mean not my mammy? But who is my mammy, then?' She only looks away again with a deep pained sadness on her face and tears showing in her eyes.

'Ah, Maureen, I'm sorry. It's so hard to tell you this. I wanted to tell you earlier, and now I've left it so late, and there's so much to say to you.'

I can't believe what I'm hearing, and I sob bitterly and silently, feeling suddenly like an orphan all over again. This isn't my mammy sitting here beside me.

She takes one of my hands in hers. 'Maureen, this is very hard for me, but what I want to tell you is that I was the one who raised you until you were three. My first husband died suddenly, and everything

196

was changed because of it. Mr Hughes is my second husband. For three years, you lived here in this very house, and . . .'

'But I want to know! I really do. Do you know who she is?'

'I do indeed. Your mammy's name is Annie, Annie Harte. That's where your name comes from.'

When I hear this name, my own name, something moves deep inside me. Something connects that I've never felt before, a terrible pang of wanting and of needing. 'Where is she now? Do you know?'

'Well, that's just it. I've not heard from your mammy in a very long time, not since before you were put in the orphanage. You were here with me and Mr Kane – he was my first husband. He died, and I wasn't able to afford to keep you.' She pauses again, staring into the fire before going on. 'Well, it wasn't long before you had to go to the orphanage, only weeks after my first husband's death. Then your mammy wrote to me, saying she'd something important to tell me. I've not kept the letter. She was sending a little money from Dublin when she could, a few shillings, but that stopped, and that was the last I ever heard of her, Maureen. I've no idea why. She never said what the something important was, and because I stopped hearing from her I never did find out what it was.

'She was working in service for a doctor in Mullingar before you were born, Maureen. But . . . when all that happened, her becoming pregnant with you, well, she couldn't stay in Mullingar then. I don't know all the details. The very last I heard, when your mammy was still sending some money to help with your keep, she had found work as a maid with another doctor in Dublin. But as I said, Maureen, the letters stopped suddenly, and I've never heard a word from her since.'

Mrs Hughes, for that is what I must now call her, drifts off into silence for a time. I can only think of my real mother: Annie Harte, my true mammy. I repeat her name to myself: Annie Harte, Annie Harte, Annie Harte. I love the sound of it. Annie Harte; Maureen Harte: a mammy and a daughter. How strange that sounds to me: that I'm someone's daughter – Annie's daughter. Why have I only felt this now and never before with Mrs Hughes? Where is Annie now? Why all this confusion and telling me this and that? It makes no sense to me.

I break the silence, filled with questions. 'Can you tell me about when I was born and what my mammy looks like?'

She looks into the low fire for a few moments, as if gathering memories that have been locked away a long while. 'It was a bad time, you see, for your mammy. When you were born, right away she gave you to us. There wasn't any waiting about. It had been decided ahead of time what would happen.'

'Why though? Why did my real mammy give me up? Was she sick?'

'You were born out of wedlock.'

'What does that mean?'

'It means your mammy wasn't married to your father.' She stops after this, sighing and looking gloomily into the fire once more. Whatever happened back then, I now see just how painful it has been for her. My mind spins wildly as I wait, trying to sort through what I'm hearing and what I know. I mustn't rush her, but how I have waited and dreamed of this, to hear these details of my past.

Her voice is low as she begins to relive aloud the painful memories. 'Your mother, Annie, had no money to keep you when you were born. She was barely able to keep herself. She didn't want to see you go into an institution, like most of the babies born to poor and unwed mothers. She asked Mr Kane and me if we would raise you. We were too old by then to have our own children, so we took you in. Oh, Maureen, we adored you. You called us Mammy and Daddy, and you were especially fond of Mr Kane.'

As I listen, things begin to click and connect in my head. On my first holiday here to Mullingar, not quite two years past now, I felt something when I stepped into the kitchen of this little house. I'd never have known if I wasn't told, but, yes, it was familiar, and I felt it. It was right here in this very house where I lived until I was three, until Mr Kane died and everything changed. My real mammy gave me up at birth, and now I know that something like this must've happened to Maggie and Lucy, and Katy and Colleen,

too. In a moment of silence, I hear myself asking, 'Do you know
who my father was?'

Mrs Hughes looks slightly surprised by this question, sitting up
and stiffening in her chair. 'I don't, Maureen. Whatever arrangements
were made at the time, we, ah, well, that was never mentioned, so I
honestly have no idea at all who your father was . . .'

'My mammy, do I look like her?'

She stands up, holding up a hand and nodding her head. 'I've got
something here. Let me get it now. As to whether you look like your
mammy, you've her lovely dark hair, I think, and her eyes.'

'Really? Do I?' I want so badly to look into a mirror when I hear
this.

Mrs Hughes returns to the fire and hands me an old photograph.
'This is my first husband,' she says proudly. 'I haven't many
photographs, though. It's a pity.' I look at a man with a very kind
face, a slightly balding head and a big moustache. 'Ah, he loved you
so much, Maureen, and after he died you'd a bad nightmare one night.
You woke up holding up your two little arms, crying for him to pick
you up.' She hands me another photograph. I look at it expecting
another one of Mr Kane, but instead I'm staring at a little girl. I hear
Mrs Hughes' voice beside me as I turn to her for an explanation. 'It's
yourself, Maureen, sure it is, taken in front here by Mrs Burke just
before I brought you to the nuns. You keep it.'

Mrs Hughes looks away again into the fire, shaking her head
sadly before she speaks again. 'It was just after that photograph was
taken, Maureen, that I had to make a decision about you. You see,
my first husband's death changed everything. We would've raised
you otherwise.'

She lets her thoughts trail off again, and I look at the picture
in my hand. In the tiny photo, no more than two inches by three,
stands a little girl in a dress. She's looking shyly up at the camera,
one finger crooked and poking into her mouth. Her hair, my hair, is
light blonde. I look happy – sure, I was happy. For the first time in
my life, I look at a photo of myself before I went to the nuns, and
it feels so strange. Would she have told me any of this if I wasn't

leaving, I wonder? She had to tell me, for my sake as well as for her own. She has kept this to herself for so many years, and it must've been difficult for her. I can only stare at myself in the picture. 'Is this really me?' I ask. 'But I've blonde hair in it.'

'You were blonde indeed, all curls and such a happy child.'

'Do you have any photographs of my mother?' I ask, feeling a deep pang to see the face of the woman who gave birth to me. But my heart sinks when I hear Mrs Hughes' reply.

'I'm sorry, Maureen, but I've no photograph of your mammy. It's a shame, but we weren't ones for the camera.'

I hold the photo of myself as we sit quietly now, the warm red glow of the fire slowly shrinking and fading before bedtime. How I long to know what my real mammy looks like. There's not a single photo of her for me to take to England. I sort through what I've heard, putting little pieces together one by one, with no reason to doubt what I've been told. So it all began here. My life started in this little terraced house in Mullingar. I called them Mammy and Daddy, and surely I bonded with them during those three years before I was taken away. They loved me. They treated me like their own, the child they never had.

My oldest memory flashes up again before me, the thing I must ask about, so tiny yet so clear, like a bright picture framed in mist. I'll never forget it. It was spring – or at least it must have been, for I remember so many colours from the flowers on either side of me – and I had on a black-and-white-chequered coat with a black collar. The nun was leading me away. I was sobbing terribly and crying for my mammy. For years, this scrap of a memory was the only hint of the past that I'm being told about now. I must know. I want to hear about that day from Mrs Hughes. She took me to the orphanage. I now have the face of the mammy Sister Elisabeth was leading me away from, but what else happened? I need to know. I reach out to touch Mrs Hughes' arm lightly. 'The day I was brought to the orphanage, I think I remember something about that day.' She smiles sadly and nods her head. Tears shine in her eyes from the glow of the turf and one escapes down her cheek. She knows what

I'm going to ask. 'I know what I had on, the little chequered coat, black and white it was, and I was walking and crying and the nun was holding my hand. So that was you, then, who took me there that day, you yourself?'

'Ah, indeed it was me, Maureen, and an awful day it was. This little house . . . it was no home to come back to with Mr Kane dead and you in that place . . .' She looks away again, lapsing into a long silence as tears fill her eyes. I want to ask what's the matter, but I can't manage it. Will she share whatever this burden is with me?

Finally, with a haunted look on her face, Mrs Hughes begins again. She doesn't try to hide her tears as she tells me about that spring day. 'My husband was dead and not long buried, and I was left with next to no money. You cried and looked for him, for his hugs and his stories, and his knee that he would set you on. How could I explain anything to you at three years old? There was nothing to be done to help or change it, and with Mrs Burke's help the decision was made.'

Another painful silence lingers. There isn't a sound now in the low kitchen, only the odd muted drone of a passing motor car outside and the silent play of shadow and light on the walls from the oil lamp on the table. Finally, she begins again, and I listen as Mrs Hughes' words remove the mist from around the one little memory I took into the orphanage with me. I hear about that day, being dressed up in the morning to go to the nuns in the black-and-white coat with the black collar. I hear about the long ride down to Longford and on to Newtownforbes. I hear about the questions I'd asked and the awareness children show when something isn't right. I hear it all, right up to the point where I had to let go of Mrs Hughes' hand and take the hand of the nun who led me away. That nun was Sister Elisabeth. Some thirteen years later, I made my leaving outfit with her, and in that outfit I returned to this house.

I listen to all of this with a kind of distant fascination as Mrs Hughes goes on. 'I went back once, Maureen, to see you in the orphanage. It wasn't long after I'd left you there, weeks only. I was waiting in the parlour, expecting to see you, when the door opened. At first, I couldn't believe the child they brought in was you. I didn't want to believe it. Your head was shaved, and they had you in some rough old dress, and you were covered from head to foot in ringworm. The worst of it was that you wouldn't look at me. Not once did you look up at me. I was shocked beyond words. And the nun was coaxing you to look up. What was it she said to you? "You've a visitor, Maureen." That was it. "You've a visitor, Maureen. Aren't you going to see who it is and say hello? Aren't you going to look up to see who's here to see you?" But you wouldn't look at me. It was terrible, the state you were in. "What have I done?" I said to myself. "My God, what have I done?" I left, Maureen. It did something to me. I left, and I never went back. I couldn't go back to that place. You were not the same child. Whatever they did to you, the beautiful chatty girl was gone, and that day has never left me. I felt terribly guilty over the years. Your poor mammy, she couldn't keep you, and I promised I would raise you. We would have a little one to bring up. We could help your mammy and give you a good home. Then it all fell apart when my first husband died. Overnight, it went to pieces. I made a promise to myself then, Maureen, that as long as I was alive I would contact you when you were within a couple of years of leaving the orphanage. That's why I sent you the Christmas parcel, and the nuns thought it might be better if you thought I was your mammy, being that you had lived here before you went into the orphanage. I don't know. I just went along with what they asked. I wanted to be able to claim you myself and give you a safe place to begin when you got out.'

She stops speaking to me and the tears now fall freely from her eyes as she sniffles and shakes her head. It all makes sense, although I have never suspected a thing. I have absolutely no memory of the day she came back, when they brought me before her with a shaved head and the ringworm. I feel for Mrs Hughes, but hearing this neither shocks nor saddens me. I've witnessed the very scene she's just described to me. I have seen three-year-old children with shaved heads and ringworm all over their little bodies. I remember the lice on me many times, and lining up in the dormitory to be doused with Jeyes Fluid, then the lice falling to the ground by the score. I remember the tapeworm crawling down the leg of a child of three or four when I was only six.

I can't help the sudden anger and resentment that fills me as I recall what I've seen. If Mrs Hughes has known where I was all these years, why didn't she come and see me when I was small? Why didn't she send a parcel then? How I want to speak out and ask her why. But my feelings and my anger are all under lock and key. I just cannot do it. Someone or something else holds the key.

Just as suddenly, my anger fades away, as I realise that she needn't have decided to send any parcel at all or claim me when I left at sixteen. It confuses me still, though, those many years in between, and I think of when I played our dandelion game with my friends, wishing and praying for a single visitor. No visitor ever came.

We sit silently for a few minutes longer, the turf fire almost out. Only a small glowing eye of red gazes dully back at us. On the way up to bed, Mrs Hughes holds the oil lamp on the stairs as she always does. We pray together, and this night I pray for Mrs Hughes and for my mammy. I lie awake afterwards, filled with joy to have learned about my past, but my joy is tinged with a terrible sadness as well. One day, when I'm able to, I will return to find out what happened to my mammy, Annie Harte. I would love more than anything to know where she is and if she is still alive, but I wouldn't have a clue as to how to go about looking for her. That is something far beyond me right now. No, I will take this opportunity of going to England to better myself. One day I will come back, and when I understand life and the world better I will search for her, and I won't let anything stop me when I do.

❖ Twenty-three ❖

I stand packing the small brown suitcase Mrs Hughes has given me to travel to England with. Except for the new dress she has bought for me and some underwear and socks, I have what I left the orphanage with six months ago. I wear the same dress, coat and beret I made with Sister Elisabeth, and, I must say, I am still proud of my outfit. Mrs Burke has arranged for me to spend tonight in a house run by the Sisters of Mercy in Dublin before my boat leaves. I think Mrs Burke must know a nun there, because she made all the arrangements. Their chauffeur, a Mr Doyle, is to meet me in Dublin. There is a name tag on my coat so he can recognise me in the crowd at the train station.

Everything about my departure is very casual and matter-of-fact, and as usual I must keep all my true feelings to myself. Tomorrow morning I'll leave from Dún Laoghaire on the ferry to England across the Irish Sea. I know this will be a sad day indeed, leaving Mullingar, the little terraced house and Mrs Hughes.

Downstairs, Mrs Burke goes over the details of my trip, asking me to repeat the name of the chauffeur. 'Mr Doyle,' I answer.

'Good, that's right, and just in case you forget, it's all written down in the envelope with all your other documents: your passport and travelling papers. And the train station in Dublin, Maureen, where is it?' She tests me to make sure I know where to go.

'Westland Row.'

Already I have tears in my eyes, feeling only the sadness and uncertainty of leaving rather than the excitement of moving on to my new life. A few other neighbours come in to say goodbye. Mrs Flynn and Mrs Lynch are here, and Mrs Wall as well. They've said many kind words to me already and are staying now to see me off. 'You will be happy in England with the O'Neills, Maureen,' Mrs Burke

promises. 'Remember all the instructions and get there safely. We'll
be saying a prayer for you that you have a safe crossing. Goodbye,
now, Maureen, and God bless.'

Through my tears, I thank her again for all she has done for me
before riding with Mrs Hughes in Michael Lynch's hired car to the
Mullingar train station. How badly I want to say something special
to her, but it's so hard to find the words. The train comes into the
station, and as it moves slowly past us Mrs Hughes leans close and
hugs me. She tells me again not to worry, reminding me to take care
of my passport and other documents. 'I will,' I say absently, smiling
because she does sound like a worried mother. I step up into the
train and turn to wave a final goodbye. She looks the same as she
did the day she met me for the first time. I wonder if I will ever
see her again.

In pouring rain, the train approaches what must be the outskirts
of Dublin. The sky hangs low and grey over a forest of tall chimneys
spouting dirty smoke, like the laundry at the orphanage only multiplied
by hundreds, and street after street of terraced houses come into view.
I see very little green. There are double-decker buses everywhere
and far more people than I have ever seen before in my life. This is
nothing like Mullingar. I get my suitcase ready, preparing to leave,
but when the conductor sees me waiting by the door he says, 'Not
quite there yet, dear. The train needs to slow down here. Fifteen
minutes till Westland Row.'

I smile and thank him but remain standing in the corridor near
the door. He glances at the name tag on my coat and asks, 'Are you
being met in Dublin, dear? Are you clear about where you're going
once we get there?'

'I am. Someone's meeting me there, thanks.'

'Right! We won't be long now. A good day to you, miss.'

'Good day.'

The train moves forward slowly in fits and starts, the wheels
grinding on the rails. Other passengers begin to appear by the door,
suitcases in hand, and finally the train inches to a stop in Westland
Row station. On the platform, I stand waiting, away from the crowd of

people, off in a corner. The station is far bigger than that in Mullingar, with more lines branching out and far more people hurrying here and there. The air smells less fresh, and there are men coming from the engine of the train in greasy overalls and with soot-covered faces.

I've been waiting ten minutes when I'm approached by a man. This must be Mr Doyle, the chauffeur. He's short and stocky, and quite friendly. 'Ah, it's grand, now, that you made it this far, Maureen!'

He takes my suitcase, and I follow him through the station to a motor car just like Michael Lynch's. We drive through the busy streets, and the traffic is heavy. People drive wildly in the heavy rain, but I soon forget to worry about it, full of wonder at the city of Dublin, the capital of Ireland. Throngs of people fill the pavements, and they all seem in such a hurry. My real mammy was living here in Dublin when Mrs Hughes lost touch with her after the last letter. She might still be living here, and me so close.

Mr Doyle lights a cigarette as we head away from the centre of the city. He opens his window a little to let the smoke out, and a rush of fresh salty air fills the car. The hostel I'm spending the night at is right in Dún Laoghaire. The chauffeur stops in front of a large neat-looking house with a wrought-iron fence. He sees me right to the front door, rings the bell and waits. A nun opens the door, and Mr Doyle, after greeting a nun named Sister Marie, turns to me and says, 'I'll be seeing you bright and early in the morning, Miss Harte. Good day now.'

I thank him before turning to Sister Marie. 'Well, come in now, Maureen. You must be tired.' I go in with only one thought: I want this one night with the nuns, the Sisters of Mercy, over with. I can only do my best and hope that they leave me alone.

After attending morning mass in the little chapel and a good breakfast, I thank Sister Marie and soon I'm on my way to the docks with Mr Doyle. The November sky is mostly grey cloud, unchanged from yesterday, and the temperature is typical for this time of the year. In less than fifteen minutes, we arrive, and Mr Doyle takes me to a waiting area of sorts, where he repeats a few details about the boarding procedure before wishing me the best and leaving. I grip my little suitcase tighter as I watch him walk away, feeling suddenly afraid and alone.

I gaze round from where I stand in a half-open area with a corrugated roof overhead. A light breeze blows across the docks, filling my head with the salty smell of the sea. All this feels dreamlike to me. It's so hard to believe, as if it's happening to someone else. Here I stand, about to board a huge boat to England. Only six months ago, I lay in the dreary dormitory on the morning of my leaving day, and now I'm here. Some of my fear gives in to curiosity, and I walk a few steps out to get a better view. I'm struck with wonder as I gaze out at the sea stretching away from the docks in greys and greens to the horizon. Above me the air is full of seagulls cutting circles round the docks and ferry, their screeches sounding like lonely music high above the water. I quite forget my fears and worries as I stare out at the sea and the gulls, almost in a trance due to the peaceful feeling it stirs in me.

The sudden shuffling behind me of the crowd of people snaps me out of my reverie, and I jump back into the line as it starts to inch slowly toward a gate. 'Have your papers ready,' I hear the man at the gate call out. I check to make certain I have them all in place. 'Keep moving along now, follow along!'

I follow the line of people onto the boat, up a walkway with ropes on the side. It is some time, though, until the boarding is completed, and when the ferry floats away from the docks it moves so slowly I can't feel the motion. With the hundreds of other passengers at the rails of the ferry, I look back towards land. All around me people are saying goodbyes, and there's much waving of hands. Some are crying, some smiling. There are families, couples and people travelling alone like me. A young woman blows a kiss to someone she's leaving back on the docks.

Gradually, as the boat moves farther out and the people on the shore become tiny figures, the passengers at the rails move off to find seats for the crossing, but I linger there, watching the Irish coast get smaller and smaller, still just able to make out the movement of the seagulls, now tiny circles above the docks. It's like a picture, my home and country there, fading away behind me. I watch until the Irish coast is little more than a heavy, uneven line of greenish blue in the distance.

Stiff and tired from the travel and in no mood to explore the ferry, I turn to search for a bench. I prefer to sit with women, so I walk over to one occupied by two ladies. They smile at me, and I nod back as I sit.

A few minutes pass before one of them turns towards me, probably to begin a conversation. I avoid meeting her eye, though she seems friendly enough. When she finally catches my eye, she says, 'Are you travelling alone, dear? You look quite young.'

'I'm gone sixteen this past April,' I say, proud to announce my birthday.

'Well! You look no more than thirteen or fourteen.'

'I know. I'm told that often.'

'You haven't travelled much, then?'

'Oh no, not much,' I answer, feeling my self-consciousness suddenly. 'I've travelled a little in Ireland, on the train,' – I pause for a moment, waving my hand toward the ferry and the sea – 'but I've never seen the sea. I mean, I've never been on a boat on the sea before, only the train.'

She watches me, listening with a warm smile on her face. 'Only the train,' she replies. 'Well, this is quite different. But tell me, are you by any chance going on to London – from Holyhead, that is? I'm going on to London, and if that's your destination, maybe you'll feel better to have someone with you, some company.'

'I am,' I answer, relieved to have someone to sit with for the crossing and the train ride to London.

'And what's your name?'

'Maureen.' It doesn't occur to me to ask her what her name is.

Farther out into the Irish Sea, the weather grows suddenly rough, and before long a terrible rain slashes across the decks of the ferry in angry sheets. The boat begins to heave up and down on the great swells, and along with it my stomach. I feel queasier each minute as

I ponder whether this is normal. No one told me I might get sick on the ferry, and the woman I've befriended is somewhere else right now. I look around at the other passengers along the deck. Some of them are utterly drenched, with spiky clumps of wet hair plastered to their faces making them look terribly odd. It gets worse and worse until finally I stagger across the heaving deck to the railings, barely making it in time. It must indeed be normal, because every single passenger seems to be at the railings and vomiting over the side.

I throw up over the railings, so sick I can think only of not being sick any longer. I don't care about the heaving swells of the storm or the angry green of the sea as it comes closer and falls away again. I don't care that people can see me like this. Behind me, little streams of vomit flow back and forth, finding their way along the deck in rhythm with the swells. Some passengers throw up on themselves, unable to make it to the side. They just lie down and throw up, surrendering to their terrible seasickness. My God, when will it stop? It seems to last for ever. When it does finally end, I feel dreadful. In my misery, I vow never again to cross the Irish Sea!

About three hours out of Dublin, the sea is quiet and calm again, as if after a bout of temper. Sickly pale passengers move about the deck again, looking shaky and unsteady as they find their legs.

The coast of Wales gets larger as we approach. I can soon make out more detail: the greenish outline of hills in the distance, then, finally, the harbour itself. My travelling friend joins me where I stand watching at the railings. She explains her plan to get me off the ferry quicker with her. 'Stay close to me when we get off. I think I can get us off a little quicker. I have an emergency telegram regarding a death in the family, and such travellers are called up first, as well as mothers with small children, so stay very close to me, dear.'

By now the boat is making ready to dock, and there is much activity on deck as the ferry drifts toward the huge moorings. With me beside her, the woman shows the telegram to the officer, and he waves the two of us along, her almost pulling me behind her, so slow am I.

Happy to be off the boat and on dry land again, I stay with my new friend, uncertain what to do next. Luckily, the train station is close to the docks, and we arrive on the platform for our train to London well ahead of the main rush of people. Behind us, a steady flow of passengers arrive from the ferry, and soon the platform is black with people. We move a little closer to the train, the woman able to time her every move almost perfectly. 'Stay with me,' she says quietly. 'Just stay close, Maureen.'

When the announcement is made to board, there's a sudden mad rush, and I realise how fortunate I am to be with this woman, otherwise I'd be crushed as I stood wondering what to do. 'C'mon, dear!' she says and grips my arm with great strength for a small woman, pulling me along with her up into the train. Inside, it is packed full of people racing to get the best seats for the long journey. But we find a compartment with five other people, and I'm lucky enough to be sitting by the window.

The scenes through the window as the train begins on its way are dim and foreign to me. I've no idea where we are: somewhere across the sea is all I know. At least I'm safe with the kind woman who took me under her wing, and I've made it this far, I think, as my eyes grow heavy with fatigue, the final leg of my journey underway. Exhausted and unconcerned with the Welsh countryside passing by outside, I allow my eyes to close to the sleepy rhythm of the train.

I wake up stiff and sore but rested, a good five hours or so later with the train stopped in a small station. Looking sleepily round me, I find the smiling face of the woman next to me. 'You've had a great sleep,' she says to me. 'That's a long time on a train. Feel better?'

'Yes, thank you. I was very tired from the travelling. Where are we now?'

'We're stopped at Stafford Station. We have about two more hours until we reach Euston Station in London. Are you hungry, dear? I was famished! I have some rather good sandwiches here. Would you like one?'

'Yes, I am. Thank you very much.' The food tastes wonderful, and after the long sleep and nourishment I'm wide awake, terribly excited now as I try again to imagine what London will be like and looking forward to seeing Julia and her mother.

For most of the remaining time, I watch the constantly changing scenes outside the window with hungry eyes. I begin to notice more and more buildings and towns closer together, one after the other almost. I ask the lady if she knows how far we are from London, and she tells me it will be another half-hour or twenty minutes. My excitement grows as we get to the outskirts of the city. The train seems to go this way then that, then under tunnels of red brick and out again. Factories come and go, and everything seems so big and so very different to my eyes: smoke stacks, street after street of houses without end, red double-deckers – yes, Julia did mention those. London, England! What a sight! I'm actually here. I made it!

After a few more lurching changes of direction, the kind woman tells me that we're almost at Euston Station. 'I'll take you to a spot where you can wait for the party that's meeting you, Maureen. I'd wait with you myself until they arrive, but I'm afraid I'm in a dreadful hurry. Just sit tight where I take you and you'll be fine, love.'

The woman takes me to a place where I can wait for the O'Neills, and I watch as she quickly vanishes into the crowds of swarming people. I stand dumbfounded, shocked by the unbelievable commotion around me. The train station is so big and frightening, with people rushing around and noisy loudspeakers calling out arrivals and departures. The air is heavy with a burned smoky smell that lingers in my nostrils and is sickly in my lungs. The seconds and minutes seem endless, and the sheer madness and rush all about me feels threatening. They'll be here. Just stay calm.

But ten minutes pass, then fifteen, then twenty. The crowds thin out, and still there's no sign of them. I'm almost trembling with fear. This isn't the station at Mullingar. I can feel the strangeness of it, the way the people ignore one another as they rush along. A half-hour, forty minutes, and nothing. No one even seems to notice me here. I wait and I wait, almost in tears, a sense of panic beginning to take me over. I keep saying to myself that they will be here soon, they will be here. I'm at the point of hysteria when a middle-aged gentleman glances at me, then again. He turns back and approaches me. He's very well dressed in a suit and a dark raincoat. 'Excuse me, miss, but are you quite all right? You look dreadfully worried. Is something the matter?'

When I begin to speak, I feel my voice tight with fear and worry. 'I don't know. I'm to be met, and they're nowhere, and I . . .'

'Who? Who is it you're waiting for? Someone whom you know?'

'Yes, Mrs O'Neill, Claire O'Neill. This isn't like her!'

'I see. Do you happen to have the address of the party who was supposed to meet you, miss?'

'I do.' My hand trembles as I give him the envelope Mrs Burke gave me with all my papers. I've not looked at them.

He sorts through the different papers quickly, finding the address among the items. 'Mrs Claire O'Neill,' he reads aloud. 'One hundred and sixty-six Kilburn Park Road. She must've missed you somehow. I can take you there by taxi. I'm going that way myself.'

Almost in tears, I agree, feeling safe with this gentleman as I did with the woman on the ferry. As we leave the station to find a taxi, he tells me that London is such a big city and that one has to be careful. I haven't the slightest clue what he means. I just want to get to Mrs O'Neill's safely.

It's quite dark now. The taxi rolls through the busy streets, with their strange noises and smells. Only now do I realise how terribly exhausted I am. The journey behind me seems stretched out over time as I pray to God to get me there safely. Eventually, the taxi stops in front of a row of tall brick buildings. 'There you go, guv: one hundred and sixty-six Kilburn Park Road,' the driver says to the gentleman, half-looking over his shoulder.

'Wait, please, driver,' the gentleman says. Then he turns to me and says, 'Sit tight, dear, while I make sure they're at home. They may have gone back down to Euston Station if there's been a mix-up.'

I watch him go up a few steps to a door, where he rings the bell before turning back to me with a smile of reassurance. Please, God, make this the right house. Oh, I just want to be safe . . . I hear some voices but can't see anything in the darkness. Then I hear, louder, 'Yes, who is it?' A woman's voice. The gentleman looks up in response. My heart pounds with prayer and hope.

'Mrs O'Neill?' he calls up to the voice. 'Claire O'Neill?'

'Yes, yes, I'm Claire O'Neill.'

That's all I need to hear! I'm out of the taxicab with my suitcase, tears of relief streaming down my cheeks. I look up to see Mrs O'Neill leaning out of a window above, and I know I've made it! 'Maureen? Is that you, Maureen? Oh, God. How worried I've been!'

I can't speak as I stand bewildered on the steps beside the gentleman, tears of relief flowing down my face. The door opens, and Julia throws herself into my arms with a big hug. 'Maureen, you're here, you've come!'

'Maureen, my God, where on earth were you?' Mrs O'Neill looks very relieved to see me, although confused about how I got here with the gentleman. Looking from him to me, she says, 'What's happened? We've just returned from the station ourselves and were on our way back just now. Oh, thank God you've made it. I was terribly worried!'

'I don't know, Mrs O'Neill, but maybe it was because I travelled with that lady who watched out for me after I met her on the ferry.'

Both Mrs O'Neill and the gentleman look at me for an explanation of this new information. 'What lady, Maureen? Who do you mean?' Mrs O'Neill asks.

'I met her on the ferry. I don't even know what her name was, but she was going to a funeral here in London, and she was able to get us off the ferry before the rest of the passengers. Then we went straight to one of the platforms and got on the train there. I felt safe with her and just did as she said. I don't know what I'd have done without her. Then when we got to Euston Station she left me and was gone, and then this man found me and brought me here.'

'That was it then!' Mrs O'Neill exclaims. 'She must have got you on a slightly later train and we'd already left the train station before you got there. Or maybe it was just delayed along the way. No matter now you've arrived safely. My God, Maureen, you gave me a fright.' Then, turning again to the gentleman, she says, 'Thank you so much for taking the time to help. That was very thoughtful of you.'

'Oh, not at all, madam. In fact, I was only doing my job.' He then reaches into his overcoat pocket and draws out an official-looking badge that he displays for Mrs O'Neill and me as Julia looks on wide-eyed. 'I'm Inspector Dennis, Graham Dennis, London police. Please allow me to explain.' I almost grow faint when I realise the man is a policeman. Fighting to keep my nerves in check, I listen as he goes on. 'Unfortunately, Mrs O'Neill, these days we are dealing with a lot of brazen kidnappings at all the large train stations and places where people travel. The targets are usually young girls and women travelling alone, innocent to the ways of the world. We believe they're being sold into what's called white slavery, though I'll spare you the details. So when I saw Miss Harte standing there crying and then heard her Irish accent, I took action and brought her here myself, just to be safe. I didn't want to tell her I was a policeman right away, given the state she was in. You see how easily she came with me. Well, I could have been anyone. That's what these people prey on: innocence. Well, she's safely here now, and that's what matters.'

All this simply overwhelms me. I feel nothing but a great sense of relief that I've arrived safely. But what kind of a place is this? The air is thick and foul smelling, and I just want to rest and gather my thoughts. Mrs O'Neill can only shake her head at the policeman's words. 'Thank you so much again, sir,' she says to him. 'It's very reassuring to know that there are police on the lookout for such dreadful things.'

'Not at all, madam. Glad to be of assistance. Good evening, now.'

With that, he is gone, back down the steps and into the waiting taxicab, which moves away into the night. I think suddenly of Sister Brendan's words. 'We will never stop praying for you, Maureen, and for all those girls who have left before you.' It seems that someone was watching over me today, and I have made it safely to the O'Neills'.

Julia, only half-understanding the commotion, is already tugging my arm in the direction of the flat upstairs. 'Come along, Maureen. We'll go upstairs, and I'll show you all around your new home. It's going to be so much fun having you live with us.'

'She's full of beans, as usual, Maureen,' Mrs O'Neill says, lighting a cigarette and nodding at Julia, who, insisting on carrying my old brown suitcase, is already through the door and heading up the steps to their flat.

The O'Neills live in a two-bedroom flat on the third floor. Julia drags me quickly round the place to show me my new home. Her room is at the back of the flat with an extra bed now for me. There is another bedroom, a lavatory, the kitchen and the front room. Mrs O'Neill soon rescues me and insists I have a bite to eat. My eyelids droop heavily as I enjoy a cup of tea and some meat called Spam from a tin, as well as beetroot and watercress, which I've not had before. After we eat, Julia takes me to the bedroom she and I will share, and the two of us sit on the bed together while she shows me her books and all her toys. I think she would chat away all night, but Mrs O'Neill, knowing how exhausted I am, explains that I need rest and that we can talk tomorrow. 'Say goodnight now, love. Maureen will be much better tomorrow.'

Julia puts her two arms round my neck and gives me an affectionate hug. 'I'm so glad you came to live with us, Maureen. What fun it's going to be. Tomorrow we'll do something nice. Goodnight!'

'Goodnight, Julia. Goodnight, Mrs O'Neill.'

I've just enough energy left to get into my nightdress, turn off the lights and crawl under the covers. I lie in the strange bed in this strange city without the slightest clue where I am. Somewhere in London is all I know and that I've made it here safely. It seems a miracle that I am in England with little Julia and her kind mother. I think of Mrs Hughes back in Mullingar in the terraced house. Is she sitting by the soft glow of the turf fire, watching the embers as they die away and worrying about me? Does she miss me already? I thank God for my safe arrival here and quickly sink into a deep, dreamless slumber.

✤ PART 2 ✤

LONDON, ENGLAND, 1946–55

❖ TWENTY-FOUR ❖

When I wake in my new surroundings, the first thing I hear is the sound of Julia's voice babbling away excitedly. For a moment, I'm confused, and then it hits me that I'm not in Mullingar but far away in England with the O'Neills. I jump up and walk from the bedroom along the hallway into the front room, straight to the window. From the O'Neills' third-floor flat, I look down on a long street of terraced houses with steps leading up to the front doors, all three-storey like this one. I see no trees or parked cars, but there must be a main road close by because I can hear the sound of traffic from the window. A number of people walk along, mammies with little children mostly. How huge London must be. It's going to be quite an adjustment for me here. 'Well, there you are!' Mrs O'Neill says, joining me at the window. 'Good morning, love.'

'Good morning, Mrs O'Neill.'

'Getting your first look at London? Different from Mullingar, isn't it?'

'It's very different. It seems so big.'

She smiles at this, taking a puff of her cigarette. 'That it is. But come on. Breakfast's on the table. I've had to keep Julia from waking you, Maureen. That's all she's talked about since she got up.'

Julia waits at the kitchen table, smiling and full of energy as usual, excited about what we should do on my first day in London. Mrs O'Neill settles her down with a promise. 'Allow Maureen to eat first, then we'll decide, all right?'

We sit down to a breakfast of eggs and beans and tea and toast, which I thoroughly enjoy. Julia gives me excited smiles as we eat, while Mrs O'Neill chats to me about everyday life in London since the war. She uses ration books to get food and clothes, and my living here will entitle her to another book of coupons. The extra coupons will mean more butter and meat to go with the canned beans and Spam. Beef, though, and whole chickens are still hard to find. When I'm told the eggs on my plate come from powder, I look at them intently and poke them a bit, which makes Julia giggle. I didn't think such a thing could be done, but they're very tasty. Mrs O'Neill promises to make me one of their favourite meals: toad-in-the-hole, a row of sausages covered in batter and roasted in the oven. Whether the food is powdered or in a can, it's much better than what we had in the orphanage, and after so many years of going hungry I feel very fortunate and blessed. I'm very grateful to Mrs O'Neill for opening her heart and home to someone like me.

The single window in the kitchen faces the back of the building, and as I help with the dishes after breakfast I lean forward to look out. Below are small high-walled cement yards, all the same size and stretching away in both directions like a row of big open boxes. Julia's footsteps sound along the hall, and she flies into the kitchen. 'Mummy,' she says, 'let's go to the park on the bus with Maureen. That'd be fun. Can we?'

'How's that sound, Maureen? It's Saturday, and it's a lovely park. You'll get your first look at London. London after the war, anyway.'

'I'd love to go,' I answer, thinking it a wonderful idea.

Julia runs ahead down the carpeted stairs outside the flat, waiting impatiently by the front door. The dark wooden banisters and red paisley carpet bring to mind the many staircases in the orphanage.

Outside seems a very different place from where I arrived last night. I remember next to nothing, only the colour of the brick in a patch of light beneath a dim streetlight and tears of relief that I'd made it safely. Now in daylight, and seen from below in the street, the terraced houses on either side of me seem taller and closer. That awful smell lingers, too. It attacks my nostrils the moment we step outside, and the grey November sky hangs oppressively low above the rooftops.

A short walk up Kilburn Park Road brings us to the Kilburn High Road. I stare, fascinated, at the busy street lined with small shops on both sides and thronged with mammies, again pushing prams, bags looped over their elbows and small children alongside. But the traffic – I've never imagined such a thing. A steady stream of cars flows along, and then, just as Julia points it out, I see my first red London double-decker bus up close.

We make our way to one of the bus stops as Julia chatters away, pointing out this sight and that. I can barely keep up, she's so excited. One of the big red buses swings in towards us, slowing a little. 'Stay close, Maureen,' Mrs O'Neill says, taking my hand tightly in hers. I gawk at the bus, thinking it will go by. 'C'mon, love!' Before I can think, I'm pulled along with her up onto a wide platform and into the still-moving bus. 'You've got to be quick hopping on and off these buses,' she says, and Julia giggles at my awkwardness. How easy they make it look.

The bus weaves back into the middle of the London traffic while we take seats on the bottom level. I stare out of the window at the streets, marvelling at the size of the city. The confusion and rush of it both excites and frightens me. The bus makes its way steadily along the same road, slowing only enough to allow the people on and off at the different stops. Curious about the uniformed man walking down the aisle with a machine strapped over his shoulder, I ask Julia who he is. 'That's the conductor, to collect the fares,' she says, smiling and bouncing in her seat, happy to tell me all about her world. The conductor sings out his words sleepily. 'Fares, please. 'Ave yer fares ready!' Mrs O'Neill says something to the conductor as he reaches us and then gives him some coins in return for tickets out of his machine. He then walks on, continuing with his song. 'Fares, please. 'Ave yer fares ready!' At our bus stop, Mrs O'Neill has to help me jump off the bus, promising me that I'll be able to manage it soon enough.

The park is lovely, and we stroll along one of the walks that wind about the small ponds either side. Julia runs on ahead with her little pail and net to look for minnows while I chat with Mrs O'Neill. She tells me how happy they both are to have me here and that I will be great company for Julia. I shouldn't worry about rushing to get a job, she says. I can walk around the neighbourhood and get used to the change first. Julia will be in school, and Mrs O'Neill will be at work during the day, so I'll have time to settle in. 'Take your time to get used to things here, Maureen,' she says. 'It won't be long until the Christmas season now, and the New Year might be a better time to begin a new job. There is the factory, where I work, but we'll talk about that later.'

'Whatever you think is best, Mrs O'Neill.'

We take our time strolling along the paths, following Julia from pond to pond in her hunt for minnows. Near one end of the park, we sit for a time on a lovely ornate bench of patterned wrought iron beside one of the bigger ponds, one just right for Julia. How strange it feels to be sitting here in this big city so far from Mullingar. This lovely park, with its ponds and fancy benches, is beautiful. If it wasn't for the awful smell of the air and the steady drone of the nearby city streets, I might think that I was in some place as quiet and peaceful as Mullingar. I already miss the little terraced house and its half-door, and Mrs Hughes' special smile and little habits. I will especially miss sitting by the fire at night with her. Even if we didn't talk a lot, I knew she cared about me.

As we sit enjoying the peace and quiet of the park, the air becomes damp and heavy and the low sky begins to darken. It looks like rain. Mrs O'Neill, thinking the same thing, waves to Julia, calling her back. Julia collects her pail and net, wiping two muddy hands together before gently pouring the trapped minnows back into the pond and freedom. Her face beams as she rushes up to us. 'I caught some minnows, Mummy! There were lots of them!'

'We're getting cold, love. Time we were off,' Mrs O'Neill says affectionately.

'Thanks, Mummy. That was lovely!'

The three of us stroll slowly back along the winding paths towards the street. Deep red and golden leaves lie strewn in patches, like blankets beneath the half-bare trees. On the path, the wind captures some of the smaller leaves, moving them in a perfect tiny circle for a moment before they fall still again.

The orphanage comes to mind for the first time in days. It will be December in a day or two, and the nuns and all the girls will be starting to think of Christmas and all the things leading up to it. Has it really been just six short months since I left? I never in my wildest dreams imagined that I would be where I am at this moment. Mrs O'Neill must believe in me, otherwise why bother to have me move here with her and Julia? I can only make the best of my opportunity and pray to God to help me through this huge change.

On Monday morning, I clean up after our breakfast of toast and tea while Julia gets dressed for school and Mrs O'Neill rushes to go to work. 'Mummy, where's my sweater for school? I've misplaced it.' Julia looks very different in her smart school uniform: a gym tunic with a white blouse, lovely knee-length socks and the crest of her Catholic school stitched smartly on the tunic.

'I don't know,' Mrs O'Neill answers from the front room. 'Check your room again, love. Did you move it getting the room ready for Maureen?'

'I don't know. I'll look.'

Mrs O'Neill hurries to say a word or two before going out of the door to work. 'Don't be afraid to go for a walk, Maureen, love. It will do you good. Not too far, right? Right! I've got to run. Oh, and Pamela will be by for Julia in a while. They walk to school together. Bye-bye.'

Mrs O'Neill rushes out of the flat, and about ten minutes later the neighbours' girl, Pam Chalmers, comes up to call on Julia. She looks at me with great curiosity when Julia introduces me, greeting me politely before the two of them leave for school. I listen as their chattering voices fade down the outer staircase, and suddenly I'm alone in the flat. It feels odd, sitting here by myself in the middle of this huge city. There's no Dublin road here, no Mrs Burke dropping by for tea and no other Irish voices that I know of. I suppose I could go into the front room and look out over the street below, but I know that it won't be the same as standing at the half-door in Mullingar. I truly miss it and the lovely quiet view of the Dublin road. It won't be like this for long, with little to do and too much time on my hands.

Soon I'll begin working, pulling my weight, contributing my share and helping with things.

Bored with the empty flat before long, I work up my nerve and decide to go for a short walk around the neighbourhood. Instead of going up to the High Road, I turn in the other direction and follow the long side street of terraced houses that way, deciding to move in a big circle so I won't get lost. With my head down and my shoulders slumped forwards, I walk nervously up one long street of terraced houses and down another, avoiding the passing faces. There are too many people in London, I realise, and maybe that's why no one says hello when they pass. Still, there's something exciting about the rush and push of it all. On many of the corners are little shops of all descriptions: sweet shops, bread shops, tailors and lots of others, and though I'm filled with curiosity I dare not venture into any of them.

Ten minutes pass, and I keep to my zigzag circle, certain it will bring me back to Kilburn Park Road and the flat. Suddenly, I'm on a quieter block, and I notice that the traffic has died away and the people seem to have vanished. Feeling strangely unsettled by this, I decide to go back the way I came. But just as the thought comes, I turn a corner round some taller buildings. I stop dead and stare. Ahead of me is a long street of ruined houses, all tumbled down, with jagged half-remaining walls jutting unevenly into the sky. I follow the ruins with my eyes to where the street ends at a huge mound of rubble and bricks. Around the houses where half of the walls are gone, warning barriers have been put up, and there has obviously been work going on to clear this. What destruction. It's thoroughly shocking, and I can't believe my eyes. This can only have been done by the bombs falling during the war. I try to think of this street as it was before, with people coming and going, children playing in the street and women pushing babies in prams. Then I imagine the bombs falling at night, the sounds and fires they must have caused. Had people been killed or hurt badly? During the war, the nuns had us pray every day for the war to end. I never dreamed I'd ever see anything like this so soon after leaving the orphanage. I'll go no further today.

✲✲✲

Spring 1937 – First Holy Communion. Maureen is in the top row,
extreme right, Maggie in the top row, second from the left,
and Katy in the bottom row, extreme left.

Maureen, aged 14,
in the orphanage.

Taken in the spring of 2004 when Maureen returned to Ireland to see her mother's grave for the first time. She put in the new gravestone you see in the photo.

This is the first photograph Maureen saw of her biological mother, Annie Harte.

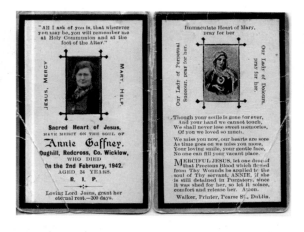

Maureen at her mother's grave in 2004.

Annie's new monument.

Taken in Ringsend, Dublin, in the late 1970s. These are the Casey sisters, with Alice in the light-green sweater, sitting to the left of Maureen.

Taken on the same trip to Ireland, this is Margo McCormack, Maureen's roommate at Warwickshire House.

Annie married at some point in her early thirties.

Mary Harte (nee McCormack), Annie's mother and the wife of James Harte.

Maureen's grandfather, Annie's father James, a cobbler by trade.

Delia Harte's house on Patrick Street in Mullingar in 2004, where Maureen and Reg drove to begin enquiries about Annie.

A photo of Annie (far right)
and Lily (far left).

Taken sometime in the 1950s in
Ringsend, Dublin, Christy and Lily Harte
with children Jimmy, right, Marie, centre,
and Pauline, left, Maureen's first cousins.

The stark ruins of Our Lady of Succour Industrial School
in Newtownforbes. A view of what the girls knew as 'the square',
photographed by Maureen in 2004.

Maureen Harte at the 'side chapel' entrance to the convent church, where the orphans entered for mass.

Another view of the square at Our Lady of Succour Industrial School in Newtownforbes.

The nuns' cemetery at Our Lady of Succour Convent and former industrial school.

Maureen with Jim Coppinger, taken within a year
of her arrival in Toronto, Canada.

Jim and Maureen met at one of the many dances thrown
then for new Irish immigrants.

Mrs O'Neill is home from the factory. I ask her about the war while we eat, curious now that I've seen the terrible damage. 'What were the sirens like?'

'Oh, we were frightened, but we got used to it,' she answers. 'The spotters were always watching, and we had drills at the start of it all, and there was always plenty of warning. By 1940, the Jerries were bombing us regularly. When a raid was coming, the sirens would begin to wail. You had so many minutes, and off you went, straight to the Underground.'

Mrs O'Neill tells me about the air raids and the noisy crowded shelters during the worst of the war years. People would be down there for hours, sleeping if they could or telling stories to the children to pass the time, and even singing sometimes. 'You were too little to remember much of that, Julia, thank God,' Mrs O'Neill says.

Julia nods her head in a dreamy way, saying nothing, which isn't like her. It must have frightened her a lot, no matter how young she was. But her father was alive then, and he'd be down there with them, surely. Or was he away fighting in the war somewhere or serving in some other way? I know nothing about him; they never mention his name or talk about him. 'A lot of women with young children were alone, their husbands off fighting.' Mrs O'Neill pauses for a moment, shaking her head. 'No, the war was not a good time here in England, Maureen, not at all.'

'The nuns had us pray for the war to end,' I say. 'Many times we prayed.'

'Oh really?' she answers. 'Yes, I can see them doing that.'

I get the feeling that that's enough talk about the war, and I ask no more. I'm beginning to see that London is very different from what I'd imagined it to be. I'd ideas of it somehow being a great place, where everything was better and there were riches to be had. But seeing those houses today, totally destroyed, has had a huge effect on me. What an awful thing to go through for the people here.

A few days later, Julia brings Pam and two other little friends into the flat for a visit. They're all Julia's age, ten or eleven, though they seem so advanced. The five of us gather in the bedroom, and Julia tells them about me – that I'm from Ireland and living with her and her mother now. They look at me closely and with much curiosity. 'Do you like it here?' one of the girls asks me, but her accented words seem to roll by me, and I look at Julia in confusion.

'Ask her again,' Julia says with a mischievous grin. 'It's your accent.'

This time I hear it, and when I answer 'I love it!' they begin to giggle. 'Are they laughing at my Irish accent?' I ask Julia.

'It's how you say "I love it",' she explains, laughing affectionately.

The girls talk about school and their teachers, and I listen, amazed by the easy confidence they show. Julia tells them that I went to school in a place where I lived all the time, and that I slept there, too, at night. 'It was an orphanage,' she tells the others. The girls look at me, quite curious about this. 'And do you know how many girls there were in the dormitory?' Julia asks, enjoying the attention of her friends. Then she has me tell them how many girls slept in our dormitory. When I tell them there were forty other girls, they all gasp. 'What? What was that like?'

I tell them all about our dormitory and the dining hall and how we ate with tin plates and porringers. It seems they've heard nothing like it before. One of the other girls, Leslie, who's been listening quietly, suddenly asks, 'What happened to your mummy and daddy, then?'

I was hoping they'd not ask me this, and I fight the sudden tears that rush up, terrified suddenly of showing my feelings in front of these sharp little English girls. 'They died,' I say into the quiet. 'They died, and I became an orphan when I was three.'

'Oh,' Leslie says, without looking at me.

There's an awkward silence in the room, so I change the subject by asking them about their school and teachers. Pamela tells me about the nuns who teach them from class five up, as she explains it. I ask her what order, and she tells me that they're called the Ursuline Sisters, who're all over Ireland as well. 'Are they hard on you in class?' I ask her. 'Will they slap you if you don't know your sums?' I hadn't really wanted to ask this question, but it just popped out.

They seem surprised by my question. 'For sums? Oh no, my mummy wouldn't like that,' Leslie answers.

A thought flashes through my mind when I hear this: the nuns that taught in the orphanage had no one to account to, and that's why we were beaten so much. So if I'd been raised like these young girls, I'd have their confident ways. I look at the girls and their clothes, and I can't help comparing us. All the years in the orphanage and being told what to do and what to wear have had a terrible effect on my whole personality. I don't really feel like I'm living in the real world yet, only getting by in it, surviving in it. I think about this a lot, and I hope and pray that soon I'll be more like other people.

My first couple of weeks in London are quiet and uneventful. I spend the daytime hours alone in the flat. When Julia returns from school she and I play cards or read some of her books in our bedroom, and sometimes Pam and Leslie join us. Julia has taken me to the library and shown me how to find and borrow books on my own, so I have taken out a couple from the children's section when we go. I feel drawn to the fairy tales because they stir my imagination. This is what we needed so badly in the orphanage. I see now that books like these would've allowed us to escape into our imaginations, and they would've maybe broadened our minds. Each day comes, and I try not to think beyond the immediate while I adjust to my new life here in London, and already the grimy air is becoming normal to me.

❖ TWENTY-FIVE ❖

With Christmas Eve a day away, I help Mrs O'Neill decorate the flat with lovely red-and-green paper chains. Through the large window, the London sky is a dull grey behind the roofs of the terraced houses, which is common it seems during the winter months. The colourful decorations in the streets and in the shops make me think about my first Christmas away from the orphanage. I'll miss being with my friends and the religious part of it. Julia, of course, at her age is terribly excited about Christmas. I'll try to enjoy it through her, watching as she opens her gifts on Christmas Day.

'What do you think, Maureen? Do they look right, hung that way?' Mrs O'Neill asks, looking over her shoulder.

'They look fine as they are. They remind me of the orphanage. We used to make garlands of real holly and red berries for the dining room at Christmas.'

'Really, that's quite fancy. These are only paper, but they do liven the old place up a bit.'

I share with her how in the orphanage we used to sit sewing each holly leaf together, then into garlands to be hung on the walls in our dining hall. I tell her about the delicious smell of Sister Michael's plum puddings. It feels good to talk of these things; I don't feel as alone with my feelings about Christmas.

'That sounds like a lot of work. All that detail.'

'Oh, we honestly didn't mind. We loved Christmas.'

'Did the nuns give you anything at Christmas?'

'They gave us a big currant bun,' I answer, 'right after our midnight mass procession by the manger.'

'That's it? That's all you got at Christmas?'

I feel ashamed suddenly, forgetting how others might react. 'Well, there were over one hundred and fifty girls.'

'Oh, right, of course. How's that corner over there look?'

Mrs O'Neill isn't too interested in my stories of the orphanage. She's very busy with Christmas, and I know she wants Julia to enjoy it. I think it's the first Christmas for them without Julia's father. I don't want to be a burden or for Mrs O'Neill to be like a mammy to me. But if I could talk, just a little, about these feelings, it would help.

It's just gone half-past seven on Christmas Eve, and Julia is terribly excited as we get ready to go next door to the Chalmers' flat for a party. It's something they've done every Christmas Eve since they became neighbours, except once or twice during the war when the city was under the strictest blackout conditions due to the bombing.

My thoughts, though, are not here in London, but back in the orphanage. Maggie is surely gone into service somewhere by now. I'm not sure about Lucy. If she's gone, her leaving day would have been recently. Why don't I know these things? If I'm still awake later tonight, at midnight, I'll close my eyes and think of the orphans in the procession. I'll say a prayer for Maggie and Lucy, that they're safe and not lonely.

Julia finds me sitting on my bed. 'Come along, Maureen, time for the party next door. Aren't you excited?'

'Of course, Julia, and I don't have to ask if you are!'

The Chalmers' second-floor flat is full of cigarette smoke and loud voices when we enter. Three other couples are visiting, and a number of children are running about playing with balloons. Julia joins them as soon as we get there, and I sit on a chair, already feeling self-conscious and out of place. There are greetings and quick introductions, but it seems the party has been going for some time now. The children run around with their balloons, bursting the odd one under foot. The adults are drinking liquor, smoking away, talking loudly and laughing. I'd seen the odd pint taken in Mullingar at the Donovans', but this seems quite wild. They tip glasses to their mouths, clinking before they all drink together – 'toasts' they call them. 'A toast!' one of the men calls out. 'To England!'

'To king and country and the end of the war!' says another.

'No! 'ang on a bit,' growls yet another, holding his drink still in the air for a moment. 'How about to real bleedin' eggs!' They all roar with laughter.

Mrs Chalmers brings food out: Spam sandwiches, watercress sandwiches, and after that mince pies and Christmas cake. The food slows things down but not for long. More drinks are poured, the children show no sign of tiring, and one of the men, Jim, has sat down at the Chalmers' battered old piano in the corner. What I thought wild before was nothing. Jim starts banging out songs, and the adults dance and sing to the tunes they all know. 'Oh . . .' they all begin together as Jim starts another one, '. . . I've got a lovely bunch of coconuts, there they are all standin' in a row. Big ones, small ones, some as big as yer 'ead. Give 'em a twist, a flick of the wrist, 'at's what the showman said . . .'

'C'mon, Jim, love. Keep it goin' now!'

'Oh, I've got a lovely bunch of coconuts. Every ball you throw will make me rich. And there stands me wife, the idol of me life, singing, roll a bowl a ball a penny a pitch. Singing, roll a bowl a ball a penny a pitch.' And they begin again with another verse.

I watch all this, amazed that a man like that has such skills at the piano. Mrs Chalmers, with a sideways look as she drinks from her glass, sees me sitting back alone. She squishes out a cigarette, blowing out the last of it before coming over. 'What's this? Join us, love, c'mon,' she says, wanting me to join in the dancing and singing. 'Get with it, love, and join the party. C'mon, on the floor, Maureen!'

'Oh no!' I cry. 'Oh no, no. I can't do it.'

'No?' Mrs Chalmers answers. 'No? It's Christmas, love!' She looks at Mrs O'Neill, who only smiles and shakes her head good-naturedly.

Mrs Chalmers gives up on me for now and goes back to dancing. I want to be enjoying myself, but I'm so terribly bashful and shy. 'Hey, Jim, love!' one of the women shouts. 'Give us "Knees Up Mother Brown".'

A roar of agreement greets this as Jim turns back to the piano. 'All right, will do. "Knees Up" it is!' he says, through the cigarette dangling from the side of his mouth. He begins to hammer out the new tune, and they all form a circle, with the women taking their skirts in both hands. At a certain place, and in time with the music, they all lift their skirts up, clearly showing their stockings and garters. Then they bend their knees up and down to the tune of the music.

'Knees up Mother Brown, your drawers are comin' down. Under the table you must go. Ee-aye, Ee-aye, Ee-aye-oh.' I blush deep red and can't find a place to look. They're roaring with laughter, lost in their wild dancing and singing and without a care in the world. 'If I catch you bending, I'll saw your legs right off. So knees up, knees up, never get a breeze up. Knees up Mother Brown. 'Ow's yer faver? All right!'

The singing and dancing goes on without pause well into the late hours. Jim plays one tune after another, filling the ashtray on top of the piano to the brim with cigarette ends and ashes. I've lost track of the time, my mind constantly drifting back to the orphanage. Just as I realise that it must be getting late, the party quietens down quickly. Everyone is suddenly subdued and thoughtful. 'Maureen,' Mrs O'Neill says, walking over. 'Come on and join us, love. It's a bit of a tradition with us to sing "Silent Night" at the turn of midnight.'

'What?' I say, so surprised at this. 'Oh, it's just . . . we sang "Silent Night", too, Mrs O'Neill, every year at our midnight mass on Christmas Eve.'

'Well, isn't that odd? That's even more special for you, then, love. Come on.'

Before I can gather my thoughts about this coincidence, Jim begins to play quietly on the piano. Abandoned balloons drift about the floor of the flat; greyish blue cigarette smoke hangs like a cloud by the naked bulb above. I turn my head to get a look at the kitchen clock: five minutes before midnight. Any moment now, far away across the Irish Sea, the nuns will walk by the manger in the chapel while all the orphans sing 'Silent Night'.

I'm brought back to the party by the sound of singing, the adults' voices blending with the children's. 'Silent night, holy night. All is calm, all is bright . . .'

I try to close my eyes and think of the procession by the manger, and of Maggie and Lucy. But I'm drawn back again to where I am and to the strange, powerful feelings that fill me as I look and listen. Mrs O'Neill's eyes are full of tears. She lets them fall without concern. Julia holds her mammy's hand tightly, squeezing it as she looks up at her singing. 'Round yon Virgin mother and child, holy infant so tender and mild, sleep in heavenly peace, sleep in heavenly peace . . .'

There are tears on the cheeks of some of the other men and women, too. I look at the faces of these people. Such emotion they're revealing – what does it mean? I feel confused and just want the night over with. The singing of 'Silent Night' ends, and there are hugs and Christmas greetings, but no more loud voices or toasts.

As we get ready to go home, Julia runs up and gives me a big hug. 'I'm so excited,' she cries. 'I'm not going to sleep tonight! Aren't you excited, Maureen, about Christmas?'

'I am,' I say. 'It's Christmas Day tomorrow.'

We say our goodnights and go back to the flat, but it takes Julia quite some time to settle down to sleep. Exhausted, I cannot sleep with my mind so full of thoughts about the past. I would have given anything to be with one friend from the orphanage tonight. Even if we couldn't share our feelings, we would be together, and that would be enough. Finally, I slip into a fitful shallow sleep.

By the new year, I feel settled enough in London to begin some kind of work. Mrs O'Neill has suggested I work where she does, in the factory where they make wooden things like chair rungs, doorknobs and table legs. I've gone along with this without question, eager to help and do my share. Sitting round the flat all day allows too much time for thinking, and I've become restless. An interview has been arranged for me with Mrs O'Neill's boss, a Mr Levitt, and I'm to go to the factory with her today.

I try to control my nerves as I sit with Mrs O'Neill on the way to the factory. Gradually, the streets of houses and shops have thinned out, and I see mostly single-storey red-brick factories around me and dingy old buildings. The streets are crowded with men in overalls coming and going, all of them smoking. We leave the bus, and I follow Mrs O'Neill straight for one of the red-brick buildings. 'Mr Levitt's office's down the back,' she says as we go into the factory. 'Just watch your step.'

Inside, I'm greeted by the sudden whine of machinery. Bright lights glare overhead, and the grinding machines almost reach the ceiling. A strong smell of wood fills my nose, and the floor is covered in wood shavings. But it's the workers I take notice of mostly, in my observant way. The men are all in overalls, standing round the machines or walking about with cigarettes hanging from their mouths, like I saw outside. The women wear pinafore dresses and wraparound aprons. Many have rollers in their hair, tied up in different-coloured scarves. The sound of shouting voices calling out over the noise and the rough-looking women bring back memories of the laundry workers at the orphanage.

We go to the back of the factory, to a small office where a man sits at a desk. When the door is closed, the roar of the machines through the glass is suddenly dulled. 'Morning, Claire,' the man says, looking up.

'Morning, Mr Levitt. This is Maureen. I've spoken to you about her.'

'Hello, Maureen. Sit down, please.'

As I take the chair beside the desk, Mr Levitt looks at me closely. 'You look quite young, love? Are you gone sixteen?' he asks, looking then at Mrs O'Neill.

'Oh yes. She'll be seventeen in April,' she answers, smiling at me.

'All right, then. Have her fill out an application.'

Mrs O'Neill helps me fill out the form then hands it to Mr Levitt. After a quick look, he sets it aside, saying I can start the following week on an assembly line and they'll see how I manage. And that's the end of my interview. I travel back to Kilburn alone, terribly afraid and worried. Will I be able to keep pace with everyone else? What will happen if I'm not able to?

❖ ❖ ❖

After a week of lying awake at night and worrying, and a lot of praying, the day I start my job at the wood factory has arrived. I'm put on the assembly line, inspecting the different pieces of wood for flaws as they come off one of the machines. My supervisor, Dotty, is a rough middle-aged woman, heavy set with a big round red face. Dot they call her. When I first see her in the distance, I have sudden nightmarish visions of the laundry workers. Immediately, I think the worst. But when Mr Levitt introduces me to Dotty, her big face breaks into a friendly toothy smile, and I relax a little. "Ello, love,' she says in greeting. 'Startin' with us, are you?'

'Yes,' is all I can manage to say.

'That's great!' Then to Mr Levitt she says, 'All right, Lev, you can leave her with me and we'll get her started. Come along, Maureen. We'll get you set up on one of the belts, love.'

The first couple of days have gone fine. Dotty's been very patient with me, taking the time to show me exactly what I'm to do. She's helped me get quicker at my task, and the other workers seem to like her. 'You all right, love,' she'll ask. 'Gettin' the 'ang of it?'

Every day, I take the bus to and from the factory with Mrs O'Neill. I earn fifteen shillings a week at the factory, ten of which I give for my keep. Mrs O'Neill works on another floor in quality control, and I rarely see her during the shift. I'm still the same with money, buying nothing for myself and always wanting to buy something nice for Julia or her mother to show my appreciation. I have little left over for new clothes and such, but it doesn't matter to me, as long as I'm managing at the factory and doing a good job.

More than anything, I'm grateful that I'm not shouted at and abused. I'd expected this, not knowing any better after so many years on the farm with Sister Joseph and old Farmer Giles. I keep to myself for the most part, shy and uncomfortable around the rough workers. They seem so strange and different to me, and sometimes I've trouble understanding their strong London accents. They call me love, and their jokes make me embarrassed. They're not saying anything about me, but I just don't like it.

* * *

A month has passed since I started at the factory. In my pinafore dress, I stand at my spot on the assembly line, watching the table legs for flaws or chips. One after the other they come, in a steady stream along the dirty belt. I turn to see a young man standing behind me, smiling down at me as he wipes his hands on a rag. "Ello there, I'm Jake,' he says, putting his hands in his pockets. 'New 'ere, are you, love?' I blush terribly and look down at the floor. 'Maureen, right? That's Irish, ain't it? Why are you always so quiet, Maureen?'

'I don't know,' I answer, not taking my eyes off the floor.

'How old are you?'

'I'm sixteen.'

'Sixteen? Well, you don't look it. Why don't you look at me?'

I look up at him shyly, and he tells me what beautiful eyes I have, which makes me blush ten times worse. I've no idea why he is talking to me this way. I just want the conversation to end. Then, to my horror, he says he'd like to take me to the pictures some weekend. 'Oh, no, no,' I stutter. Jake's smile broadens at this, and with a shake of his head he turns away. He seems nice enough, but I pray he never comes near me again. I just can't handle such things at the moment.

Often, when the loud siren sounds to signal a break, I join one of the groups of women, sitting near them but still keeping to myself. I try to stay invisible around them, because if they're in the mood they'll tease me about my shyness and innocence. I don't like attention being drawn to me, being made aware of how different I am, though they mean no harm. This afternoon, as they gossip among themselves and smoke cigarettes, they start talking about some of the men here. I know it has something to do with sex, and I try not to listen. In my curious way, though, I glance quickly at the one doing most of the talking. Bette sits confidently on the table, with a cigarette in her hand, chewing away on gum at one side of her mouth. For an instant, I think of one of the cows in the paddock and how they'd chomp the grass in the summertime, their mouths moving sideways. 'Blimey, look at that bloke!' Bette says about a man passing a ways off. 'What's under 'is overalls, I wonder. Roger 'e is, that one.'

Just then she catches my eye and winks at me. I turn away, my face purpling with embarrassment, but it's too late. 'Maureen, love,' she calls out, elbowing another woman and winking again. 'What d'you make of 'im? Not half bad, he ain't!'

I can only look back, blushing even worse as they laugh and tease me, wanting only to be left alone. But I say nothing. I know they're not really being mean. They know how naive and bashful I am. But they don't know why, and they know nothing about where I come from. I want to run off when this happens, to be anywhere but here.

The winter months pass without much change, although by the beginning of March I'm beginning to feel restless at the factory. Is this what I left Ireland for, so peaceful and full of fresh air? Am I to stay in this old factory with the rough workers and nothing better for me? I'm not much better here than in the old laundry in the orphanage. No, I want to better myself and learn, but how? I have to rely on Mrs O'Neill's help and her understanding to make a change, but she may think me ungrateful.

❖ TWENTY-SIX ❖

As April has waned and my seventeenth birthday has passed unnoticed, I have become more and more restless at the factory. The job here has been good for me in some ways. Being around real people, real life, and the things I've learned have made me feel more grown up. The workers in the wood factory are true Londoners, but they've been kind and have watched over me. However, in my heart, I know I want to move on and improve myself somehow. When I'm out with Mrs O'Neill and Julia at the shops, I look at the assistants. That's something I could do: work in a nice place, maybe a shop, where it isn't as rough. My biggest worry is that Mrs O'Neill will think me ungrateful for saying I'm unhappy where she works. But I must try to find a way to better myself. So, I've decided to speak to Mrs O'Neill about how I feel at the factory over tea this evening.

'Mrs O'Neill,' I begin nervously, 'I . . . I want to speak to you about my job at the factory . . .' A long pause hangs while I summon my courage. 'I think I'd like to try something else, another job.'

She seems surprised, coming out of her dreamy look, as she sits silently on the settee, looking off at nothing. 'Changing jobs? Well, what's the matter, Maureen? Where's this coming from? Is something wrong there?'

'I want to better myself,' I reply, my eyes on the floor as usual.

'Better yourself? Of course. That's fine. But what can you do, Maureen?' She knows how little experience I have.

I go on in a rush to speak my true feelings and explain that I'd love to work as a shop girl, that I'm not happy in the factory. The women, I explain, laugh at me because I'm so bashful. Mrs O'Neill sits back and lights a cigarette. 'So you really want to change then?'

'I do,' I reply, more confidently now. 'I've thought about it a lot. I've watched the shop girls when we're out.'

'A shop girl? All right, but I'd no idea you were feeling like this, Maureen.'

'But I didn't know,' I say, not looking up, 'if you'd make me stay at the factory . . .'

'Of course not, Maureen,' she says. 'Of course I wouldn't make you stay, not if you're unhappy. Tell you what, then: we'll read the adverts and start to look right away.'

'Oh, thank you, Mrs O'Neill,' I reply. 'Thanks for helping me. I'll try hard to make my next job work for me.'

'I know you will, love.'

We have bought different papers each day, and I've helped Mrs O'Neill to look through all the job listings over tea. I don't think I could find something on my own. There are so many shops and areas of London, and it's very confusing to me still. She doesn't want me travelling too far from Kilburn, so we are looking for something close by. After a couple of weeks of looking, we've still not found anything. Maybe tonight?

Mrs O'Neill talks to me from behind the advert section, opened wide in both her hands. 'Here's one that may be something.'

My ears perk up, and my praying begins. Please, God, make it work.

'A toyshop,' she says, looking at me for a moment over the paper. 'Oliver's. That sounds familiar.'

We head off to the public payphone up on the High Road. Outside the red booth, my silent prayers continue while Mrs O'Neill rings the toyshop. 'Good news, love,' she says, stepping out of the booth. 'They say to bring you in to meet them tomorrow. They'd like to do that first, then maybe you can apply.'

Oliver's toyshop is only a short bus ride along Kilburn High Road. Behind a large shop window, lovely handmade toys are on display, including a beautiful wooden rocking horse. A bell sounds as we walk into the shop, and a tall middle-aged woman with light-brown hair steps out of a small office to greet us. She looks smart in her tweed suit and has kind eyes. Mrs O'Neill gives her name then introduces me to Mrs Oliver. She offers her hand, and I feel comfortable with her warm, polite way. Have I any experience as a clerk or something similar, she wants to know. I explain that I'm not long over from Ireland and working where Mrs O'Neill works in the factory. 'And why are you leaving your job there?'

'Because I want to better myself.' My words are out before I can think about them.

'I see,' she answers, smiling warmly. 'I see.'

'Yes,' Mrs O'Neill puts in, sounding a little nervous. 'Maureen has been wanting to work in a shop for a while now. She wants to be a shop girl, she does.'

Mrs Oliver thinks for a moment. 'All right. I'll arrange an interview for you next Monday, Maureen. We can talk more about the position then. Mr Oliver, my husband, may interview you as well. Let's say half-past eight.'

'That's fine,' Mrs O'Neill answers. 'I'll have Maureen here for half-eight.'

I thank Mrs Oliver, leaving the store feeling so happy. Having an interview means I might get the job. It's a lovely little shop, and I really want to work there. Oh please, God, help me get this job. I'll do my best. I promise I will.

On the morning of my interview, I meet Mr Oliver, who seems just as warm and caring as his wife does. Mrs Oliver interviews me first, in the office off one side of the shop. 'So, you're working in a factory, Maureen? You've told me a little about that. What about yourself? How do you spend your free time? Do you have hobbies?'

I tell her that I love to read and that I go to the library and to church with the O'Neills. I explain that I'm only six months here and haven't made any friends yet. She seems to understand this and, with little more to ask about, gives me an application form to fill in. When I finish, she leaves with the application to talk it over with Mr Oliver in another office. Mrs Oliver isn't gone long, and she's smiling when she comes back into the room. They've looked over the application, are pleased with it and I can start a week from tomorrow. This seems almost too good to be true. Suddenly, my future seems different, and the weight and worry of working at the factory is already leaving me. Mrs Oliver says one or two other things, standing then as we finish. 'Before you go today, Maureen, I'll show you around the shop. Oliver's is a specialist toy carrier of almost exclusively wooden toys but also books, games and other interesting things. I think you'll like it here. Come on, I'll give you the tour.'

As we walk about the small shop, Mrs Oliver shows me all the beautifully made items: rocking horses for toddlers, puzzles, children's tables, dollhouses, genuine china dolls, tea services, special books and more. When we're finished, I already know that I'm going to love working here.

I leave feeling very relieved. Mrs O'Neill will be happy for me. I hadn't thought of the earnings, but I'll be increasing my weekly pay from fifteen shillings to a pound. I'll be working in a lovely toyshop where there are plenty of books and lots of nice families coming in, I expect. How I've bettered myself in one day. Sister Brendan would be proud of me, she would. 'You will do well, Maureen. Always keep your faith.' She always said that to me. I feel pleased that I am living up to her expectations.

With the wood factory and its haunting reminders of the orphanage laundry behind me, I travel on the bus to Oliver's toyshop for my first day at work. Clutched tightly in my hand is a medal of the Virgin Mary, given to me by the nuns at my First Communion. Please, Our Lady, help me through my first day at this important new job. I repeat this to myself again and again. Surely Mrs Oliver saw that I wanted to better myself, otherwise why would she hire me?

I arrive a half-hour before opening time. 'Good morning, Maureen,' Mrs Oliver says. 'You're early. That's good. I can show you some important things before the customers arrive.'

Already familiar with the look of the shop, I watch and listen carefully to everything I'm told. Most of the drawers and the shelved book displays are clearly marked, and the larger toys are well organised, too. I am to watch Mrs Oliver when the store opens to see how she speaks to the customers about the goods and learn where the stock is located. 'Most importantly, Maureen,' she says, 'ask if you're not sure. Don't be afraid. It's part of learning and part of bettering yourself.' Her smile says she understands me a little.

I love my new job, and I learn quickly, feeling a little more confident with every passing day. Well-to-do customers come into Oliver's, families or a young child with a mammy or daddy, all well dressed and polite. I observe them, fascinated by how they behave and the love they show each other. However, seeing these happy families often makes me realise how much we were deprived of in the orphanage. It makes me so sad to realise I will never be part of one. When these feelings come, I block them out. I have so much to keep me busy here that it keeps my mind off such thoughts. If I have a spare minute as I tidy up the shelves in the book section, I'll open one of the fairy-tale or fable books. I never tire of them. I love the mystery of these stories and the feeling of letting my imagination run free as I flip through the pages.

Often, a mammy with little children will come into Oliver's to look at the selection of children's books. Today as I'm working, a mother comes in with a little girl no more than five years old. The girl has beautiful pink ribbons in her hair and shiny black patent-leather shoes. They walk straight towards the children's books, the expensive sets and collections. With the little girl smiling up at her, the mother says, 'Would you like the Beatrix Potter set, Angela? The Peter Rabbit one?'

The girl tugs at her mother's dress. 'Does it have the tale of Mrs Tiggy-Winkle, Mummy? What about Pigling Bland and Squirrel Nutkin and the Flopsy Bunnies?'

The mother smiles down patiently, as if playing a little game they're used to. 'Well, aren't you forgetting Mrs Tittlemouse? What about her?'

'Yes, yes, Mrs Tittlemouse, too!' the girl sings up at her mother, throwing her head back with a little stamp of her foot and laughing.

'We'll get the entire set then, shall we? They'll be your bedtime stories.'

When the girl and her mother leave, I swallow the lump in my throat and walk to the Beatrix Potter collection. I gaze at the beautiful drawings on the cover, realising I haven't had a look at these yet. I stand there, reading the incredible stories of little animals that behave like people. All the while, I think of the little girl and her mammy. I see the little girl curled up warm in a lovely cotton nightdress. I see her in her own bed, maybe, her own bedroom, surrounded by clean sheets and stuffed toys, like the Wall children had in Mullingar. The mother will read these stories to her daughter at night, and the child will fall asleep with her head full of the lovely tales and her mother's love. Mrs Oliver's voice calling me ends my daydreaming. I walk away feeling heavy. The girl and her mother are one more reminder of what has been lost to me.

After having worked at my new job for a few weeks, I finally feel more settled in London. My work at Oliver's is everything to me, and my self-confidence is growing, at least a little. Although it hasn't quite worked out the way I'd imagined it with Mrs O'Neill, I feel happy. I thought I might be able to talk about my feelings a little and confide in her, but it hasn't quite happened that way. I still do nothing on my own. I've not met anyone my own age, and I haven't a clue how to change any of this.

Julia seems to be growing up overnight. She plays more and more with her many school friends and has started dressing in the latest fashions. She's beginning to wonder about me: the way I dress so plainly and never buy clothes for myself. It puzzles her that I don't dress up and wear make-up. I'd look nice, she says, wearing high heels or the new fashions. I can only say to her that I don't long for new clothes and things like that right now. She always gives her head a little shake and goes back to reading her book.

I have stood in front of the mirror when I'm alone in the flat, looking at my figure and my face. I've imagined what I'd look like with make-up on. I've looked down at my feet, seeing high heels on them, and tried to picture one of the latest young women's fashions on me. A part of me wants to change and try new things, but the rest of me is so scared and unsure, terrified to try anything new. If I told Julia that I don't know how to buy clothes, she would think me more backward still. How can I tell people about my deep shame when I cannot face it myself — it is too painful.

I see how other girls my age look and behave, how they carry themselves. I see the difference clearly. I see that they are at ease with life, and I wish I could be like them. But survival is still the first thing on my mind. I know now, though, that this world I'm in, the real world, is the place where I must find a way to be me, to be real and perhaps to thrive.

❧ TWENTY-SEVEN ❧

I t is late on Saturday afternoon, and Mrs O'Neill has come into the flat full of energy and looking very happy. I've never seen her like this before. 'Hello, Maureen!' she says, greeting me in the front room. She tosses the brown-paper parcel in her hand onto the settee before lighting a cigarette. 'How are you this afternoon, love? Good?'

While I stand gawking, she paces the floor humming a tune. The next moment, she flies by me into the kitchen still humming away, continuing to talk to me from there. 'Do you know, love, they're building Kilburn back up as if there was never a war at all. Isn't that lovely? Life really does go on, yes it does.' There's a pause and a clattering of mugs as the kettle is boiled before she continues. 'Guess what's opened up on the High Road, love? A new dry cleaners. Look on the settee at the clothes in the brown paper!'

'And, Maureen,' she says, coming back into the front room, 'this new dry cleaners is owned by two single blokes. It's right up on Kilburn High Road. Two brothers from Wales, Alec and Graham Ewans. Single men, love! Not easy to find after the war, single men ain't – good ones, that's to say! Anyway, Alec, the oldest, he fancies me, and I fancy him!'

She sits down for a moment, but then jumps up again, going back into the kitchen and laughing at my amazed look. 'I'll take you and Julia up with me next time. She don't know yet, so let me tell her, right?' And off she goes to make tea, humming away to herself.

Mrs O'Neill rushes about getting ready to take Julia and me up to the dry cleaners. Julia giggles as she teases her mother about wearing more make-up. 'Never mind that, cheeky!' Mrs O'Neill mockingly scolds her. 'You'll know the reason soon enough.' I've noticed this, too: that she is dressing up more and spending more time in front of the mirror.

244

The new shop isn't far at all, just up to Kilburn High Road and a short walk from there. Mrs O'Neill points to a big window with a sign above saying 'Ewans Quality Dry Cleaning'. She checks her reflection quickly in a window before we reach the shop. Julia, seeing this, hurries her mother along impatiently, thinking it all a great adventure, and I'm just as curious. 'You behave yourself, Miss,' Mrs O'Neill whispers as we enter.

A bell on the door jingles as we go in, the noise of the street dying away as it closes again. A tall, heavyset man with dark thinning hair and a moustache stands smiling behind the counter. He's not particularly attractive, and he must be at least ten years older than Mrs O'Neill. 'There she is,' he says, smiling at Mrs O'Neill. This has to be the one named Alec. 'And this must be little Julia,' he goes on, 'who I've heard all sorts of lovely things about.'

I detect the Welsh accent right away, remembering the people round the docks at Holyhead speaking with a sing-song lilt. 'It is indeed, Alec,' Mrs O'Neill answers. 'And this is Maureen, not long over from Ireland and living with us.'

I step forward shyly to shake hands with Alec. Just as I do, a younger man walks out from behind the steamy machinery in the back. He stands just behind Alec and wipes his hands on a towel. 'My brother Graham. Graham, this is Claire's little one, Julia, and, I'm sorry, ah, Maureen, was it?'

'That's right,' Mrs O'Neill answers. 'I wanted to bring the girls up to the shop so you could meet them. We won't keep you long. I know you're very busy.'

Graham greets Julia kindly but ignores me. He turns to return to work in the back, and as he does so his gaze falls on me. He scans me from head to foot. I meet his eyes for just an instant then look down, blushing red and feeling terribly self-conscious. Something about the way he's looking at me isn't right, and I feel it. Finally, he's gone, and I only want to leave this place.

But Alec and Mrs O'Neill just stand gazing at one another. They're lost in their own world, like no one else is here. It's obvious how attracted they are to one another. She's certainly a very good-looking woman, still in her thirties, and this Alec is quite taken with her – that's obvious even to me. He seems very pleasant and friendly, and he certainly made a big fuss of Julia. Before long, we leave the shop, walking on to do a little shopping before going back to the flat.

Alec and Mrs O'Neill have been seeing one another regularly for a while now, and they're obviously quite smitten with one another. After closing the dry cleaners, or when he can leave there alone, Alec walks down to the flat to pick up Mrs O'Neill for a date, and sometimes Julia goes along with them. Until today, I've not been asked to join them on these outings. However, I'm delighted to have been invited along for a picnic at the nearby park.

The four of us take the short bus ride along Kilburn High Road towards the park. It's quite familiar to me now, after many leisurely afternoon outings on a Saturday or after mass on Sundays. On a grassy spot beside one of the ponds, we lay a blanket out. Julia is already off to look in the pond in search of minnows. Left with Alec and Mrs O'Neill, I feel a little uncomfortable. He hasn't said a word since we left the flat, and on the bus he only stared out of the window, ignoring our chatter. Then, as I try to make sense of this, I realise that there's a strain between the couple. With her two legs folded beneath her on the blanket, Mrs O'Neill smokes her cigarette nervously and smiles awkwardly at me while Alec remains silent.

When Julia is anywhere near us, running back and forth with reports about her minnow hunt, Alec is all smiles. He seems to go out of his way to be nice to her. I've seen this at the flat: his showering her with attention and promising little treats. But now, as soon as Julia runs off again, he looks away and goes quiet. 'Maureen works at Oliver's, Alec,' Mrs O'Neill begins, breaking the awkward silence. 'Do you know that shop? It's so interesting. All wooden toys. Handmade, aren't they, love?' Alec nods, grunting something and not turning to look at us.

'They are, Mrs O'Neill, and the books are lovely as well.'

'How are things there for you, Maureen? The Olivers are dears. My goodness, we got lucky getting you a job there, didn't we? A shop girl you wanted to be!' She laughs nervously, glancing at Alec. I can see that Mrs O'Neill is trying to include me in this family outing, but Alec just looks up at the sky and pours out more tea for himself.

I get up, mentioning quietly that I'm going to join Julia at the pond. Once there, I take quick looks over at the two of them while Julia busies herself catching minnows. They appear to be arguing quietly and trying not to show it. Alec keeps shaking his head, and Mrs O'Neill looks as if she's pleading with him. Then, with a sinking feeling inside me, I realise that whatever's the matter it has something to do with me. For a moment, I feel afraid. Maybe it will be better if I don't join them in future; perhaps they'd rather be out with just Julia. But that would mean then that I'm not a part of this family. Is that it? Does Alec just not want me around? Mrs O'Neill made sure that I was included this time, but it's obvious now how he feels about me. It would've been better had I not come at all.

Since the picnic outing, I haven't joined them for any more outings. I stay home alone or with Julia when the two of them go out on their own. But when Alec is at the flat for dinner, and when we're at the table eating, I notice that he never looks at me directly, as though I'm not there. I say very little, but when I do say something he'll look away suddenly like he's annoyed or I've interrupted. Once or twice, he's spoken over me before I've finished what I was saying, raising his voice in a threatening manner. It frightens me when he does this, and I don't dare open my mouth again. I think that's what he wants. To cope with this, I do what I've always done: I shut it all out and worry only about what I'm doing each moment of each day. The best escape for me is my job at the toyshop, as it was even before this awkward situation with Alec began.

This afternoon, the three of us are eating in the kitchen when Mrs O'Neill suddenly sets down her knife and fork. Then, looking seriously at Julia and me, she announces that Alec has asked her to marry him and that she's accepted. It's been two weeks since he proposed, and only a few months since they started seeing one another, but she just made her mind up yesterday. Julia, of course, bubbles over with excitement at her mother's announcement, but this news of marriage shocks me. It seems so sudden. Of course, I don't say anything.

This hasty decision does say one thing for certain: that Mrs O'Neill is feeling the strain of being a widow and trying to make a go of it alone. I'm sure she's thinking of Julia and the long years ahead. It will be so much easier with a husband to share the burden with. But with Alec's attitude towards me getting more obvious each day, I am worried what it will be like with him living with us in the small flat. If he doesn't accept me now, I can only wonder what it will be like when he and Mrs O'Neill are married and this becomes his home.

Alec and Claire O'Neill are married at a small local registrar's office, and Alec has moved into the flat from the place he shared with his brother. Julia seems happy and content, and Alec still gives her a great deal of love and affection. I'm happy for her, of course, but I wish he'd try to accept me, too.

However, as the weeks have gone by, a very different and frightening Alec has gradually begun to emerge. He has started to take over and change everything. His temper is bad and unpredictable, and he seems a bit of a bully. Often, he'll behave in a very domineering way towards Mrs O'Neill and then charm her after he's gone too far. She always forgives him. If Mrs O'Neill disagrees with him on some small matter, he'll say things to her like, 'What do you know, Claire? What do you know about it, eh?' One of his favourites is, 'And what would a woman know about such things?' which he says with a sort of snort. It must surely make her feel foolish. I mostly hear this from the bedroom, where I hide out trying to forget about the real world in my books and fairy tales. I feel as though I'm living in a nightmare, and the tension in the flat is building almost daily. I pray to God for help, for I can do nothing else. I was just beginning to settle in, but it's all changed now. I never expected Mrs O'Neill to marry. It was the last thing I thought would happen.

And there's a noticeable change in Mrs O'Neill. All the happiness and joy she showed just before the wedding is gone. Now she's tense and sad, and there are dark puffy rings of worry under her eyes. Julia has caught on, and, although she doesn't show it, she's upset and quite worried about her mother. Terrified of Alec and his violent temper, I've begun to stay away, not wanting to go home. I walk just to get away from it, often ending up by the bombed-out houses to pass the time away. I feel trapped and suffocated and more alone than I ever have before. I want to run away somewhere, anywhere, but where can I go? I have no friends other than Julia and her mother.

After coming in from Sunday mass this morning, I make my way up the stairs to the flat and hear them arguing again. Once inside, I stand still, as I've done so often, waiting to see if it's clear to hurry into the safety of the bedroom. Suddenly, Alec's voice gets louder, and I hear him say, 'Why, Claire? Why do you feel responsible for her?'

'You don't understand, Alec!' Mrs O'Neill shrieks back, her voice high and shrill. 'What you don't understand is . . .'

'I bloody well don't care! This is my home, too, or don't you care about that, eh? Doesn't that matter to you, Claire? Just tell me why! Why can't you just get rid of that bastard out there? Why do you have to keep her? Why do I have to keep her? Tell me!'

I'm suddenly terrified. He's heard me come in. My legs feel weak and an awful feeling fills me. I turn round and slip quietly out the door, down the stairs and out into the street. I've no idea what 'bastard' means, but I feel ashamed just because of the way he spat it out. I know I'm being called something very bad.

I shake with fear as I hurry along toward the library. Mrs O'Neill is fighting for me, standing up for me as best she can, but she'll not win. I'll have to leave.

As I walk, the fear lessens, and I begin to feel a strange empty feeling, as if the ground has suddenly fallen away. What am I going to do now? I feel alone in the world again, the way I did when Mrs Hughes told me she wasn't my real mammy. I feel like I am no one again.

The next day, I slip like a shadow from my bedroom into the front room to sneak a look at Mrs O'Neill's tattered old Oxford School

Dictionary. I have to know what the word bastard means and why he called me that. It must be very bad. My heart flutters as my finger moves down the page: bass, basset, bassoon. There it is: bastard. I read the definitions: '1. a person born of unmarried parents. 2. informal an unpleasant person'. Suddenly, I understand more than I want to. Mrs Hughes' words come back to me: 'It means your mammy wasn't married to your father.'

I decide to look up the word wedlock while I've got the dictionary open, although I know what it means. My hands shake with emotion as I turn to the back pages. I find 'the state of being married' and then below that 'PHRASES: born in (or out of) wedlock – born of married (or unmarried) parents'.

I let the book slip from my hand. Everything is clear to me now. I understand how Alec feels – I'm inferior. I'm a bastard, a girl born out of wedlock. I remember the postulants took vows to become nuns. A vow is something very serious and sacred. My real mammy, Annie Harte, she'd none of these things: no husband, no marriage vow, just me born out of wedlock, an orphan. So, it's everywhere, then, how people feel about children born wrong like this . . . like me. This is why I was put in the orphanage, and maybe that's the reason my mammy didn't keep me and why she doesn't want me now: because of the shame of it. I could be called this by anyone. I have no choices left. I'll have to leave here – but to where? I fall with my face in my hands and sob, sweeping the dictionary onto the floor.

❈ TWENTY-EIGHT ❈

On yet another late summer evening, I walk slowly towards the bombed-out section of Kilburn, feeling strangely drawn there once again. I feel numb and empty inside, and I don't pray any more, or at least it doesn't feel like God is listening when I do. I feel no connection to my prayers, and that's never happened before this terrible mess. Never in my life have I felt so trapped. It feels as if everything good in my life has vanished and that the world is closing in on me.

I cross an empty street, turn a final time and stop. The heavy summer rain drizzles slowly above me as I stare once again down the same bombed-out street. Above the shattered buildings and broken walls, the sky is cold grey in the twilight. People must've died here during the bombings, when the war was on.

My eyes fill with tears, and an awful emptiness wells up in me again. God is far away, and he doesn't care. I don't want to live any more. I'll not get out of this awful situation. How can I? Even if I wrote to Mrs Hughes, what could she do? She'd only get Mrs Burke to read the letter, and that'll make a worse mess of it. Wanting to take your own life is called suicide, I know, but surely it must be a sin, and I've no idea how I might follow through on it. Why won't you help me, God? Why have you left me here like this, gone away when I need you most?

I turn and walk away down another street, not thinking where I'm going. What will I do now? Where will I go? What will happen to me? This is all that goes through my head. At a corner, I look up at one of the street signs on the side of a building. Dimly visible in the fading light, rain slants across the words 'Quex Road'. I'm somewhere near Sacred Heart Church, where we attend mass on Sundays. Perhaps if I seek counsel, they'll give me advice. With a tiny bit of hope in my heart, I decide to try. I get my bearings and walk with a quicker step toward the lovely old church.

At the vestibule entrance, I brush the rain from my coat before stepping inside to where it's dry. I walk silently down a quiet carpeted hallway toward a sign above a door that reads 'secretary', relieved to see light streaming through from the cubicle's half-opened window. I stand there until the secretary notices me. 'Yes, dear, may I help you?' she asks, looking up from her desk.

'Yes, I've a problem . . .' My words falter as a flood of sudden emotion rushes up in me like a dam bursting, and I break down in tears. 'I just want to kill myself. I've no one to turn to, no one to go to . . .'

She stands and rushes over to open her door. 'What on earth! Come in here, dear. Come on in here, and we can talk about this. Now then, dear, sit down and tell me what your name is.'

'Maureen Harte,' I answer, sobbing and looking at the floor.

'Now, dear,' she says, 'tell me what's wrong. Do you have parents, dear? Where are they?'

'No, no, I'm an orphan. I want to see a priest!'

'Don't even think about killing yourself, Maureen,' she says. 'I'm sure we can get help for you here, but tell me why you want to do such a thing to yourself. What has caused all this?'

'I live in this home, and I'm not wanted there. I can hear them fighting about me . . .'

'Who?' the secretary asks me. 'Who is fighting?'

'It's Alec! He married Mrs O'Neill and doesn't want me there any more . . . he calls me a bastard . . .'

'Maureen,' the secretary says to me, putting her hands on my shoulders. 'Look at me, Maureen. Look at me, dear. If we're to help you at all, you must calm yourself a little and explain slowly what has happened. I'm sure we can do something for you, all right?'

She hands me some tissues from a box, and I wipe my nose and face. I calm down enough to tell her all the things that brought me to the church for help. She seems kind, and she listens closely to what I say. 'Well, I'll tell you what, Maureen. I can get you in to see Father Browne tomorrow, at half-six, due to the urgency of your situation. But only on the condition you promise not to do anything in the meantime. I am sure there are many reasons for you to have hope. Do you think that's what God would want for a young girl like you? Now, you must look at me and tell me that.'

'I promise.'

'Right, dear. We'll see you tomorrow at half-six. You'll be here?'

'I will, I promise.'

I leave the church feeling such relief. The secretary was so kind and thoughtful. She'll get me the right help, I know she will. I must have hope.

I sit waiting quietly for my appointment with the priest, praying hard. After ten minutes, I'm shown into a small office with a couple of chairs and a small desk. The priest is a heavyset man in his mid-forties with a stern look and a fair complexion. He sits on the desk directly in front of me, where I sit facing him. 'Maureen,' he says, looking for a moment at a sheet of paper on the desk. 'Maureen Harte. You would like to talk to me about a problem you're going through? Tell me about it.'

'Yes, Father. I was raised in Ireland in an orphanage, and I was brought over to England with Mrs O'Neill to live with her and her daughter. But now she's married a man who wants me out of the house, and he calls me a bastard and shouts at Mrs O'Neill all the time, but it's about me he shouts . . .'

'Maureen,' the priest interrupts me, tapping two fingers on the desk. 'Tell me, slowly, please, and from the beginning, what this difficulty's about. You're Irish, you say, and raised in an orphanage? Tell me about that, Maureen, and how you came to be living here in London. Go on.'

I tell him about everything as clearly as I'm able. But when I get to the part about Alec, I begin to cry, all the fear and worry of the past weeks stirring inside me again. 'I've no one to turn to, Father, absolutely no one. I've not been round many men, and I'm afraid of Alec. His temper frightens me.'

His eyes open wide at this, pushing his heavy red brows up for a moment. He begins to shift restlessly and rolls his fingers silently on the desk, moving even closer so that he is almost directly in front of me, only a foot away. 'Yes, I see, you are quite young . . . umm . . . I see . . . So you really know nothing about men, then, do you?'

'No, Father,' I reply respectfully, beginning to feel uncomfortable. I have an awful fluttering in my stomach, and my heart begins to pound for no reason. What is happening to me?

'Umm . . . I see . . . so you've never seen what a man looks like, then?'

Again, the heavy eyebrows rise and fall with the question as he gazes down at me. There are more shifting movements. Oh my God, what does he want with me? It seems he's after something, but he's a priest. No, it couldn't be. His eyes are piercing and predatory. I start to tremble, feeling the room closing in on me. Now his hand is running up and down the inside of his trousers, up high along his inner thigh, near his privates. Oh my God, please help me! He just squeezed himself . . . there! My eyes fly to the floor, where they remain riveted. Each second feels like an hour, bringing me closer to some awful danger with this man, I know it. My God, this is a nightmare. Is he going to try to take advantage of me somehow? What will I do?

As I'm about to answer his last question, a loud knock sounds on the door, making me jump inside. 'Your next appointment, Father. You've gone well over,' the secretary says, sticking her head into the room for a moment. She leaves the door open for the priest's next appointment. I don't miss my chance. 'Thank you, Father,' I say without meeting his eyes and walk out.

'Will you be coming back, Maureen?' the secretary asks as I walk by her booth.

'Oh, I don't know. I don't think so. I'll be fine now.'

'Well, I hope it has worked out for you, dear. Please take good care of yourself.'

'Thank you. Thank you very much.'

My legs feel weak as I leave the church, stepping out into the drizzle. What has just happened? How lucky for me the secretary knocked when she did. Why has the priest confused me this way? What terrifies me most is that had he tried to take advantage of me, I'm not sure if I would've been able to protect myself. I know nothing of such things or the evil ways in which some people can behave. I won't go back to the church again for help, that's for sure.

I walk slowly back towards the flat, knowing now that I must do something on my own. No one else is going to get me out of this. I must find a way on my own. I go back past the sullen ruins in the failing light, my mind working feverishly, trying to sort through the possibilities. I must confront the problem head on and control my fears. An idea strikes me: the only thing we believed and were told we were good for, and now it just might be the answer. But how will I find the courage to approach Mrs O'Neill? Taking my time, and going up one familiar street and down another, I use all my wits to try and put the pieces together. Tonight is one of Alec's late nights at the cleaners, so if I hurry home, I might catch Mrs O'Neill alone. I quicken my pace, not wanting to be out in the streets after dark and desperately working up my courage as I go.

I find Mrs O'Neill in an all too familiar place these days: sitting alone on the settee in the front room and gazing forlornly through the window at nothing. I get right to the point for fear of losing my nerve. 'Mrs O'Neill, I have to talk to you.'

'Yes, Maureen, what is it?'

I look at the floor, trying to find the right words and holding my feelings in check. 'Well, it's this situation with Alec. I know he doesn't like me. I've not said anything, but I know there have been arguments between you about me . . . and . . . I heard him shouting at you one morning about me . . .' I begin to cry as I blurt out my feelings. 'I just can't stay here any longer, Mrs O'Neill. I can't. I don't know what to do!'

She says nothing, turning toward the window for a moment. Then she bursts into tears, putting her head in her hands. 'Oh, Maureen, this is so god-awful. It's all my fault. I know you're very unhappy. Of course I know. I feel helpless. I didn't think . . . I don't know what to do about it. Honestly, it's just awful.'

'But I have an idea,' I say. 'Do you remember the last time you were in Mullingar, when you asked me to come to London to live with you?'

'Yes, I remember.'

'Do you remember how I told you I was working for the Wall family as a maid? Well, I can do that again. I know I can! I wasn't really in service with the Walls. I didn't live with them, but they liked me, and I did a good job there. I can go into service, Mrs O'Neill, here in London!'

Still crying, she reaches out and takes my hand in hers. 'Oh, Maureen,' she says, 'I feel this is all my fault. I should have . . .'

I don't want her to feel like this. 'No, it isn't,' I say. 'It isn't your fault.'

'Oh, it is, it is,' she sobs, crying harder.

Both of us cry as I pour my heart out, all the feelings and emotions of the past weeks flowing out of me like a river. I explain, as best as I'm able, how much I love being with her and Julia but that I can stay no longer. Through her sobbing and tears, Mrs O'Neill can only nod her head as she presses a sopping handkerchief to her face. She keeps saying how terribly bad and guilty she feels, explaining how she brought me here to begin a new life and as my guardian is responsible for me, and now all of this is happening. Julia, she tells me, though I of course know, has been very troubled by the quarrels and shouting, and for the first time since I've known her Mrs O'Neill mentions her late husband and how Julia changed after his death, worrying about everything since then. I suddenly feel a deep sense of pity for them both, but it will only be worse for all of us if I stay – we both know that. How sad she looks now, and how changed she is. I think she might've been better off as she was.

I gave notice to the Olivers, telling them only that Mrs O'Neill is remarried, that the flat is crowded and that I'll be better off in service. They don't ask any questions, agreeing that I'm doing the right thing and wishing me the best. They tell me how good a worker I've been and that they promise to give me an excellent reference.

There are plenty of jobs for servants in London, but Mrs O'Neill wanted to make sure to find me the right place. We looked through the papers every day, sometimes leaving the flat for tea if Alec was home, and then, about a week after starting to look, Mrs O'Neill found an advert she really liked. She's already spoken to the woman. Mrs Davies is her name, and the family live in an area called Willesden.

I travel with Mrs O'Neill and Julia to Willesden, where we step off the bus onto a main street full of shops and people walking about. Following the directions, we walk along a street of lovely two-storey houses with beautifully kept gardens. 'Number one hundred and ten Stanley Gardens,' Mrs O'Neill says, stopping to look round at the numbers. 'There it is. That one across there.'

A tall, thin smart-looking lady with light-brown, slightly greying hair and a sharp nose opens the door. 'Hello,' she says with a nice smile, looking at each of us. 'You must be Mrs O'Neill.'

'Yes, I am.'

'I'm Mrs Davies, Elizabeth Davies. Did you have any trouble finding us?'

'None at all, Mrs Davies. This is Maureen Harte. I've spoken to you about her.'

'Hello, Maureen, do come in.'

'We'll leave Maureen with you,' Mrs O'Neill says. 'My daughter and I can walk about for a while until you've finished.'

'Very well. Come on in, Maureen. We can sit in the drawing room and have a talk.'

I step inside and am reminded right away of Professor Wall's house in Mullingar, but this is even larger.

'Well, Maureen,' Mrs Davies begins when we're sitting, 'Mrs O'Neill has told me a little about you when she rang about the position. You've worked as a maid for a professor in Ireland?'

'Yes, Mrs Davies,' I reply with my eyes down. 'It was in Mullingar.'

'I see,' she replies. 'Can you provide me with an address? I'll have to write them down for a reference.'

'Oh yes, I know the address,' I reply, reciting it from memory.

'So, more recently, then, here in England,' she continues, 'you've been working in a toyshop. Is that correct? I will need that address as well if you can.'

I give her the information. 'You have a good memory,' she says, smiling as she writes. 'My situation, Maureen, is that until recently I've had a Welsh girl here. Three years she was with us, and she was very happy here. She would not have left but for family reasons.'

Mrs Davies talks some more about my references, before suddenly sitting back and telling me that she'd like to hire me. This really surprises me. I'd expected a long and involved interview, but maybe she sees something in me that she likes or perhaps she just wants to give me a chance. Before I can react, she goes on to say, 'So you were raised with the nuns in an orphanage? I was told that by Mrs O'Neill, of course. I like to know a little about the history of someone I might have working for me.'

'Yes, Mrs Davies. I was there for thirteen years.'

'I see,' she replies. 'So you have no one here in England?'

'No.'

She stands up. 'I will take care of securing these references, and assuming all goes well I see little reason why you can't begin with us in a couple of weeks.'

'Thank you so very much, Mrs Davies.'

She walks me to the door, and I hurry off to share the good news with Mrs O'Neill and Julia, finding them waiting near the bus stop. 'I think I've got the position! Mrs Davies has to contact my references, but I think I've got it!'

'That's wonderful, Maureen,' Mrs O'Neill says smiling. 'I get the impression she's a decent person and a real lady as well. She'll be good to work for – fair, I'd say. I feel so much better.'

We jump onto the next double-decker heading back to Kilburn, something I do almost as well as the Londoners now. I try not to show how excited I feel inside, seeing how quiet Julia and her mammy are. I look over at them for a moment, at their expressions and the tired lost look they both have. I will miss them, it's true, and I hope Alec will be different now that I'm leaving. But something in me doubts it very much.

✳ ✳ ✳

It is two weeks since my interview. I close my little brown suitcase, my mind far away with worry about what lies ahead. The familiar sounds of Julia's running steps along the hall bring me out of my thoughts. 'Mummy wants to know if you're ready, Maureen.'

'I am, Julia.'

She turns to leave but then stops herself, staring silently at the floor and unable to look at me. 'Oh, Maureen,' she says finally, turning to me as she breaks into tears. 'I'll miss you.' Julia cries now without any attempt to hide it. She rushes up to me and gives me a big hug just as she's done so many times since I've known her. My own tears fall freely then, but like so many other times I can find no words to go with my feelings. I always feel so crippled when this happens, and just once, now when it is needed most, I wish I had something to say to her, but it's hopeless. As usual, I find no words and say nothing. I will pray hard for them.

The three of us leave the flat for the bus to Willesden. I have only my suitcase packed with my leaving outfit and some new clothes I got in Mullingar after my leaving day. The ride over to the Davies' in Willesden is quiet and awkward, and I pass the time thinking about all that has happened lately and what my life will be like in service. I feel a sense of relief that I've at least solved the problem of Alec by moving out of the flat. Yet I feel as though it's a terrible setback for me at the same time. Going into service was not what I expected out of my move to England.

The experience with Alec has hurt me deeply. All my life I've been made to feel different, less than others, unwanted and illegitimate. But no single beating or abusive word ever made me feel the way Alec Ewans did. 'Why can't you just get rid of that bastard out there?' I fear now that when others find out that I'm illegitimate, they will treat me the same as Alec did. I honestly think that as soon as the priest learned of my background, he too felt the same as Alec – that I was nobody, something to be used then disposed of. Now I'm facing new people again and feeling so insecure about my background. What will this family think of me? Will it always be like this?

All these wearisome things drift through my mind as the bus moves toward Willesden. I have to survive now, just as I always have. Survival comes first. Without survival, there is nothing else.

❖ TWENTY-NINE ❖

I report to the Davies' wearing the coat that I made with Sister Elisabeth in the orphanage. On this beautiful street, so different from the terraced houses and flats of Kilburn, I say goodbye to Julia and Mrs O'Neill. With a last hug for Julia, I pick up my suitcase and walk to the door of the Davies' house to press the doorbell. Julia and her mammy are already walking away as I turn to look – another sad parting. I wonder if I will ever see them again.

The door opens, and Mrs Davies greets me. 'Hello, Maureen, do come in. Just leave your suitcase at the foot of the stairs. We'll get you settled shortly. But first I'll introduce you to the rest of the family, just to let them know you've arrived.'

I recognise the room where I was interviewed as Mrs Davies opens the door. 'This is Maureen Harte,' she announces to the family. 'She'll be starting with us as of today. Maureen, this is my husband, Andrew Davies, my sister, Beatrice, and my father, Harry.'

'Nice to have you here, Maureen,' Mr Davies says, looking up from a newspaper amidst nods and hellos from the sister and father. 'I hope you'll be comfortable with us.'

Mrs Davies closes the door of the drawing room. 'I'll show you around the house now, Maureen, but I won't spend too much time today with all the little details. You'll soon know our home quite well, I suspect. I'll go over your specific duties a little later. Let's start at the front here, shall we, in the hall.'

The four-bedroom house isn't a mansion, but it's very nice indeed, with a lot of polished-wood mouldings and banisters and beautiful lamps. Inside the front door is a lovely foyer, and to the right of that, across from the drawing room where I met the family, is a formal dining room. Again, I'm struck by the way Mrs Davies speaks with such ease and confidence, and how she dresses and walks with such

261

grace. She seems a real lady. Towards the back of the ground floor are a smaller dining area and the kitchen, with all the latest equipment: a big mixer, an electric kettle and a toaster. Two big doors – French doors, Mrs Davies tells me – lead out to a garden, but she doesn't open them.

Upstairs, there are four bedrooms, a lavatory and some big closets off the hall. 'This is your room, Maureen,' Mrs Davies says, stopping in front of one of the closed doors. 'I think you will find it comfortable. I'll give you time to unpack. Come down to the drawing room in an hour. We'll go over your daily duties and schedules then. I'll see you downstairs.'

'Thank you, Mrs Davies. I'll be down in an hour.'

She closes the door softly behind her. I stand in the middle of a tidy, colourful room, the worn suitcase looking out of place sitting on the bright bedclothes. The room has a single bed, a dresser, a mirror, a small wardrobe and a bright-coloured carpet on the floor. I walk over to a big window and pull the drawn curtains across. There below me, in the late evening light, is a beautiful garden full of pretty flowers and shrubs. And what's that? Yes, a sundial, right in the middle. Oh, how special! My own room, my own privacy. I've never known such a thing. If Maggie and Lucy could see this.

There's something different about this room, though. What is it? Of course, it's the colours. They all match one another, and the bedding, too. This room is a girl's room, made up specially and so pretty-looking.

I start putting my things away, feeling very nervous about doing my job well – everything depends on it. As Mrs Davies was showing me round the house, I put on a brave face, but I'm afraid and alone.

Exactly an hour later, I arrive downstairs and knock lightly on the closed drawing-room door. 'Come in!' I hear Mrs Davies answer. I step into the drawing room to find Mr Davies and Beatrice sitting with Mrs Davies, but it seems the old man has gone off to bed. 'Sit down, please, Maureen,' Mrs Davies says, and I take the chair across from her. 'I'll take you through your duties as they are to be done. I find that the most sensible.'

I am to begin at seven o'clock in the morning, and Mrs Davies will give me a small alarm to set. Most days I'll start by helping to prepare breakfast and setting the table in the small dining room off the kitchen. After breakfast, there is a regular cleaning routine, starting with the front door, outside and in, including all the brass parts, then on to the big front hall and the other rooms. She promises to take me through the routine herself. 'Do you understand everything I'm telling you so far, Maureen?'

'Yes, Mrs Davies, but I might have to ask you again. Only if I forget something. If I don't understand.'

'That's perfectly fine. We'll get along much better and understand one another if you do. It will take some time to get into the routine. It's only that, a daily routine, so don't worry about it.'

Mr Davies has said nothing. He only looked up from his newspaper when I came in, with a smile and a nod of his head. He seems kind enough, and I don't think he'll be mean to me. The sister seems more serious: she's only looked up once or twice from her sewing in another corner of the room. I guess it's Mrs Davies who runs this house and gives the orders.

When she finishes going over my duties, Mrs Davies surprises me by mentioning the orphanage again. 'So, you were raised in an orphanage. How long did you spend there? Thirteen years?'

'Yes, thirteen years.' I feel terribly unprepared for this.

'That's a long time, Maureen. Do you stay in touch with the nuns?'

'No. I've not had the time to think much about it so far.' I hadn't expected such questions, and suddenly I'm barely able to hold back the tears that rush up. At times like this I can only curse the place that made me like I am. With my head down, I wait for her to speak. Surely she's noticed my reaction. I can't begin crying right now. The tears will be so embarrassing and so hard to stop. I'll not talk of the orphanage in front of these people.

'Have you considered writing to them, Maureen?' she goes on.

'No, I haven't written yet, but maybe I will one day.' I hear in my own voice a tone that says 'I won't speak of this'. What an awkward moment. My throat feels as though it's being squeezed by a metal band. I can see Beatrice's eyes flicking up occasionally as she takes this all in.

'I see. All right.'

Is Mrs Davies interested in my life or is she worried that my past will affect my duties here? I'm not sure, but I'll not talk about my life with these strangers. She stands up. 'Well, Maureen, you must be exhausted after all this. Why don't you get yourself a good night's rest? And not to worry. Things will be fine once you've settled into your routine.'

Finally alone in my colourful room, so quiet and private, I sit on the bed, which is so comfortable. There is a big puffy comforter covered in pink satin and a puffy pillow in a pink satin case as well. I hold the soft pillow to my cheek, realising it's filled with feathers.

As I undress, my whole body sags, and I can barely get into bed, so drained am I from all the weeks of worry and the desperate lonely walks among the ruins of Kilburn. Now suddenly I'm here, in this beautiful home, in service. How strange to have this little room all to myself, with its bright girlish colours. With the soft satin on my cheek and the feather pillow under my head, I fall into a deep sleep, feeling as though I will like it here in service with this family.

In my plain grey maid's outfit, I steadily settle into my duties. Though Mrs Davies teaches me my routine and I catch on quickly, I worry constantly. If I don't succeed here with this family, maybe they'll send me off to a home not as nice. I might wind up going from place to place to survive.

Only when the first month passes do I dare believe I might be good enough to be kept on. This makes me do even better and try harder. I'm fortunate, I realise, to be in service with Mrs Davies and her family. They don't make me feel judged or looked down upon. Surely this must mean I'm not as different as I thought and a much better person than I believe myself to be?

In the mornings, I help with the breakfast preparations, though I don't cook myself. Mrs Davies is an excellent cook and loves to prepare all her own meals. Beatrice, who is older than Mrs Davies and unmarried, often helps prepare the meals while I lay the table in the breakfast room, the small dining area off the kitchen. There's a sideboard, a china cabinet with glass doors and the French doors opening out to the back garden. All the family's meals are taken in the breakfast room, except for the formal dinner parties in the main dining room. I eat the same food as the family but alone in the kitchen, and I've never seen or tasted such fancy dishes.

Beatrice, or Bee as the family knows her, is short, stooped and wizened, her dark-brown hair lashed with streaks of iron grey. She doesn't have much of a sense of humour, and she's the most formal with me. I have to know my place with her. She doesn't miss a thing through her wire-rimmed glasses perched on her small bird-like face. Always dressed in skirts with blouses and cardigans, she does a lot of knitting and crochet. Her work is everywhere in the house, the embroidered lace doilies covering the chair backs in each room.

The family spend a lot of their time in the drawing room, where a big bay window faces the front of the house and the street. There are four high-backed chairs spread out around a very comfortable and expensive-looking settee, and a carpet with a floral design covers the middle of the polished wooden floor. They also have a beautiful phonograph and radio, a console model – it is an actual piece of furniture. Mrs Davies had to show me how to clean it properly.

The Davies have their regular routines: listening to the BBC news in the mornings or sitting round together for the radio plays on *Saturday Night Theatre*. I can hear the radio through the closed door and smell burning wood from the fireplace in the drawing room now that the days are getting colder. The Davies are of the Anglican faith, and they usually make it to Sunday evening service. They're good about giving me time to attend mass on Sunday mornings, though I've not returned to the lovely old Sacred Heart Church on Quex Road.

Mrs Davies' father is such a sweet, friendly man. With a full head of the whitest hair and a sharp mind and wit for his age, I'm sure he must've been very handsome when he was younger. Each morning before breakfast, he takes his time getting dressed in a suit. His clothes are always perfect, his shirts clean and pressed. Down the stairs he comes, his walking stick with the ornamental top flicking out before him with each step. The first few mornings here, I thought he was off to some special occasion and kept waiting for him to leave. But this is just his daily routine. After breakfast, he goes back up to his room, where he'll sit and read. Always the perfect gentleman, he doesn't say much, but he always gives me a big smile, and I think he likes me.

Mr Davies himself is a tall, very good-looking man with a square pleasant face, his hair thin and greying. He loves to read his newspaper, hidden behind the open pages in his own world, sitting in one of the tall high-backed chairs in the drawing room. I hear the regular flick of the pages as I go about my duties.

As soon as I began in service, Mrs Davies started training me for the formal dinner parties they often have in the main dining room. I was fitted right away for a black formal maid's dress and cap. She taught me, when we'd a few spare minutes during the daytime, what she called etiquette. This is the exact and proper way for a maid to behave at a formal dinner party: how to set the table, where and how to stand, and how to serve the different courses during the meal. I was told that I did quite well on my first dinner party. I made no mistakes and everything went well for me. In fact, I really enjoyed it. It was very exciting, the guests treated me well and Mr Davies was so funny and generous.

Today, I've been rushing around preparing ahead of their return from the races at Epsom. I hear them coming in, with Mr Davies leading the way. 'Hello, kid. Holdin' down the fort!' he says to me, a wide grin on his red-flushed face. 'How are ya? Good, what?'

I smile back at him then hurry off into the kitchen, not missing the frown on Beatrice's face. Once in the house and settled, the family head into the drawing room, but Mrs Davies pops out now and then to see how everything's going for the dinner party, which will be attended by just the family tonight. 'Nothing like a good wager on the ponies, what!' says Mr Davies, chortling as he goes into the drawing room. 'A good wager! A good pony! A jolly good day at the races!'

Through the closed door, I hear bits and pieces of lively conversation between Mr Davies and Beatrice. Normally, Mr Davies is a perfect gentleman, sitting in the drawing room with the others and flicking through the wide pages of his newspaper. But a profitable day at Epsom, and the few drinks that go with it, make him fun-loving and talkative, as if the whole world had a good day at the races. I'm sure he must be having a couple more drinks in there, because the lively chatter through the closed doors of the drawing room is getting louder and louder, only falling again when Beatrice responds to Mr Davies' teasing banter.

The family seat themselves for the first course, and I bring in a big bowl to set on the side table. While they're having soup, I get the main course ready. Everything has to be just so. I must remember my etiquette. After dessert, Mr Davies sits back with his hands on his vest looking very contented. Then, spying me at the sideboard, he reaches into his vest pocket and pulls out a five-pound note.

'Here, kid!' he announces. 'Buy yourself something nice!'

'Oh no, Mr Davies,' I say, looking awkwardly at Mrs Davies for rescue. 'I can't take it, I . . .'

'Take it, Maureen,' she says, waving her hand casually. 'Take it while he's being generous. Go ahead and take it.'

I take the bill and quickly find a reason to leave the dining room. As I hurry off with some dessert dishes, I hear Beatrice say to Mr Davies, 'You're quite giving today, Andy Davies, aren't you? Quite generous when you've had a few.'

I walk back in for more dishes to find Mr Davies looking straight up into the air and smiling at the ceiling. His face is flushed and very red. 'Hush, hush, now, Bee! I simply know how to have a good time. Relax, let go and all that, unlike some I know . . .'

'Oh, please,' responds Beatrice. 'It's frightfully obvious, Andy, that when you indulge in alcohol you're suddenly a philanthropist, so generous and . . .'

'Hush, Bee, hush!' He continues to smile and stare at the ceiling.

'Oh, it's true, Andy Davies, and you very well know it. Don't argue with me, for God's sake!'

'Now, Bee, leave the man alone,' Mrs Davies' father interjects, his old voice thin and dry. 'He's quite under the influence!' The old man's fond of this, looking back and forth, closely following their conversation and smiling away as if he's watching a game of tennis.

Suddenly, Mr Davies pushes his chair back and stands up. Oh no, is there going to be an argument? How terrible if I'm to be the cause of it. I stack the plates slowly, one at a time. Mr Davies holds his long arms out and stares up as if about to make a blessing. 'I have a proclamation, something to assert,' he begins in a deep loud voice, smiling at the old man. 'I shall stand here Promethean, Promethean I say, and assert, dear Bee, that you are far too prudish, too goody goody, stick in the mud, wet blanket, et cetera, et cetera.'

Mr Davies sits back down, still talking away. 'Now I'll sit Promethean, content as a king after a regal meal, to proclaim further sound advice to Bee, my dear sister-in-law. You too should have a few drinks from time to time, some of the sauce you so disdain. 'Tis the nectar of the gods, a bacchanalian rite. You'd be transformed, and I'd pay a few quid to see it, by jove!'

'Really, that's too much,' Beatrice says as she tosses her handkerchief on her plate, only mildly annoyed by Mr Davies' teasing. It seems she has seen it many times before and is playing her part. 'Ridiculous. You'll be as quiet as a church mouse tomorrow, Andrew Davies, that's for certain.'

Mr Davies sighs as he leans back. 'Occasionally a few drinks, Bee, occasionally.'

Mrs Davies watches all this with a small grin on her face, and it all happens when I am right here in the room, as if I am invisible. I puzzle over this, but I already know how different the English are from the Irish. They always go on like this in front of me or when I can hear. They're just themselves. But I know my place here. I just take it all in, watching and learning.

❈ THIRTY ❈

As I finish my early chores, Mrs Davies comes into the kitchen. 'Everything all right?' she asks easily.

'Fine, Mrs Davies.'

'I think, Maureen, it's time that you bought some new clothes.'

'Oh yes,' I reply, looking up for a moment. 'I should do that soon, I suppose.'

'Well, I think we should do it today. We can go to Bourne & Hollingsworth on Oxford Street, a lovely big store with all kinds of clothing and much to choose from.'

I stop what I'm doing without looking up, not certain what to say to this. Is she really going to take me shopping? Why would she want to do such a thing for me?

'I would like to see you in some new clothes, Maureen,' she continues. 'Those clothes you're wearing are far too old-fashioned for someone your age. You're young, and you should dress more stylishly. You must've saved some money by now. Perhaps I might help you choose the right kind of outfits, and, really, that coat you constantly wear must go!'

I'm certain Mrs Davies knows I haven't a clue about fashion or styles in clothing. I've bought next to nothing since I've been here. But that coat is the one I made for my leaving day. Since starting in service, I've saved most of my two pounds weekly earnings. I never go anywhere to spend money and have no friends or social life yet.

'Come on then, Maureen,' she says, already leaving the kitchen to get ready. 'Finish up and we'll take the bus.'

As we walk through the entrance of Bourne & Hollingsworth, a place I've never set foot in before, I'm stunned by the colour and glamour of it all. I follow Mrs Davies through the different areas and displays, staring round at the latest fashions with wide eyes. 'We'll go straight to ladies fashions, Maureen,' she says. 'I'd like to see you in a sweater set. There are nice ones over here for younger people.' In one of the many areas of ladies fashions, she removes a lovely beige cardigan and sweater set from one of the racks for me to try on, holding it up for me. 'What about this one, Maureen?'

'It's beautiful, Mrs Davies.' As I put on the sweater and then the cardigan, I begin to feel different. The smell of the clean new fabric reaches me as I turn to look into a mirror. 'What's it look like on me?' I ask, turning to Mrs Davies.

She stands looking at me intently, one arm across her chest and her chin resting in the other hand. 'Turn, Maureen, let me see. Do you know what? It's perfect. That's the one. Take it. Now we'll go over to the skirt section.'

We walk on to another section and straight over to one of the racks of skirts. She seems to know exactly what would look good on me, picking out a lovely plaid skirt and holding it out for me. 'These skirts are midi length,' Mrs Davies explains, 'worn to the mid-calf. All the young girls wear them since the war. They are the very latest in London fashion, and these colours will look good on you with your dark hair.'

I'm barely able to believe all this. Not two hours ago I was standing doing my work in the kitchen and now I'm in this beautiful store with Mrs Davies. I put both the skirt and sweater on then turn to one of the full-length mirrors. My goodness, what a difference! I catch Mrs Davies' smile in the mirror as she looks at me. 'You look wonderful. Turn round. Very nice, very nice indeed. You wear it well, Maureen. What do you think?'

'I love it, Mrs Davies. I do. It's so beautiful!'

I buy the outfit immediately, thinking how different and grown up Mrs Hughes would think me if she could see me in it. As I follow Mrs Davies through the store, I watch the young women working as clerks in their fine outfits. This is very different from Oliver's toyshop. It's huge and sprawling, and everywhere I turn there is a different display or department.

After purchasing a brown fitted coat of the same midi length to go with the skirt and sweater set, I expect we'll start home, all my new possessions secure in the lovely bags. But Mrs Davies says something about getting me some 'pumps' to go with my purchases. What are pumps? Not clothing surely? My curiosity wins out, and I ask Mrs Davies what they are.

'A pump, Maureen,' she says, chuckling, 'is a high-heeled shoe without a strap.'

'Oh,' is all I can think to say as I follow her into a large shoe department. She chooses a pair of pumps in a lovely tan shade and suggests I try them on. Sure, how can I stand in those, let alone take a step? Seeing that I can make neither head nor tail of them, Mrs Davies chuckles again in her warm way. 'Don't worry, Maureen, you'll get used to walking in them, and when you do you'll love them.'

'All right,' I say. I sit down and squeeze them on. I then put out my hand to Mrs Davies as I stand up slowly. Straight away, I go over on my ankles, feeling like a tree about to fall and looking at her for help.

'Take a step or two, Maureen,' she encourages. 'You'll be surprised how quickly you'll learn to walk in them.'

I actually do take a few steps across the carpet on my own, thinking it a great accomplishment, but not before throwing out an arm once or twice to Mrs Davies for balance and rescue. Without hesitating, I buy the pumps, adding to my new clothes.

As we walk from the store, I search for a way to tell Mrs Davies how much this means to me, but it isn't easy. I'm just a maid, and it's understood that I can't be too familiar with the Davies. But this incredibly thoughtful gesture on her part is such a special thing to do for me. Who else could have helped me like this? I was never taught to think about clothes, though I can see now how they can make a person feel confident and good about themselves. I wouldn't have done this on my own; I'd have gone on without knowing about clothes and fashion. Finally, I find the courage to say, 'Mrs Davies, I can't thank you enough for taking me shopping today. I love all the clothes. I love them very much. Thank you.'

'I know, Maureen,' she answers. 'I know you do. That's quite all right.'

How I wish there was a way for her to know, to really know, what this means to me. I could cry because of the feelings bubbling inside me. The past always comes up. In the orphanage, we would cling to every little act of kindness. It was like a ray of hope to keep us going.

This morning, not long after our day at Bourne & Hollingsworth, Mrs Davies suggests that I take up ballroom dancing, telling me that a friend's daughter has been taking lessons. 'Oh no, Mrs Davies, no!' I answer, terrified by the thought. 'I'm too shy for that sort of thing.'

'Then that's even more reason for you to try it. You don't go anywhere at all, really, and it would give you a little confidence.'

'Oh, honestly, I really don't know if I'd be able to learn something like ballroom dancing.'

'Well, give it some thought, and we'll talk again about the possibility.'

When Mrs Davies leaves the room, I begin to imagine what it would be like to learn ballroom dancing. I would have to dance with a partner, surely. No, it's too much. I'm far too shy. But the thought of learning to dance won't leave me as I go about my cleaning duties, and I begin to argue with myself whether or not I might be able to do such a thing. I always loved Irish dancing at school. Maybe they will teach us in a group first before we dance with a partner. If so, I might be all right. I have to start socialising with people my own age, and this could be a start.

Why am I doing this? Why did I agree to go along with it? I have no answer for myself as I walk into the building for my first dancing lesson. Eventually, after a few little comments by Mrs Davies, I've decided to try it, signing up for ten one-hour lessons at five shillings each. I go up to the second floor and walk into a place about the size of a large classroom. A few other young girls sit on a bench beside the dance floor. I hurry over to sit among them, hoping to get lost in the crowd. Oh, how will I get through this, and why am I here? I feel my nerves stretched tightly, and the panic starts as the instructor walks towards us.

'Good evening, ladies. My name is Mrs Taylor, and I'd like to welcome you to the Bellaire Dance Academy. I think you've made a good decision to decide to learn about the art and enjoyment of ballroom dancing. You do not have to be the best dancer ever to step out upon a ballroom floor or be a professional stage performer to enjoy dance. Dance is quite a natural thing to do, although it might not appear easy at first. It can do much for one's social life, posture, confidence and more. Now, you're here to learn dancing. I have all your names recorded, and I want you to sign in each time you come. Give me one minute, ladies, and then we'll begin.'

Mrs Taylor is a glamorous woman in her fifties, wearing a long flowing satin skirt. She turns away from us and strolls over to a phonograph player. All of us just gawk at one another with the same look, as if to say, 'What am I doing here?' At the moment, I'd rather be anywhere but here, and my shyness is so obvious to me. I'm sure the others must notice it. But as I look around at the other girls, it seems they're a little shy as well. The instructor comes back towards us, all business this time. She claps her hands and says, 'Now, onto the floor, ladies, for a stretch to warm up.'

No one moves, the lot of us just looking stupidly at each other and waiting for someone else to get up first. 'Now, ladies,' Mrs Taylor says, taking a couple of slow serious steps to where we sit foolishly on the bench. 'Everyone must get up. No one sits around here. This is a dance class. We dance here, not sit. You won't learn that way.' I get up with the others, and Mrs Taylor has us stand in a line. 'Good, that's much better, much better!' she exclaims.

After putting us through some gentle stretches, she teaches us to hold our arms a certain way to help us balance. Then we're shown the basic steps of a modern waltz. I feel very awkward at first, unable to finish a whole series of steps. A few of the others seem to be catching on faster than I am. But as the lesson goes on, I forget some of my nervousness and lose myself in concentrating on the instructor. The hour goes by quickly, and at the end I feel quite proud to have got through it. Mrs Taylor assures us that we've all done well and encourages us to keep attending regularly. I promise myself as I leave that I will enjoy these lessons. Perhaps they'll help me fit in when I do meet a friend.

By lesson five, I begin to feel like I can dance. By the end of the ten weeks, I'm able to do a modern waltz, the foxtrot, the samba and the rumba. How quickly my life is changing! How quickly I am changing. I look better, which makes me feel more confident. The dancing lessons have even helped me improve my posture, and I can hold my head up a little more when I look at people. Will my new confidence last? I hope so, because I feel good for the first time since I left the orphanage.

❖ THIRTY-ONE ❖

I've seen different youth groups advertised in the church bulletin. The one that has attracted me most is called the Sodality of Mary. So, after Sunday mass today, knowing I have to begin somewhere, I find the courage to ask about the group and decide to join right away. The sodality meets on Sunday evenings, so I'll return later before I have time to lose my nerve.

I arrive early for the meeting and sit at the back of the hall watching the young women trickle in, slowly filling the empty chairs. I'm not used to mingling with so many new people, and I feel very uneasy. I know there are young women from Ireland here, working alone in London in different positions as maids and such in service for well-off families.

While I'm lost in my thoughts, a girl about my age sits down right beside me and greets me with a smile. I have no time to get nervous. 'Hello, how are you?' she asks in an Irish accent.

'I'm fine, thank you.'

'Are you Irish?' she asks, smiling. 'You sound Irish! I'm Abby, Abby Collins.'

'Maureen Harte,' I answer. 'And, yes, I'm Irish.'

'Where are you from, Maureen?'

'Mullingar.'

'Are you? I know of Mullingar. Never been there, though.'

'And yourself?'

'Enniscrone.'

'Have you just started in the sodality?' I ask her.

'I have, yes. I began three weeks ago, and yourself?'

'It's my very first night.'

'Ah, that's why. I thought I didn't recognise you. It's a good group. You'll like it. What do you do for a living, Maureen?'

'I'm in service, working for a very nice family in Willesden. No children, though. I'm quite happy there for the moment, and yourself?'

'I'm a nanny. Ah, it's all right, sure it is. I like the children. I'm comfortable with them, and don't you have to be. But I've only the one night off each week.'

'Myself, as well.'

Our talk is interrupted by the start of the meeting, and there's a shuffling of chairs as everyone gets seated. Abby quickly leans over to me, and in a quiet voice says, 'The meeting's going to start in a moment, Maureen. We could go for a quick cup of tea after it ends. Are you able to?'

'Sure, I've a half-hour or so,' I say, trying to sound casual. But I'm shocked and thrilled by her offer. Maybe she's a little lonely here in London, too.

'Good evening, ladies. Will you please stand for prayer.'

Immediately after the Hail Mary, the meeting begins, and I listen carefully to all that is said. I don't want to miss anything that might embarrass me or put me on the spot the next time. It seems I'll have to attend many meetings to learn what it takes to become a 'Child of Mary'. My mind wanders, though, as I think of Abby beside me. She seems so nice and friendly. I'd love to be her friend, and I wonder if she feels the same way. She's my own age, and it would be wonderful to finally have a real friend.

Sitting with Abby after the meeting, the two of us chat over tea. I feel excited. Having a friend my own age is totally new for me, as my friendships in the orphanage cannot be compared with friendship in the real world. Friendship and survival was the same thing for me and my friends in the orphanage.

'What's it like being a nanny?' I ask quietly.

'I'm happy enough, Maureen, and Mr and Mrs Wilson, the people I work for, treat me very well indeed. I like looking after children.'

'How old are the children?'

'The girl is five and the little boy three. I don't do anything other than look after them. There's a maid who does all the cleaning and some of the meals. I take the children walking in Hyde Park, which is very close by, and I've a full day off each week and time off in the evenings, too. That's how I make it to the sodality meetings.'

'Me too, Abby, but will we see each other at the next meeting?'

'Indeed we will, but what about the pictures? Would you like to go on our next day off?'

'I would love to, Abby, sure!'

In the restaurant after the pictures, Abby finally asks the dreaded question about my past and my family. How this question can change me in an instant. It's always the same when I meet someone new, as if they can see through me to all my shame and secret thoughts. And so, like an actor with poorly rehearsed lines, I give Abby my made-up story about 'my family', something that will fit the truth of my upbringing in the orphanage. 'Oh, my mother died when I was born, and my father died when I was three years old. That's when I went to live in Longford in an orphanage,' I explain.

'Oh, Maureen, I'm so sorry! When I asked you about your family, I'd no idea, honestly.'

'Oh, that's all right. I'm used to it when people ask me.'

Abby quickly changes the subject, and I suspect she's seen through my mask and knows this subject makes me uncomfortable. She'd have been fine if I'd said more about it, I know, but I'll not show that side of myself to anyone. My background isn't something I can speak of with ease. It's constantly on my mind, and I switch some of the details around to make it sound better, especially the part about my father dying when I was aged three. In my mind, that's exactly what did happen. But this is the first time I've had to tell the lie in the real world to someone I might develop a true friendship with.

Abby Collins has become my first real friend since I left the orphanage. With jet-black hair, a lovely oval face and deep green eyes, she's beautiful, almost Spanish-looking. I'm certain she has no idea how striking she is. She's a very warm person, and I felt comfortable with her right away. I know she's likely had a good education. I can tell by how well spoken she is and by the confident way she carries herself. Together, Abby and I gradually come out of our shells, both of us not having much of a social life, and we begin to settle into living in London. How nice it feels to have a friend like this. We've so much in common, especially our religious beliefs. We go to the pictures or the theatre and then always have a quick tea somewhere afterwards.

This evening, quite ignorant of the arts, the two of us have boldly decided to go to a ballet. Well, the performance starts, and a male dancer in tights appears on the stage, completely embarrassing us. We know that the people around us will think little of us laughing, but it's impossible to be serious during the performance. I can't look at Abby, but I can see in the corner of my eye her shoulders shaking and a hand over her face as if she'll burst at any moment. If she does, I'll run out of here, I will!

'Oh, Maureen, I'm so ashamed of the way I behaved. Wasn't I awful?' Abby confesses outside after the ballet, feeling humiliated about her behaviour. 'But when I saw him come on in those tights, I was finished. We must've appeared like two complete ignoramuses.'

'Sure, I was as bad, Abby,' I laughingly admit. 'When I saw your shoulders shaking, I couldn't go on watching without giggling.' We laugh about this on the way to Marble Arch tube station, where we part for home.

I actually laughed! I laughed with a friend and shared my feelings, something I've not done since I left the orphanage. I feel so alive, and I thank God for my new friend Abby.

We have many more nights like that at the ballet, sharing great times together and laughing our way through the situations we get into. This kind of friendship is something totally new in my life and very special to me. Before meeting Abby, I'd nothing to compare my friendships in the orphanage to. There we were suffocated and smothered. We had to whisper our friendship and laugh when it was safe to laugh.

As I go through my cleaning routine each day, I find my mind drifting back a little more, now that I've a friend in the outside world, to Maggie, Lucy and Katy. I see the truth of just how forgotten we were in that place for so many years. I wonder if Maggie has made a good close friend, too. I hope so. I wonder where she is now? And Katy Fallon – where is she? Is she still in County Roscommon? Does she have a job? Is she happy? I'd love to know how my old friends are. How I long to see them again. It feels as if a little part of me that I shut down tightly when I left the orphanage is opening back up again.

I've been in service for almost a year now, and Mrs Davies' father has become quite ill. Before a week passes, the old man takes a turn for the worse. Due to his age, the family doctor has said that he can stay at home rather than in hospital as long as he's watched around the clock. Mrs Davies has been spending the long nights sitting alone with her father. I know she must be very tired, so tonight I've offered to sit with her father while she gets a little sleep. She really appreciates this, and thanks me wholeheartedly. 'Yes, Maureen, I am quite exhausted. Thank you for offering. He's comfortable. Just keep an eye on him. You know where I am if you need me. Goodnight, and thank you again.'

I sit by the bed watching her father closely. Poor old man. I've come to be very fond of him, seeing him come down for breakfast every morning with his fancy walking stick and all dressed up in his suits, or enjoying watching the battles between Beatrice and Mr Davies. I've grown to love him. But he is old. He must be nearly ninety, or gone that maybe.

He lies still for a while, but then his eyes open and close again. He does this once or twice more and then begins to speak. At first, I pay no attention, thinking he's just delirious. But I start to listen as he goes on about his past, reliving his old days and mentioning his dead wife – 'Gladys', it sounds like. 'Ah, love, dear ole Gladys, love. Ah, my Glad,' he says, with great sighs of affection as his glassy, far-away eyes open and close. He's having a whole conversation: laughing aloud, and questioning and answering. But I'm not worried: I know that he's been like this before tonight, and after a time it stops.

Feeling a powerful tiredness come over me, I start to doze a little, but a moment later I'm woken by a strange, deep throaty noise coming from the old man. I've not heard that before. I rub my eyes to stay awake. This goes on for a few minutes, and I move over to him sleepily, trying to make him more comfortable by adjusting the pillows. The noises soon stop, and he seems restful. By now it's gone four in the morning, and I drift off to sleep again myself.

'Maureen! Maureen! Wake up, dear. Wake up!'

I come out of a deep sleep to find Mrs Davies kneeling beside my chair and gently shaking me. The whole family is standing around the bed. Only half awake, I stare, not yet understanding the situation. Then I realise: it's the deathbed! The old man has died! Mrs Davies takes me into the hall and quietly tells me that her father has died in the night.

'Oh no! Oh no!' I blurt out, feeling shocked, then terrified, weak-kneed and nauseous. 'I thought he was just sleeping, Mrs Davies. Oh, I'm sorry!'

'Now, Maureen, listen, dear. It wasn't your fault. You just happened to be with him. He was very elderly . . .'

But I don't hear her as I suddenly remember those odd sounds, those awful throaty noises the old man made in the early hours. Oh no! He died right then, and I adjusted his pillows. Things start to spin, and Mrs Davies is walking me down to the kitchen, trying to calm me down and saying something about a nice cup of tea. But the kitchen starts to spin about me, too, and suddenly I begin to vomit and feel rushes of panic and dizziness, almost passing out. Meanwhile, the doctor has been called, and when he arrives Mrs Davies tells him about the state I'm in. I can hear them speaking, but they seem far away. 'She'll be fine,' I hear the doctor say. 'A delayed shock response, I suspect. I'll give her a mild sedative, then get her into bed and she should be all right in a little while.'

Mrs Davies comes over to give me a tablet. 'The doctor assures me, Maureen,' she says, making sure I swallow the pill, 'that you'll be fine with some rest. I'm sorry you've had to go through all this. Now let's get you up to your room. Everything is fine now. My father was very old, and he was going to go some time. Come on now, dear.'

Even in the state I'm in, Mrs Davies' concern touches me deeply. It feels nice that someone cares when I'm not well. She walks with me up to my room to see me into bed. 'I'll leave the small light on, Maureen. Just rest now. You'll be fine. We're not going anywhere. You're a religious young woman, Maureen. Rest now, and say a quick little prayer for my father. He was fond of you.'

She smiles warmly and closes my bedroom door. Whatever the doctor gave me quickly sends me into a deep sleep. Some time in the afternoon, I wake feeling fine. It was the fact of knowing that I'd slept beside the dead old man for at least three hours before Mrs Davies came in to find me asleep that really upset me.

I'm now eighteen, and I finally feel ready to take Mrs Davies' advice to write a letter to Sister Brendan. I sit with pen and paper in the privacy of my room. How strange it feels to be writing a letter to Sister Brendan, as if I am writing home. I want her to know how well I'm doing. She'll be proud of me when I tell her what I've accomplished. I just haven't been ready to write before now, even to Maggie as I promised I would. A friend of Mrs Davies has taken a photo of me standing by the sundial in the garden, and I'll send it with the letter. I begin slowly, giving each word a lot of thought.

Dear Sister Brendan,

I'm writing this letter to let you know how very well I'm getting along here in London. I've been here since November 1946, the year I left the orphanage. An English lady, Mrs O'Neill, came to Mullingar on holiday with her only daughter, Julia. Mrs O'Neill was a widow at that time and offered me a chance to live with her and Julia in their flat in the Kilburn area of London. But about six months later, Mrs O'Neill got married again, and I had to leave the flat.

I am now in service with a lovely family, and they treat me very well. I'm learning so much from them. I never forget my faith, and I attend mass every Sunday. Do you hear from Maggie O'Rourke or Lucy Nolan, and do you happen to know anything of Katy Fallon, who was adopted when I was ten? I would like to write to them, and if you're able, could you please send me their addresses. I would be very grateful. I think often of all the help and encouragement you gave to me in my last two years in the orphanage, and I thank you. I hope this letter finds you in good health.

Sincerely,

Maureen Harte

When I finish the letter, I feel greatly relieved and so glad I've finally done it. I also write to Mrs Hughes, telling her how happy I am in England, sending another photo of myself along with greetings to Mrs Burke.

✹ THIRTY-TWO ✹

Almost two years have passed since I left the flat to go into service as a maid. Though I love working for Mrs Davies, I feel tied down by my life here. Over the last six months especially, I have found myself reflecting constantly on the circumstances that forced me back into service. But things are so different now. In fact, it is because of Mrs Davies' help and my blossoming friendship with Abby that I'm able to think this way at all – of moving on and bettering myself. I'm so much more self-aware. I look and feel better, and the few new clothes I have bought make me feel better inside. I feel prettier, more fashionable and more like other girls my age. All of this has shown me that I can be like other people. I can be liked and appreciated by them, and I don't always need to feel so different and separate from others.

But besides wanting more freedom and a job out in real society, there is a deeper reason why I want out of service. It is the shame attached to it for me. After all, growing up as illegitimate orphans, the only thing we believed ourselves good enough for was being servants for the fortunate and the wealthy. As long as I remain a maid, that shame will control me. It will completely define who I am as a person, and that would be like a death sentence, a way of reliving my childhood indefinitely.

And yet how strange it is that Mrs Davies, the very woman whose maid I am, should be the one to teach me so much. And she has done it all willingly, out of the goodness of her own heart.

As always, I don't have a clue how to broach the subject or how Mrs Davies will react to my approaching her. I worry about hurting her feelings and that she'll think me ungrateful after all she's done. And yet she's always been very approachable and supportive, encouraging me to improve myself. So why, then, would she react negatively to my urge to move on?

The days pass and the nagging thoughts of moving mount inside me. I can see that I will just have to go ahead and confront it, say a prayer, take a big breath and speak to her today. Right after lunch seems the best time.

I find her in the breakfast room, facing the back garden. I've decided to be direct and honest with her. 'Mrs Davies,' I begin, and it takes all my courage to continue. 'I would like to speak to you about something.'

'Of course, Maureen,' she answers with her easy, elegant smile. 'Sit down and join me. I'm enjoying the sun while it's still out.'

'I've been thinking a lot lately,' I begin, taking one of the chairs, 'about what I want to do in the future.'

'Like what, Maureen? What do you want to do?'

'I feel sometimes,' I hesitate, with my eyes downcast, 'that I want to leave being in service and work as a shop assistant. But I wanted to speak to you because I just don't know how to go about it or where to start. But I know I want to better myself by getting a regular job and standing on my own two feet.'

'Well, Maureen,' she answers when I finish, 'I understand that you want to move on to something else, and that's fine, but we don't want to be too hasty. I wouldn't be comfortable with you taking the very first thing that pops up. That won't do in your case. Otherwise, you shouldn't worry about how you feel. It's perfectly natural for someone your age to be concerned about the future. The most important thing is to try to set yourself up to succeed, to better yourself as you put it, and not make a decision that would set you back instead of helping you move forward. Does that make sense?'

'It does, Mrs Davies. It's been on my mind for some time. But, as I said, I really wouldn't know how to go about it.'

'That's perfectly reasonable. It sounds as if you've given it a lot of thought, and you did the right thing by approaching me, Maureen. Leave it with me for a time. I promise I'll not forget our discussion, but I really would like to give it some thought and not rush things.'

'Thank you so much, Mrs Davies. I'm so glad I spoke to you, and I'm more than happy to leave it with you for now.'

❖ ❖ ❖

Three months have gone by since our talk. I've waited, greatly relieved just to have spoken to her about it and sleeping much better at night, with hope in my heart. Today, Mrs Davies approaches me, assuring me that she hasn't forgotten the talk we had and repeating her concern about where I might go from here. 'When you spoke to me initially, Maureen, my immediate concern was your living arrangements. I don't think you should be on your own just yet. You're far too young, and, quite frankly, you know absolutely no one in England other than Mrs O'Neill, and she will not likely be able to help you. Am I right?'

I nod my head in agreement, realising that Mrs Davies must indeed have sensed that something deeper was going on with the O'Neills. It wouldn't take much for a shrewd woman like her to figure it out. 'Now, Maureen, I have made inquiries at Bourne & Hollingsworth on Oxford Street. They have quite a good hostel for employees to live in while they work for the company.'

As I listen to this, I almost hold my breath. Could Mrs Davies have really done this for me? I'm shocked that she would go to so much trouble.

She continues, 'Of course, there are rules – curfews and such things. They will deduct your room and board from your pay, but it is a very good hostel, and you wouldn't be on your own, Maureen. I would relax knowing you're looked after.'

She stops speaking, waiting for me to say something. But I can only look at her in amazement, as moved by her concern as delighted at what I'm hearing. 'Do you think . . .' I trip over my words. 'Would they perhaps hire me, Mrs Davies?'

She smiles at me, then laughs quietly in her elegant way. 'Yes, Maureen, I think it might be just the right place for you now. Of course, you will have to have an interview, but not to worry. I will arrange that. In fact, Mr Pendleton, who does the hiring, is a friend of the family. Now let me tell you more about the actual hostel. I want you to know what you will be going into . . .'

I'm so excited I could float off my chair. I try to see myself in that beautiful store, dressed just like the young women I saw when Mrs Davies took me shopping for new clothes. How smart they looked in their uniforms, and so confident. Bourne & Hollingsworth! This is like a dream. It must be a dream, surely?

'They take in girls from all over Europe, including many Irish girls your age, and I think you'll share a room with another girl. Yes, that's right, and they have a swimming pool, a gymnasium, a hairdressing salon, a lounge, a snack bar to entertain friends and more I've forgotten.' I can barely believe what I'm hearing, and I can scarcely pay attention to what Mrs Davies is saying. 'Now, Maureen, I can see how excited you are about this, but do think about it, please. It is indeed a lovely place, but it will be a significant change for you nonetheless. We can arrange an interview as soon as you're ready.'

With our talk over, I stand to leave the drawing room to go back to my duties. Before I leave the room, though, I turn back to Mrs Davies shyly and say, 'Mrs Davies, I really don't have to think about it. I'd love to try it. I really would.'

She smiles again and nods her head. 'All right then, Maureen. We'll go right ahead with it.'

'Thank you, Mrs Davies. Thank you very much.'

My stomach flutters as I leave the drawing room, so full of hope and light of heart. I have choices now, and I can make the most of good luck when it comes my way. If I'm fortunate to get this position with Bourne & Hollingsworth, I will make the very best of it. I will better myself.

About a week later, I travel on the bus with Mrs Davies for my interview with Mr Pendleton, dressed in the fine outfit I bought with Mrs Davies' help. She talks encouragingly to me as the double-decker fights the London traffic. 'Just be yourself in the interview, Maureen. You will be fine.' Her words and the fact she's accompanied me to my interview mean so much to me. I repeat her words silently to myself, taking them very much to heart. Just be yourself, Maureen. As we approach the entrance to the glitzy Bourne & Hollingsworth department store, my heart races with excited nervousness and anticipation of what's ahead.

Having arranged to meet Mrs Davies afterwards, I sit waiting in an outer office, terribly nervous about how I'll do. I can't lose this chance. A woman opens the door and looks at me. 'Maureen Harte?'

'Yes,' I answer as I stand, forcing myself to look straight at her and not at the floor.

'Do come in, Miss Harte, and take a seat at the desk. Mr Pendleton will be with you shortly.'

'Thank you.' I sit in the single chair in front of a large and very tidy mahogany desk. The seconds feel like hours.

A minute or so later, Mr Pendleton appears from an adjoining office, nodding curtly and sitting down across from me. A tall thin man in his fifties, I'd guess, he's dressed in a dark-grey pinstriped suit, with dark greying hair and glasses. With a very business-like manner, he picks up a file and opens it. His movements are quick and exact. 'Ah, yes,' he says, looking at my file and speaking in a clipped tone that's almost in tune with his movements. 'Maureen Harte, recommended to us by Elizabeth Davies. Yes, of course. Good, very good.'

He looks over my application for a moment longer then places it on the desk. I expect my very difficult interview to begin, but Mr Pendleton asks only a few quick questions about my sales experience. 'So, Miss Harte, I see you've worked at Oliver's, a toyshop. I've heard of them. Wooden toys a speciality, correct?'

'Yes, Mr Pendleton, wooden toys mostly and books. I served the customers, stocked the shelves and filled out the sales slips sometimes as well.'

'Very good.' He listens to my answers distractedly, nodding politely and pushing his glasses up his nose with one finger as he smiles. After one or two more similar exchanges, he opens my file again, looks at something else, closes it again and then tells me I'm hired. My heart leaps, although I try not to show it. I'm hired! I'm hired! I cannot believe this.

He continues, going over some of the store's rules and a few other details. 'You'll be given a shop name,' he says. What is a shop name? Puzzled, I just nod my head as he provides an explanation. 'Here at Bourne & Hollingsworth all our clerks are given a shop name, usually something beginning with the same first letter as their surname.

It is a bit easier for our personnel files, you see. Also, Miss Harte, occasionally we're not able to secure immediate accommodation at Warwickshire House when employment commences. But not to worry. I know you'll need to give Mrs Davies one or two weeks' notice. If there is no opening by the time you begin work, alternative arrangements will be made for temporary accommodation at the Good Shepherd Hostel in Soho Square. These situations are common, Miss Harte. The turnover of our hostel employees is ongoing, and openings occur regularly, if not frequently. Your shop name will be assigned when you begin in two weeks' time.'

Mr Pendleton then calls in his secretary. 'Would you take Miss Harte here down to haberdashery, please, to meet Miss Ridelle. She's to begin work in two weeks' time. Thank you.' He turns to give me a final smile and a nod, and off I go with the secretary to the haberdashery department.

On the way down, Mr Pendleton's secretary tells me I'm to attend a tour of Warwickshire House on the following Saturday, giving me directions and a time in the afternoon. 'The hostel's only two underground stops away from Bourne & Hollingsworth,' she tells me. 'All the girls there get on at Goodge Street station, and two stops later at Tottenham Court Road station you're right there on Oxford Street. It's very convenient.'

We walk to an area that must be the haberdashery department, consisting of one big oval counter between two smaller square ones laid out in a half-circle. Two or three sales clerks work behind each counter, with displays and items all the way around. It seems a busy place, selling mostly small, fine items such as pins, needles and thread, ribbon, elastic, buttons, and other such things.

The secretary asks me to wait a moment while she locates the supervisor, and a minute later I'm introduced to Miss Ridelle, a pleasant-looking woman dressed in a smart black suit. She thanks the secretary, and turning to me says, 'Come with me, Miss Harte, and I'll show you the department and go over your specific duties and our expectations of you: dress code, punctuality and all that.'

I listen attentively as I follow Miss Ridelle along the counters, trying not to feel overwhelmed by everything. I am aware of the curious glances of the girls working at the counters as I pass. I'm told that I'll be wearing a black skirt and a white blouse at work but that all the supervisors wear proper suits with their names on the lapel. Miss Ridelle explains to me that each new girl at Bourne & Hollingsworth starts in the haberdashery department. If she shows promise as a salesperson, she'll be moved to a better department, such as jewellery, perfumes, cosmetics or even one of the clothing departments.

Finally, the brief tour is over, and Miss Ridelle turns to me with a warm, encouraging smile. 'We'll see you in two weeks, then, Miss Harte, and have a shop name for you. Just come here to my cubicle on your first day, and we'll get you started, right?'

'Yes, thank you, Miss Ridelle. I'll see you then. Thank you again.'

I walk from the haberdashery department with my feet barely touching the ground, looking round me at all the people, the elegant departments and the fine clothing. I don't know whether to laugh or cry. Everything went so perfectly, and I got the job. I did it. I think of Sister Brendan, knowing how proud she would be of me for accomplishing this. Not only will I be leaving service, but I will be working in one of the finest stores in London, and that is most definitely bettering oneself.

I have to refocus my eyes to get my bearings and find the right way to the main entrance. Mrs Davies is waiting there and is very happy to hear the good news. Indeed, she seems proud of me. 'That's wonderful, Maureen, just wonderful. That's the worst of it over now. How does it feel?'

What I really feel is the old familiar lump form in my throat, but I catch my emotions quickly. Not here, Maureen, and not now. 'Oh, I feel such relief that the interview is over, Mrs Davies. It was actually much simpler than I imagined, and Mr Pendleton didn't ask me too many difficult questions. Just a little about my sales experience at Oliver's and then it was over. I feel wonderful. Thank you so much. I can't tell you enough how grateful I am for all your help.'

'You are more than welcome, Maureen. This will be the perfect place for you to live and work – and meet many friends, I hope. I know that each new girl is carefully trained when they begin. You'll be fine.'

'I'm to be given a shop name, Mrs Davies, though I won't know what it is until the day I begin.'

Mrs Davies laughs affectionately at my excitement. 'Yes, all the floor-staff girls are given shop names, and you must remember to tell me what yours is when I come into the store. I'll be sure to stop by your department and say a quick hello.'

On the Saturday before I am to start my new job, I travel to the hostel for my tour and orientation day. I'm to meet the woman who runs the hostel when I arrive, a Miss Nicholas. Coming out of a small street, I spot the front entrance and walk up the steps and through the big double-doors. Inside, to my right, I notice a security desk and decide to report there. A short bald man in a dark security uniform greets me. 'Good morning, Miss. How may I help you?' he asks pleasantly, with a definite twinkle in his eye.

'My name is Maureen Harte. I'm here to meet a Miss Nicholas for the tour. I'm new.'

'Well then, Miss Harte,' he says, looking at something below him on the desk, 'you're in the right place. Miss Nicholas is indeed expecting you, and you're right on time. I'm Mr Henning. You'll be seeing a lot of me. Always about during the day, I am. Please just sign your name here, Miss Harte. There's a lot of signing in and out here. It's just part of the routine.'

I sign where he indicates on a ledger and look up at him for more instructions. 'Great, thank you, Miss Harte. Now turn right around and go to that office across the way. Miss Nicholas will be in there.'

Miss Nicholas is an elegant woman in her fifties, dressed in a beautiful black suit and white blouse with a frill down the front. She is tall and thin and wears glasses with light silver frames. She speaks with a soft, quiet voice, but right away I can see that she's firm. I have to fight the fear that comes up in me every time I meet someone in authority. I can't help it. Authority figures mean one thing only to me, especially female authority figures.

There are four other girls with me for the tour. Miss Nicholas walks us through the hostel slowly, pointing out different areas and telling us a little of its history. The hostel itself is a three-storey building on Gower Street, running the length of the block and backing onto Mallet Street, which faces the University of London. She mentions there are more than two hundred girls from all over Europe, ranging from eighteen to thirty years of age. I smile to myself as I realise that the orphanage had almost the same number of girls.

Inside the entrance to the hostel is a nice lounge, with comfortable chairs, sofas and artwork on the walls. Off to the side of the lounge are a big snack bar and the main dining hall, which is huge and is set up for buffet-style serving. Miss Nicholas explains that all the girls must sign in and out on a large ledger with Mr Henning the security man. 'Mr Henning reports directly to me regarding curfew violation. Curfew, ladies, is 11 p.m. sharp, and we believe it is reasonable. Consistent violations over a period of time may be reported to Mr Pendleton and disciplinary action will be taken if required.'

When the tour is over, Miss Nicholas turns to our small group. 'Well, ladies, I hope that you'll all settle down well in Warwickshire House and respect the rules. Experience has taught us that there are good reasons why the rules are the way they are. Thank you again, and good luck to each of you.'

I turn to leave with the others, but Miss Nicholas catches my eye with a raised forefinger. 'Ah, Miss Harte, could you remain behind for a moment. I need to have a word with you about your accommodation. Do step into my office, please.'

I follow Miss Nicholas, again fighting the irrational impulse that somehow I've been a bad girl and am going to be reprimanded. 'Unfortunately, Miss Harte, we won't have a bed for you by Monday when you start work. We will need to place you at the Good Shepherd Hostel in Soho Square. It won't be more than a month or so, I should think. So, when you report on Monday, bring your belongings here to my office, and after your first shift we'll see that you get over to the Good Shepherd and settled there.'

'Yes, Miss Nicholas,' I reply, a little disappointed by this news. The

Good Shepherd Hostel: it's probably still a lovely big place, given that it's connected with Bourne & Hollingsworth. I'm not going to worry about it.

It is my final day as a maid in service with the Davies. I stand at the big window in my bedroom and gaze sadly out at the evening summer sky and the lovely garden with the sundial in the middle. Tonight will be the last time I sleep in the cosy bedroom that was my very own, and Mrs Davies has asked me to come down to the drawing room after the family has tea so they can say goodbye. I will miss them all very much. They've watched me develop and grow into the more confident person I am today. I am especially grateful to Mrs Davies for treating me as more than just her maid and for all she's done for me.

When the time comes to go down to the drawing room, I descend the stairs and knock lightly on the door. I wait for Mrs Davies' reply before entering. 'Do come in, Maureen, and sit down,' she says as I walk in, gesturing to one of the high-backed chairs. When I'm seated, Mrs Davies glances round at the other family members before beginning. 'Since this will be your last night with us, Maureen, we want to take a moment to thank you, all of us together. And I know my father wouldn't have missed this if he were still with us.'

Already I feel sad and weepy. It's time for another wrenching goodbye and a new start. 'On behalf of us all, I'd like to thank you for your hard work and your dedication while working for us.'

'Yes, kid, that's right,' Mr Davies says to me. 'I wish you all the best in your new position at Bourne & Hollingsworth. They are a good firm to work for, good people indeed.' He reaches into his vest pocket and hands me a ten-pound note. 'And buy yourself something, kid.'

'Oh, thank you very much, Mr Davies. That's so kind of you.'

Then Beatrice shakes hands with me, presenting me with a lace doily she's made. 'I wish you the very best, Maureen.'

'We shall miss you, Maureen,' Mrs Davies says. 'But we know you have to move on now, as you said, to better yourself. I have no doubts at all that you will do just that. As a gesture of our appreciation, we have a small gift for you to take away when you leave us.'

She hands me a box, which I open right away. Inside is a beautiful mirror-and-hairbrush set, with shiny pearl handles. I've seen a similar set on Mrs Davies' dressing table in her bedroom. I'd always admired them when I was doing the dusting, but never did I think I would own a set like it. 'Thank you so much. I just love it . . .'

My words trail off as I struggle to contain my emotions and find a way to express a simple thank you, but I can't stop some of the tears from falling.

'Now, Maureen,' Mrs Davies says, taking my hand. 'This is a joyful occasion, hardly a sad one. It's a new beginning for you. And I will drop by the haberdashery department to see how you are doing.'

Still teary-eyed, I thank the family again before leaving and going back up to my room. My old brown suitcase, which has lain under the bed for the last two years, is out and packed, ready to leave in the morning. I sit on the bed, looking at my reflection in the little mirror that came with the gift. Who am I? I look at my eyes, my nose, my hair and my skin. My face comes from two other people: my mother and my father. Who are they? Where are they? How did they meet one another? Will I ever know what they look like? I often think about my mother somewhere in Ireland and pray that she's still alive. The more I learn about life and the more time that passes, the stronger the feeling of wanting to know and wanting to meet her. Never have I felt it as strongly as I do now.

I think of the orphanage and of meeting my mother one day and telling her all about the long years there and that I always thought of her. To know who I am, I must know who she is. I'm part of her and can never fully know myself until I know what happened to her. All I know is that my mother is Annie Harte, the woman who gave birth to me and brought me into this world. If I am anyone, I'm her daughter. I'm Annie's girl.

❖ THIRTY-THREE ❖

I stand beside Miss Ridelle, feeling incredibly nervous before starting my first day of work at Bourne & Hollingsworth. 'The first thing, Maureen, is to assign you your shop name. Yours will be Miss Hatton.' She spells out the name for me, explaining that it is the one used on the company records and that while at work I'm to use only my shop name and to address all fellow employees by their shop names. Over the years growing up in the orphanage, I dreamed of becoming many different things once I made it to the outside world. Becoming a 'Miss Hatton' wasn't one of them. It will take time getting used to it. But it is a title, after all, and I've never been given a title before. Miss Harte is now Miss Hatton of the haberdashery department of Bourne & Hollingsworth.

Miss Ridelle takes me directly across to the counters and introduces me to an older girl there by the name of Miss Blake. 'Miss Blake,' Miss Ridelle announces, 'this is Miss Hatton. Today is her first day with us, and I'm assigning her to you for her training.'

'Hello, Miss Blake. Pleased to meet you,' I say, trying to take the initiative a little. My nerves, though, are getting the better of me, and I can barely look at her. I feel the heat rise to my face as I blush deeply.

'Hello, Miss Hatton,' Miss Blake says. Right away I detect her Irish accent. She's very cheerful and friendly, but she's certainly noticed my shyness and the fact I'm blushing every time I'm spoken to.

'Now, Miss Hatton,' Miss Ridelle says, 'Miss Blake will keep an eye on you and help you to learn all about the stock. She's the senior clerk in the department, so feel free to ask her any questions at all if you're uncertain. It will take you some time, but you'll soon catch on.' Miss Ridelle nods to Miss Blake and leaves the two of us at the counter.

As she walks away, I suddenly feel the immediacy of my situation, especially the glances of the girls at the other counters. As if drawn by magnets, my eyes keep moving to the ground, and I realise that this will not do. I must get over my shyness with the other girls in the department. This isn't Oliver's toyshop; this is one of the top department stores in London.

'Don't worry about selling anything today, Miss Hatton,' Miss Blake is saying to me. 'Just watch what I and the other clerks do and concentrate mostly on learning the stock for the first few days.'

'Yes, Miss Blake,' I answer, trying my best to look confident, but my extreme self-consciousness makes me feel naked in front of these smart, confident women, like a glass person with every nook and cranny exposed. Because I'm new, they're sure to be curious about me, but any attention makes me feel defenceless. I must get over this. I'll use the one skill I have that is sharp as a knife and has been since I was three years old. I'll watch. I'll observe. I'll see what's coming, and I'll survive this.

When it comes time for my first break, Miss Blake brings the tall girl from the far counter over to meet me. I'd noticed her as soon as I started this morning. It was hard not to with her striking looks. As soon as I laid eyes on her, I knew her to be full of confidence and personality. 'Miss Hatton, this is Miss Manley,' Miss Blake says, introducing us. 'She's going to take you upstairs and show you the staff room, where most of the girls take their break.'

'Nice to meet you, Miss Manley,' I say.

'Nice to meet you, Miss Hatton,' she answers pleasantly as she shakes my hand, a hint of mischief in yet another noticeably Irish accent.

'Now bring her back on time, do you hear, Miss Manley?' Miss Blake says, pretending to be stern as she winks at her.

'I will indeed, Miss Blake. You're not to worry at all.'

I like Miss Manley right away, and as the two of us go up to the huge staff room on the floor above I let her do most of the talking. 'Miss Manley' in real life is Margo McCormack from Killimor, County Galway, in the west of Ireland. She began working at Bourne & Hollingsworth just a few weeks before I did. Margo, a tall, slender, striking young woman with lovely shoulder-length hair that she wears to one side, is two weeks younger than I am. I immediately have the same feeling I did when I met Abby: a sense that here is a decent and honest girl. 'Oh, you're Irish. You'll like it here,' she says, chattering away easily to me. 'There's a lot of Irish here. Miss Blake, now, she's Deirdre Burns from Cork.'

Margo tells me not to be shy. All the girls in haberdashery are great, she assures me, and they all get along well. She's heard already that I couldn't get into Warwickshire House just yet and will be staying at the Good Shepherd Hostel. 'Yes, this will be my first night there,' I tell her. 'I hope the wait isn't too long.'

'I was lucky,' Margo says. 'There was an opening for me when I first started here. But my roommate, an English girl, might be leaving to travel on the Continent. So who knows, Maureen. If the timing's right, you might end up stuck with me!' She laughs at this, entirely confident in herself. I feel infected by the lightness of Margo's personality. She's so friendly and direct, and I'm sure she'd make a great roommate.

As the conversation goes on in a lopsided fashion, my shyness is so obvious and my discomfort so apparent that she asks, 'Are you always this quiet, Maureen?'

This only makes me worse as my mind races for a quick way out. 'Ah, no. When I first meet people, I'm usually like this, and I've been very worried about the new job, getting it right and . . .'

'Ah, well now, you won't be shy round us for very long. That just won't do!' And she brushes off my worrying about the job with the wave of an arm. 'Don't be worried. You'll catch on in no time.'

Our short break is soon over, and on the way back to the haberdashery counters Margo continues to encourage me and tell me little things about the job. I feel so much better already, realising that with each passing hour things will improve.

At the end of the day, Miss Ridelle comes to the counter and asks, 'How did the first day go, Maureen? Are things coming along?'

'Very well, Miss Ridelle. I'm still learning the system and where all the stock is kept and the names of all the items. There's quite a few of them.'

She chuckles good-naturedly at this. 'There is indeed a lot of stock and a lot of names, but that will come with repetition, and each shift will be better. Well, goodnight, Miss Hatton.'

'Goodnight, Miss Ridelle.'

I pick up my suitcase and head off to the Good Shepherd Hostel. I have no trouble with the directions Miss Nicholas gave me, but as I get into Soho I feel uneasy. It looks so dirty, with narrow streets and tiny cluttered alleys everywhere. The odour of curry drifts from the many Indian restaurants and seems to hang heavily in the air. Though I feel the fatigue and strain of the day begin to creep into my bones, I start to walk quickly, wanting to remove myself from this close atmosphere and eager to settle into my new lodgings.

Finally, I locate the large hostel. I climb the few steps slowly, feeling hesitant and slightly uneasy for no particular reason. Then, just as I pull back the heavy brass knocker, bringing it down twice, I repeat the name of the hostel to myself: the Good Shepherd. No, it couldn't be, could it? Oh no, why didn't I think of this before? Nuns! As I wait, praying against hope that I'm wrong, an old familiar feeling washes over me. My heart seems to thud as loud as the heavy knocker did. The door opens, and I'm greeted by a stern-looking nun. Immediately, my old identity starts to wrap itself around me like unwanted skin.

'Hello,' the nun begins, 'you must be the new girl from Bourne & Hollingsworth.' She glances down at the suitcase in my hand.

'Yes, Sister. I'm Maureen Harte.'

'I'm Sister Margarita. I'm in charge here. Do come in, and we'll get you settled.'

As I follow her down a hall, I fight to get my sense of balance, like a person suddenly walking on a ship in stormy seas. Breathe, Maureen, breathe. It's just a hostel, not the orphanage. But then I notice a large statue of the Sacred Heart at the far end of the hall, yet another concrete reminder of my past.

Sister Margarita is chattering away to me, but already I feel the familiar weakness and closed-in feeling, the swish of robes and the rattle of beads bringing a rush of emotions back. I fight to focus on what Sister Margarita is saying. 'You'll meet Sister Loretta and Sister

Eleanor at the evening meal. But first we'll go on up to your room. It's on the second floor.'

I follow the nun on up the stairs, wishing I were anywhere else, but I've no choice in the matter, and I must make the best of it. 'This is your room, and the bathroom is along the hall. When you're ready, please come down to the front room. It's on the left side of the hall near the front door.'

'I will. Thank you, Sister,' I answer obediently, feeling like I am ten years old again. At least the room will be my own. It is small and narrow with a single bed on a wooden floor. A crucifix hangs on the wall above the bed, and an old wardrobe and dresser sit across from it. I have only half an hour, so instead of unpacking I lie on the bed going over in my head all that I saw and learned today in the haberdashery department. I think of the products I was shown and try to remember what they cost and where they were kept beneath the counters. I want to remember as much as possible for my next shift.

The half-hour passes quickly, and I descend the stairs to face Sister Margarita in the front room. I knock lightly on the door and enter when instructed. 'Please sit down, Maureen, and I will go over the rules of the hostel with you.' Waiting until I'm seated in the nearest chair, she continues, 'We are early risers here: 6.30 every morning. Then mass in the chapel at 7 a.m. and breakfast at 8 a.m. sharp. Prayers before bed each evening will be at nine, unless you have to go out for the evening. Then you must be in by eleven o'clock. All doors are then shut for the night.'

'Yes, Sister,' I say quietly, the memories of the orphanage smothering me. Oh, I must get out of this room before I break down in front of her. Her tone of voice is so imperious and judging, and I feel as though she can see right through me. Almost every nun I have ever known seems to have spoken down to me, as if from a pedestal, and has had a direct and penetrating look that has seemed able to read my thoughts. I'm sure it's more me than anything else.

'We'll see you for supper, Maureen. You may leave now.'

'You may leave now.' How many hundreds of times have I heard that exact phrase?

I quickly escape upstairs to the privacy of my own room. I throw myself back on the bed and try to relax. I'll be fine in a little while. I'm not going to be here very long.

Despite my nervous disposition and my obvious shyness, I settle well into the daily routine of my job at Bourne & Hollingsworth. With Miss Blake as my guide and the other girls offering tips and helpful advice, I soon learn the system. I write out sales slips and handle money with growing confidence. On top of our salary, every girl receives a small commission for each sale made at the counter. I soon learn that a couple of the more aggressive girls at the counters are known as 'rushers'. They watch for approaching customers and intercept them for the sale and a little commission. 'There goes herself, Miss Knightly,' Margo will whisper to me. 'She's a real rusher that one, piling up all the commission.'

We get two fifteen-minute breaks, one in the morning and one in the afternoon, and a forty-five-minute break for lunch. The food in the staff room is good, and inexpensive. Each day I go on break with Margo, sitting with her and some of the other girls from the haberdashery department. Margo has chosen to take me under her wing, and she always arranges it so that our breaks land at the same time. I listen to the lively chatter of conversation at break or during lunch. When I do open my mouth, it's usually to ask a girl where she's from or a question about our department. The conversation often switches to the goings on at the hostel, and the girls keep telling me how much I will love it there when I finally move in.

The girls at Bourne & Hollingsworth are from all over Europe, and sitting with them is both an education as well as a reminder of my terribly sheltered past. What for them must be normal girlish chatter – usually about men – is frequently a revelation to me. My two years in service have done little to make me more worldly, and even my social life with Abby is very tame. Some of the English girls are quite worldly, and they come out with some things that burn my ears a little.

However, I feel as though I'm coming out of my shell more than ever before, especially because of Margo, who never ceases to be amazed at my genuine innocence. She often has me in tears with laughter. Usually it's a remark about a good-looking young man, after he's walked off, of course, and I'm left shaking with laughter to the point where I can't count the money in my hand and put it in the cash register. It's how she says things and her boldness and razor-sharp wit that gets me going. I'm just as much embarrassed by her remarks as I am amused by her craziness.

And then there's Mr Baxter, the handsome supervisor in his late twenties who all the girls go on about. He slowly walks by our counter, his arms folded across his chest and dressed in his lovely grey pinstriped suit. We follow him with our eyes. He's so quiet and shy, and this makes him even more attractive to all us girls in haberdashery.

Already I have a reputation as a great blusher, reddening at the drop of a hat. I'm mortified when I have to serve a young man, and I can feel Margo's eyes looking across from her counter whenever this happens. She gets the biggest laugh out of my unease around men. I wish I could be as confident as she is. She is able to look the male customers right in the eye. But overall I'm doing well, and at the end of two weeks Miss Ridelle tells Miss Blake how pleased she is with my progress. This is great news, as it means that I can handle the job and can worry less.

After an evening out at the pictures with Abby, my mind drifts during the short walk from the bus stop to the hostel. Suddenly, a quick, sharp movement to the right of me catches my eye. I turn to look, and to my horror an Indian man is reaching out from a doorway and grabbing at me. He tries desperately to pull me back into the shadows. 'Come 'ere! Come 'ere!' he hisses at me harshly, his voice low and menacing.

He has a handful of my coat sleeve in his grasp, and I twist away, screaming, 'Get away from me! Get away from me!' With more strength than I knew I had, I finally free myself then turn to run. Before I can think again, I'm back in Oxford Street, and right there, thank God, is a policeman standing at the corner. I can barely speak to him in my panic. 'Excuse me,' I manage to get out, my chest heaving and my heart thudding, 'I can't go back down that side street! A man tried to pull me into a doorway, and I have to be in by eleven!'

'Calm down,' the policeman says. 'Calm down and tell me what the trouble is, Miss.'

'This man, back there, down that way. He came out of a doorway! I'm on my way to the hostel . . .' I have to stop and catch my breath while tears begin to stream down my face.

'First of all,' the policeman says, 'tell me your name?'

'Maureen Harte.'

'Now tell me, Maureen, what you're doing walkin' down there to begin with? You're far too young to be hangin' about round Soho. Calm down now and tell me why you're in Soho?'

I explain my situation to him, and he offers to walk me to the hostel. On the way, he asks me a question or two, and I tell him I'm waiting for a place at Warwickshire House and that I work for Bourne & Hollingsworth. He says he knows of Warwickshire House and that I'll be a lot safer there and that I should try to get in a little earlier. As we arrive in front of the hostel, I thank him again for his help and for taking me home. He wishes me the best and walks off into the night, tapping his short stick on the side of his leg.

I lie awake in my quiet room reliving the attack and feeling terrified about what I'll do tomorrow. I must've scared him away in time by shouting out the way I did. There's a word for that kind of attack on a woman: rape, it's called, and I suspect that that's what he was after. The thought sickens and terrifies me: that there are people in the world creeping around with the likes of that in their head. I decide to tell no one about this. I wouldn't know how to or what to say.

One thing is for certain: I'll never again feel safe as long as I have to live in Soho. I worry that the man who attacked me has been watching me and that he could still be out there, stalking me each day as I go to and from my job.

To my great relief, a few days after I am attacked, my supervisor informs me that a bed has become available in Warwickshire House and will be ready for me at the end of the week. Margo McCormack will indeed be my roommate, and I couldn't be happier with the news.

'I'm certain the two of you will get along great,' Miss Ridelle is saying. 'We try to find the best matches we can. What do you think, Maureen? Will it be a good fit for you?'

'I think it will be a perfect fit, Miss Ridelle. I probably know Margo the best so far of all the girls. I'm sure it will work fine. She's great.' I glance quickly across to see Margo at her counter, winking furiously and nodding her head in exaggerated gestures of approval. I have to fight to keep a straight face.

'That's wonderful, Miss Hatton,' Miss Ridelle continues. 'Be prepared to bring your things across from the Good Shepherd on Saturday. We like to do all our room transfers then. I'm sure Miss Manley will acquaint you with all the little details you'll need to know when you move in. Good luck.'

'Thank you very much, Miss Ridelle.'

As soon as she can, Margo comes over to my counter to tell me how pleased she is to get me for a roommate, too. 'You're a bit quiet for me, all the same, Maureen,' she teases, 'but I'm sure living with me will change all that!'

On Saturday morning, I walk into the Warwickshire with the same brown suitcase, delighted to finally be moving into the lovely hostel. I knock on the door of room 207 on the second floor. 'Come on in!' I hear her familiar voice call out. 'There you are, Maureen! Welcome. Let me help you with your luggage. Where's the rest of it? Outside the door?'

'This is it, Margo.'

'What? Well, you'll have lots of space in your wardrobe,' she says, laughing and throwing her head back. 'This is your end of the room, with a bed, a chair and a double wardrobe, and we share the sink and cupboard under it.'

The room is rectangular, with a single window facing Mallet Street and the University of London grounds. The floors are wooden, and the sink and vanity are built right into the wall as part of two large wardrobe closets. My bed is on one side of the room just inside the door, while the headboard of Margo's bed is by the window. 'Come on,' she says, 'I'll show you the bathroom and showers now, and later I'll take you down to the snack bar and lounge.'

'Oh thanks, Margo. I'm so happy to be here. I hated walking through Soho after dark.'

'I can imagine, Maureen. What a place to house young women.'

Margo shows me around the second floor, telling me about the rush for the showers in the mornings. There are three shower stalls and washroom facilities at the far end of the corridor. I think she'll be the perfect roommate for me, and she has quite a few friends, so maybe they'll accept me as one of their crowd for social outings. And yet I sense that Margo still doesn't know quite what to make of me. We're both nineteen, though she's so worldly and I'm still so naive.

As we get ready for bed that night, Margo takes a break from her joking to put a serious question to me. 'You know, Maureen, for someone with an obviously good sense of humour who loves to laugh, you're very shy. Why is that?'

'Oh, I don't know. It could be my upbringing. I was raised in an orphanage.' I wasn't expecting this question, and I know it will lead to the dreaded family questions that were bound to come up eventually. Oh well, I'd rather get it over with now on our first night as roommates.

'What happened to your family?' Margo asks. 'Did your mother die?'

'Yes, when I was born, and then my father died when I was three. But I remember practically nothing about him, so it's like I was always in the orphanage. It's not like I really know who they were.'

I hope Margo doesn't ask me any more questions or I'll have to come up with more lies to cover the last ones. But she goes on. 'Where was the orphanage where you were raised, Maureen?'

'In County Longford. Not in Mullingar, where I was born.'

'Oh, how very sad,' she says sincerely. 'When I think of the size of my family, I can't imagine what it would have been like growing up without them.'

'Oh, I'm used to it by now,' I say, but inside I feel like a fool who's only covering up this deep shame, this secret I carry with me.

'How many are there in your family?' I ask.

'Nine of us, all girls.'

'What?' I cry. 'Nine? And all girls?'

'Yes, but this is my father's second family. I'm part of the second lot. His first wife died, and there are four girls from that family.'

Margo lets out a lazy yawn, and our conversation slowly fades. Soon, we say goodnight and turn off the lights. In the stillness of the darkened room, I think about my conversation with Margo and how I've lied again about the past. All I really want to do now is bury it. I don't want to drag it around with me everywhere I go. Warwickshire House is full of young women living their lives to the fullest, and I want to do the same.

I think it will be a perfect fit for me here. I've lived with rules all my life, so the curfew and the other limitations will mean little to me. Finally, I will be able to look in the mirror and see a person who fits in. That's what I crave more than anything else: to be one of the crowd and to have a great time being young and free. There are so many opportunities for me now, and I won't waste them thinking about a past I cannot change. I know that one day I will want to find my mother or find out where in Ireland my family are, but right now I want to live, and this beautiful hostel is the perfect place to do just that. I feel wonderfully contented, happy and proud of the changes I've made. 'Thank you, Mrs Davies,' I whisper to myself in the darkened room. 'If only you knew.'

❖ THIRTY-FOUR ❖

When we wake up, we decide to go out and take in the many sights of London. Margo then suggests we go boating on the Serpentine in Hyde Park along with Miss Manning, also known as Elaine Matheson. Elaine is an English girl from another department, and she is an absolute riot to be around.

The three of us go out in a rowing boat for about a mile in one direction, taking turns at the oars before coming back to where we started. All along the way, people are enjoying the lovely spring weather, picnicking near the banks or walking in pairs along the paths that follow the bend of the lake. Afterwards, we stroll through the park, stopping to listen to the soapbox preachers for a little while.

'There are so many things to do during the day on a Sunday, Maureen,' Margo explains as we walk. 'Some days we just sit and watch the pigeons at Piccadilly Circus flying in circles around the statue of Eros or go to watch the changing of the guard at Buckingham Palace.'

'And those are only the things we can do in the daytime, Maureen!' Elaine adds. 'You haven't lived at Warwickshire House until you've had an evening of dancing, especially at the Lyceum Ballroom. Isn't that right, Miss Manley?'

'Quite right, Miss Manning,' Margo replies, mocking the manner of speech at Bourne & Hollingsworth. 'We must indeed initiate Miss Hatton here in the nightlife side of things, and that means the ballrooms!'

Margo and Elaine begin to do a mock waltz along the path in front of me, totally unconcerned about the turning heads around them. I laugh at their antics, feeling content and happy to be out socialising like this. This is just how I imagined it would be, taking advantage of being young and having fun with other girls my age. And this is only the start of it.

Margo and Elaine waltz back to me, picking up the conversation where they left off. 'Next Saturday, then, Maureen. It's settled,' Margo proclaims. 'You'll join Elaine, me and God knows who else for a night out at the Lyceum Ballroom over on the Strand. Agreed?'

At seven o'clock on Monday morning, a loud electric bell shatters the sleeping peace of Warwickshire House. I wake with a start, feeling slightly confused in my new surroundings. For a good two minutes, it sounds in long bursts. Then, a low groan and a familiar voice reminds me where I am. 'God, that's enough to wake the dead, that thing is. Time to get up.'

'Does it ring every morning?' I ask Margo, already on my feet and at the sink.

'Every morning at seven,' she answers through a yawn. 'Except on Sundays. It's what you might call the communal alarm clock.'

By twenty past seven, Margo and I are in line with our trays in the cafeteria. The food is very good, and even the powdered eggs are delicious. We take our trays to one of the many tables, each one seating about six people. I listen to the buzz of lively chatter and talk as girls come and go, rushing in for breakfast before work. I'm going to love meal times here, although it's a bit strange that I'm again living communally with so many females. That the atmosphere is one of such freedom is why I take joy in the simple act of having a meal in a crowded cafeteria.

After breakfast, it's back upstairs to our room for a final touch up before joining the general flight of girls on their way to the Underground and on to work. Miss Ridelle always stands smiling, waiting for us to appear. She greets us with a polite but formal, 'Good morning, ladies,' and another day at the haberdashery counters begins.

About an hour after I begin my shift, I finish serving an elderly lady who has just purchased a package of hairnets and a card of assorted needles. I look up to greet the next customer, and to my surprise and delight I see Mrs Davies standing smiling at me. 'Good morning, Maureen. I assume all has worked out well for you, then?'

'Mrs Davies! What a surprise it is to see you. Good morning!' I struggle to regain my composure – my haberdashery Miss Hatton composure. Inside, though, I suddenly feel emotional as a result of this unexpected visit. My mind races to find the right words to say. 'Yes, I've settled in nicely, and Warwickshire has been everything you said it would be and so much more. I can't even begin to tell you how much I love being here. I've met so many nice friends, and many of them are Irish like myself. Oh, and my shop name is Miss Hatton. I promised I'd tell you. And, Mrs Davies, you'll be happy to know that I'm going out ballroom dancing for the first time with some friends this coming Saturday. They go almost every week.'

'Oh, that's so lovely to hear, Maureen. I had a good feeling that you would make good use of it. Now wasn't it worth the effort?'

'It was, Mrs Davies, and so much more.'

'Well, Maureen, I shan't hold you up. It's wonderful to see how well you've made the adjustment, and you're obviously doing a wonderful job. Do keep it up, and the best of luck to you. I will give your regards to Mr Davies and Beatrice. Bye, Maureen, and God bless.'

'Goodbye, Mrs Davies. Thanks so much for thinking of me and stopping by.'

I watch her walk away, knowing as I always have that I can never fully express to her my gratitude and thanks. It is to her that I owe my being here at Bourne & Hollingsworth and my new life at the hostel. I could scarcely tell her in a few minutes how much she has changed my life, but I'm sure she knows and that means the world to me.

It's Saturday evening, and I feel giddy and nervous dressed in my best plaid skirt and sweater. Margo looks so much more sophisticated than I do in her long flowing skirt and dressy blouse. Her wardrobe is full of the most beautiful clothes, and she has an almost movie-star glamour about her. I still don't have many clothes: only a couple of skirts and blouses that I wear all the time. Now I'll have to put some money aside and update my own wardrobe as soon as possible. My gross pay is six pounds a week, only three pounds of which I take home, plus the pittance of commission I make. The remainder is deducted for room and board.

Elaine Matheson is joining us as planned, as is another English girl from a different department, Diana Stanley. The four of us hit the Underground and head off towards the Strand and the Lyceum Ballroom full of chatter and anticipation. 'Now, Maureen,' Margo begins, 'at the Lyceum Ballroom, the hordes of handsome young men who are sure to be there all congregate in one spot. They gawk at all the young women who gather in another spot, waiting to be asked for a dance and . . .'

'But, Margo, dear, you must caution Maureen on the asking etiquette!' This is Elaine, butting in with some further advice for me. 'If a man asks you to dance once or twice, well, that's fine. But if after a third dance he asks, "Can I buy you a mineral?" that means he wants to take you home. Home as in back to Warwickshire before eleven and curfew. He's trying to tell you while remaining within proper etiquette that he would like to see you again, just the two of you, for a date.'

'Why tell me all this? I'll be lucky to get a single dance in tonight. I think I'll just watch everything and take it all in.'

'Watch? Take it all in?' Diana repeats in mock reproach. 'Why, Maureen, love, you will dance a waltz tonight at the Lyceum!'

'Or a foxtrot or the quickstep, the samba or the cha-cha, and perhaps you'll even jive! Can you handle all that in a single night, Maureen?' Elaine says, playfully interrogating me.

'Stop it! My head is spinning!'

This good-natured teasing increases both my curiosity and my nervousness, and after a brief walk from Charing Cross station Margo points out the flashing lights of the Lyceum's dazzling marquee just ahead. 'We're here,' she announces. 'Everyone get out your five shillings!'

After paying at one of the two windows, we enter the ballroom lobby, and my breath is taken away by everything I see. I fall instantly in love with it. I can't believe I'm in a place like this! I feel more awe-struck than anything. What glamour! We check our coats in, and the four of us go from the lobby to the main ballroom. The twelve-piece band is already in full swing, belting out an up-tempo number. The four of us make our way to the obvious throng of women crowded on one side at the back. Across the floor are all the men, some seeming to watch like hawks for any new arrivals, and I actually blush as I feel distant eyes cast upon us.

'Well, Maureen, what do you think?' Margo shouts out over the pulse of the music. 'The stage rotates! When the one band is finished, the entire thing turns round and the next band strikes up! It's wonderful!'

'Oh, Margo, it's incredible. I love it, I really do. Look at the ceiling!'

High above the dancers hang enormous chandeliers and placed around them like tiny silver planets around a sun are globes that glitter and sparkle. I watch with amazement as the glitter balls reflect light in little beams across the floor as they turn. I can feel the energy and the charged atmosphere in the air, and I begin to feed off it. As we watch and wait by the benches at the wall near the back, I can't help but notice the few men who walk slowly by the girls as if window-shopping. My eyes look to the floor as they pass. 'Don't mind those blokes, Maureen,' Elaine quips, but still I shrink back as they pass. 'They're all ego, little else. They're what we call the cattle buyers.'

'That's right,' Margo chimes in. 'They walk by looking the girls up and down as if we were a load of cows at auction!' This is met with roars of hearty laughter from all of us, and I know without doubt that ballroom dancing is going to be a big part of my social life from now on.

The band continues to play all the hits: the big-band music of Glenn Miller, Tommy Dorsey, Nat King Cole and others. I sit with Margo and the others on the long benches at the side of the dance floor, waiting for the young men to come and ask us for a dance. I'm told that when a man asks a girl to dance, she would never think of refusing. And indeed it isn't long before all three of my friends have been asked out onto the dance floor. I don't think about being asked to dance, and as the night passes I find reasons to hide at the very back. I'm content to stay sitting as Margo, Elaine and Diana dance up a storm. It's nothing to them with their abundance of confidence. 'Maybe the next one,' I say with a casual wave of my arm when they try to get me to look interested, or, 'Ah, sure, I'm just taking everything in.'

But eventually, thanks to some serious detective work, Margo thinks she spots an equally shy young man hanging back across the way, and she all but pushes me out into his line of sight. Her crazy ploy works, and I find myself being approached by a slim young man. 'Would you like to have this waltz with me?'

'I would,' I reply, easily outdoing him in the shyness department and hoping my blushing doesn't show under the lights. We take to the floor, and I allow the easy familiar music and the rhythm of the waltz to move me around the floor. I feel elated just to be able to do it and to be dancing with this bashful young man across from me. Thank you again, Mrs Davies, for talking me into taking dancing lessons! I can't even imagine now not being able to dance and having to miss out on all this.

I can feel the stray beams from the ceiling globes pass over my face, and as we spin I fix my best smile and avoid my partner's coy glances as I bask in the mood and atmosphere. The dance finishes, we thank one another and part. I walk back to find my friends, entirely pleased with my performance. Now that I've actually had my first dance with a young man, I love it. I love everything about the Lyceum and will definitely look forward to many more nights like this one.

The four of us pour out of the ballroom just before half-past ten in time to make our curfew. We chatter away amidst much giggling after what was nothing short of a magical night out. 'Well, Maureen,' Diana enquires, 'now that you've been introduced to ballroom dancing officially, how does it feel?'

'Oh, Diana, I loved it so much. It was wonderful! What a beautiful place. I can't wait to go again.'

'One night we'll take you over to the Hammersmith Palais,' Elaine adds, 'another lovely ballroom.'

'Oh, we won't be leaving it too long,' Margo says. 'And if you ever want to borrow a dress, Maureen, I'll loan you one of mine.'

'Thank you, Miss Manley. I might just take you up on that offer.'

'Don't mention it, Miss Hatton,' she replies in a posh voice. 'Now let us be gone before the golden carriage – that's the tube – turns into a pumpkin. Miss Nicholas will be there looking at her watch and proclaiming, "Miss Hatton, Miss Manning, Miss Manley and Miss Stoughton! What are you doing in that decrepit pumpkin? It's one minute after curfew!"' We all laugh at Margo's endlessly imaginative humour and quickly make our way to Charing Cross station and home before curfew strikes.

❧ THIRTY-FIVE ❧

Life is never lonely at the hostel. When Margo is out doing something without me, there's always someone knocking at my door wanting to go to the pictures or any of the number of other things going on in London. I also begin to go to Irish dance clubs, which is a totally different experience from that at the flashy Lyceum. The Blarney Club, a place off Tottenham Court Road, down some steps, is a lot smaller than the huge ballrooms we go to. There is a stage where accordion and fiddle groups play old-time Irish waltzes and quicksteps. Later, when things get going, sets are played and 'The Siege of Ennis' and 'The Walls of Limerick' are sung. The Blarney Club throws both afternoon and evening dances on a Sunday, and sometimes we'll end up going to both. Margo or one of the other Irish girls will meet a man, usually an Irishman, at the afternoon dance. 'Will you meet me here this evening?' he'll ask her, and a date is made. It's accepted that the fellow will pay the girl's way for the evening dance.

For the young Irish men and women in London, it's a great way to be among our own kind and support one another. Sometimes, the atmosphere gets quite lively, and occasionally it can be a bit rough, what with many of the Irishmen arriving at the afternoon and evening dances by way of the local pubs first. The dances themselves are without drink. The Round Tower is another famous Irish dance club, situated in Hammersmith at Seven Sisters Road and Holloway Road, although I've only been there once so far.

Abby Collins has also moved on. She's left her position in service as a nanny for a job at Selfridges, a major competitor of Bourne & Hollingsworth. She did try to get into Bourne & Hollingsworth and would have joined me at the hostel, but the timing wasn't right. She and Margo hit it off right away, and we're part of a larger group of friends now.

Around the same time, one of Margo's many sisters was hired by the department store, and she shares a room with another girl on the floor above us. Isobel, or Izzy as we call her, is an absolute delight. I just adore her. She's tall and thin, with dark hair and brown, laughing eyes, and she's so talkative. These Galway girls: they'd talk you into knots if you listened long enough. Izzy has an amazing sense of humour, and we're often on the floor with laughter, watching her mimic the funny characters from back home. I could listen all day to the tales she and Margo tell about the local people in their village and their funny country ways, and the kitchen ceilidhs, where friends and neighbours gather to sing and dance to fiddle and accordion music. Margo herself has a beautiful singing voice, and she belts out all the latest tunes. And when she and her sister get excited, their west Ireland accents get faster and faster until they're almost firing the words out at you.

Through Mrs Burke's occasional letters, I've managed to stay in touch with Mrs Hughes in Mullingar. I've also written twice more to Sister Brendan, who's now a full reverend mother. I asked her again in my most recent letter if she might send me addresses for Maggie, Lucy and Katy Fallon. When I write to Mrs Burke these days, I can't resist the impulse to mention my successes big and small. It's very important to me that they know I am doing well in England. Naturally, Mrs Burke will share my news with all the neighbours in Mullingar, and that makes me feel good. I want them to know that Maureen Harte the orphan is doing well and making it on her own, and though I can't say that I miss Mrs Hughes in a truly emotional sense, I still feel a very strong connection to her.

All mail for the girls in the hostel goes through Mr Henning, and today he hands me two letters at the front desk as I sign in after work. One I know is from Mullingar, as I recognise Mrs Burke's familiar hand. The other has the return address 'Convent of Mercy, Newtownforbes, Co. Longford, Eire' and is obviously from Reverend Mother Brendan. I rush impatiently up to my room, where I can read them in privacy. I pray with all my heart that Mother Brendan's letter has what I've been waiting for: Maggie, Lucy and Katy's addresses.

Opening Mrs Burke's letter first, I skim through the lines quickly, knowing that she'll have much the same news for me as always: Mrs Hughes is fine, I'm welcome back any time and all the neighbours remember me and send their best wishes. I read on but stop abruptly, saddened to read of Mr Hughes' sudden passing. Poor Mrs Hughes, alone again after the death of her second husband. She'll miss him dearly, and I must write back to offer my condolences and try to say something to let her know I'm thinking of her. Or better still, perhaps I can find time and enough money to go back for a visit.

Saddened by this news, I put Mrs Burke's letter down on the dresser and take up the other one with less excitement. I open the envelope and unfold the thin blue writing paper Reverend Mother Brendan always uses and begin to read.

Dear Maureen,

I'm delighted to hear you are getting along so well in London and very blessed I see that the family you were in service with have done what they have for you and got you the job you now have. What a lovely family they seem. Each day all the sisters and myself pray for all of the girls who've gone out into the world and for the protection of God over you all. With respect to your queries, I have heard from Maggie O'Rourke and Katy Fallon and have enclosed both addresses should you want to write to them. You will be very pleased to hear that Maggie is living in London and working in a hospital. She is on the cleaning staff there, so perhaps the two of you will find time to meet should you choose to contact her. Katy doesn't write very often, and she tells me very little about her life. However, Maureen, now you may write yourself to both of them. We are all praying for you.

May God bless you always,

Sincerely in Christ,

Rev. M. Brendan

By the time I read the last line of the letter, I'm pacing the room with restless excitement and tears fill my eyes. Maggie in London – I can't believe it. She's so close. She's actually living here in London. What incredible news this is! I sit on my bed and cry, touched by Reverend Mother Brendan's words that all the nuns pray for us. I am also stunned by the news that Maggie is here, and so pleased to have received Katy's address as well. In truth, I didn't hold out much hope that I would hear news this wonderful. But what about Lucy? I asked for her address as well. I wonder why Reverend Mother Brendan didn't mention her. There's no way to know. I must write to Maggie and Katy immediately.

Some little thing I've held onto has given way inside me, and my tears are of pure relief and joy. I've found my dear friends. My leaving day flashes before me, as vividly as if I were living it all again. That was the last time I saw Maggie's face, the moment before I walked out of Reverend Mother Brendan's classroom and into the outside world.

I wish I could run down to Mr Henning's desk and phone Maggie right now, but that isn't possible. Now that I know that I can reach them, I'm going to go ahead and do something I've dreamed of doing for a long time now. I'm going to write to Maggie and Katy and suggest that the three of us meet in Ireland and return to the orphanage. How I've dreamed of doing that. I want to show Reverend Mother Brendan how well I've done in the world, and I want her to be proud of me when I return. If I can arrange such a reunion, I will go to visit Mrs Hughes, too, but the truth is that I feel much more drawn to the orphanage than to Mullingar. In many ways, it will be like going home, the only home I knew for thirteen years. More than anything, though, I long to hear those coveted words of approval from Reverend Mother Brendan and some of the others. That is the magnet that is pulling me back to the old grey buildings.

The next day, I sent two quick letters off, hoping to hear back from Maggie right away and only briefly mentioning the idea of a reunion to her. If I'd known where exactly to find her, I'd have gone right over, but London is a big place, and after the incident in Soho I didn't want to take any chances and wander off to the East End on my own.

Then, this evening while lounging alone in my room, after having waited for two anxious weeks, I hear the familiar static of the hostel's public address system crackle into life. 'Miss Hatton, room two-zero-seven, phone call. Please come down to the front desk. Miss Hatton, phone call.'

I fly out of the room and down to Mr Henning's desk. I'd left Maggie the number here, and it surely couldn't be anyone else. 'Well, that was fast, Miss Hatton,' Mr Henning says in his friendly way. 'Go ahead. You can pick up now.'

I pick up the telephone, shaking with excitement and emotion. 'Hello?'

'Hello, Maureen. It's Maggie calling.' I hear the same quiet voice, but I can detect the nervous excited edge in her voice. Surely she feels as strange as I do after all this time.

'Hello, Maggie! How are you? I was expecting a letter. I didn't know if you'd call and take a chance on getting me in at the hostel. I just can't believe I'm hearing your voice again. This is so wonderful! I'm glad you remembered to ask for Miss Hatton.'

Maggie chuckles quietly on the other end of the line. She sounds so happy to be talking to me. 'I laughed at that, Maureen, when you explained it in the letter. Miss Hatton indeed.'

'I know! I've been given a title! But listen, Maggie, when do you think we can meet?'

'I work odd shifts here at the hospital, but maybe in a week's time I can come up to the hostel to see you. I know my way around a bit better now, and I'll try to make it on a Sunday when you have the whole day off.'

'Oh, that would be wonderful, and maybe I'll have a letter from Katy soon. Is there a number where I can call you and leave a message or maybe arrange a time to call?'

'There is. I'll give it to you now!'

As I write down the number, I blurt out in my enthusiasm, 'Wouldn't it be something if you, Katy and me could have a reunion and go back to Ireland and see Reverend Mother Brendan?'

This is greeted by dead silence on the other end. I must have taken her totally off guard, though I did broach the subject in my letter. Finally, she says something. 'Well, Maureen, I'll see. I have mixed feelings about it, you know? I'd never thought about going back before you suggested it, though I do admit that I'd like to see some of the sisters I was fond of: Mother Brendan and Sister Michael. But listen, my break's almost over. I'll think about it and see what time would be best to travel. I wish we had an hour to talk. I can't believe I'm actually hearing your voice. It's so . . . unbelievable! But, really, I must go now or I'll hear about it. I'll see you in a week. Goodbye, and God bless, Maureen!'

'Bye, Maggie. God bless!'

I put down the telephone with great hopes that our reunion will take place. I hadn't considered when I asked Maggie that she might not ever want to see the orphanage again, but she seems fairly interested for the same reasons as me: to see those nuns who meant a lot to her. I forget that maybe some orphans might not feel as I do. Maggie and I have grown away from one another, and we're making our own choices in life now.

A week after my telephone call with Maggie, I receive a reply from Katy. It's a very short letter, and all I learn is that she's still living with her adopted family in Cloonfad. It must be hard for her to know what to say to me after all these years. It's been almost ten years since I've laid eyes on her. When I get together with Maggie, I'll bring up my idea of going back to Ireland again, and we can discuss how best to convince Katy to join us.

❖ THIRTY-SIX ❖

I tremble with anticipation every time the door swings open, waiting for Maggie to walk into the front lobby of Warwickshire House. What will she look like, and how will she be dressed? What will we talk about after all this time? Then I see her: Maggie O'Rourke, who is like a sister to me and has shared a childhood with me. She walks up to me smiling, and we just stand looking at one another, speechless and wondering where to begin. 'Maggie,' I begin, 'I . . . I can't believe we're together again and that you're here living in London at the same time as me. I can't believe it!' I can't resist moving forward and giving her a warm hug. She shrinks a little from my embrace before saying, 'I know, Maureen, I know.'

Her face is a struggling mask of shifting emotions: joy, shyness and delight. She seems close to tears, but she won't let herself go that far. 'Oh, Maureen!' she says finally, after standing like that for a time. 'I'm sorry. This is hard for me. I feel shocked, and I can't believe we're together. The last time I saw you . . . it was your leaving day, and there you were . . .'

We both begin to cry quietly, and we hug again. We stand back and just gaze into each other's bewildered faces, almost unable to accept the fact that we're together again, here in the outside world. We quickly wipe away the tears, regaining the shared composure we are so much more comfortable with. 'Come on,' I say. 'We'll go into the lounge and sit and talk before my friends come down. They're looking forward to meeting you.'

'So, do you think I've changed a lot?' I ask her when we're seated.

'Oh yes,' she answers. 'You dress so nicely now, and you look so grown up, but I'd still know you. Your face hasn't changed much. What about me? Do you think I've changed?'

'You have, but your hair looks just the same.'

'Ah,' she answers, 'it is, and I haven't grown much. Not like you.'

We chat easily, but we are both aware of the strangeness of this reunion. I feel like I'm meeting a family member I've not seen in a long time. A part of me, which I hide well, is surprised at Maggie's appearance. She still has the look of the orphan about her, and the way she carries herself and her hair is just the same as we all wore it at the orphanage. Her personality is exactly the same: kind, warm and unassuming. It occurs to me as we sit across from one another that I likely expected her to be a lot like I am now: more stylish and outgoing, chatty and maybe even a little giggly. But she has a frumpy look about her. She's dressed drably, and her manner is still more reserved and quieter than mine. She seems almost old fashioned. It occurs to me that Maggie had no one like Mrs Davies to teach her how to be fashionable. How very fortunate I've been.

'Oh, Maureen, I must tell you,' Maggie says, 'how Lucy and I envied you so much on your leaving day. We cried many a night after you left and missed you awfully. But tell me why you're not still living with your mother in Mullingar? What caused you to leave there, Maureen? You said nothing of it in your letter.'

'She's not my mother,' I quietly admit.

'What?' She's stunned by this response.

'It's a long story. Mrs Hughes is the one who brought me to the orphanage when I was three. My real mother gave me up to her and her first husband. She and her first husband agreed to raise me, since I was a baby, so by rights she was my legal guardian. But he died, and I was brought to the nuns. Don't ask me about all the years in between. I haven't a clue why she stayed away. It's all very strange and mysterious. But listen to this, Maggie. I was only out of the orphanage and living in Mullingar for six months before I moved to England. I spent some months in service, as a maid for a professor and his family. Then, with only weeks to go before my departure, Mrs Hughes tells me one night, right out of the blue, that she's not my real mother! I was so shocked and heartbroken. It is almost three years ago now since I found out the truth.'

Maggie shakes her head sadly as she hears this. 'Goodness, Maureen, I can't believe what you're telling me. I'm so sorry. Why on earth did the nuns tell you that she was your mother? What could their reasoning have been?'

'I've no answers to that question, either. There's so much I don't know or wasn't told. I've no idea where my real mother is, but I know her name. It's Annie, Annie Harte, and I want to find her some day. There's a very good chance she's still alive. I believe she is, or at least I pray to God every day that she is and that I will find her.'

'Annie Harte.' Maggie repeats the name almost in a whisper to herself. I know she's thinking that I now know the name of my biological mother and that it's something she'll likely never discover about herself.

I tell Maggie about the long talk with Mrs Hughes by the fire, and all I discovered about the day I came to the orphanage. I tell her of Mrs Hughes' one return visit and how she found me in such terrible shape, with a shaved head and covered in ringworm. She listens in total fascination to the story, wondering, I'm sure, what it was like for me to be told so much about my past. 'Do you ever want to know about your background?' I ask her.

'Oh, I think about it sometimes, but I wouldn't know where to begin looking,' she answers, looking aside and shaking her head in a dismissive gesture. 'I know nothing of where or how I was born. I must have been only a baby when I was placed in the orphanage. I have no other memories at all.'

We don't linger on the subject, nor do we bring up our past in the orphanage. It's enough just being together for now and being a world away from the place where those terrible memories stem from. The past is frightening, and we are not at all ready to deal with it. The memories are with us, but where do we begin?

When I raise the matter of a reunion at the orphanage, I'm delighted when Maggie agrees in her easy-going way. She admits that she'd never make the move on her own. 'I honestly try to forget the place,' she says bitterly. 'Except for Mother Brendan, Sister Carmel and Sister Michael. It's too upsetting to think about. I'm already becoming nervous at the thought of going back there.'

The others are late coming down, and growing more comfortable with one another by the minute Maggie and I sit chatting and catching up on our lives. She speaks of her leaving day four months after mine, admitting that for her the biggest worry was her placement in service. She worried herself sick, wondering whether the people would accept her and treat her decently. 'Where was that, where they placed you?' I ask her, dying to know, for wasn't that all we spoke of as older girls outside in the cloisters?

'In County Sligo, it was, with a doctor, his wife and their three children. They treated me well, but right from the start I wanted out of service. I was there for two years when I met a girl home from England, and luck was with me, thank God. We became friends, and she told me about the hospital. She helped with everything I had to do to get over here: writing for a position, the passport, the accommodation, all of it. I had to go, Maureen, and that was my chance. So I went. And here I am.'

'How lucky you were to get that break, and how brave of you to act on it.'

'I know, and I'll never go back to Ireland to live, Maureen, never! I love it in England. And I've made friends, too. I share a room close to the hospital with a nice English girl. She's in housekeeping, like me.'

A voice behind me brings us back to the present. 'Oh, there you are, Maureen,' Margo says, walking over to us.

'This is my friend, Margo McCormack, and her sister, Izzy,' I say, introducing Maggie. 'Margo's my roommate.'

'Hello,' Maggie answers shyly. In her sudden discomfort, I suddenly see what I must seem like when I meet people, and she seems even less outgoing than I am.

'It's lovely to meet you, Maggie,' Margo says. 'Come on, let's go, Maureen. Do you still want to go to Lyon's Corner first? Or do you want to go walking in the park and then go to Lyon's Corner?'

'Let's head to Lyon's Corner first. Then we'll go to the park.'

Then, to Maggie, I say, 'Don't mind Margo. She's always like this. Never stops, that one.'

The four of us head off towards the Lyon's Corner House restaurant in Leicester Square. The Corner House, as we call it, is situated right in the heart of the West End and is very popular with young people, especially after the theatre or a night at the pictures. It's one of our favourite hangouts and a great meeting place. 'I'll meet you at the Corner House' is a familiar phrase among my crowd at Warwickshire House. The restaurant has a huge number of tables, a long rail at the buffet-type brasserie and lovely brass work throughout.

The four of us head in the general direction of Leicester Square, looking forward to spending a lovely day together. 'Do you have any idea what happened to Lucy?' I ask Maggie quietly as the others move off ahead, leaving us space to talk.

'I honestly don't,' she says, shaking her head. 'Mother Brendan would've given me her address had she known, surely. Or maybe there's a reason why she can't or won't give us her address. You never know, Maureen, with the sisters. They never were ones for telling us much.'

'I wonder how Lucy made out and if she's all right?' I say. 'She'd a very nervous temperament, didn't she?'

'We can only hope she got a good placement and has found some peace.'

We walk on through London, the same familiar quiet between us that we're so used to. We need no words to share our memories. Margo and Izzy walk ahead of us, laughing and carrying on as usual.

'Won't it be lovely, the three of us together again,' I say, looking across at Maggie.

'It will be strange,' she answers softly, pausing a moment. 'It will be so strange to go back there, the three of us together. I'm happy you wrote for my address, Maureen.'

'Yoo-hoo, you two!' Margo calls back at us. 'Christ, will ye's come on! You're as slow as a wet week!'

Maggie and I race to catch up with the others. We move off into the crowds of London, four Irish girls laughing and happy and enjoying being young and alive.

❦ THIRTY-SEVEN ❦

It is gone half-past three in the morning, and Maggie and I are standing on the docks at Holyhead, waiting in line to board the ferry to Dún Laoghaire in Dublin. The ferry is bathed in floodlights as workers move about getting the boat ready to depart. Beyond the docks, all is cloaked in night. Tiny distant points of light fade into the distance, dotted like stars against the blackness. They could be anything: maybe the lights of a small sleeping seaside town. The heavy salt air and the smell of the sea round the docks sharpens my memories of that first journey to England.

'Have your passports and any papers ready, please!' The line inches forward, and we begin to board the ferry. I have butterflies in my tummy I feel so wound up. Not able to afford berths, we find a section of benches in a large covered area of the upper deck for this night crossing of the Irish Sea. We'll not sleep much, I suspect, both of us anxious and with much still to talk about.

As the ferry moves slowly away from the docks at Holyhead towards the open sea, a light salty sea breeze blows across the open upper decks. Maggie gazes off with that thoughtful far-away look on her face, an expression I know well. The time and the mood seems right, and I decide to feel her out a little about our shared past in the orphanage. I'm very curious to know how she feels about it now. 'Do you think often,' I begin, 'of what we've been through?'

'Every day, Maureen. Now that I've left and have seen what life is really like, I can't believe all that we saw in there.' She wraps her sweater tighter, as if chilled by the memories. 'But it's so different now.'

I turn to look at her. 'How so?'

She stares ahead silently for a moment before answering. 'I don't know. It all seemed the same in the orphanage. One day was the same as the next, and all there was to think about was the day we would leave for good. But when I got out, I realised how bad it really was in there. My God, Maureen, they treated us terribly.'

'It's strange you should say that,' I tell her. 'I've thought about it that way so many times.' A long silence hangs between us. Only the salt breeze and the easy motion of the ship moving through the water whisper in the night. 'Poor Colleen. She never had a chance. I wonder if she's alive today.'

'She didn't, did she?' Maggie says. 'It was terrible what happened to her.'

Another long silence seems to bring it all closer, here in the middle of an August night on the open sea. This mention of Colleen, sent to the mad house at the age of twelve, strikes a note of sudden anger in me, and I can feel the bitter emotions begin to rise. 'She was a normal enough child, Maggie, until Anthony turned her into the total cripple she became.'

'I know, Maureen. I feel like we watched them take her life away, right in front of our eyes. The only reason that she and the other bed-wetters couldn't stop was because they were terrified. Every single day of their life was lived in fear.'

I feel the old lump in my throat. Colleen might be sitting here in place of either of us had things been slightly different. I think of this often: why some of us made it out while others met with such terrible odds. 'How very innocent we were when we first left the orphanage,' I say. 'How on earth did we get so far?'

'I don't know, but I couldn't say a word to anyone when I left. I always felt different, like people were staring at me and knew about my past – the same way I felt when the nuns took us through the village and the people gawked at us. The shame of it all. But I'm getting better. I am a lot better now. But, Maureen, I'm better because I left Ireland. Had I stayed a maid in Sligo, I'm not so sure I would have changed at all.'

Her words tell me a lot: that we were right to get out of Ireland and that we experienced the same problems after leaving. The ferry floats lazily up and down over the gentle swells. I stare into the distance towards the horizon, the sky a shade lighter where it meets the water. I am looking forward to seeing Mrs Hughes and Mrs Burke and all the friendly neighbours in Mullingar. But my mind is on the orphanage and Reverend Mother Brendan and the old grey buildings that were my only home for thirteen long years. I wrap my light coat tighter around me, pulling up the collar and closing my eyes in the hope of a little sleep on the hard bench before we reach Dublin.

It is daylight when we dock at Dún Laoghaire, and though stiff and tired we're grateful that at least the wicked Irish Sea was kinder on this summer crossing and neither of us was seasick during the night. At Westland Row, we board the train to Newtownforbes, the final leg of our journey. The train ride brings back many good memories of my first time away from the orphanage, but so much has changed inside me now, and I see the same passing sights through different eyes. Maggie and I chat throughout the journey, both of us trying to hide our anxiety. 'Where do you think they'll put us up for the night?' I ask her. 'It won't be in the dormitory, will it?'

'It might be that room off the senior dormitory,' she answers. 'It was a sickroom, wasn't it? The little spare one the nuns never used.'

'That means we'll be right inside the dormitory still and locked down for the night. I wonder what that'll feel like?'

'We'll know soon enough, Maureen.'

The month of August is often beautiful in Ireland, and upon arriving at the little station of Newtownforbes there are roses in full bloom and other wild flowers growing along the hedges running each side of the railway tracks. The station hasn't changed. It's still as pretty as I remember it, with the climbing roses on the outside walls of the old building and the lovely colourful flowerbeds. With our battered old suitcases in tow, we step onto the platform from the train. We stand for a few moments looking at the pretty old station. Suddenly, I feel a strong sense of the Irish in me. I am truly home. 'Oh, Maggie, I'd no idea how much I missed these little things! Can you smell the air? I'd almost forgotten all this. The fields, the flowers and the sheer greenness of it all.'

Taking a deep breath of fresh air, we start down the quiet country road towards the orphanage. We pass the boarding school, and then the convent farm comes into view just beyond the school. Here we stop, staring in silence at the cow byres and the outbuildings and sheds we remember so well. Maggie and I say nothing to one another, lost in memories of the past. We lived it all together, and we need no words now. I think of my cow Primrose, wondering if she's still alive, and I have to resist the impulse to run down to the paddock to look for her. We walk on silently.

As we round the final bend, the drab old buildings show themselves as grey and threatening as ever. 'Almost there,' I say, instantly nervous and my stomach churning. Maggie's expression is blank, revealing nothing as we stand a few yards back from the high black wrought-iron gates at the entrance to the convent.

'Oh, Maureen, it just hit me. We're really here. I feel so nervous. It's seeing the old buildings again. My God, did we really spend so many years here? I don't like it.'

'I know. Let's just stand here a moment and take a few deep breaths before we go in.' Both of us had underestimated the effect coming back here would have on us. We stand and stare for a good minute before finally going through the gates.

Just inside is the big statue of the Sacred Heart, standing with arms open as if welcoming us home. It takes me a further moment standing before the beautiful ornamental doors to find the courage to ring the bell. It booms and echoes eerily through the halls within, and I distract myself by looking at the patterns in the door's woodwork. Long moments pass before the door opens, and a young novice greets us. 'Good morning. Is someone expecting you?'

'Yes. I'm Maureen Harte, and this is Maggie O'Rourke.'

'Reverend Mother Brendan is expecting you. Come in, please.'

We are shown into the beautiful parlour that we haven't seen since our Confirmation day, some seven or eight years ago now. The novice leaves us to summon Reverend Mother Brendan, and the two of us sit like statues, afraid to open our mouths. We're like two orphans again: frightened, fearful and waiting to be punished.

The silence is broken by the sound of footsteps and rattling rosary beads getting closer and louder before being joined by the dry swishing of robes. Only when Reverend Mother Brendan enters the parlour and I see her warm smile and brown eyes do I relax. We stand as she enters, reaching out to shake hands with her. I feel a thrill go through me, and the feeling that I've come home rises up in me strongly. I can even smell the fresh soapy smell that fascinated me as a little girl. I know at this moment that she alone is the reason I've come back.

'You are both very welcome, girls. Please sit down. Look at you both. You look wonderful, so grown up! I know you must be wondering about Katy. She will be here shortly. I've sent for some refreshments, girls, now please sit down.'

This warm welcome puts me more at ease, and we take our seats again, waiting respectfully for Reverend Mother Brendan to speak. She looks at the two of us, smiling in a way that takes me back many years. 'Well, look at the two of you,' she says. 'I'd hardly know you at all. Two lovely young ladies, you really are, and look how smartly you're dressed.'

We beam inside hearing this compliment from her. She must think that we've done well. There are more rustling sounds outside the door, and the novice walks in with a tray of drinks and a tea set. Reverend Mother Brendan smiles and nods to the novice as she sets the tray down quietly before leaving the parlour. As we chat, I begin to feel very strange sitting here as a free person and a visitor. It seems odd, and I almost feel out of place.

'Girls,' Reverend Mother Brendan begins, 'there are many temptations in a big city like London. You'll meet all kinds, and you must watch the company you keep and always keep your faith. A special devotion to the Virgin Mary will help you be stronger and to resist those temptations.'

'Yes, Reverend Mother,' I answer, reassuring her. 'I go to mass every Sunday, and all of my closest friends in the hostel are Irish and Catholics, and I belong to a sodality as well.'

'And you, Maggie?' Reverend Mother Brendan asks, turning to await a response.

'Well,' replies Maggie, 'at the hospital there are a lot of Irish girls, and I go to church with them regularly.'

'Oh, this is very good news indeed,' she says, leaning back in her chair and clasping her hands in her lap. 'We do pray for every girl who leaves here.'

The deep boom of the doorbell echoes again through the halls. I hear more rattling beads and the rustle of garments and footsteps as the novice goes to answer it. Moments later, there's a soft knock on the parlour door and in walks Katy. I stand up, but when our eyes meet I start to cry. I can't help it. Maggie's eyes mist up, and Katy has some tears in her eyes, too. But my joy at seeing Katy is mingled with a terrible, almost unbelievable shock at her appearance. I feel confused by my own eyes, and I fight to hide my reaction. Katy is so much heavier than I'd imagined she'd be, and she hasn't grown very tall. Dressed in outdated and drab clothing, her hair is exactly the way it was ten years ago, parted on the side and pulled back from her face with a plain black clip. Her shoes are the same as the ones we all wore in the orphanage: a plain, low black boot. How can this be? I'd expected a very different Katy to walk through that door: a grown-up version of the bright beautiful girl who was my best friend before they took her away. What has happened to her? Please, Maureen, don't show your shock. Something tells me Katy doesn't need that. I don't dare look at Maggie.

'Hello, Katy,' Reverend Mother Brendan says. 'I am delighted to see you, just delighted.' She looks from one of us to the other. 'This is really great, having the three of you together again. It's wonderful. Katy, won't you sit down beside Maggie?'

'Thank you, Reverend Mother,' Katy answers quietly.

'Now, girls, I've ordered a nice lunch for us. But before we eat, Katy, I've just been hearing about Maggie and Maureen and their new lives in England. Will you tell us a little of your life now? You left here when you were ten. It's been, what, ten years now? What have you been doing in that time?'

'Yes, Reverend Mother. Ten years it's been since I was adopted from here.' Katy seems uneasy, keeping her head down and avoiding looking at any of us. The directness of her next words shocks me further. 'Well, I've not really been treated like a daughter. It wasn't like that, not at all. What I mean is . . .' She stops talking and looks down at the floor, turning the toes of her worn black boots towards one another. My shock deepens, and I feel almost numb. Katy's speech seems slow and backward. I feel like I'm staring at a grown version of what we looked like then in the orphanage.

'Go on, Katy, tell us. It's all right,' Mother Brendan says encouragingly.

'What I mean is,' Katy goes on, 'that they adopted me out of the orphanage so I could do farm work for them and be their maid. I've never felt like anything else but that – a maid. I've been treated like a skivvy, Reverend Mother . . . that's the truth of it.'

Maggie and I glance at one another in disbelief, while Reverend Mother Brendan cannot hide her own shock and obvious discomfort at this announcement. Katy talks slowly, and her voice is flat with no emotion in it. But I can sense the dull anger as she continues. 'And that's all I am today, and that's all I've been since the day they adopted me when I was ten. They didn't allow me to stay in school or have any other life than being a servant. You know, Reverend Mother, how I loved school. I was good in school, I was. I missed my friends terribly, and the loneliness was awful!'

Katy stops talking again, and there is silence. She looks down at the floor, sad but not crying. She seems full of shame and humiliation. Only now, through the numbness and shock of seeing her like this, does it hit me. My God, Maggie must be thinking the same thing. The morning Katy was adopted, ten of us were placed in a circle. I will never forget how I had prayed to God to be the one who was picked. My whole future hung there for a moment, and for some reason they didn't pick me. Everything that has happened to me rushes by in an instant: the parcel, Mrs Hughes, the O'Neills, Mrs Davies. I'm very glad I'm sitting down, because I don't know what to feel or think right now. Only that we must somehow try to help Katy.

Reverend Mother Brendan must realise how this has made us feel, and she says quietly, 'Now girls, this news has been difficult for all of you, and it will be enough for now. I think that a good meal will help. The nuns who know you and have taught you will be dropping by to see you later, here in the parlour.'

The three of us are distracted by the beautiful meal and by the special treatment we're receiving. But what we've just heard about Katy's sad fate and the truth of our past in this place seems at odds with the good food and the fancy furniture of the parlour. 'You can go down for the evening recreation period and join the children for the Rosary,' Reverend Mother Brendan is saying. 'Sister Sacred Heart will be with them.'

Shortly after our meal, the nuns begin to appear, one by one, starting with Sister Carmel. 'Good afternoon, girls,' Sister Carmel says in greeting. 'I cannot believe the three of you are here together. What a lovely reunion.'

'Aren't they looking wonderful?' Reverend Mother Brendan says. 'Look how tall Maureen is.'

Sister Carmel takes hold of our hands in hers. 'It's absolutely wonderful to see you. Tell me what you've been doing.'

After Sister Carmel leaves, Sister Sacred Heart enters the parlour. Sister Sacred Heart is followed by Sister Edna, then another and so on. Just as I'm thinking I'll be spared a visit from Sister Anthony, I look up to see her walking into the parlour. My stomach churns at the sight of her, and I'm not prepared for what happens to me. I suddenly feel detached from the parlour and very weak. Things seem far away. My head feels dizzy, and my skin is all cold and tingling. I try to talk myself out of it. Come on, Maureen. Don't let her do this to you. She can't hurt you any more. She can't touch you. The feeling slowly recedes, and I get a hold of myself.

When our eyes finally meet, some of my fear has turned to anger. How dare you stand there and smile at me like that, so mildly, so . . . calmly! For only a moment, our eyes lock. I know exactly what she's thinking. She's remembering the terrible beating she gave me that night in the dormitory, and we both know it. I could barely walk the next morning.

Sister Anthony doesn't stay long. Duty done, she turns and leaves the parlour politely. She can no longer hurt me, but my heart feels for those she's surely still hurting.

'Now, girls,' Reverend Mother Brendan says, 'we've had our dinner, and the rest of the day is your own. What would you like to do?'

'Well,' I answer, 'we were thinking we'd like to walk down to the Shannon. That was always our favourite outing.'

'That sounds wonderful. Make sure you are back here before nine o'clock when we lock up the orphanage.'

❦ THIRTY-EIGHT ❦

The three of us go off down the Sligo road on this lovely late August afternoon toward the River Shannon, along a stretch of road that brings back so many memories for me. Katy's much slower than Maggie and me, being a true country girl who's never had to rush for anyone in her life. When we reach the lane that leads down to the river, I run on ahead of the others, just as I did every year. I'm already in the water and sitting on a big rock when Maggie and Katy reach me. 'What's the water like?' Katy asks.

'Beautiful, like always. You must remember coming down here, surely?'

'Oh, I do, Maureen. I remember.'

We paddle about in the shallow water, loving every minute. We talk about our picnics here, bringing up the names of girls our own age, wondering how this one and that one are doing and how they're surviving. 'Colleen Carey!' Katy says suddenly, looking at the two of us. 'How could I forget her? How did she do?'

We both fall silent, staring out at the slow-moving water and feeling unprepared for Katy's sudden mention of Colleen. She wouldn't know, of course, how bad Colleen became in the end. 'Ah, Katy, you know what she was like. I mean, you must remember . . .'

'Well, what happened, then? What happened to her, Maureen?'

'They took her away to the asylum in Longford when she was twelve . . .'

'The asylum!' Katy exclaims, her eyes wide with dismay. 'Why, that's a horrible place! The worst of places imaginable. I've heard stories about such places in Ireland! My God, the poor thing. What happened to her? Twelve years old, you say?'

'Yes, Katy. She got very bad in the end. It was really awful. She'd roam the dormitory at night and fight to get out. She'd get into my bed and disrupt all the others, and you know what they were like. One night she was very bad, and I stayed up with her into the wee hours. Then, the next day, she was gone. Anthony was still beating her, right up until the end. It was terrible, Katy. At least you missed all that. There was nothing we could do . . .'

Katy listens to this, staring down at the ground and seeming more saddened than shocked. She was very fond of Colleen. Maggie and I take turns sharing all the details of Colleen's final two years with us in the orphanage. Katy is deeply troubled by the news, finding it hard to believe that Colleen got so bad and that the nuns allowed it to reach that point. In the silence that settles over us, I stare across at the swaying bulrushes on the far bank as the light breeze moves through my hair. How many times, I think, have we sat like we are now, with no words for the way we are feeling?

Maggie turns suddenly to Katy. 'Katy,' she blurts out, 'the way the nuns took you from us was so cruel!'

'It was terrible,' I say. 'That was the cruellest thing I ever saw, whisking you away without even a goodbye to your friends. I was so angry with Sister Edna, Katy. I used to think she wasn't as mean to us, but after that incident I changed towards her.'

In her slow defeated way, Katy begins to tell us the details of the day she was adopted. 'I was in shock. I can't explain it. It was like a dream or something. I thought I was going to come back and say goodbye to my friends. But then we just kept going. I was sitting in the back seat of a car and driving away with them to God knows where. I had no idea what was going on. We got to the McCanns' place in Cloonfad, and they explained that I was to be a worker for them, on their farm and other things. They hardly spoke a word to me, and right away I felt like a slave. They just fed me and ignored me and gave me orders. I was left alone with no one to play with and so lonely without you when I first arrived. I knew right away that they hadn't adopted me to get me out of the orphanage or to love me and give me a new home and a good life. That wasn't it at all. They wanted a skivvy, that's all, and they got one, from the orphanage and the nuns.'

We listen to this with heavy hearts, on a beautiful summer day down on the banks of the Shannon. How terribly tragic, Katy being forced from one hell to another. She would've been better off with us. I want to reach out to her somehow, to take care of her and help her to find herself. If only we could help her break free from this nothing life she's been living. She is obviously still hurting badly, and I thank God that I organised this reunion. How much can one person take before they just give up and quit, with nothing left to hope or fight for? Is it too late? We must try.

The three of us gaze silently out at the gentle flow of the river for a time, seeing only the weary past move by, the slowly moving current lulling each of us into our own thoughts. I finally break the silence with a question I must ask. 'Do you think, Katy, you might want to leave Ireland and start over with us in England? Would you consider it?'

She lowers her head, avoiding our pleading eyes. 'Oh, I don't know,' she says, almost in a whisper. 'I would really have to think about it.'

'We better be leaving now, before it gets much later,' Maggie says, and I smile knowing she'd be the first to remind us of the time. We decide to leave things as they are for now. Katy will think about it, she promises us. We gather our things and head up the lane back to the Sligo road, less talkative than we had been earlier that afternoon.

We arrive back at the orphanage at about six in the evening, and the same novice informs us that Reverend Mother Brendan will have tea with us and instructs us to wait again in the parlour for her. She joins us there, and we chat casually. Not wanting to lose a chance to receive the advice and support of Reverend Mother Brendan, I bring up the possibility of helping Katy by getting her to come to England to begin a new life. Maggie assures her she would likely be able to guarantee a position for Katy at Hackney Hospital.

Mother Brendan sits back to think about this before looking back up at Katy. 'Would you be able to take on something like that, Katy? What do you think?'

'I don't know,' she answers quietly, apparently unable to focus on any sort of a decision.

'Well, Katy, you see how well Maggie and Maureen are getting along in London. It might be just the break you need, and you are still young enough to start over.'

'I know, Reverend Mother. I'll think about it,' Katy answers, not convincing anyone.

'Now you've had your tea, girls, this would be a good time to see the children you might know. It is their recreation time now, I believe. I'll walk you over myself.'

The four of us leave the parlour, walking outside and through the nuns' garden near one of the cloisters, saying hello to Sister Ignatius and Sister Patrick as we pass. We stroll along the cloister past Sister Michael's kitchen, and I remind myself that we must find time to visit her before we leave. When we enter the recreation hall, Sister Sacred Heart claps her hands, and all the children stop what they are doing. 'Good evening, Reverend Mother Brendan,' they all chant together as she enters the room.

Reverend Mother Brendan explains our presence to the orphans, and I immediately see the hunger and curiosity in them as they devour us with their eyes. Any little thing that is new or different is special to them. Don't the three of us know it well. 'They are former residents here, girls, like yourselves, and they will be spending a little time with you today. Some of you may remember Maureen and Maggie, though Katy left us ten years ago.' Turning back to us, she says, 'Well, girls, I'll leave you now. The spare room has been made up for you. Have a good evening with the children and get a good night's rest, now. I will see you at mass in the morning. God bless you.'

The girls stare at Maggie and me, especially at our clothes. They see little fashion in the way Katy's dressed. They know we've been living in the outside world, and they search for any slight sign of that, something to tell them what it's like.

How small the old recreation hall seems now. I look over at the younger orphans as they play, trying to be happy and trying to forget. My heart goes out to them, and I pray to God to keep them safe from the suffering and cruelty I experienced here, thinking of the years they have yet to go.

Sister Sacred Heart invites us to stay with her and the orphans for evening Rosary before going to our room for the night. After Rosary, the children are lined up in silence as we were so many times. I fight to hide the tears that well up in my eyes when I see Sister Anthony appear to take charge for the remainder of the evening. There is dead silence in the recreation hall as the orphans fall into line, the grim presence of Anthony filling the hall like a dark cloud. The three of us say goodnight to Sister Sacred Heart, nod respectfully to Sister Anthony and leave immediately for the dormitory.

At the top of the wide wooden staircase, we enter the dormitory, stopping just inside and staring numbly. It's all here, even for Katy – all the memories, collected like dust among the rows of beds. I can almost hear the voices and the nightmares and the scurry of rats at night on the floor and along the pipes, sounds I'll never forget. I look at the rows and the bed that would have been Colleen's back then. They look like the exact same beds, and again I feel tears well up and sad helpless memories rush forward. I wonder what Maggie and Katy are thinking about. They have their own pasts here, their own ghosts and unforgettable memories.

I tell the others to go on without an explanation so I can stop to stand at my special window for a few moments. I look out over the sleepy village and the patchwork of green fields that go as far as the eye can see. But it doesn't feel the same now, and my heart sinks a little. After all the initial excitement of the reunion, I feel somewhat deflated and depressed here in the dreary old dormitory. Seeing the orphans in the recreation hall, saying the Rosary with them and having to look at their expressions has been a dreadful reminder of what life was like here. Nothing has changed in this place, and now the nuns are putting us up as if we were orphans still. We'll sleep behind the locked door tonight and at the same old bedtime. There are ghosts everywhere here and not the kind I believed I saw as a little girl. They are deep inside me and very much awakened now. I take a final look out across the village before I turn away, watching the green of the fields blend with the fading summer night.

The three of us settle in for the night in the old sickroom, chatting and unpacking a few things while the sounds of the bedtime routine can be heard through the closed door. We hear Sister Anthony clapping and warning the girls to hurry along and not to whisper. Then all the familiar sounds return: the pulling back of bedclothes, the sounds of broken springs from the old beds and the coughing and wheezing of the children who're sick and ignored. The rattle of Sister Anthony's beads as she walks swiftly among the rows of beds is a chilly reminder to my ears. I listen to her footsteps as she strides towards the large door and the sound of the deadbolt slamming from the outside.

We chat quietly and into the night. I tell Katy everything, from the parcel and the grand feast that night to all I've shared with Maggie about Mrs Hughes in Mullingar. She listens silently, saying only when I'm finished, 'Another act of cruelty by the Sisters of Mercy, I see. So, you've been through hard times, too, Maureen.'

'I'd say I'm over the worst of them now, Katy, and at least I know where I was born, and I'm grateful for that. But I'm coming back some day to look for my mother, Annie Harte.'

We doze off after trying a final time to convince Katy to leave Cloonfad and come join us in England. I try to go to sleep, back behind the locked door of the dormitory where I spent so many years. But my mind is overworked with all I've learned today: the wretchedness of this place and of Katy and of Lucy's absence. It's a wonder we've come back at all. All these thoughts seem to burn grimly in me, like a flame in my heart, before a familiar summer music rescues me. From somewhere below, in the warm silence of the fields, comes the sound of a braying donkey. It is a lullaby that once filled me with hope and made me dream of the outside world.

❖ THIRTY-NINE ❖

We walk to the chapel for mass. It still looks lovely to me, just as it always has. I pray hard for all the orphans who are still suffering here at the hands of Sister Anthony and the other cruel nuns. And I pray hard for Katy, that we might help her find freedom from her enslaved life on the farm.

We go off to the kitchen to see if we can find Sister Michael. I knock on the big wooden door, very anxious to see this kind nun. 'Hello, hello,' Sister Michael says, opening the door. 'I heard the three of you were here!' She looks the same as she always has, her round pleasant face flushed and a big warm smile for us. 'So you've come back to visit us. Isn't that nice to see. And aren't you all looking grand,' she says. 'Just look at you. So grand!'

She asks us about our lives, saying that she remembers Katy but that it's been a long time. 'And what do you work at in London?' she asks us.

'I'm in the housekeeping department at a big hospital in the East End of London, the Hackney Hospital,' Maggie explains.

'And, Maureen, where do you work?'

'I'm in a department store in London, Bourne & Hollingsworth. I live in the hostel they have there for their employees, with over two hundred other girls.'

'Now, Katy, I know you were adopted. Are you still there with the same family?'

'I am,' she answers quietly. As I turn to face her, she looks so forlorn and lonely. She's been listening to Maggie and me tell Sister Michael about our lives in England. She seems almost to squirm with shame, her eyes looking downward, the way we always did as orphans. Her two feet habitually turn inward towards one another, a sad mannerism of defeat she cannot hide. Before we leave, I find

338

the courage to say to Sister Michael something I've waited a long time to say. 'I've never forgotten your kindness to us, Sister, especially when you gave us vegetables from your garden.'

She brushes this off. 'Oh, you were always such good little girls,' she says. 'You were happy little girls, you were.' She shakes our hands. 'God bless you, now. God bless the three of you. I'll pray for you.' I feel a strange sadness as we say goodbye and walk away, one that I don't quite understand.

Before leaving the orphanage, we are treated to a lovely breakfast with Reverend Mother Brendan. Afterwards, she walks us to the front gate. 'Keep your faith, and may God go with you always,' Reverend Mother Brendan says. 'We will pray for all of you, and you two have a safe trip back to England.'

We say our final goodbyes and walk through the gate. Here Maggie and I will part with Katy to walk back to the train station, while she'll walk the other way through Newtownforbes to catch a bus back to Cloonfad. In front of the iron gates, and with many tears and promises we hope to keep, we say our own special goodbyes. 'I hope you enjoy your time in Mullingar together. Goodbye, now,' Katy says, then she walks away in her slow, defeated fashion.

'We must help her,' I say, watching Katy plod off, 'to change and free herself from that life of slavery.'

'We can at least try,' answers Maggie.

We do not look back at the old grey buildings as we start in the other direction, deep in our own thoughts. I look across at Maggie, my fond smile unnoticed by her. We are two free spirits who have survived the orphanage, and as we walk away in silence I wonder what she's thinking. I know Maggie is happy to be on her way to Mullingar with me. We didn't like to show our excitement in front of Katy, knowing how miserable it would make her feel.

At the station in Mullingar, Mrs Hughes is waiting for us in her usual style, with Michael Lynch's hired car. She comes forward to hug me as I introduce Maggie. She's aged since I last saw her and is more stooped now. I've prepared Maggie for her deafness, which can only be getting worse.

In fifteen minutes, we arrive in front of the terraced house on the Dublin road. 'This is the half-door you always spoke of, Maureen!' Maggie exclaims on exiting the car and seeing the house.

'Oh, you remembered it!'

'Oh yes! You spoke about it so much, especially after your first trip.'

I'm filled with happy feelings and joy as I look round at the familiar scene inside: the turf fire burning, the lovely wooden table and the smell of Mrs Hughes' home-made bread – all of it is just as I remembered it to be, and all I had hoped it would be when I returned here. 'Well, what do you think? What do you think?' I ask Maggie, scarcely able to contain my excitement.

'It's everything you've ever told me, Maureen,' she replies. 'I love it!'

Mrs Hughes stands watching us, smiling warmly. 'Maureen, you really have grown up,' she says. 'I would hardly know you in those lovely clothes, and look at the height of you. You've changed so much!'

She tells us to go upstairs with our belongings to the bigger room, where I slept with Mrs Hughes when I was here. She'll use the extra room, empty now since Mr Hughes' passing. We are delighted at the idea of sharing the room alone, as it means we can chat late into the night. We talk for a while upstairs while Mrs Hughes cooks dinner, content to be here. I've waited for this day since Mrs Hughes took me out of the orphanage for the first time in 1944, the day when I could bring Maggie here and show her what I so desperately wanted to be able to show her and Lucy back then.

I bring Maggie down to stand at the half-door. 'See that house over there,' I say, pointing across the way. 'That's where Sarah Flynn was visiting her mother. She's the one who took me to the pictures on my second trip here.

'And you can't see it from here, but a few houses up, just past the Lynches' place, is the sweet shop. I'll take you there. And the canal is down to the right there, where Julia and I went walking with her mother. Do you remember I told you about that? How I'd walked with her and her dolls?'

I point out as much as I can to Maggie, telling her that tomorrow we can go into town and see more. She's already heard a lot about Mrs Burke and about all the neighbours and the things I've done on my holidays here, but she was never sure that she would see it herself one day with me.

Only Mrs Hughes' delicious cooking can tear us away from the famous half-door, and we sit down to a lovely meal. As we help to clean up after dinner, Mrs Burke comes in for a visit, and I introduce Maggie right away.

'Will you look at yourself, Maureen!' she says, amazed at how much I've changed. 'I'm delighted to see you. You've grown up so much, and so stylish! Turn round while I get a good look at you again.'

Mrs Hughes simply stands there, smiling with pride. Again, I feel a craving in me for this approval and experience the sheer joy of hearing it given so freely and honestly. It's like being handed a sum of gold – that's how much it means to me. Mrs Burke talks casually to Maggie as we sit at the big wooden table, asking her a little about her life since leaving the orphanage. She also speaks of Mr Hughes' death, admitting to us that Mrs Hughes is missing him terribly. 'She gets quite lonely at times, she does, Maureen, but she'll be fine. I keep a good eye on her. She loves to hear from you, and your visit means so much to her. It will help her greatly.'

After a good hour and a cup or two of tea, Mrs Burke stands to leave. 'Well, now, Maureen,' she says, 'I must be off. You and Maggie have a wonderful time here on your holiday, and be sure to say goodbye before you leave. God bless, now.'

The two of us enjoy every moment of our three days in Mullingar, taking in all the sights and going from one end of the little town to the other. I take Maggie for walks along the banks of the canal and to the lovely Christ the King Cathedral, where we pray together. With very little money, we do no shopping, but we do get to the pictures.

During our stay, all the neighbours drop in one at a time to see me, and I bask in their compliments on my appearance. 'Look at the height of you, Maureen, and so stylish. Why, we wouldn't know you to see. You've changed so much!'

'How well you must be doing in London now. That sounds like a wonderful place you're living in and such an exciting life.'

'The height of fashion, you are . . .'

How I wanted to fit in when I came back, to walk down any street in Mullingar and to have them look out their windows and doors and think, 'That one must be off in England doing well, like so many of the young people since the war.' I remember how I idolised Sarah Flynn as a fifteen-year-old orphan, and I know that I look like her now. But what would everything I've accomplished mean if I didn't come back here to get this approval, and what does that say about me? I have their approval and more, and yet I will return to London no closer to finding my mother or family than I was before.

From the window of the train as it leaves the station, Maggie and I watch Mrs Hughes walk away. I wonder if I will ever see her again.

Almost all the way to Dublin, Maggie and I talk about our trip and about Katy. We vow to try and help her. First, Maggie must try to get a position for Katy at Hackney Hospital, and then there's the matter of convincing her to make the move.

As our conversation slowly fades, we drift off into our private thoughts to the slow sleepy rhythm of the train as it rolls on towards Dublin.

❧ FORTY ❧

It feels wonderful to be back in London again, with the familiar routine of work and my social life. This time of year, in the late summer, the flowers are still in bloom in the parks, the shops are full of people and the streets full of visitors. There are hints in the air, though, of the coming autumn when the infamous London fog will come to cover the city like a slimy blanket.

Overall, I have felt refreshed during my first week back to work. Today, though, is a Friday, and my haberdashery counter has been exceptionally busy all day long. Almost every customer, it seems, has been difficult or annoying, and for whatever reason I've struggled to keep thoughts of Katy Fallon and memories of my childhood at bay. They are like wakened ghosts in me now, stirred up and restless with nowhere to go, and today they are haunting me. I didn't expect this.

After work, Margo goes out with some other friends, but I choose to stay in for a quiet evening alone in our room. I try reading, but I can't concentrate. Later, when Margo arrives home and both of us are in bed, I toss and turn endlessly. Finally, I slip into fitful sleep.

I'm in a bed. A tall figure is standing over me. The figure terrifies me and threatens me. I want to get up, to get up and run, but I can't move. I try and try again as the tall figure raises an arm very slowly. It's holding something. I try to scream, but my scream is mute – silent and futile. Then the figure moves closer to me. It's closer and smiling . . .

I wake to the sound of my own screaming voice. 'Someone's in the room! Someone's in the room! Margo, Margo, wake up! There's someone in the room!'

The lights blaze on. 'Maureen! For God's sake, calm down. There's nobody here. What's the matter? What is it?'

I realise I'm in my room at Warwickshire House and that I am with Margo. 'Oh, Margo, there was a . . . someone was here.' I look around, absolutely terrified.

'Maureen, you were screaming that someone was in the room. You're just having a bad nightmare, that's all. Listen, I'll get you a glass of water. Just calm down and . . .'

'No! Please take a look in the wardrobes! Just look in each wardrobe for me, Margo.'

She is visibly shocked by my behaviour. 'Check the wardrobes, Maureen?'

'Please! Just please do it for me, will you?'

'I've never seen you like this, but, all right, if it'll help, I'll check them.'

She walks over to the wardrobes as I follow her every move. 'There,' she says, going from one to the other and swinging open each door. 'Look, nothing at all. Nothing scary, no monsters, nothing.' She throws out her arms and shrugs her shoulders.

'Oh, don't joke, Margo. I'm sorry. It was so frightening.'

'What's caused this, Maureen?' she asks with genuine concern.

'I don't know. It's probably nothing, just a nightmare. I'll leave my light on for a minute or so. I'll be all right.'

'That's fine. No rush. You turn off the light when you're ready. I'm going back to sleep.'

I finally calm down and turn out the light above my bed. But as I try to fall asleep again, I think about my nightmare. I don't want to believe it, but I can't pretend that it was anything else but about the orphanage and a certain nun I'd rather forget.

It will settle down, I tell myself the next morning, surely it will. But only days later, the same nightmare comes back. A tall, ghost-like figure is standing over my bed, and I cannot move. Just as the figure is about to strike me, I wake, terrified and screaming. Margo has to check the wardrobes before I can think of sleeping again, and then I face another long night of feeling restless and haunted.

✳ ✳ ✳

Saturdays are sacred at the hostel due to the short half-day at work, and tonight Margo and I are going dancing at the Lyceum Ballroom with some friends. As we rush about preparing to go, Margo watches me take out my favourite plaid skirt and cream-coloured blouse, which I lay carefully on my bed. 'You're very fond of that outfit, Maureen,' she says good-naturedly.

'Well, it isn't as if I have a huge amount of choice, Margo. I'm putting aside all of my commission earnings to buy some new outfits.'

'Well, why don't I loan you something of mine for tonight?' She reaches into her considerable collection of clothing and takes out a lovely green dress that she hands to me. 'How about this one? It will be stunning with your dark hair.'

'Oh, that's lovely! Thank you. I hope it fits.'

Later that evening at the ballroom, I feel very flattered when a tall young soldier approaches me for a dance. I follow him out onto the dance floor, excited at the prospect of dancing with a young man in uniform for the first time. 'I'm David, David Redmond,' he says, introducing himself as we turn to a lively waltz beneath the dazzling lights.

'Maureen Harte,' I answer, looking up shyly for a moment and realising that David's quite young. He is also very tall, well over six feet, with short light-brown hair and a mouth full of lovely white teeth. But I quickly look away again, afraid to talk to him let alone look at him. Dancing I love, but conversation is another matter. I smile a lot and say very little to my dancing partners.

David starts telling me he's serving his two years' conscription in the army. I nod my head in response, content to let him chat away while carefully avoiding questions and any talk about myself. I feel attracted to this tall easy-going soldier, and this makes me feel shyer than usual. Not to worry. When the music stops, I'll have an excuse to escape back to the bench and lose myself in the crowd of young women. But as the waltz ends and I turn away after thanking David, he asks, 'Will you have the next one with me, Maureen?'

'Of course,' I answer, flattered and pleased that he wants to continue dancing with me!

David buys me a mineral after the third dance, a foxtrot, and after that we have many more dances until finally at the end of the evening he asks if he might take me home. Though taken off guard by his offer, I'm delighted and readily agree to let him escort me home before curfew. I've hardly opened my mouth all night, but he's been more than able to talk for both of us. 'Will you come over and meet my friends, David? I'm always here with a crowd.'

'I'd love to!'

We walk towards where Margo and the others stand talking and laughing, getting ready to return to the hostel. As we approach them, I feel all my painful shyness and awkwardness come back to me. But Margo and the others have seen me with David all evening, giving me subtle knowing looks as we passed them on the dance floor. I stumble and grope my way through the introductions to nods and hellos from my friends. As soon as she gets a chance, Margo moves closer to me. 'It must be the green dress, Maureen,' she says with a wink of admiration and an elbow of approval.

I wave goodnight to the others as they head off towards Leicester Square station, but Margo finds a moment to wag a finger at me and says, 'Don't get lost, Maureen, and remember curfew.' This only makes me want to crawl under the nearest table with embarrassment.

David and I leave just behind them, walking slowly towards the Underground. For the first time I'm being escorted home by a young man, and it feels wonderful, another sign that I'm fitting in, although it's odd to not be heading home with my girlfriends as always. David is so clean-cut and sincere, and I find him very attractive indeed. I like the attention he's showing me. He must enjoy my company.

As our train pulls out of Leicester Square station, David turns to me. 'How old are you, Maureen?'

'Twenty, this past April,' I tell him, seeing his surprise.

'Really? Twenty? Eighteen I'd have said, no more!'

'Oh, I know. I don't look my age.'

We're both silent for a few moments, as the train moves through the darkened tunnel under the London streets. 'How old are you, then?' I ask quietly, getting my nerve up.

'Eighteen, just gone.'

We continue in this hesitant way, and I try to say the right thing or ask the right question. I'm awkwardly feeling my way along, nervous but fascinated, too.

The scene outside the hostel when I arrive with David just before curfew is a common one. On both sides of us couples are necking and hugging in doorways, saying their goodnights before eleven o'clock when the doors will be shut for the night. Aware of the time, I turn to David. 'Well, David, I must leave and . . .' Suddenly, his face is closing in on mine, his eyes closed and his lips slightly parted. My God, he wants to kiss me! 'What are you doing?' I ask, pulling away. 'I don't even know you!'

He looks surprised for a moment, then suddenly sulky. 'What's the matter with you, Maureen?'

'With me? Nothing's the matter with me!' I say, looking around nervously. 'I would rather get to know you better, that's all! I must go now.'

He runs a hand quickly over his mouth and chin, as if looking for the kiss he thought would be there. 'God, that's right, you're under curfew here. Maureen, listen, might I have a number so I can contact you again?'

I agree to give him the number at Warwickshire House, scratching it out on a napkin from the ballroom before rushing to make it in. 'Here you are. This will get you through to the front desk. Ask if I'm in residence, and they'll call up to my room on the public address. If I'm in, I'll come down and take the call. Now, I've got to go. Oh, David, I'm Miss Hatton. When you call the desk, ask for Miss Hatton, not Maureen!'

'What? Miss what?'

'Miss Hatton. That's my shop name at Bourne & Hollingsworth. Have you got it? Hatton, not Harte and not Maureen Hatton, just Miss Hatton! Thank you for bringing me home.'

'Got it! Miss Hatton it is, Maureen Harte. Right, goodnight. I'll call you on my next leave of absence.'

'Goodnight.'

I turn to rush in, passing the long rows of necking couples. I find Margo in our room, lounging on the bed. 'So, Maureen, a tall handsome soldier. Well now, I think it must be the lovely dress I loaned you.'

'He tried to kiss me! As soon as we got to the front! Bold they are, some of them!'

She throws her head back laughing as I tell her what happened with David and my refusing him his kiss. 'Oh, Maureen, you're so funny!'

A month went by before David called, and he asked if he could take me to the pictures. 'I've got this weekend off, and I'd love to see you again. I thought this Saturday evening, if it's all right.'

'Yes, that's fine, David. I'd like that.'

'Good, I'll come pick you up at the hostel, then.'

After meeting David, I found myself hoping he'd call one day and the next day convincing myself that I could do without the intense feeling of dating one on one. Still, I did enjoy his attentions and knowing that he found me attractive. So now that I'm to go out on my first date tonight, I promise myself I'll make the best of it and try to have fun.

I find David standing a few feet from the reception desk. In his crisp neat uniform, he greets me with a big smile, showing his lovely white teeth. He greets me warmly, suggesting we take the Underground to Piccadilly Circus and see a film at the Odeon. During the film, David puts his arm around me, and I begin to feel uncomfortable. I've never been this close to a young man, but when I glance quickly about the dark rows of the theatre I see that many of the young men are doing the same, and I realise it must be fine. Sensing my discomfort, he turns and smiles down at me as if to reassure me.

After the pictures, we go for tea to the Corner House. We find a table facing the busy street after selecting from the buffet. David makes easy conversation as we sip our tea, talking about his family and how he's the proud uncle of his married brother's two-year-old boy. He immediately takes out a picture of his little nephew, a beam of pride on his young features as he shows it to me. Then the question I dread but fully expect comes. 'What about your family back in Ireland, Maureen? Where are you from?'

'I don't have a family. I was raised in an orphanage in Ireland.'

'Oh, I'm sorry,' he replies, looking shocked.

'Oh, not at all. That's all right. I'm well used to it by now.'

David gives me a warm, sincere smile that makes me feel strangely exposed before him. 'Are you always this shy, Maureen?' he asks.

'Only when I first meet people. My friends wouldn't consider me too shy now, I don't think.' But even as I hear the words come from my mouth, I feel the old wall rise before me. I'm running away from a past I don't want to explain because it shames me. How could I explain it anyway? Am I supposed to admit, at twenty, that he's my first boyfriend? What would he think of me then?

I look away, sensing by his open gaze that if he knew, it wouldn't matter to him, but no . . .

Rescuing me again from my awkwardness, he asks, 'So what are your plans for Christmas Day?'

'Oh, I'll be fine. The hostel puts on a lovely dinner, and, besides, I'll have the company of girls like myself.'

'I have an idea, Maureen. I'll ask my parents if you can come to ours for Christmas. They'll make you welcome, just Mum and Dad and my brother and sister-in-law and their little one, my nephew. What do you say? Sound like a plan?'

'Oh, I don't know . . .'

'Well, you can't stay at the hostel! Not on Christmas Day, Maureen. I won't take no for an answer! Do come, won't you?' Again, I hear the sincerity in his voice. He seems to be such a family person. So I agree to spend Christmas Day with him and his family.

Later, outside the hostel, I allow him to kiss me goodnight this time, and I actually like it. I like kissing. I'm sure he knows it's my first kiss, as he smiles tenderly down at me, making me feel relaxed about it. I look about and see other girls in doorways kissing their boyfriends goodnight, and I again feel more like one of them.

✳ ✳ ✳

David and I date for three months, from our early October meeting at the Lyceum into the new year of 1950. He's a sweet, sincere person, and I am very fond of him, but the feeling of dating one on one begins to be a strain for me, and our conversations are often one-sided. There is little I can do to change what goes on inside me. It's always the same when I try to play a role I'm not comfortable with. A great weariness and a desire to put things off to another day comes over me at such times. I look towards my friends and to losing myself in the crowd and doing things together in large groups, where the feelings that haunt me are lost in the fun and laughter. These wonderful days at Warwickshire House will end at some point, I know, so I will enjoy them while they last.

❖ FORTY-ONE ❖

The spring of my second year with Bourne & Hollingsworth finds me receiving my first promotion since starting with the company. Though it is referred to as a transfer to another department, Miss Ridelle assures me that the move is a promotion. She tells me that my performance has been exceptional and that management have been waiting to find a suitable department for me. That department will be men's and ladies' shoes, and I'll need to attend a seminar to learn about feet and fitting shoes properly, which is mandatory for all new sales personnel. 'Report to Mr Miller Monday next, and good luck, Maureen. I know you'll do well there,' Miss Ridelle says, shaking my hand.

Around the same time as my promotion, my friends surprise me by announcing that they are taking me out to celebrate my twenty-first birthday. It is Margo's idea. I've told her in passing that I've never had a single birthday marked in my life. I'm deeply touched by the gesture, and it will be enough just to go out and have a good time to mark the occasion. If not for Margo's insistence, this year would've been the same as every other, and I would barely have given it a thought. It feels strange to me to celebrate my birthday, I must admit, and a part of me struggles to give it the meaning the others say it should have.

After meeting in the lobby of the hostel, we head off in a group, and soon we're at the Corner House chatting loudly and enjoying a lovely meal. Over dessert, Margo surprises me with a beautiful birthday cake, while everyone sings 'Happy Birthday' to me. They present me with a small box with a stylish silver brooch inside. I'm in awe of this gesture, barely able to voice my thanks to them. 'Put it on now, Maureen, so we can see it.' I pin the brooch onto my white blouse, and they tell me how pretty it looks on me. I cry as Margo hugs me and says, 'Happy birthday, Maureen. You deserve it, you really do. Enjoy this one and the many more to come. D'you hear me, now?'

'I will, Margo, and I'll never forget the kindness you and the others have shown me. Thank you so much.'

How blessed I am to have such good friends as these.

On yet another Saturday night at the Lyceum Ballroom, we're having the time of our lives dancing to our favourite numbers as the bands play continually on the rotating stage. A variety of different men frequent the Lyceum: young and not so young, educated and otherwise, and it's always a good spot to meet someone. On this particular evening, half-way through the night, I'm asked to dance by an older man whose flashy appearance catches my eye. 'What's your name, love?' he asks as we take to the dance floor beneath the chandeliers and spinning globes. He sounds like a true Londoner, judging by his accent.

'Maureen Harte.'

'Ah, that's an Irish lilt in your voice! So you're from Ireland, Maureen?'

'I am.'

'Well, Maureen Harte, I'm Reg, Reg Walker. Is this your first time here?'

'Oh, no, I've been here a number of times.'

'Really, that's odd. I haven't seen you here before. I come here all the time with my partner Charles. Are you having me on? Are you sure it's not your first time here? I'm not likely to have missed such an attractive woman!'

I smile at this, not as embarrassed as I might've been by the comment. 'Oh, we like a change, my friends and I. We're not regulars here. Sometimes we go to the Irish dances at the Blarney Club and the Round Tower.'

'How long have you lived here in London?'

'Almost five years now,' I answer, becoming more fascinated by the minute with the roguish charm of this Londoner and totally at ease with his open confidence. He's certainly unlike any man I've met to date, and I rather like him, even if he's got to be a good ten years older than I am. He is about five-feet-ten-inches tall and slender. He has straight brown thinning hair, a very sharp nose and sparkling brown eyes that are obviously full of devilment and humour. A sharp dresser, he has on a broad, bright-coloured tie, a dark jacket and trousers.

Reg is very chatty and friendly, and after many trips to the dance floor with him throughout the evening he asks to take me home. Though I think about it for a moment or two, I continue to feel drawn to this easy-going character. 'Well, love, what do you say?'

'Yes, all right, then. I think I'd like that, Reg.'

'Blimey, that's wonderful,' he says, and I chuckle at this brash openness. 'Say, you're very shy, Maureen.'

'Yes, I am at first, and, well . . . I've not met anyone quite like you before. But don't mind me. I'm always a little shy at first, then I get over it.'

He pushes me back a little to take a closer look at me. 'And you don't talk a whole lot. That's the most you've said all evening. Not that I'm complaining. Not at all, in fact. I probably talk too much anyway. That's what I'm always being told!'

We have the last dance together, and I take Reg over to meet my friends and let them know he's taking me home. 'Hello, girls. So you're all Irish, too?' he asks them while offering his hand to each of them.

Immediately, I sense my friends don't approve of the flashy older man I've brought over. They're giving Reg a real going over, but my mind's made up. I'm going home with him anyhow. 'Remember, you have to be in by eleven, Maureen,' Margo warns as she leaves with the others, giving Reg a final look of obvious disapproval as if to punctuate her words.

'What's this "be in by eleven" mean?' Reg asks as we walk away, either not noticing Margo's reaction or not caring about it.

'Oh, we all live in a hostel on Gower Street,' I answer. 'It's owned by Bourne & Hollingsworth, the department store where we all work, and there's a curfew.'

'Oh, right, I've got you. Not to worry. I'll have you there on time.'

'Thanks, Reg. I'm in serious trouble if I'm late.'

Reg takes me over to meet his friend and business partner Charles Gibson. 'Delighted to meet you, Maureen,' Charles says, shaking my hand and introducing me to his girlfriend Susan.

Immediately I note how Charles speaks with a much more refined English accent, like Mr Pendleton our store manager, while Reg is calling me love. His 'blimeys' remind me of the workers in the wood factory and how they spoke. Now, what have I got myself into?

The men get our coats, and the four of us leave the ballroom together. I notice the expensive-looking camel-hair coat Reg's wearing, comparing it to Charles's more conservative navy-blue coat. Expecting we'll walk across to the Underground station, I'm surprised when we turn to go to a car park instead. We say goodnight and part with Charles and his girlfriend. 'I'm parked over this way, Maureen,' Reg says, gesturing to a beautiful dark-blue two-door sports car.

'I've never dated anyone who owned a car before,' I say, not thinking before I speak for a change and not caring, which is the more surprising.

'Blimey! You're kidding! Well, jump in, love, and enjoy the ride home.'

I get into the car while Reg, glancing over at my expression of awe, chuckles. 'What d'you think of it?'

'Oh, I love it!'

'Well, love, you see it's a thing with me and cars. I'm in the car-park business, and Charles, he's my partner.'

'Oh, really, car parks? I don't know much about the car business.'

'Ah, but that's it, love! You and the rest of London don't know much about it, because it's something new, and it's going to expand, we hope. Charles and I are among the first to do this. We're using old bombsites to build on, though not exclusively bombsites. All's changed since the war. We're based in the West End, not at all far from Oxford Street, where you work.'

Reg looks at his watch and tells me we'll take the scenic route back to the hostel, seeing as we've some time before the curfew. He chats about his business as we drive, and while I listen to him I feel more at ease with him. He seems to be exactly as he appears on the surface, and I like that about him. I sit back in the plush new interior of the car and allow myself to enjoy this brief exposure to genuine luxury. I find myself wishing we had an extra hour, just to go riding about in Reg's sports car or maybe to go for a late cup of tea somewhere. Maureen Harte, what has got into you? I feel carefree and happy with this Reg Walker, and I already know I'll want to see him again should he ask me.

We finally reach Warwickshire House, and Reg starts laughing. 'Hang on! What's all this? Will you look at all the girls in doorways, necking with their blokes! What kind of place is this, Maureen? Blimey, this is funny. Wait'll I tell Charles tomorrow.'

'I have to rush in now, Reg.'

'Right, that eleven o'clock thing! Wait, love, give me your phone number. I'd love to see you again.'

I give Reg the number and say goodnight. Then I rush up the stairs to find Margo reading, with her feet up on the end of her bed. 'Oh, Margo, you should see the car I just came home in!'

'He brought you home in a taxi, did he?'

Margo's lingering disapproval is obvious. 'No, his car. Reg's own car. He has his own business, in car parks. It's new here in London.'

'His own car?'

'Yes, a navy-blue one. A Martin Eston or something!'

'My, you hit it good this time, Maureen.'

'Yes, I know. So, what do you think?'

'Think?'

'Of Reg! What do you think of him? Tell me.'

'Well,' she says, sitting up and stretching, 'since you ask, he does seem a little old and sophisticated for you. And that's all I can tell you. I mean, you just met him tonight.'

'He's very different, don't you think?'

But Margo simply looks at me like a protective sister. What is she thinking? 'Are you seeing him again, Maureen?'

'Yes, I gave him the number here, and he's calling me this week.'

'He's a good few years older than you, Maureen, don't you think?'

'I don't know. I never asked him how old he is. He mostly talked about his business. He and Charles are partners.'

'I'm thinking he's close to thirty,' she says.

'Really? Do you think? Oh, I guess I'll find out when I see him again. It doesn't really matter to me, to be honest. He seems such a nice man, and I think he's very funny. Maybe it's because he's a Londoner. They're so witty.'

'Oh, yes, maybe they are witty, Maureen, and worldly and forward. Just be careful.'

'I will, Margo.'

I wonder why she's telling me to be so careful. Reg doesn't seem like a mean person to me.

Reg calls me the following week, and we decide to see each other on the Wednesday evening. He arranges to pick me up right outside Warwickshire House. 'Did he say where he's taking you, Maureen?' Margo asks when I run back upstairs, excited by the news.

'No, we never talked about that.'

'He'll surely take you somewhere nice. I'd say he can afford to.'

'Do you really think so, Margo?'

'I'm sure of it, Maureen.' She seems to know so much more about these things, yet I still feel she's not overly fond of the idea of me going out with Reg. But I can't think too deeply about what others think, even those I admire, or I'll never make my own decisions in life.

In the lobby of the hostel, I stand waiting, unbelievably excited as I watch for any sign of Reg's approach. I've chosen my beige sweater set and plaid skirt, the outfit Mrs Davies chose for me. At last, he pulls up in his lovely car, and I can't help but look around to see if anyone's watching me being picked up in such a stylish fashion. I wave to him and walk nervously toward the car. 'Well, love, don't you look nice this evening,' he says as I get in.

I feel myself blush deeply, hoping it doesn't show in the darkened interior. Reg talks easily as we pull away into traffic. He has the whole evening planned. We're going for a drive in the country to a place called the Grasshopper Inn out in Kent, where we'll meet Charles and Susan. 'How does that sound?' he asks, but I just smile and agree. 'You're still not saying too much, Maureen Harte. Just relax and enjoy the evening. Charles and Susan are easy to be with. Just be yourself. That's always the best policy, I say, and you don't have to be shy with me. I don't bite.'

During the hour drive out to Kent, Reg never stops talking: about his business, about the passing sights, about anything that comes to his busy mind. When he finally asks about my family, I tell him the same story I've told many times before, but his response to this catches me unaware. 'You know, Maureen, when I met you at the Lyceum that night I thought there was something different about you. A shyness, yes, but an openness as well. It showed when we danced for the first time.'

Whether I show my alarm at this or not, Reg seems to sense my unease with the subject. We drive on in silence for a minute or so before he speaks again. 'So, tell me a little about yourself, Maureen. I mean, if you're comfortable with that.'

I feel the same sense of ease with Reg as I did the night I met him, and I soon relax. I tell him a carefully chosen version of my life since coming to England. I talk of how shy I was at first and how it was a very difficult adjustment after leaving the orphanage and that I've come a long way since then. Without being aware of it, my guard is soon almost completely down with Reg. He has an almost fatherly way about him, and he's able to draw things out of me. In truth, he's easier to be around than any man I've met. I thoroughly enjoy the ride through the countryside, taking in the beautiful scenery as we get to know each other. I find that he has so much more confidence than a man my age, and this instils a sense of confidence in me, too.

We eventually arrive at the Grasshopper Inn and meet up with Charles and Susan. I just follow Reg's lead, letting him order the roast beef and Yorkshire pudding for me. He promises me that I'm sure to love the way it's done here. The rest of the evening goes very well. I even find myself able to speak more easily to Charles and Susan, and I ask questions as well, instead of just responding when spoken to. Susan in particular has a lovely personality and makes me feel accepted and comfortable. The drive home is just as pleasant, and when Reg finally drops me off on time in front of the hostel I'm more than pleased when we agree to continue seeing one another. I decide with conviction that I'm going to follow my instincts and enjoy myself even more with this new man in my life. Why not?

And so begins a steady relationship with Reg Walker, a flashy Londoner ten years older than me, with a caring and deeply sincere nature. He drives a shiny new Aston Martin, takes me to gorgeous restaurants, buys balcony seats at the pictures and above all he makes me laugh like no one ever has before. My friends are slowly getting used to seeing me with him, grudgingly accepting his presence when he drops by the lounge in Warwickshire to say hello. Reg himself is indifferent to their approval, and I like him even more because of this.

Margo and her current boyfriend Tom join Reg and me on dates. The four of us have very lovely and often lavish nights out on the town. But Margo stubbornly feels that Reg isn't suited to me and that I am too good for him, though she tries to say so in a kind way. For my part, I'm feeling more attached to Reg, more trusting during our moments of physical intimacy, and I cannot help but admit that I also enjoy the luxurious lifestyle he's providing me with. Though he isn't Catholic, he always displays respect for my faith, and I often speak to him of my beliefs, feeling comfortable in doing so. Sometimes he'll tease me, always affectionately, saying things like, 'Maureen, you are so Irish and so Catholic!'

Despite these little differences between me and Reg and the fact that my friends don't really approve of the relationship, I love his company and friendship, and I have no desire to be with anyone else. I'm not going to change a thing.

❧ FORTY-TWO ❧

When I hear from Maggie that Katy is coming to London, I have a difficult time believing it. She's made the decision to move here, and I am ecstatic to hear it. Maggie and I don't get together often, mostly because we live such different lives now. The truth of it is that Maggie has done the most for Katy. I've been caught up in seeing Reg and enjoying my life and haven't made much effort to help Katy. I'm sure there must have been a lot of correspondence between them, because Katy would never have made the move on her own.

The fact that she is now moving here says an awful lot about Maggie's deep concern for Katy. I can't help but worry, though, about how she will manage once she's here. I'm fearful that London might swallow up this sadly defeated former orphan. I think of her little village of Cloonfad and of the pace of life there, and I can only hope that Katy will manage to make her new life here work out. What a huge undertaking this must have been for her: the long journey, the big change and leaving everything she knows behind her. I desperately pray that she will be able to begin again and find new hope.

A few anxious days go by before I find a note at the front desk with instructions to call a number this evening at Hackney Hospital at a set time. Maggie will put Katy on the telephone when I call. As I read the note, my eyes fill with tears. She's done it. She's made it here. She's taken the first and biggest step.

I call the number at the set time, and Maggie answers it after a couple of rings. After a quick few words, she puts Katy on. There's a slight pause before I hear Katy's voice. 'Hello, Maureen,' she begins in the same slow manner. 'I'm here at last.'

'Katy!' I reply. 'I'm so happy to hear from you! You did it. You took the plunge, and you're actually here in London. I can't believe it!'

'I am. It's scary here. The trip was very long and tiresome. I don't know, Maureen, it's awfully big here and so noisy. Do you think I'll get used to it? I honestly don't know . . .'

'Of course you will! Stop worrying, now, do you hear? Please give it a try, won't you?'

'I will, Maureen, I will,' she promises.

'Listen, Katy,' I say, trying to reassure her. 'When you get settled, the three of us will get together. There's no rush. There's a lot we can help you with. We were the same when we first got here – totally lost and frightened by all of it. But it will be fine, don't worry.'

'All right, Maureen. I'll put Maggie back on.'

Maggie and I make arrangements to meet the following Saturday afternoon before saying goodbye. I hang up with mixed feelings. She appears so unchanged and anxious, as if she's locked in the past. I try to convince myself that it might just be the long trip. Give her a little time . . .

Today is the big day. It's Saturday, and I'm to meet with my two dear friends from the orphanage at Lyon's Corner House. I step off the bus in Piccadilly Square and immediately spot them by the restaurant. There beside Maggie, looking awkward and out of place, stands Katy. I rush to them with a big smile, greeting them with affectionate hugs. My first reaction to Katy is again one of shock, though I fight to disguise it. She hasn't changed at all since arriving here. She's wearing the same old-fashioned clothes she wore when I last saw her and has the exact same heavy black shoes and plain dull hair. She looks like she belongs in a different world. She has a fixed stunned expression on her face, the look of someone totally lost.

The restaurant is noisy and crowded as always. People move quickly along, choosing their food from the buffet, getting their money ready, pushing forward – nothing to it. I pick up my tray, with Katy behind me and Maggie after her. I expect Katy to follow me. Instead, she stands there, fumbling about at the stack of trays. She looks at the trays, reaches for one and puts it down. She looks at her money and then behind her in a slow confused manner. Maggie tells the other people to move on ahead, helping Katy choose her food and carry out the simple act of getting lunch.

As I watch this unfold, it seems she's become even more introverted since our reunion. I feel a harsh pang of utter helplessness at the extent of her crippled nature. How did she ever travel to London alone? It upsets me to see her so unchanged. I'd hoped to see her a little more outgoing, with a hint of excitement and a desire to experience more. I can see the strain on Maggie's face. She must be totally stressed from trying to get Katy settled and up to speed with her new surroundings.

Finally, the three of us are seated, and I look across at Katy. 'Well, how are you getting along so far? Do you like living in London?'

She glances nervously about and then back at me. 'Oh, Maureen,' she says, 'the city is so big. It's hard for me to get around, and I'm so slow and afraid to speak to people. I just . . . I honestly don't know yet.'

I question her about her job, and she tells me that the girls she works with have little patience with her slowness. 'And then I get upset, and it makes me even more nervous. I really don't know. I don't know what else to do, Maureen. Honestly, I don't.'

So this is what's been going on. Now I begin to see. Katy's trying to tell me she's about to give up, that's it. Maggie speaks up. 'As I've told you, Katy,' she begins, 'I was very shy and very slow when I first started at the hospital. I thought I'd never be able to handle the job.'

Katy listens with a kind of sluggish nervousness, glancing about the restaurant as if expecting some unknown intrusion. She looks at me then at Maggie, a pleading, heartbreaking look of defeat playing across her features. 'I kept saying to myself,' continues Maggie, 'you are not giving in. There's nothing back in Ireland for you, nothing!'

I speak up again, feeling like I'm trying to save a drowning person. 'Why don't you stop worrying and just concentrate on moving a little faster on the job? Then your confidence will follow. Just you wait and see.'

'I hope so,' she replies. 'You've both caught on to the pace of life here, but my slowness bothers everyone.'

'Listen,' I add quickly, not wanting to lose this flicker of hope, 'I had to be pushed in the same manner when I arrived. Please try, Katy! Please just try.'

After lunch, we hop on a bus to Hyde Park for a leisurely walk along the Serpentine. Katy has trouble getting on and off the moving double-deckers, and we share a laugh as I recall for her my own initial experience with the buses in London. Strolling through the park, our worries disappear for a time, and we continue chatting easily together. We turn onto a lovely path fringing the river, walking for a while before stopping under a large ash tree, where we sit and rest.

In the unusually warm autumn afternoon, an easy breeze moves through the leaves of the tree above our heads. I glance at Katy. This beautiful green parkland, with no hustle and bustle, is just what she needs now. Curious, I ask her how her adopted parents reacted to her leaving for England. 'They were shocked,' she responds, picking at the grass. 'They asked me how I thought I'd survive.'

She explains how she'd told them that Maggie could guarantee her employment at Hackney Hospital and that she was leaving in three weeks' time. The parents, who were cold to her after hearing of her plans, helped her get all the necessary papers. But before she left, they casually mentioned that she was welcome back if things didn't work out. Yes, I'm sure they did. They didn't want to lose their skivvy. So why not let her know she's more than welcome back, back to where there's nothing for her.

Beneath the tree, we sit silently, picking up small stones and idly tossing them up and down in our hands. We talk more of the orphanage, and for the first time ever it is easy for us to do so. We talk of the fun times and sad times, the kind nuns and the evil nuns, the beatings and the special days. We speak of Lucy Nolan with deep affection, regretting that she somehow got lost to us. Still idly tossing the stones, we drift into silence again, each of us deep in thought. Maggie turns to Katy, reminding her of the time she won first prize for being top in religious studies. 'You were always top of the class and well liked by all your friends. Your hand was constantly raised in that class, and you always gave the right answers,' I add.

Katy recalls another pleasant memory. 'Maureen, I'll never forget one time during recreation period. Do you remember how we loved to play see-saw on the long benches inside?'

'How could I forget?' I answer, thinking of it with fondness.

'Well, one afternoon,' Katy continues, 'you wanted us all to sit the same way, instead of two facing the wall and the other two facing out towards the hall. Well, of course we all fell back, our feet flying into the air as we landed against the radiators laughing. You slit your head open that night, Maureen, and you still kept laughing.'

'Oh yes! I do remember that evening,' I say, giggling as if it were yesterday.

We continue to remind Katy of her achievements in the orphanage, trying desperately to get her to see a self she can no longer recognise. But something inside me feels that this is hopeless. There must be a way. We could help her and teach her social skills. She's only twenty-one years old. Surely she can unlearn this terrible conditioning, as we did. It will be hard, but she could do it . . .

My heart feels an emptiness I haven't known since my leaving day, an utter helplessness I can do nothing about. Although I've never expressed it aloud or recognised it myself, I suddenly realise how much I love these two girls. These two dear and special friends, who shared and survived an entire childhood with me.

We stand and turn to leave. I toss the few stones I'd been clutching to the ground. None of us speaks as we make our way back along the winding path towards the crowded streets. Gradually, the peaceful setting of the tree beside the river is lost in the din of the city. I say goodbye to my two friends, watching them until they disappear into the Underground station. As I watch them go, I have a feeling that I will never see Katy Fallon again.

It is less than two weeks since I met with Katy and Maggie. On my way into the hostel after work, I check with Mr Henning at the front desk for messages. 'Yes, Miss Hatton, in fact I do have a message for you. She said it was very important and to get it to you as soon as I could. Here it is.'

I take the folded note from him. 'Thank you, Mr Henning.'

Alone in my room, I sit on the edge of my bed, fearful of opening Maggie's note. As I read, I learn that Katy has been let go at the hospital and is preparing to leave London to go back to Ireland. Maggie's arranged a time for me to call and say goodbye to Katy. I stare silently and helplessly at the words for a moment. Then I set the note down, put my head in my hands and weep.

I call at the agreed time, and during our brief conversation I experience the torment of the past in a way that couldn't be described in a thousand years. Mr Henning gazes at me silently as the tears roll down my cheeks. 'I'm so sorry, Katy,' I get out between sobs. 'I . . . I wish you the best, and . . . I'll try to make it over to Cloonfad to see you, all right?'

Her voice is flat on the other end. 'I'm sorry, too, Maureen. I suppose it just wasn't for me. I'll be better off where I was.'

No you won't! No you won't! I have to end the call because my heart is breaking. 'You take good care of yourself, Katy,' I say. 'I'll let you go now, all right?'

'All right, Maureen. I'm so glad things worked out here for you and Maggie. Goodbye, now, and God bless.'

'Goodbye, Katy.' I put down the phone and rush upstairs, the tears still streaming from my eyes.

I sit alone in my room. How will it be for Katy to return in humiliation to the adopted parents who likely knew she would fail? It will be worse, and I feel guilty because of what's happened, though we tried our very best. Now Katy will return to the small gossipy world of Cloonfad as a failure, as if she needs that. But she's not a failure. She's a victim! She will know now without doubt her place in this world, and she will probably never again be free. She may marry or, more likely, be married off. She may become an old maid, sitting in front of a dirty hearth day after day. Who can say what her fate will be, other than it is and always will be a tragic one. But Katy's fate isn't just that of one girl or one illegitimate child. God himself only knows how many there are like her and how many yet to come. I felt it, all of it, when I had to say goodbye to her.

I put the note away and leave Warwickshire House to go walking alone, something I rarely do. Our failure to help Katy has affected me deeply. As I walk, I look about at the endless faces. I watch children with their mothers and fathers, and old people near the end of life but smiling, chatting and happy. I promise myself I will always remember Katy in a positive light. In many ways, her fate is my own as well, and Maggie's, even if what we look like on the outside says something different. It hurts me too deeply to think of what Katy might have been. I want to remember her only as she was, so many years ago before she left us. I'll never forget her then rosy cheeks, laughing green eyes, jet-black hair and bright, hopeful smile. I see her in class, an exceptionally intelligent little girl but unwanted. We were all unwanted. We were illegitimate. How I hate the word – unlawful, it means to me, without purpose or function in this world. The injustice done to Katy and the others was a crime. Tears fall down my cheeks, but I quickly wipe them away. I turn back towards the hostel and the life I have to get on with.

After a night out down at the Tilbury Docks, Reg and I go for a long, leisurely stroll. Since Katy's departure, I just haven't been myself. Never has the urge to share my deepest thoughts been so strong in me, and I feel right now that I can only trust Reg. I just need someone to say it all to, to hear the truth, and if I can find my voice, then tonight will be that night. 'Do you ever pray to God for what you want, Reg?' I ask him, trying to find the right footing to begin my torturous story.

'Of course, Maureen. I was brought up in the Protestant faith. We had to go to church on Sunday evenings when we were little, so I've kept my faith, and I pray in my own way. But I don't go to church every Sunday, like you do. In fact, I don't go at all.'

'Tell me some more about how you grew up,' I go on, making casual conversation as I tremble inside.

'We never had much growing up in the East End. It was a rough area, and things were very tight.' Reg shakes his head, looking distant. 'The war years, Maureen. My God, the war years. The rations, the bombings and blackouts. It was terrible here. After Dunkirk, well, for a while all of England trembled with fear. There was talk of concessions to Hitler then. Thank God it never happened. It's all behind us now, I suppose, and some of those bombsites are making us money.' Reg chuckles as he glances over at me, bending down to kiss my cheek.

'I saw some of the bombed-out streets,' I say absently. 'In Kilburn, right after I arrived here.'

As we walk, I glance quickly across at Reg. He hasn't a clue about the storm of emotions whirling inside me at this moment. Why would he? I've kept my true emotions deeply hidden for so long that I've become an expert. I've never trusted another soul enough to say what I feel I'm close to saying to him. Stopping him suddenly, and in a rush of awkward words, half sentences and desperate tears I reveal the terrible restlessness within me. The constant longing I can no longer keep to myself and the hunger to find my family. He listens to the whole tale, quietly and patiently.

He seems shocked at first, but as I desperately search his eyes for a response I see the compassion I sensed was there. 'Ah, love,' he says, taking me in his arms. 'I can't imagine what it must be like not to have any family and to be all alone in this world. And don't feel ashamed, Maureen. It's not your fault, do you hear?'

I sob into his shoulder, and it feels good to finally let it go. 'I do, Reg, but the shame does haunt me constantly. The shame is the worst of it. I can never say a thing about it to my friends. They're great, don't get me wrong . . .' I cry even worse now, sobbing like he's never seen before. The floodgates have opened, and I cannot stop. I realise now just how strangled the trip back to the orphanage was for Maggie, Katy and me.

Reg takes me by the shoulders and wipes my face with his sleeve. 'I can't say I understand your past, Maureen. Only you know that. But what is perfectly normal is that these feelings inside you were bound to come out, especially after so much time.'

'I'm sorry, Reg. I shouldn't have said a word.'

'Nonsense, Maureen, don't think like that at all. You had to tell someone, and I'm just happy that you trusted me enough to share this. I know it was difficult. I just don't like to see you cry, all upset like this, that's all.'

Reg glances at his watch. 'If we don't get you back soon, you'll be upset with me for making you miss the curfew at the hostel.'

As we walk back to the car, I feel a weight has lifted from my shoulders. Just sharing this awful burden with someone who cares has made a huge difference. I feel slightly more whole and hopeful, now that he understands me so much more.

❖ FORTY-THREE ❖

Reg's Aston Martin sits idling outside of Warwickshire House.
We've just returned from my twenty-second birthday
celebration, which we shared with Charles and Susan. Reg and I have
been dating steadily now for nine months, and even my friends are
grudgingly accepting that I care deeply for this flashy Londoner from
the East End. At half-past ten, with some time yet before curfew,
Reg turns off the car and looks thoughtfully through the windscreen.
What comes out of his mouth next takes me completely by surprise.
'I honestly think, Maureen, that you should start the search for your
family. It's about time, don't you think?' He turns to look at me. I
open my mouth to answer, but he holds up a hand. 'We could take
a short trip back to Ireland and begin the enquiries from Mullingar.
Well, what do you say? Sound like a plan?'

'Are you having me on or do you honestly mean this, Reg? Of course
I'd love to go back to Mullingar. But you must know that I can't afford it.
I mean, I hadn't expected to go for some time yet. Who knows . . .'

'Happy birthday, Maureen! I know your money situation, that's
why I'm offering to take you! It's a little birthday present!'

'Little,' I say, almost in a whisper. 'Oh, that would be absolutely
wonderful, Reg. It's not a little present at all. It's the greatest gift. I
can't believe this. I don't know what to say!' I can see the sincerity in
his face. This means a lot to him, and it seems he's given it a great
deal of thought already.

'Just say, "Yes, Reg, darling, of course I will go!"' Without waiting
for a response, he continues. 'We'll rent a car in Dublin and get about
much quicker that way. We might have to do a bit of running about.
And I can't leave Charles alone for more than three days.'

'But, Reg, it will take a few days just to get there and back, what
with the train to Holyhead and then across the Irish sea and . . .'

'Fly, love, fly! We'll take a flight from London to Dublin in no time at all.'

'Fly?'

'Like two birds. I hope you won't have trouble getting the time off from your job, will you, love?'

'I'll get it off somehow. It won't be a problem. I'll not let anything get in the way of this chance. I must write to Mrs Hughes immediately to tell her we are coming. We can start the search for my family there. Yes, it makes sense.'

Reg glances at his watch. 'You better run, Maureen. It's five to eleven. I don't want to get you in trouble with the warden. I'll sit here for a while and watch the neckers.'

'You're terrible,' I tell him, as I reach over and give him a long kiss. 'Thanks so much for doing this.'

He gives me a long kiss back. 'Don't mention it, love. I'm delighted to help you out this way. Let's just hope for the best and make the most of it.'

'We will. Now, one more kiss and then I have to run.' The kiss is another long one, and then I fly up the stairs to sign in and make curfew. I burst into the room, not allowing Margo a moment before spilling out the great news. 'I've wonderful news!'

'What? Well, will you tell me, for God's sake, Maureen! Goodness, I've not seen you this excited before!'

'I'm just so happy. Reg is taking me to Ireland to help me search for my family! Isn't that wonderful? Oh, Margo, this is . . .'

'Wait,' she says, holding up her hand. 'Wait just a minute. What do you mean search for your family? You told me they were dead, your parents. Who is this other family you're going off to find? An uncle, an aunt?'

Suddenly, a little of the joy is gone, and I realise I must now explain the whole shameful story to Margo. She'll be the first of my friends to discover the truth, and I'm so afraid to tell her. I sit on the bed and look over at her. 'Well, you see, Margo, it's not quite the way I told you. Oh, listen, I'm so sorry, but what I told you was a lie. I made it all up. I always do, I . . .'

'Made what up, Maureen? What are you talking about? I'm totally
lost now!'

'Let me explain. The truth is I don't know who my father is. I'm
illegitimate. I do know that my mother gave me up when I was born.
I know her name is Annie Harte. She gave me away to a couple in
Mullingar to be raised with them. They'd no children. Their name
was Kane. Well, that was fine, but then Mr Kane, he . . . he died,
and I was put into the orphanage at the age of three.'

I can go no further, and I start to sob uncontrollably. 'I'm sorry,
Margo. I've never told anyone this before. Only Reg knows. I'm so
ashamed of who I am, and I don't even know who that is. I want to
belong to someone. He's going to take me to Ireland, and we'll try
to find my family . . .'

'Maureen, just a moment, calm down. It's all right,' Margo sits
beside me on the edge of the bed. 'My God, you should've told me
the truth, all of us. It makes no difference to me, and I know the
others will feel the same. We accept you for who you are, not because
of your past. My goodness, if I'd known.'

We talk late into the night, and I tell her the whole story. Sitting
back on her bed now with her arms crossed on her knees, she listens
with a look of sympathy and fascination, shaking her head in disbelief
at times. 'My God, you've been keeping an awful lot inside. It was
terrible what they did to you. I don't know how you got through it.
I can't even begin to imagine going through that myself. You're a
very brave person. I feel I know you better now you've shared this
with me.'

A long silence hangs between us before Margo continues. 'Tell me
one thing,' she says. 'You spent all that time with this Mrs Hughes
– your two holidays from the orphanage and then living with her
after you left. Why did you not ask her? Why didn't you ask all the
questions you have: who, what, when, where? Who was my mother?
Is she alive? Where are my living relations?' Margo shakes her head
in total amazement, like she cannot fathom someone not asking those
questions. I suddenly feel very tired. The weight of years of memories
and events that are impossible to share or explain overwhelms me.

'Oh, Margo, don't you think I've thought about that and wondered why? The truth is I don't know why. I could never bring myself to do it. It was the way we were raised in the orphanage. You didn't open your mouth in the orphanage – ever. You didn't question things or ask why things were the way they were. We were beaten for the smallest things: speaking up, making a noise, asking questions. You've no idea what it was like, what I've seen. I didn't grow up in the same world as you. It may have been the same country, but it was a different world altogether . . . I wish . . . I . . . of course I should have asked more questions.'

'I'm sorry. I'm seeing it through my own eyes, not yours. I didn't go through it. Thank you for trusting me with this. And the others won't judge you because of your past. You're one of us, and we all think the world of you. Please don't worry. But it's late now. Let's go to sleep. And, Maureen, thank you.'

I toss and turn into the night, too restless and overrun with thoughts to sleep, wondering what this search for my family will turn up, if anything at all. I've come a long way since my leaving day, but the orphanage has followed me like a shadow. When I look inside myself, beyond the laughter and the good times, I see only Maureen the orphan, the illegitimate child with a shameful past.

I have a name: Harte. I am Maureen Harte, but I'm so alone with that name. I want to know what became of my mother. I want to belong and to say I am a member of that family, that I am a Harte, too. But there's also the chance I may not be welcomed by my mother or any of my other relations. It's a very real possibility I have to face: to be rejected now, after all the years of longing and hoping to be reunited and accepted. It would devastate me, and it fills me with dread. But I'm going ahead with it. I'll take the risk of rejection. I must.

On an early May day, with the sun shining brightly and the flowers in full bloom, Reg and I start out on our exciting trip to Ireland to look for my family. 'Come on, Maureen, or we'll be late,' he says patiently, as we rush through the airport to the boarding area.

'I'm sorry, Reg. This is all so interesting to me, and I've not . . .'

'I know, I know. You've never been in an airport before or on a plane before, but if you keep sightseeing, we'll be standing watching our flight leave without us!' Reg laughs at my excitement. I must seem like a gawking little child as I look about, and I'm not even on the plane yet.

After about forty minutes in the waiting area, we begin to board, and soon we're seated, buckled in and comfortable. 'What happens next?' I ask Reg as I look through the small window beside me.

He takes my hand and squeezes it reassuringly. 'Well, they'll seal up all the doors, the pilot will taxi out to the runway and then voom, off we go down the runway and into the clouds. That's all there is to it. Don't worry. After take off, you won't feel much at all, and the weather's clear. There's not likely to be any turbulence today.'

The plane finds its way out to the runway, turns slowly and then stops. Suddenly, the engines roar, and I'm pushed back into my seat. Reg doesn't have to tell me that the plane is taking off. I hold his hand and my breath, looking out of the thick little window and watching the ground beside the runway become a blur. Then the plane lifts off the runway into the air. My stomach jumps as I watch the ground change out of the window. The houses and roads begin to resemble a map the higher we go into the sky. 'Look, Reg, at the houses and roads. It all looks so different from up here. I can see for miles. It's incredible.'

'I know, that's why I gave you the window seat. It's quite something when you see it for the first time.'

About an hour later, we safely touch down at Dublin Airport, and Reg wastes no time in renting a car. Without any fuss or delays, we start out on our journey to the little town of Mullingar in County Westmeath, fifty miles from Dublin. As we get nearer to Mullingar, I watch for the high spire of Christ the King Cathedral, a familiar landmark. 'I hope you know where we're going, Maureen, because I haven't got a bloody clue.'

'Look, there's the cathedral spire in the distance. You can see it as you reach this bridge we're crossing.'

'Never mind the cathedral, just tell me where I'm going! Are we close to Mrs Hughes' house?'

'Yes, we are. This isn't exactly the way I came in Michael Lynch's hired car, but I recognise where I am. It's just round the next bend. You'll see a street of small two-storey terraced houses on your left. Slow down, Reg. There it is on the left! That little house with the half-door.'

I know Mrs Hughes will have difficulty hearing us, so I knock hard on the inner door. She opens the door, greeting us with a big smile on her face. Seeing that warm and genuine smile brings back everything I've grown to love about her and this house. She's aged since I was here last, but I'm just pleased she's still alive and will be able to help me search for my family.

'Ah, sure, there you are, Maureen, and this must be your friend, Reg. You are indeed welcome. Now, Maureen, take Reg upstairs while I set the table for tea. It won't be long. You must be hungry indeed after the long drive.'

Later that evening, Reg and I sit by the fire discussing where to begin the search for my family with Mrs Hughes. 'Well, Maureen,' he begins, 'where do you think we'll start? Have you any ideas?'

'This is the most likely place, right here in Mullingar, but I don't even know how to begin.'

He gazes thoughtfully into the turf fire before turning to me. 'Didn't you tell me that your mother had gone to Dublin for a time? Might there be someone there?'

'She did go to Dublin and kept in touch with Mrs Hughes, but then Annie sent her a letter saying she'd something important to tell her. But there were no further letters after that, not a thing. It was as if she'd disappeared.'

Mrs Hughes sits down and joins us beside the fire, and I fill her in on what Reg and I are talking about. I explain to her that we're wondering where to start looking, hoping that this will pry some old titbit loose. 'Ah, yes, indeed now, isn't that why you came all this way,' she says, sitting back and thinking. And then, very casually, as if it was an afterthought, she says, 'Ah, sure, isn't there a Della Harte here in Mullingar, up on Patrick Street. Now, she's a cousin of Annie's, your mammy, Maureen, and she might be able to help you, though I don't know. Sure, you could go up and talk to her.'

Reg and I quickly exchange a stunned look, both of us thinking the same thing: that this was the last thing we expected to hear from Mrs Hughes. 'A Harte you say? A distant cousin?' I try hard to hide my excitement and surprise. I'd never considered there would be any Hartes this close by, and never even a casual mention of it to me, my God.

'That's right, up on Patrick Street near the railway station,' she answers, before gazing back into the fire. We could be talking about the weather, and Reg must think this is all quite odd.

A Harte living by the railway station. How many times have I driven by there in Michael Lynch's hired car, coming and going to the train station on my holidays here? This is most promising. If this Della Harte is a cousin of Annie's, then she'd be fairly close in age to my mother. 'We could get an early start in the morning,' Reg says. 'If she does know something, we might have to go somewhere after that. What do you think, Maureen?'

'We will, Reg. We'll start early, like you say, in case she knows something.'

Early the next morning, I feel wrought with anxiety as we drive away from the house towards Della Harte's on Patrick Street. Doubts and the fear of disappointment fill my mind. Less than five minutes later, we turn into Patrick Street, and I recognise it immediately. 'I know this street. Number twenty-five, right?'

'That's right, love. There it is.' Reg parks directly in front of the house before taking my hand to reassure me. 'Good luck, and don't be afraid to speak up and ask about your mother.'

I walk from the car to the front door, ring the doorbell and say a quick prayer. A tall woman, in her mid-sixties, perhaps, wearing glasses and with an apron on, opens the door. 'Yes?' she asks, peering intently into my face.

'Good morning. I'm Maureen Harte. I've come from Mrs Hughes' house on Austin Friars Street to ask if you know anything about my mother, Annie, or any of her family's whereabouts?' There, I did it. I got it out.

Della Harte looks shocked for a moment, her eyes widening behind her glasses and her jaw falling slightly open. But she collects herself quickly. 'Your mother, you say? Annie Harte? Oh, good gracious, are you Annie's . . . the one . . . you're her daughter?'

'I am, yes, and I'm trying to find out where my family are.'

For what seems like a long time, we remain standing in the door. She stares into my face in disbelief, as if she's trying to see my mother in me. 'Will you come in? Forgive me, it's a bit of a shock, you see,' she says finally, peering past my shoulder at the car parked outside her door.

'I've someone waiting outside and mustn't stay long,' I explain as I follow her into the kitchen.

'Ah, yes, I saw the car, right enough. Where are you coming from, dear?'

'I'm living in London now.'

'Oh, I see. Well, sit yourself down. Well, yes, in fact I can help you. I'm a third cousin to your mother. Annie had five brothers, but I knew only one of them: Christy Harte, the oldest. He worked here in Mullingar. Your mother worked here, too, as a maid for a doctor.' She stops talking and looks right at me. 'Ah, sure those were dreadful times.' She looks very serious, pausing to reflect on years gone by.

What is she trying to tell me by saying that? I decide to be direct and bold. 'Do you know where my mother is now? Or any of my uncles?'

'Ah, sure that I wouldn't know. I lost touch with Annie a long time ago, but I do hear from your uncle Christy now and again. Not too often, now. He went off to Dublin around the same time as your mother. I've no idea about the other lads at all, though, I'm sorry. Sure, that was a long time ago.'

I listen to this in agony, waiting for her to get to the point, not knowing whether to have any hope yet or not. Does she know something that will actually help or is she just reliving old times? Then she says, 'Christy, your uncle, drives a bus in Dublin. That much

I do know. I've his address, now, if you'll give me a moment.'

A tremor of joy surges up in me as I watch her walk to a little table in the corner of the kitchen. An address! My uncle's address in Dublin! That's what I was waiting for. What a feeling. I have to fight hard not to show my excitement as Della returns and hands me a piece of paper.

'If you're willing to go to Dublin, that's where you'll find your uncle, all right. In a place called Ringsend in the city.'

I can only nod and stare at the address. It doesn't occur to me to ask anything else about my mother. I feel blank, and I can only think of getting to Dublin and going straight to this address. 'Thank you so much, Della. This is so helpful. I'd no idea at all that there was anyone who knew my mother living so close to Mrs Hughes. Thank you so very much! I'd better go now. I think we'll head straight to Dublin from here.'

She walks me to her front door, again looking hard into my face. 'Good luck to you, now, Maureen.'

'Thank you. Goodbye.'

I run to the car and blurt out in a single breath that I have the address of one Christy Harte, my mother's brother in Dublin. Reg smiles broadly, taking the paper from my hand. 'That's great. But let's go. We're being watched, we are!'

I wave a final time to Della Harte. She's still standing in her doorway, looking as if someone from beyond the grave has just paid a visit to her door. 'Well, that was easy enough,' Reg says, smiling. 'Did you ask any questions about your mother?'

'No! I didn't even think of it. I was too excited, and when she handed me the address I could hardly think. Oh, this is so amazing, Reg!'

'It is, love, but what's more amazing is that you were never told about this Della Harte. She was living here all this time and not even a mention, eh?'

'I know. I was thinking about that last night. But you have to understand the Irish and what they're like in these small towns. It's not that unusual for them, especially when it has to do with secrets and the whole illegitimate thing, you know?'

'I'm learning as we go, love. It's quite different here in Ireland, and it's good for me to see it. It's too bad, though, that you didn't just blurt out a question or two to old Della while you had the chance. If she does know anything about back then, she might have taken great delight in being the one to share it with you. Oh, well, too late for that now. We've got what we were after.'

'I'm sure we've given Della Harte enough to think and talk about for quite some time. She knew right away. She said something like, "You're the one." And then she stopped herself from saying something else, but I know what she was going to say.'

'Ah, now, you oughtn't to worry about that,' he says. 'For you to show up now, over twenty years later, that would shock the bleedin' life out of her, I'd say. It was a stroke of luck, you know, to get this address.' He squeezes my hand in reassurance. 'So, it's off to Dublin!'

✤ FORTY-FOUR ✤

O nce in the Dublin area, we have little trouble finding the neighbourhood of Ringsend, and after some twists and turns through the narrow, busy streets and 'blimey loves' we find Ringsend Road. Reg pulls onto the curb, stopping a few doors away from number ninety-one. He turns to me. 'Are you really ready for this?'

'I don't know, Reg. All my life I've been ready, but now that it's here I'm shaking like a leaf. I don't know what to expect from my uncle. Suppose they turn me away and want nothing to do with me. That's always been at the back of my mind. They're not even expecting me. They don't know me.'

'Take a few deep breaths, love. That's it. Just calm down and sit for a few minutes longer.'

What will this be like for me? After all the years and the dreaming, all the waiting and tears, what will it feel like to finally meet my family? Mustering some final courage, I look at the immediate scene: the old bridge spanning the Liffey ahead in the distance, a bottle factory immediately next to us and across the road a line of terraced houses. I stare at number ninety-one for a moment. 'All right, I'm going up there.'

'I'll be right here, Maureen, no matter how it goes. I'll be here, just remember that. Good luck. Now go on.'

As I walk up the path to the house, I feel much the way I did when I stepped from the train on my first trip to Mullingar: alone, scared and with no idea of what to expect. On the glass section above the door is the inscription 'St Jude'. That Saint Jude is the patron saint of hopeless cases flashes through my mind. Reg will find it very funny that I thought of this at such a time. Well, there's no turning back now. I close my eyes, and my lips move in silent prayer as I ring the doorbell.

Moments later, a tall man with thinning hair and a broad, friendly face opens the door. He looks at me without recognition, waiting. 'Are you Christy Harte?' I ask.

'I am.'

'I'm Annie's daughter, Maureen Harte.'

There's dead silence for a moment, and my entire world shrinks to this scene at the door. Then, beginning to understand, he repeats my words, almost in a whisper. 'Maureen . . . Annie's daughter . . .' His eyes fill with tears, and we stare at one another in silence.

Suddenly, a woman's voice intrudes, breaking the spell. 'Will you for God's sake ask them in, Christy, whoever it is!' The woman can only be my uncle's wife. She appears at the front door, wiping her hands on an apron.

Looking stunned and shocked, Christy says, 'This is Maureen, Annie's daughter.' And to me he says, 'My wife, Lily Harte.'

'What!' she cries with disbelief. 'Annie's daughter! Annie's . . . my God! Why, Jesus, Mary and Joseph, would you believe it! Come in, come in! How on earth did you find us?'

'I've a friend waiting in the car,' I explain, gesturing back towards Reg.

'Well, sure, go and ask him in,' Lily says in a strong Dublin accent, stretching her neck out to get a good look.

I run down the path to the car. 'This is the place, Reg,' I say, breathless. 'This is my uncle's place! They've asked us in. Come and meet them!'

Reg's face breaks into a big smile, and I've never seen him look so relieved. Christy shows us into the front parlour, and as I introduce Reg, Lily goes off to bring us tea and sandwiches. Christy sits opposite us in his armchair, looking a bit like he's just been told of a death in the family. In the awkward silence, I nervously explain how we were led through Mrs Hughes to Della Harte and from her right here to Ringsend. 'Hughes?' my uncle repeats weakly. 'Sure, I know no Hughes in Mullingar.'

'She's the woman my mother gave me to when I was born. She was Mrs Kane then, and she still lives on the Dublin road in Mullingar.'

I watch my uncle to see if he reacts to the name Kane or Hughes, but he seems only stunned, pained by the events he's being forced to think about.

'Ah, sure, I see now,' Christy replies, sitting back in his chair with his hands on his knees and looking at a spot on the carpet.

I go on, hoping to warm him to the whole idea. 'Della Harte told me that she knew you but not your brothers, that my mother worked for a doctor there in Mullingar and that you eventually moved to Dublin. She said that she stayed in contact with you for a time.' As I watch Christy struggle with his emotions and his memory, I begin to feel bad about the way I've arrived: unannounced and out of the past.

'Della Harte is a third cousin of mine,' Christy says, 'and your mother's, but I've not written to her for a long time now.'

'Yes, that's what she told me. She knew only that you drove a bus . . . and your address.' I look at Reg quickly, then down at the ground. There is something unreal here in this room. I can feel it. My uncle's eyes when he looks at me reveal a heavy sadness. What is it?

'I'm glad that you did, Maureen,' Christy says numbly.

'You see, Uncle Christy, Reg has brought me over to Ireland for the purpose of finding my family. Before meeting Della Harte today, I've known not a single detail about my family, and I have no idea where my mother is, either.'

'I see, I see. Yes, I used to keep in touch with Della, after I left Mullingar, but then we had the children, and raising a family has kept us very busy.'

Lily returns to the parlour with a tray of tea and sandwiches, setting them down and asking us to help ourselves before sitting herself. I look over again at Reg. He nods his head slightly: go ahead and ask the question you must, he's telling me. I feel the answer throughout the room and in the way my uncle looks at me. I look up at my uncle, trying to meet his eyes, but I can't. Suddenly, I feel very alone, far apart from Reg and the whole world. An invisible wall shoots up around me. I steel myself inside and blurt out, 'Is my mother still alive?'

'Oh no,' Lily says, in a matter-of-fact tone. 'Your mammy's dead, but, sure, how could you know that? She died very young, at the age of thirty-four, twelve years ago.'

'Twelve years ago,' I say to no one in particular, and then it hits me coldly: my mother is dead. I feel only numbness and disbelief.

Silence fills the cosy little parlour. Lily jumps up from her chair. 'Would you like to see a picture of your mammy, Maureen? I'm sure you must do.'

'Yes, please,' I answer, not prepared for any of this. My mother is dead and gone for ever. I will never, ever meet her. The news slowly starts to sink in, and I feel the shock begin to settle upon me. This is happening too fast . . .

I look up to see Christy's eyes fill silently with tears as he watches Lily root about in the drawer for the photos. He wipes one away as it escapes down his cheek, obviously very moved and embarrassed by the entire situation. 'Ah, here it is,' she says in a wistful voice. 'Her memorial card.'

She hands me a small card. As I reach out to take it from her, everything I've ever been or known seems to come sharply into focus, and suddenly I feel very alone and disconnected from everyone around me. For the first time in my life, I look at the woman who gave me life. My mother, Annie Harte. The photo is tiny, no more than an inch by an inch and a half, black and white and set into the middle of the first open page. I stare into the image. Annie has a full round face, and her hair is dark like mine, cut short but full and piled up neatly in a plain, old-fashioned style. The photo is slightly blurry, and it is hard to get an impression of Annie's personality from the two eyes set back behind the large round eyeglasses. The neutral expression seems to belie an inner sadness but a mysterious intelligence as well. Below the image are the words 'Sacred Heart of Jesus, have mercy on the soul of Annie Gaffney, Oughill, Redcross, Co. Wicklow, who died on the 2nd February, 1942, aged 34 years. R.I.P. Loving Lord Jesus, grant her eternal rest.' I look back at her face, scanning every detail of a mother I will never know.

Uncle Christy begins to speak, his voice hushed and low. 'She died,

Maureen. She was young, too young. She married John Gaffney, from Wicklow, and died just over a year later. She was thirty-four.'

'She died from an ectopic pregnancy,' Lily adds. 'The child as well. On her way to the Rotunda Hospital here in Dublin. She was too young to die, God bless her. There were no other children by the marriage.'

I scarcely note these details as I look towards my uncle, the shock turning to agony. 'I honestly thought I'd find her alive,' I say, then the dam breaks, and I can no longer hold back the tears and the pain. I cry and cry, not caring or wanting to stop.

'I'm so sorry, Maureen,' Christy says.

I look down again at the memorial card. 'This is all I'll ever have of her now, this picture.'

Reg gets up, goes down on one knee and takes my hand. 'I'm sorry, Maureen. This is a hard way for you to find out. But at least you know now, and you've found your family. Isn't this what you wanted all these years, to find someone to belong to you?'

I say nothing to him. I know he's right, but my loss is so agonising I cannot see any positive side. Deep inside, I begin to recognise old feelings – frightening and lonely feelings that I've known long before this day. The sense of abandonment is complete now and overwhelming. I was twelve when she died and still in the orphanage. Why did she not come to see me? Where was she while I was longing and hoping for a single visitor? Why did she not try to contact me through Mrs Hughes? Why had Mrs Hughes never put me in touch with my family? She could have done so, many times.

Before I can help it, my bitter thoughts rush out as spoken words as I look up at Reg. 'I know, Reg, but I was twelve years old when she died. You don't understand!' Then, to my uncle, 'Why didn't my mother come to see me in the orphanage? I was there for thirteen years, and no one ever came to see me, ever!'

Even through the tears in Christy's eyes, I can see his shock at the mention of the orphanage. 'Orphanage? What! I always believed you were being raised in Mullingar with this woman you just mentioned, and I felt at that time it wasn't my place to interfere or change what was arranged for you by your mother.' Christy's voice sounds distant and evasive. I have no idea if he's telling me the whole truth. He sounds like a man caught entirely by surprise, by a past he thought was buried. My eyes remain fixed on the little memorial card, at the small picture and the still face. Am I trying to see into my mother's soul and hoping she will somehow speak to me from this image? What would she say to me if she could? Would she be sorry? Would she be proud of me? Will she watch over me? Does she care? I read more words on the little card, on the page opposite the one with her picture.

> Though your smile is gone for ever,
> And your hand we cannot touch,
> We shall never lose sweet memories,
> Of you we loved so much.

> We miss you now, our hearts are sore,
> As time goes on, we miss you more.
> Your loving smile, your gentle face,
> No one can fill your vacant place.

The shallow rhymes and words on the card are hollow and empty to me, without meaning. I have never known her to miss her, but I do. I have no memories of her, none at all. I look up to see my uncle gazing at me with a strange, forlorn look on his face as he wipes more silent tears away.

'Yes, I was there for thirteen years,' I manage to say in a flat voice, looking back again at the card in my hand. 'You don't know how much I longed for this day. To sit with people who were family, to find out who I am, and now my mother isn't alive to see me.'

'I'd no idea, Maureen, no idea at all,' Christy continues to speak softly to me, shaking his head sadly and reliving all these painful memories that had surely been fading before I showed up.

The tense sombre mood in the parlour is shattered by a sudden commotion from somewhere else in the house. I can hear the sound of doors opening and children's voices. Lily stands up, smiling at me. 'Ah, now, Maureen, sure you'd not expected to meet any first cousins today. Won't they be tickled. Give me a minute, and I'll tell them.'

'Our children, home from school for their dinner,' Christy says, with more than a hint of pride.

Lily opens the parlour door, motioning me to follow. 'Sure, they can't wait to meet you. Come along to the kitchen, pet.'

I hadn't thought about this, having first cousins. It's an odd feeling, and I'm immediately curious. Lily takes me down to the kitchen to meet my three young cousins: Jimmy, age eleven, Marie, age nine, and Pauline, the youngest, age five. Jimmy is in his schoolboy's short pants, and Marie beams at me with a smile that reminds me right away of Christy. Little Pauline gazes up at me with her beautiful dark hair full of ringlets. 'Where does Maureen live, then?' Marie asks her mammy shyly, avoiding looking at me.

'Maureen doesn't live in Ireland,' Lily explains, and they have to hear more about this.

'I live in London, England. But I'm Irish, too, just like you are,' I explain, spending some time chatting with them in the kitchen as they eat and telling them how happy I am to have found them.

'When are you coming to visit us again?' little Pauline wants to know as Lily bustles about the kitchen collecting bags and coats to get them ready for their return to school.

'I hope it won't be too long, Pauline,' I answer, pleased they seem to have taken to me.

'All right, you three, it's back to school now, so say goodbye, and you'll see Maureen again soon, God willing.'

I say goodbye to the three of them as they rush to leave for school, feeling very touched by their excited reaction to me. I have first cousins and a family now, and I begin to feel a little better as I walk back along the narrow hall to the parlour with Aunt Lily.

The arrival of the children seems to have broken the terrible heaviness that hung in the parlour earlier. Reg and Christy have been talking about cars and buses and what not. As Christy turns casually to look at me, I see in his face a kind and caring man. He didn't turn me away and close the door in my face. I see also the pain that I brought with me into his home. Christy must have loved my mother, his only sister whom he lost so young.

'You know, Maureen,' he says, 'that you've two uncles living in London, not far from you. Paddy and Jimmy, my two younger brothers. And if you're interested, there's another relation here in Ireland, a great-uncle to you. Uncle Joe Harte, he lives in Milltownpass in Westmeath on a couple of acres of land.'

'Della Harte told me that my mother had five brothers. Where are the other two?'

'Dead, I'm sorry to say. Tommy and Sean. They died of tuberculosis at a very young age, and so did your grandparents, my mother and father.'

I listen carefully to my uncle, watching his sombre expression as he tells me some of the Harte family background. So much suffering and tragedy; we've all suffered in our own way. I begin to calm down as I listen to his soft voice speaking in a melodious Dublin accent, and the mood in the parlour seems like that of a simple visit. But as I gaze at the memorial card and the other photos, I hear myself asking, 'Do you know, Uncle Christy, who my father is?'

'No,' he answers, rather abruptly, as he glances quickly at Reg. 'Well, there were rumours, Maureen, that it might be a man by the name of Logan. He lived as a boarder in the same house as your mother, but I'm not sure.' It's obvious he doesn't want to pursue the subject, likely embarrassed, especially in front of Reg, an Englishman.

My head is spinning with questions, none of which I feel are safe enough to ask. You're the same, Maureen. You're playing the same game of burying the past. It's what you've been taught, and it's all you know. Damn it all, I feel so crippled! The questions stream silently past like a rushing river. What happened? Who was my father? Where was Christy when I was born and how old was he? What role did he truly play? Where was this mysterious boarding house, and was my father really this man Logan? What became of him? Did he seduce Annie one night and I am the unacceptable result who had to be hidden away? Had Annie fallen head over heels in love with my father? Was Logan perhaps penniless and left with nothing to do but flee after the unfortunate news was out? Had Annie been forced into her decision? Was my father driven away by an infuriated, dishonoured brother?

But I can only utter a single, feeble question. 'What was my mother like? As a person, I mean. I'd love to know. As a little girl growing up there, I always wondered . . . there were so many things that I wondered about.'

'Ah, Maureen, pet, everybody loved your mammy. She was very gentle. We missed her terribly when she died. She was a very kind woman, and any time she came to visit she would always bring some little trinket for us.'

It's strange listening to someone talking about my mother, about her personality and what she was like. I'm happy in one way, hearing all this, and yet I burn inside with the need to find out more. They must know something, and it's just too difficult for them to go into, and too shameful, maybe. I'll try a final time, to see if I can wring anything from Christy. 'Do you know anything at all about when I was born, where my mother was born and what she did?'

Christy leans back in his chair, the tension obvious in his movements. 'Well, your mammy was of course born in Milltownpass. All of us were. You were born in Mullingar because Annie had moved there to be a maid for a doctor in town . . . and . . . well, that's where it all took place. After that, well, I wasn't involved at all really.'

'You say there was a boarding house, where my mother lived. Do you . . .'

Christy cuts me off, quietly but definitely. 'Yes, that's where your mammy lived, and maybe this fellow Logan lived there at the same time. That's all I really know. It was such a difficult time . . .' He lets his words die, and the parlour goes quiet, like a tomb full of shameful secrets.

A sudden surge of anger ripples through me. How evasive he's being. If I had more nerve, I'd challenge him, beg him even. We came all this way to find only bits and pieces of a shattered past and the news that my mother is long dead. I know Christy knows more than he's letting on. Why? Why this silence? Do they not feel I deserve the truth after all those years of waiting and wondering and hoping? I'll get no more answers today.

Lily hands me photos of my uncle Paddy and uncle Jimmy, the two living close to me in London. 'Jimmy's so like my mother,' I say, studying the picture.

'You're right,' Lily agrees. 'They're the spitting image of one another.'

I see some other photos of my mother, looking happy in family group shots. I see her in these pictures getting on with her life and looking happy. It only makes it even more difficult. The anger returns. Thirteen years and not a card or a visit: it's like I didn't even exist in her mind. It's a simple fact that I will leave here today still in the dark about so many things.

'Take that memorial card with you, Maureen, and these ones,' Lily says, her words bringing the parlour back into focus before me. I glance across at Reg, feeling almost as emotionally spent as I did on my leaving day. Sensing my mood and that this is probably enough now for all of us, he hints at leaving. I turn to Lily. 'I'll look forward to meeting my uncles in London, Paddy and Jimmy. What's the best way to go about contacting them do you think?'

'Not to worry, pet,' Lily assures me. 'You just leave me the address of where you're living and any telephone numbers there. We'll write to them straight away and tell them about your visit here. I'm sure you'll hear from them before long.'

'Thanks so much for offering to do that for me,' I say, scribbling out my address at the hostel in London.

'You're quite welcome, pet,' Lily says, taking my hand in hers. 'It's the least we can do, and I know they'll be as surprised as we were, Maureen.' She smiles as she says this, and I know she means surprise in a nice way. I feel comforted by her gentle support and her kind manner.

Christy and Lily walk us back to the car amidst promises to meet again and many thanks from me and Reg. 'Have a safe trip back,'

Christy says with a final wave. As we pull away into the Dublin traffic, I watch his form become smaller and smaller. I wave back to them a final time and settle into quiet contemplation, without words to describe what I've just been through. It's been remarkable and unsettling: the joy of finding my family tempered by the terrible truth that I will never know my mother.

Reg is very proud of what we have accomplished and extremely happy for me. What we thought would be a long search for my family is over in less than a day. I've found my family and the truth about my mother, but it hasn't turned out the way I imagined it. I feel shocked and wrung out. I hold the little memorial card in my palm like a precious jewel, gazing at the silent image of my mother and unable to tear my eyes away. 'I don't look like her, Reg, do I? I must look like my father, Logan or whoever he was.'

'Show it to me again. Just hold it up.' He looks quickly at the little card. 'I suppose not, but she's your mother, and you do have the same dark hair, certainly.' We drive on past the outskirts of Dublin and westward. The city scenes slowly give way to a patchwork of green fields, farms and villages. As the scenery rushes past us, my mind whirls with images and questions – so many questions still. 'What are you thinking about, Maureen?' Reg asks, looking across at me. 'Tell me now. Don't keep it all in, love. Do you regret coming and finding out what we have?'

'No, never think that. Not in a million years. It's just that all this time I had such hope, and she's been dead for so long already.' I pause for moment in thought. 'Do you believe Christy? That they didn't know I was in the orphanage and that I was being raised in Mullingar by someone else?'

He doesn't hesitate with his response. 'How could they not have known? I mean, they may have known you were given to someone who would raise you, but that only lasted three years, love. They must have known that you were sent away. It's a small town, and word spreads quickly. They didn't want to know, Maureen. People can force themselves to forget things, unpleasant and embarrassing things, shameful things. And Christy seemed to contradict himself once or twice, you know, in the memory department. And listen, love. I think I understand now why it was so hard for you to ask them more questions. Oh, I felt it in there. The shame and denial. Believe me I felt it, and I do understand.'

I turn my head away, watching the passing scenes, the beautiful fields and scenery indifferent to my heartache. 'And why didn't a single member of your family ever check with Mrs Hughes?' Reg continues. 'Why did Mrs Hughes never tell them, even just to let them know how you were doing from time to time, if they really did think you were growing up in Mullingar?' He reaches across and rests his hand on mine. 'I know this is hard, love, but really now. Don't you think it unlikely? Not one word in thirteen years? Very unlikely.'

'It's all beginning to fit, Reg, you're right. It was all just covered up, from Mullingar to Dublin to the orphanage.'

I begin to relive the events of the day, and again I feel angry with my mother instead of sadness over her death. My mood swings crazily back and forth between a terrible sense of loss and utter abandonment. Thank God I'm with Reg. His honest appraisal of the meeting at Christy's helps me think more clearly about it all. I look down again at the memorial card in my hand, thinking of my mother and her death. Then it hits me: how close my faked stories are to the actual details of Annie's death. 'Oh no,' I say aloud, my hand over my mouth.

'What is it, love?'

My heart starts to pound strangely, and my breathing becomes frighteningly shallow. I stare unbelievingly at the picture and the words: 'Annie Gaffney . . . died February 2nd . . .'

'Maureen, what is it? What's wrong?'

This is more than I can take right now, and my head starts spinning. 'Reg, oh Reg. How my mother died: that's what I told you and everyone else for years. Oh, I don't feel well. I feel sick . . .' The sudden realisation seems to break through the last remaining bastion of my ability to stay in control. My whole world is shrinking in on me and terrifying me. I've never known a feeling like this!

'What is it?'

'Pull over, Reg! I don't feel well.' I begin to disassociate from my immediate surroundings, feeling only terror, as if I'm completely alone in the universe. Reg stops the car. I feel my heart pounding wildly. I can't get my breath. I dig my nails into the seat as I clutch for the door handle. 'Reg, what's happening, my heart! What's happening to me?'

'Maureen!' he almost shouts at me. 'You're panicked, that's all. Just breathe or it'll get worse!' He gets out of the car and comes round to my side. He opens the door, gets down on one knee and holds both my hands in his. 'Just take deep breaths. You'll be all right. It's a panic attack or something. It'll pass. You'll be fine!' He seems far away as I start to think that I might die from the terror of this moment. 'Look at me. Look into my face. Just breathe and let it go. It's all in your mind, that's all. It's just the shock, love!'

I stare at his face as if it's a far off place I must somehow get to. Slowly, so slowly, I feel my breathing return to normal, and I eventually slump back in a flood of exhaustion and tears. How tired I am. How wrung out by all of this. 'We'll stop in the next town, love, at the first place, and get you some tea.'

'Oh, Reg, what would I have done without you here with me?' I try to thank him. I try to put the events of this day into a place in my head where they will make sense, but they don't and they can't. Instead, I simply curl up and sleep as Reg drives through the countryside toward Mullingar and the little terraced house.

Back at Mrs Hughes', I feel like a limp rag doll, emotionally drained and looking forward to sleep. Sitting down for tea, I tell her all about finding Christy in Dublin and of Annie Harte's death. I show her all the pictures my Aunt Lily gave me.

'Ah, sure that's your mammy all right, Maureen,' she sighs, looking closely at the memorial card. 'I'm happy you found Christy. He's a good man, and he was kind to your mammy when you were born. I'm so sorry. I honestly had no idea, Maureen, that she had died.'

What does that mean exactly? How was he kind to my mammy when I was born? Why could he not have told me that? I'm almost too exhausted to care at this moment, but it does rather suggest that

Reg's suspicions are accurate. But we don't go on about it, and I spare Mrs Hughes all the details of the visit with Christy and Lily Harte. It seems I may never know the whole truth. My father may remain for ever a name without a face, another ghost from the past. We sit quietly by the fire, and even Reg seems lost in his own thoughts.

I watch the glimmering light on the walls of the kitchen, breathing in the earthy scent of the burning turf so familiar to me. All the warm and sad feelings flicker in me, like the play of shadows on the walls. I glance over at Mrs Hughes, realising that she is the closest thing to a mother I will ever know now and that I would've grown up here in this house had fate not shrugged the way it did.

'Maureen?' Reg's voice breaks the gloomy silence. 'Why don't we take a run down to the orphanage tomorrow. We still have a whole day. What do you think?'

'Oh, I don't know if I'm up to it, although I would like to see Mother Brendan, of course.'

'It might do you good,' he encourages. 'And who knows when you'll be back again? It's only about thirty-five miles from here. I've been studying the map.'

'You have, have you? Well, you're a regular London tourist, Reg. Your interest is just getting going!'

'So, it's settled then. We leave here early in the morning!'

❧ FORTY-FIVE ❧

After a pleasant drive from Mullingar to Newtownforbes, we drive slowly through the quiet little village, along the main road, and I point out all the familiar sights for Reg. In a few blinks, we are through the village, and all my nervousness comes back to me as we get closer to the orphanage. As we round the final bend, the grim old buildings come into view, seemingly staring at me in recognition. I stare back at them. 'Take a look at those buildings, Reg, my home for thirteen years.'

'It's just a visit, Maureen. No one can hurt you now.'

We drive over to the main entrance of the convent and park the car. A young novice opens the ornate wooden door. She greets us pleasantly, asking who we are. 'I'm a former orphan, Maureen Harte, and I keep in touch with Reverend Mother Brendan. We happen to be here in Ireland for a few days, and I would love to see her.'

'I see. Do come in. I'm Sister Angela. I'll send for Reverend Mother Brendan. I'm sure she won't be long.'

The young novice shows us into the parlour, asking us to take a seat before leaving and closing the door behind her. Reg is immediately impressed with the furnishings in the parlour. 'Blimey, love, these sofas are worth a few quid, eh?' Before I can answer, he notices the huge stuffed pheasant perched on the sideboard and whistles in quiet admiration. He and Charles often go pheasant hunting in the English countryside. 'Not half bad, that one ain't!'

'Reg, please, this is a convent, a place of reverence.' I can't help but smile at his behaviour. He's always so jovial, and I'm blessed to have him as a friend. Fortunately, the approaching sounds of footsteps prevent him from committing any further blasphemy in the parlour. 'Mother Brendan's coming in,' I whisper. 'Behave.'

She opens the door, greeting us warmly with a welcoming smile as Reg and I stand to greet her. How is it, I wonder yet again, that the nuns never seem to age at all? Her skin is still the same as I've always remembered it since I was a little girl. 'Maureen Harte, well, what a lovely surprise. What brings you back to Ireland again?'

'Hello, Reverend Mother,' I say, shaking hands and introducing Reg as a friend from London.

'Very pleased to meet you, Reg. You are welcome. Do sit down. And tell me, what brings you back this time?'

I've already thought of how I should reply to this, but here in the presence of Reverend Mother Brendan I'm surprised by how difficult I find it. I explain that I have returned to attempt to find my mother and family. I tell Reverend Mother Brendan about my successful discovery of Uncle Christy in Dublin, but when she asks specifically about my mother I feel my emotions suddenly rise again.

'She married a John Gaffney from County Wicklow,' I say, continuing with my nervous report. 'But she died a year and a half later at the age of thirty-four, from an ectopic pregnancy.' I pause before adding sadly and with my eyes downcast, 'I was twelve when she died.'

'How very tragic,' Mother Brendan says. At this, I almost break down again into a fit of crying. When she sees my reaction, she changes the conversation immediately. 'Well, you both must be ready for some dinner. Sister Angela will be in soon with a tray. Tell me, where are you staying?'

'In Mullingar, Reverend Mother, with Mrs Hughes, the woman who claimed me when I was sixteen.'

'Of course, yes, I do remember her. So, you've remained in contact with her, then?'

'Yes, I wouldn't have known where to begin the search for my family if it wasn't for her. It was Mrs Hughes who raised me until I was three, in the same house where we're staying now,' I explain. I hear the sound of my own words as I speak, with Reg listening silently beside me. 'They would have raised me as their own, but her husband died in 1933 when I was just three.'

I go on filling in all the details for Reverend Mother Brendan, but she shows no indication that she feels compelled to add a single fact.

'I see, Maureen, and of course that is when you were placed here in the orphanage with us.'

'Yes, Reverend Mother, that's exactly what happened.'

'How tragic indeed,' she continues in her soft voice.

The young novice arrives with a large tray of food: roast beef and mashed potatoes with carrots and gravy, accompanied by home-made brown bread. Reverend Mother Brendan remains while we eat, chatting casually. 'I often wonder, Maureen,' she goes on, 'how many of the girls have the courage to search for family like you have done.'

I beam inside at this remark. 'I couldn't have done it without Reg's help,' I say, looking across at him and smiling.

'Yes, of course. Sure, how would you get around from one place to the other without someone driving you? I think it's very kind of you, Reg, very kind indeed.' Reverend Mother Brendan continues talking to Reg – about politics, business and current affairs in general. I can see the little dance of words going on between them, and I know she's anxious to discover if Reg is a Catholic. I know that Reg senses this too, and finally he tells her what she wants to know. 'I'm not Catholic myself, Reverend Mother,' he says, looking directly at her, 'but I respect Maureen's faith deeply. It's not a problem between us.'

She looks down, avoiding his eyes. 'I'm sure you do, and I know that you, Maureen, are very strong in your beliefs, and I pray that you will remain so.'

'Thank you, Mother Brendan,' I answer. 'I know you pray for all of us girls, and it's a big comfort.'

'Before I forget, Maureen,' Reverend Mother Brendan continues, 'what's the news with Katy Fallon? Did she make the move to England?'

'She's been and gone, Reverend Mother. It just didn't work out, though she did try . . .' My words trail off into uncomfortable silence.

Reverend Mother Brendan looks away, a strangely forlorn look on her face. 'I know you and Maggie did your very best to help her, Maureen. Perhaps it is for the best.'

As we stand to leave, Reverend Mother Brendan and Reg shake hands, and she thanks him for coming with me to visit her and the sisters. But this isn't the only thing she hopes to influence by prayer. As Reg walks on ahead of me, allowing me a final word, Reverend Mother Brendan holds on to my hand and whispers, 'Perhaps with your prayers, Maureen, Reg will convert to Catholicism.' I'm shocked by this comment, but I don't show it, easy enough to do after all my years of practice with the nuns. I'm glad Reg didn't hear the remark.

I cry as I say goodbye, promising as always to remain in touch. As we pull away from the old grey buildings, I have a quick look up towards my old dormitory window. Who knows when I'll come back again to this place – maybe never. Reg chatters away, impressed by the hospitality shown to us and full of questions about my life in the orphanage. But something about his tone strikes a bitter chord in me. I want to tell him that he didn't see the real orphanage, the place where I grew up. He hasn't really had a glimpse into what life was like for me or how I grew up. He's never been near a religious order in his whole life.

Something inside me wants to scream out 'What about me?' I was the one who spent thirteen years locked away in a prison. I was the one who witnessed and experienced cruelty and neglect on a daily basis. He can never really understand what it was like for me there, and the enormity of this realisation saddens me. No matter what I tell him, he will never really understand my pain. The news of my mother's death seems to have darkened my memories of the orphanage even more, and the anger and rage I feel frightens me.

I keep seeing the photos of my mother standing with her family and friends, smiling and living in the outside world so free and happy. When those pictures were taken, I was rotting in the orphanage, alone and dreaming of a single visit . . .

Maybe we shouldn't have come back here. I feel my nails bite into my palms, and I have to check myself. Fifty little miles: she was only fifty miles away from the orphanage. She abandoned me because I was illegitimate, born out of wedlock. I feel myself drowning in a torrent of abandonment, more than I ever have before. I take deep slow breaths, dreading another panic attack. Gradually, I push the feelings and pictures away and force the door closed, like I always do, like I've been taught to do.

Through the car windows, I look out at Newtownforbes as we leave it behind. It hasn't changed very much over the years. Now, though, at this very moment, it seems washed in a painful haze of memory. The village falls away behind me as I stare out, leaving only the odd house or cottage in the moving frame of the car window. Then it's gone and only the open country and the fields remain. If only some memories were like that – if I could simply keep moving on and away from them until they were no longer there – then maybe I could be like most other people. I could let my past go and watch the ghosts fade like mirages in the distance.

Reg's gloating about our visit and how well the nuns treated us is getting to me. I know he doesn't mean it, but his open and accepting attitude of the whole place is infuriating. 'That place weren't all that bad, Maureen,' he comments. 'I found them to be quite normal people and very hospitable.'

I let out a short, bitter laugh despite myself, hearing the angry edge in my voice. 'Well, of course you did, Reg. The nuns know how to make an impression, even on short notice. And, yes, of course everything you saw today was fine and hospitable and normal. Very normal! But you were only in the nuns' beautiful parlour, with their lovely furniture, and you were treated very specially. You did not experience the convent as I did.'

'I know, love, and . . .'

'Do you know, Reg?' I ask quietly but sharply. 'Do you know? You haven't seen inside the orphanage itself, and if you haven't seen inside the orphanage, you haven't seen where I was raised. And even if Mother Brendan had allowed you to go over, and I doubt she would have, you wouldn't see it, Reg, because the orphans would be too terrified to open their mouths!'

'What's the matter, love? What . . .'

'Just let me finish, please! You did not see that place. You didn't see the beatings, the hunger, the sickness, the lice, the sores. Not the way I did for years. Do you know that during the whole thirteen years I was there, I only saw the nuns' parlour twice as an orphan? Yes, the parlour you so admire! We were allowed in there twice: on my first Holy Communion day and on my Confirmation day! And do you know what? On the second occasion, on our Confirmation day, they had to lock up my friend Colleen Carey in the sickroom so the bishop wouldn't see that she'd gone insane from all the beatings. That's what they did: they beat her until she was mad and then they hid her away so no one would know the truth. This is what the orphanage was really like. For us, it was nothing like what you've just experienced today.'

'Ah, Maureen, I'm sorry. I . . .'

'And that's what you saw today: a nice parlour in front of all the truth, and just beyond all that, a little way down the hall and through a door, is the real orphanage. It's all so . . . You just can't even begin to . . .' I can take this no farther. The dark cloud of rage in me erupts, and I burst into tears, howling with the injustice and frustration of it all.

Reg stops the car. He doesn't say a word, and he doesn't touch me. He just waits for it to pass, this letting of poison and demons. When finally I can look over at him, I tell him I'm sorry. 'I don't know what's caused this, Reg. That place has a power over me. Please don't think me ungrateful. I'm so sorry.' I place a trembling hand on his shoulder. 'Please!'

'No, I'm sorry, love. Sometimes I talk when I should be thinking, you know? But no matter, it'll help to let go of some of this. A lot has happened, and quickly, in less than two days. You were afraid to come back here, weren't you?'

'At first, yes . . . I'm just so tired from it all, especially since coming back from my uncle Christy's.' I stop and smile – I don't seem to know whether to laugh or cry at the moment. 'Listen to what I just said. "My uncle Christy"! I can't believe this! They're my family, and I have three little cousins and two uncles in London and another little cousin, Brian! Am I not so rich now that I've found my family? I can't thank you enough for everything. It's just that . . . it's very painful to know I'll never meet my mother. How I've held onto that one dream: of one day meeting her and putting my arms around her and . . . it's all gone now.' The tears come again, silently.

'I do understand how you must feel. Never doubt it.' He leans over and draws me into a warm, protective embrace, kissing me softly on the forehead. 'I do understand, love.'

We sit there in the rented car, stopped at the side of the road in the sleepy Irish countryside not far from the orphanage. The fields roll away on both sides of us. An occasional farmer goes by in an ass and cart, nodding or tipping his cap. No one here would think of passing without greeting another person. I close my eyes, listening to the occasional musical clip-clop of hooves. That's a sound I'll not forget. It is in my soul now, in the deepest part of who I am. A light breeze carries the fresh country air through the open window of the car.

Reg talks about how much this trip has meant to him, how happy he is to have seen the orphanage, my home. He says it has given him a new understanding of my past and my background, even my religious side, something he's always teased me about. He now understands my belief in God and how it gives me strength. It will never leave me, he says, and he's right. We drive off through the beautiful countryside, past the stunning scenery and quilt-work shades of green toward Mullingar.

I'm deeply saddened about my mother, and there will be new feelings to come: fear and anger and whys and what ifs. But I will never have to imagine again what it's like to have a family. They've accepted me. I've been adrift alone on an ocean for my whole life. Now, finally, I've found a place on a welcoming shore where the people say, 'You are of us. You're a Harte, too, and you belong here.' I know now that belonging to a family, to other human beings with a common past, is something so very special and as deeply needed as the air we breathe.

Before leaving the next morning, Reg squeezes three twenty-pound notes into Mrs Hughes' hand. I see the shock on her face as she looks down at the money. 'No, Reg, please. Sure, you were hardly here at all.' But he'll have it no other way, closing her hand again and smiling at her appreciation. He tells her loudly how much he loved the town of Mullingar and Ireland. I give her a big hug as we stand at the half-door. 'Goodbye now, Maureen. I'm so happy for you. Do come back again to see me.'

'I will, please God,' I say, tears filling my eyes.

Then, right on cue, Mrs Burke appears from her doorway in her typical way of appearing just as someone is leaving. I'd be disappointed if she said goodbye any other way. 'Ah, sure, it's yourself, Maureen, off again to England! You must be very happy having found your uncle up in Dublin. I'm delighted for you.'

With final and heartfelt goodbyes, we pull away from the little house, waving a final time. Reg squeezes my hand, knowing how I feel at this moment. I will never forget a single detail of this house or the little street and all the wonderful and uncomplicated people who live there. 'That Mrs Burke's a very smart lady,' Reg comments as we move down the main road. 'Yeah, I can see how she'd be in control of things, and she seems very fond of you, Maureen.'

'Yes, I know that only too well. She's made most of the decisions concerning my life. Mrs Hughes can't read or write, the poor thing, so Mrs Burke has been very much in my life since I first arrived.'

'How heartbreaking it must have been,' Reg says, taking hold of my hand, 'when Mrs Hughes' first husband died. I mean, it changed so many lives. But never mind that. Think what we've done! And now you can look forward to seeing your two uncles when we get back to London.'

'Yes, but before I'm ready for that, I'm going to recover from all this for a few days. I'll wait to hear from them, and then maybe go and meet them. If they'll have me. And my little cousin, Brian Harte, is English. He's a Londoner, like you, Reg.' I laugh as I say this, patting his hand.

'A Londoner like me? That's bad. Right outta the Old Blighty. Englishmen are mad, love, beware!'

'The old what?'

'The Old Blighty. You know, old England herself. Britannia and all that.'

Reg starts singing in a ridiculous voice, loud enough for all of Mullingar to hear him. 'Rule, Britannia! Britannia rule the waves. Britons never, never, never shall be slaves!' His singing gets louder and more ridiculous until finally he breaks down into raucous laughter, and then both of us are laughing, harder and harder, without knowing why and caring even less.

Reg, almost in tears, finally stops. 'Blimey, they'll never let me back! But listen, Maureen, in all seriousness, I'm so happy you found what you wanted. I really am. We did it!'

I close my eyes and breathe in the crisp Irish air, wanting to taste it and remember it. I haven't felt so changed since the day I left the orphanage for the first time when I was fourteen. 'Yes, Reg,' I say, my eyes still closed. 'We did it.'

❖ FORTY-SIX ❖

Last night, less than a week after returning to London, I was handed a postcard by Mr Henning at the front desk. To my surprise and delight, it was from my aunt Kathy, Paddy Harte's wife, asking me to send back a response to set up a telephone call. I wrote back immediately, suggesting she call me this evening at the hostel.

The call comes as expected, and Mr Henning connects me at the front desk. My hand trembles as I pick up the receiver. 'Hello?'

'Hello, Maureen?'

'Yes, this is Maureen.'

'Maureen, oh thank God I've got you! It's Kathy Harte. We got a letter from Christy in Dublin. We were shocked, totally shocked. I'd no idea you even existed. My goodness, it's strange to hear your voice. I don't know what to say to you . . .'

I am so touched by this response that it takes me a moment to find my voice. 'Oh, I'd no idea when Christy was going to contact you,' I blurt out. 'I'm so happy to hear from you. You've no idea what this means.'

Then in a rush of words and emotion she says, 'If only someone in the family had told me, I would've taken you out of the orphanage. Never doubt it.'

I sense the emotion in her voice and her sincerity, and I get a sharp pain in my chest. I mustn't start crying or I'll never stop. For a split second, I see a flash of what my life could have been. I can only tell her how much I appreciate what she's saying and how happy I am just to have found them. 'I know that, Maureen,' she responds, her voice faltering again. 'I'd have raised you as my own,' she reiterates. 'I swear I would have. But, listen, Paddy and young Brian, my husband and son, they can't wait to meet you. Will you come for dinner next Sunday?'

'I would love to!'

'That's wonderful. I'll give you the directions to our flat.'

So, Christy has written to his brother in London to tell him all about me showing up on his doorstep in Dublin. How interesting it would be to read that letter.

All this time living in London, thinking I didn't have a soul in the world, and I had family so close by. Imagine if I'd been raised with Uncle Paddy? Then Brian would be like my brother, and I would speak with an English accent. I would've been better educated and, who knows, maybe have chosen a career in something I was good at, something I truly loved. I would've had choices and freedom.

I walk out of Ladbroke Grove station, checking my written directions a final time. It's not far from the station to Uncle Paddy's flat at number twenty-one Bonchurch Road. I pull the knocker back and strike: once, twice. I hear an excited child's voice. It must be Brian. Uncle Paddy opens the door. He stands for a moment, much as Christy had, as if trying to convince himself I am indeed his niece, his long-dead sister's daughter. He's slighter in build than Christy, with no obvious physical resemblance. He smiles broadly after a few seconds. 'You are welcome, Maureen. Come on in,' he says, shaking my hand warmly.

Almost immediately, Brian, who is only seven, pulls me inside and along to the kitchen where his mother's preparing the dinner. I'm a little taken aback but overjoyed by this affectionate reception. Kathy greets me very warmly, taking my two hands in her own and looking at me intently for a long moment. 'Maureen Harte,' she says, shaking her head as Brian continues to tug at me, already wanting me all to himself. 'I still can't believe this. Annie's girl. Who would've thought after all this time? I'm without words other than to say how very welcome you are, and that had we known we would've had you out of that place long ago.' Paddy stands in the kitchen doorway, smiling warmly as he listens.

'Let's go into the sitting room with Maureen,' Brian insists, still tugging at me.

'He's talked of nothing else all week,' Kathy says, tousling his hair and smiling down proudly at him. 'Nothing but meeting his new cousin. Isn't that right, Brian?'

'That's right!' he answers.

Kathy is tall and slim. She wears dark-rimmed glasses, and it looks to me like she must have been red-haired when she was younger. Her smile is so bright and inviting, and I realise that she is truly happy that I've appeared in their lives. Kathy turns to open the oven door to remove the roast beef for dinner. 'Will it be ready soon, Mummy?' Brian asks, still clinging to me. It's obvious that his mother simply adores him, looking at him with pride as he unabashedly displays his excitement at my visit. Brian is an only child and doesn't have any other family his age in London. He seems delighted to have discovered me. Maybe he hopes I can be like an elder sister to him. I love his accent and the way he looks directly at me when speaking to me. But he's not overly patient with this arrangement in the kitchen. Determined to have me to himself, he tugs me by the hand towards the sitting room, where Paddy waits patiently.

As soon as I'm seated, Brian plops himself comfortably on my knee, frequently smiling up at me as he fumbles with a toy car. Aunt Kathy joins us a minute later with tea. 'Maureen,' Paddy begins hesitantly, 'I didn't know about you. I mean, we didn't know you'd been born – not at all. I left Ireland very young, you see. And Annie, your mammy, was the oldest. She and Christy were closer in age, and they stayed behind.'

My emotions start to churn again as I listen to this, but I remain composed. Aunt Kathy listens from her chair in the corner, affirming Paddy's words with occasional nods of her head. My uncle talks a little about what it was like back then and how difficult times were. Annie and her brothers lost their parents, my grandparents, James and Mary Harte, to tuberculosis. They died not more than a year apart. Though nothing is mentioned, it suddenly strikes me that my mother named me after her own mother, Maureen meaning 'little Mary' in Irish. My concentration drifts for a moment, fighting yet another lump of deep sadness in my throat. My mother named me after her own mother. She must have loved me, then, but she couldn't keep me. I don't know how to feel about this.

Paddy goes on. 'It was everyone for themselves then, Maureen,' he says, looking directly at me. 'And, well, I got the hell out of there.'

My uncle has a simple and honest nature, and a soft-spoken, gentle manner about him. He often ends what he's said with a quiet laugh. Christy was gentle, too. We chat easily for a while, me avidly listening to stories of my family history as if I could never get enough. I learn that Uncle Paddy fought in the war in the Tank Corps of the British Army. He spent two years fighting the Germans across North Africa and survived to return to England but with chronic lung problems from exposure to toxic chemicals. He was away a lot, and Kathy tells me how difficult it was to conceive Brian – it took them nine years to have their much-adored little boy. It almost seems, as she shares this, that she's thinking how easily she might have raised me during what must have been long and often lonely years.

I keep my emotions in check for a time, but finally the tears start to fall. Not as bitterly as they had in Christy's parlour on Ringsend Road, but sadly and quietly as I resign myself to the facts. I try to express to my new-found family that I understand they never knew about me and what matters to me most is having found them now. I don't want them to feel guilty or awkward.

Changing the subject somewhat, Paddy praises me for how far I've come, saying how well I've done for myself, despite my beginnings. I gladly tell him about my time in England and of some of the trials I've been through. I feel a common bond with these other Hartes, something that is far removed from anything I've experienced before.

Some time later, Aunt Kathy informs us that dinner is ready. Brian is determined to take good care of his cousin, and he leaps from my lap and escorts me into the kitchen. 'Come on, Maureen,' he says. 'You're sitting next to me!'

During the meal, we don't talk much about the past. I feel like Uncle Paddy is unwilling to go too far back into it. In the short period since I discovered my uncles, I can see my own life more clearly and the reasons for what happened to me in a very different light. My mother's family were torn apart in such a brutal way. This was and is Ireland. When the family was broken to pieces by disease and poverty, they went where the work was. Every day people died of the consumption. Families disintegrated overnight. Poverty tore people apart, and unwanted and illegitimate children were thrown into orphanages and forgotten. Uncle Paddy was a survivor. He left, and he survived. My mother was not so lucky.

Kathy and I follow a skipping and still excited Brian back into the sitting room to join Paddy. Kathy takes out a box of old photos, removing a stack to sort through before handing the box over to Paddy. He goes through them until he finds one of Jimmy Harte, his brother and my other uncle here in London. Jimmy Harte and his wife Irene, a childless couple, live with Irene's two maiden aunts not far from here. Looking at the photo, I'm immediately struck by the resemblance between Uncle Jimmy and my mother. They share almost identical facial features. 'I'd love to meet them,' I say as I stare closely at the photo.

'Ah, you most certainly will, Maureen,' Paddy replies, with a sly glint in his eye as he glances at his wife.

Young Brian, perched on my knee all the while, is determined to get all the time he can with me. Suddenly, though, he makes a funny face, and then he's all arms and legs as he lets out a great sneeze. After looking down at my lap, he jumps up and flies out of the parlour, having left dollops of snot on my skirt. The poor child is simply mortified. By now, both Paddy and Kathy are laughing at their son's embarrassment. Kathy tries to stop her laughter as she follows Brian to assure him he hasn't permanently offended his new cousin. Paddy chuckles quietly. 'He's left a great load of snot on you, Maureen. That was nice of him.'

'Ah, sure, it's nothing really,' I say, laughing.

'Ah, he'll be back in soon,' Paddy says. 'He's too curious, I think, to stay away from you long.'

As I clean my skirt, Kathy manages to get Brian to come back into the room, and I give him a big smile to let him know that everything is fine. I laugh out loud as Kathy fusses over me, making certain that the small mess is cleaned up.

As we relax in the sitting room, looking at old photos, I think of how much warmth and sincerity both my uncles have displayed towards me. But despite discovering members of my family, my mother still remains a mystery to me. In a private part of myself, in a place I could never share with these lovely kind people, I curse those past times that made life so difficult.

My visit at Uncle Paddy's over, I travel back to the hostel with much to think about. Before leaving, I mention Uncle Jimmy and that I haven't heard from him. Aunt Kathy says they have written to Jimmy themselves, immediately after hearing from Christy, and that they're waiting to hear back. They suggest that I leave it with them to deal with. It will be better that way. And so I'll wait and hope for another positive reception at the home of Jimmy Harte, the man who looks so much like my mother.

Two weeks after my visit to Paddy Harte's, I receive a message from Aunt Kathy inviting me and Reg to join them at Uncle Jimmy's house. All the arrangements, as I expected, have been made through Aunt Kathy, which suggests to me that Jimmy Harte might not be as welcoming towards me as Christy and Paddy have been. My curiosity to meet more family wins me over, though, and I can't help but go. I'll be with Reg, Paddy and Kathy, which is reassuring. No matter what, I simply must see in person this man who looks so much like my mother. It will be the closest to her I'll ever get.

Jimmy Harte's house is in north London in an area called Edmonton. When Reg and I arrive, it is Irene, Jimmy's wife, who opens the door. Aunt Kathy, Paddy and Brian are already there, and Brian rushes out to greet us. My uncle Jimmy, I can see as we step in, is sitting comfortably in his armchair by the fire in his slippers. He stands and walks over to greet us, shaking hands with me and Reg before casually returning to his place by the fireside, his first duty of the visit over and done with.

The house belongs to Irene's family and two of her aunts,

unmarried spinsters who live here with them. Uncle Paddy had previously joked about Jimmy being pampered, with three women waiting on him and meeting him each night at the door with his slippers. It isn't long after we arrive when the two aunts walk into the room. They just stand there like stone statues, waiting to be introduced. They must be in their seventies but are both spry and fit looking. Greetings and introductions over with, they disappear back to where they came from.

While Irene and Kathy prepare evening tea in the kitchen, Reg and I stay in the sitting room with Uncle Jimmy, Paddy and Brian. It's a lovely room, with a beautiful fireplace, a mantelpiece with an old antique clock and quaint little china figurines displayed on it. At each end of the sofa are pretty antique tables, with more figurines and ornaments on them, centred delicately on lace doilies. More doilies are draped here and there over the back of the chairs and sofa.

After we're seated, Jimmy says very little to me, and I begin to feel uncomfortable. It is obvious that he isn't overjoyed at discovering his niece, showing up as I have to disturb the murky waters of the past and expecting some sign of acceptance. Is it too much to ask that he at least make a gesture of acceptance towards me? Even though I was born with the curse of illegitimacy on my head, I too am a part of this family. I never asked for things to turn out this way.

I force the thought aside, trying not to stare at my uncle. Without a doubt, he looks very much like Annie, with his heavy-set features and round face. As we sit chatting, I see expressions pass across his face that could be my mother's in the photos I've seen.

Eventually, he stiffly turns to face me. 'Well, Maureen, how are you getting along here in London? How long is it that you've been here now?'

'Gone five years,' I answer hesitantly.

This kind of small talk goes on as he asks me some general questions. 'Do you like living here? What part of London are you working in?' And so on. It is so casual we might be old acquaintances talking over an afternoon cup of tea and not long-lost family meeting for the first time.

Not once does Jimmy raise the subject of the past. He just sits there quietly withdrawn while Paddy and Reg talk about sport, the weather, cars and safe subjects that don't raise any ghosts. It doesn't surprise me. After all, it's the same reaction as Christy and Paddy had, just a bit more obvious. I begin to realise that I am the same in so many ways. I've never looked back since the age of sixteen. I was gone the first opportunity that came my way. Why would my three uncles think of Milltownpass with fondness, a place of so many painful memories? They regard their past in the same way that I do the orphanage – a place of ghosts that should be laid to rest. Don't expect regular invitations from Uncle Jimmy Harte.

❖ FORTY-SEVEN ❖

As the New Year begins, I start to look ahead and think more about the future. Some of the girls have moved on, finding work elsewhere and living in flats now. Am I ready for this? I watch as most of my friends slowly grow tired of the curfew and the restrictive lifestyle that's part of living at the hostel. But until they began to comment on getting restless and wanting to move on, I'd never considered it. I'm still entirely comfortable with a lifestyle where everything is controlled for me: meals, finances and living arrangements. And, most importantly, I'm never alone here, and I've never enjoyed being alone.

Margo, who's a store detective now, is getting restless and tiring of living in residence at the hostel. I've known this for a while. We are all getting older, but I can't help the pang of anxiety I feel whenever the subject of moving on comes up. Margo's mentioned Boots the Chemists, remarking that they're a good company to work for and that they pay good wages. I sit listening to Margo, agreeing with her wholeheartedly. I mention that I too have been pondering a change but go out of my way to state that I feel too afraid to make any decisions. 'It's not looking for another job that bothers me,' I explain. 'It's living alone that worries me.'

'I know, Maureen,' she answers. 'Now that you've explained your past, I do understand that, I really do. But for me, well, I'm getting to the point where I've got to try it. Really, it seems the natural thing to do. It will be nice to try living on my own for a change.'

'That's fine, Margo, but I'll never share a room with anyone else as long as I'm still here at Warwickshire. I'm going to leave when you leave.'

'What's stopping you from moving on yourself?' Before I can reply, she continues in her confident manner. 'Listen, Maureen, I know

409

Madeleine Wood is getting restless as well. Maybe she'll consider sharing a flat with you.'

'Do you really think so?'

'I do. You know Madeleine well enough from working with her in the shoe department. Tell you what, I'll think it over and then discuss it with her. I honestly do want to find a small flat of my own, somewhere in the West End. I really don't want to go too far, and I'm definitely going to apply at Boots for a position.'

Hearing Margo talk like this, I feel an irrational sense of loss, even a mild feeling of abandonment. I feel silly and childish for feeling the way I do. It all comes so easy to her, and it's not her fault that I'm so afraid of moving forward. 'Maybe, Margo,' I begin, fighting not to betray my insecurity, 'I could apply at Boots, too?'

'Why not, Maureen? I think we've outgrown living in residence at our age, and it is always good to try something new.' Yes, it's always good to try something new if you've been raised from birth to believe in yourself.

Something will come up. I've been through much worse, and I know that with God's help I'll make it through this change as well.

Margo left Warwickshire House without much fuss. She's doing well at a classy Boots location in the West End, and she has a nice little flat of her own close by. Before I could leave the hostel, though, I had to secure a job, so I decided to follow Margo's example and managed to find a position at Boots. It's not the same shop as the one she works at, and maybe that's just as well. God only knows what mischief the two of us would get ourselves into if we worked together.

Madeleine did agree to live with me, and after working out all the details we left Warwickshire House and moved into a flat close to the Clapham South Underground station.

I truly like Madeleine. She's extremely forthright, independent and confident. In that way, she's very much like Margo. It will be good for me to share a place with someone like her, and the two of us have a similar sense of humour. Our landlord is a former priest from Poland. A fifty-something man, he is, with thinning hair and a definite glint in his eye. Well, that's what Madeleine thought when we met him, but she can be a bit of a flirt. Though the bed-sitter flat was advertised as furnished, it is only sparsely so, with a basic sitting room, bathroom and a kitchen with a small gas stove. The few personal things we have brought with us add little to the bare look of the place. The sitting room where we sleep on a pull-out couch has two large windows that face out to the front of the house. There is an old bathtub in the small lavatory, and the only way to have a hot bath is to put a shilling in the meter, which then grudgingly surrenders half a tub of almost-hot water.

Madeleine works in the West End at a fine jewellery store, and we travel together to work each day. Life in the little flat is a huge change for us both. Without doubt, we miss the whole scene at Warwickshire: the constant knocking on the door to go out, all the different recreational facilities, listening to records in the gym and all the noise and constant activity. But now we are totally free from the restrictions of hostel living, and it's very enjoyable.

The biggest challenge for me now is that for the first time ever I'm responsible for all my basic needs: my rent, feeding myself, managing my money and more. But it will force me to become more independent. Neither of us are great cooks, and we certainly didn't learn to cook in the hostel, where all our meals were prepared for us. But we soon learn, and with necessity our new mother we have to get a little inventive. We buy a cookbook and work our way through its pages as if it was a foreign map. Though I would be content to bake pastries all the time, Madeleine suggests we try to learn some more practical dishes.

Both Madeleine and I love music, and recently we bought ourselves a portable record player so we can listen to all the latest hit records. One of our favourites is 'The Blue Tango', which we play frequently. One Sunday, we played the song so many times that by evening there was a loud knocking on our door. We opened it to find the landlord standing there on the landing, gesturing wildly as if he might tear his hair out. 'Why you play "The Blue Tango" twelve times?' he cried out to us in his broken English. 'Twelve times you play "The Blue Tango"! Why? Why?'

We apologised immediately and promised him we'd be quieter from then on. But as soon as the door was closed and his footsteps had gone down the stairs, Madeleine was already crying out in imitation "'Why you play 'The Blue Tango'? Why? Why?" Maureen, he must have been down there counting. "Once 'The Blue Tango', twice 'The Blue Tango', seven, eight, nine 'The Blue Tango'! Oh God, please, no more 'The Blue Tango'! Twelve enough, enough!'"

'Stop it, Madeleine!' I said, doubling over with laughter. 'Stop or we'll be looking for another place to live!'

The Boots where I work is a small shop with only eight full-time staff, near Leicester Square at the corner of Rupert Street and Berwick Street. My boss is Mr Chambers, a pleasant, quiet man in his early fifties. The Boots is next to Berwick Market, where the so-called barrow boys operate their stalls, selling fruit and vegetables and small clothing items, such as purses and scarves. The market is famous for the art of bargaining, and voices ring out all day as vendors and customers haggle over prices. The barrow boys are in a class of their own, dressing in long suit jackets and wearing their hair sleeked back in a style called 'the duck's arse'. They're rough in manner and very bold, speaking loudly in their strong accents. I feel a little afraid of them and not overly thrilled about the location of the shop.

It is my first week in the job, and Vera, one of the full-time employees, has been training me. In her late forties, she's been at Boots for seven years and knows the job very well. She's kind and patient, taking her time to teach me about different products and showing me where things are stored beneath the counter.

Vera motions me over to her. Curious, I walk over and stand close, wondering what her secretive manner is all about. 'This drawer here,' she begins, pointing to one just beneath the counter, 'is called the "naughty drawer".'

'Now, why is it called that, Vera?' I respond innocently.

Just then, the counter gets busy, and she doesn't have time to explain the mysterious drawer. I follow along to help her with the rush of customers. As people keep coming up to our counter, Vera says, 'Maureen, right now it's too busy. As soon as I get a moment, I'll show you the naughty drawer, all right?'

'All right, Vera,' I answer, although I remain mystified. What's inside it that could be so naughty?

Ten minutes later, Vera hurries over to where I stand waiting by the naughty drawer. 'All right, Maureen, the naughty drawer.' She goes on to explain all its contents. It's full of contraceptive items, mostly: things such as condoms, spermicidal gels, ointments and the like. 'Anti-pregnancy products,' Vera adds, with a smile and a wink.

'Honestly, Vera,' I reply. 'I'm glad you explained all this to me.'

Vera moves off to another counter, suggesting I familiarise myself with the naughty drawer while I have a moment. I know next to nothing about these things. I know that sex leads to pregnancy. I'm not that daft. So all these naughty products are to allow sex while avoiding pregnancy, is that it? And all the naughty items are kept apart because they're naughty? It's all a bit confusing. My friends never discuss sex with me. It's just the way we all are, so I certainly haven't learned anything from them. Maybe they're just as ignorant about it as I am.

Vera asks me to cover the middle counter during the lunch hour. She thinks me confident enough by now to serve customers alone, and I know most of the products and where they're stored. But I've not had a chance to learn all the different products sold at this middle counter. Deciding to do this now, I note razor blades, shaving cream and some colognes and deodorants for men on the shelves. I'm in the middle of doing this when a young man walks up to me. Without looking directly at me and keeping his voice low, he says politely but nervously, 'A pack of Durex, please.'

Ah, Gillette – they're men's razors. I just saw them a moment ago. I'll try to practise a good professional voice with this young man. 'Yes, sir, we have them in different sizes, tens and twenties, with swivelling heads and in blue and red. Which would you like, sir?'

He flushes deeply and seems uncomfortable. 'Durex,' he says, a low edge of urgency in his voice. 'I said a package of Durex!'

Oh dear, he's not after razors. 'Just a moment, sir. I'll ask another girl.'

I turn to see Vera at the far counter, just getting back from her lunch break. I hurry over, not wanting to keep the young gentleman waiting. 'Vera, I'm so glad you're back. This young man at my counter, he's asking . . .'

'What young man, Maureen?' she asks, perplexed. 'There's no one at your counter.'

I look over to where he had been moments before. 'He's gone? He was there a moment ago.'

It doesn't take long for Vera to figure it all out. She finds it terribly funny, and I blush deeply as I put all the clues together. 'What he wanted was in the naughty drawer, Maureen!' As I re-enact what happened, we're both laughing so much that Mr Chambers gives us one of his chastising looks from the dispensary. Perched in his world of medicines, he wears half-lens eyeglasses for filling out the prescriptions. He stands there in his white lab smock most of the day, never bothering us as long as we do our job well. But now he gives us a long, silent gaze, with his chin on his chest, his face expressionless and his two eyes finding us from above the half-lenses. It says more than any words could. And Vera makes sure that I learn the difference between Gillette and Durex!

❖ FORTY-EIGHT ❖

The summer months soon pass, and the autumn rolls in like a slow tide. The London skies are greyer and the air damper. Without fail, as surely as the bitter frost will mantle the Irish midlands this time of year, the London fog will come. It is November now, and seven years ago this month I arrived here in London. But these wonderful times seem to be slowly ending, and all my friends are thinking of settling down. I don't feel quite the way they do, and far from resolving the deep restlessness that's always been a part of me I feel it close to the surface again and demanding attention. Though I now know what this feeling is and why I have it, I never really have a clue just when and how it will affect me. I can only say that I have always felt different from my friends in this way – a little bit off to the side, a little way behind them and always grappling with the nagging worry that when this all ends I'll be left on my own again. I shouldn't fret so much, though. I still have Reg. Where will it all lead to, and where will everyone go?

I rarely meet with Maggie. She is still working at Hackney Hospital. The last time we spoke on the phone she had met a young English sailor named Robert and had been seeing a lot of him. She seems to be quite happy. In truth, after our trip back to the orphanage, we haven't shared a close connection together here in London. We became very different people after leaving the orphanage as young girls, though I often wonder had Katy made it work here whether that would have brought us closer together. Neither Maggie nor I have received a letter from her since she went back to Ireland.

During an evening out with Reg at the lavish Grasshopper Inn in Kent, we sit relaxing in a private booth, sipping rich coffee with our dessert. I see his eyes light up as he reaches into his pocket to take out a small blue box. 'What's that, Reg?' I ask playfully, trying to peer into his closed hand to see. Has he bought yet another piece of jewellery for me? I'm forever telling him not to.

To my absolute shock, he opens it slowly and asks, 'Will you marry me, love?'

I'm dumbstruck by this. In the beautiful little box is a breathtaking five-diamond engagement ring. I can only stare at the glittering ring as he removes it, almost afraid to touch it let alone slip it on my finger. 'Reg, it's so beautiful! I don't know what to say. It's just so . . . beautiful!'

'Well, you gotta say something, love. Give me some sort of answer!' He laughs at my shock and my stunned expression. 'Well, will you marry me, Maureen Harte?'

I hear myself answer, 'Yes, Reg,' so easily and without a thought in the world. I'm totally swept away by the sheer romance of the moment that I can't think about anything else. Reg is delighted, and clapping his hands together he says, 'Well, let me see it on your hand, love. That's what it's for.'

'I never expected this,' I say. 'What a surprise.'

Still in shock, I slip the glittering ring onto my finger and hold it out for him to see. I feel truly special at this moment to think that Reg wants to marry me. I look into his eyes, smiling tenderly at him and seeing his own eyes glitter with delight and love. I see someone who really cares about me, and I become overjoyed and emotional. I reach out to take his hand. 'Oh, Reg, thank you so very much. This is so incredible!' I look down at the beautiful ring again – not just one diamond but five beautiful glittery stones on my finger.

'It looks beautiful on you, Maureen. Perfect!' He takes my hand and kisses it. 'Now I can call you my fiancée. How does that sound?'

'It sounds . . . different. I mean, it's wonderful. I just didn't expect this, not in a thousand years.' I gaze at the ring on my finger, turning it about and letting the soft light play off it. Five diamonds. Five beautiful jewels.

But as I gaze at the beautiful ring, an inner voice begins to wonder at this and ask questions. Why does Reg want to marry me? I've never thought about this as a possibility. I've never thought about things going this far. But I quickly push these thoughts aside. Reg and I will make it work somehow. At the moment, I have eyes only for the ring, and I feel such joy at being engaged. How special and important this makes me feel. That seems to be enough for me for now, and both of us are extremely happy about our engagement. I keep looking down at my hand the rest of the night, the five glittering diamonds putting me into an almost hypnotic trance. Is this really happening to me? Never in my entire life have I owned anything so beautiful. I can't even afford costume jewellery.

Margo, Abby and I go out to celebrate my engagement. My friends can't get enough of the ring, and they all examine it intensely. They too think it is gorgeous, but when Abby asks me about the religion question and whether Reg is going to convert I will only say that we haven't given it any thought yet. Then Margo voices her concerns that I'm rushing into something too soon. I brush these concerns aside casually, repeating again that a date hasn't been set and that we have no plans to wed immediately.

Dismissing the serious questions, we all continue to chatter away about our relationships. Abby shares with us that though she and John are quite serious about one another, it will be a couple of years at least before marriage plans are discussed. She and Margo haven't a notion of settling down, not quite yet anyway, but I know they're both thinking about it. We continue to celebrate all our exciting news well into the evening, enjoying each other's good fortune and making plans for the future.

With Reg and me newly engaged, I can hardly refuse his offer to meet his parents for a Christmas Day celebration at their place, which is somewhere in the East End. His younger brother William and his wife Barbara, whom we already know, and another brother Allan and their only sister Delia will be there. After a long courtship of two years, I will finally meet Reg Walker's parents. It's partly been my own fault. I've always found reasons to avoid it, mostly because I worried that I'd be asked about my past. And Reg has never pushed the matter, seemingly content to leave his parents out of the picture – until now, that is.

I awake early on Christmas morning to prepare myself for the visit to Reg's parents, making sure I look my very best for the occasion. Meeting new people is still a concern for me, although it's not quite as bad as it was three or four years ago. Reg is to formally announce our engagement during dinner, although his parents might already know. I'm not sure. He does everything like that with a lot of class, always toasting birthdays and such when we're out at nice restaurants. I know how much this means to him, and I've not seen him so nervous in a long time. It won't help for me to show him how nervous I am.

Christmas Day this year is a rather typical one for December in London, and a depressing blanket of fog lies dirty and wet over the sprawling city. In Reg's Aston Martin, we set out for his family's home in the East End. While he talks excitedly about the day ahead, I sit quietly with my thoughts, feeling uneasy about the visit. I know I look fine. Reg's compliment when he picked me up assured me that my efforts had paid off, but my worries are of a different nature. After driving for about half an hour, we arrive in front of a row of council houses, where Reg grew up. 'Well, here we are, Maureen,' he announces as he pulls the car to a stop. 'This is the place where your darling Reg was reared!'

I look around at the rows of bleak cement houses without any lawns or greenery anywhere near them. Further up the road are apartments with lines of washing hanging out everywhere, criss-crossing each other in strange, chaotic patterns of colour against the grey December morning. At the front door, the familiar face of Reg's brother William appears, and he greets us with a large welcoming grin. With the same sense of humour as Reg, he teases his brother about the pending announcement of our engagement. 'Well, this is it, mate! This is it!'

'Get out of it!' Reg brushes by him, playfully knocking him aside. 'Don't mind him, Maureen. Well, you know what this geezer's like!'

We go into the sitting room, where some of the family are already celebrating. Reg introduces me to his father, who gets up from the fireside where he'd been enjoying a pint of ale. 'Hello, Maureen. It's a pleasure to finally meet you. Reg's told us so much about you. You're very welcome here, and Happy Christmas!'

'Thank you. It's lovely to meet you, Mr Walker. Happy Christmas.'

After meeting all the others, Reg takes me to the kitchen to meet his mother, who is preparing Christmas dinner. Her greeting is far from warm, though, and she barely raises her head as Reg introduces me. She's just busy, I convince myself as we join the family again in the sitting room, making small talk and exchanging pleasantries. Christmas decorations cover the home, and without a doubt I sense a real Christmas spirit here and a family closeness. We spend quite a while in the front room before eating, and though Reg's mother comes in and out she seems content to stay in the kitchen. The men talk amongst themselves, and Reg's father says very little to me. But Barbara tries to put me at ease by coming to stand with me now and then, making casual conversation, which I'm grateful for.

Finally, at close to half-past three, we sit down to a beautiful Christmas dinner. On the table beside each plate are Christmas crackers, and Reg has to explain to me what they are. Each little cylinder is wrapped in colourful pretty paper decorated for the season. With one person holding each end of the cracker it's pulled apart and makes a bang, then some little trinket or novelty falls out. Inside the one I pull with Reg is a little folded tissue hat like a crown. I think this tradition is fun, and I begin to feel myself getting into the spirit of Christmas. The meal is delicious, and after a while my nerves settle, and I relax more. There are the usual toasts I had expected from Reg, many it seems directed at his mother, complimenting her on the beautiful Christmas dinner. She smiles at each toast made to her, basking in the attention from Reg and seeming accustomed to it. The rest of the meal goes well, and finally tea and Christmas cake are brought in.

Eventually, whether by plan or not, William proposes a toast to mark the occasion of our engagement. Glasses are raised and cheers sound all around. Everyone turns to us in expectation of a formal announcement now that it's been mentioned. I don't open my mouth, smiling and enjoying this playful teasing of Reg by his family. I'll allow him his moment. He stands, beaming proudly at me as he squeezes my hand. 'Maureen and I haven't set a date yet, but I would like, now, in the presence of my family on this lovely Christmas Day, to announce to you all that I have asked Maureen for her hand in marriage, and she has accepted.'

There are more cheers and toasts all round the table, but as I glance just for an instant at his mother I see her mouth is set in a thin line of disapproval as she looks directly at Reg. Though I feel uncomfortable, I brush it off, telling myself it's only my nerves getting the better of me again. But then in the middle of one of Reg's jokey comments, I suddenly feel his mother's eyes on me. I glance up as she begins to speak, raising her voice just above the lively conversation at the table. 'No son of mine is going to marry an Irish Catholic,' she says, looking right into my eyes. Nothing I have ever heard in my life has stunned me more.

There is a sudden deathly silence at the table. It is broken only when Reg, as if unable to believe what he's just heard, says, 'Mum, what are you saying?'

Her tone is casual, one of a mother scolding a boy who should know better. 'You heard me, Reg! I don't want you marrying an Irish Catholic, full stop!'

I cannot find my voice at this point. I'm literally stunned silent by the hatred I can see so clearly etched on her face. One thing flashes through my head, and that is that she hates me for two reasons and two reasons only: because I'm Irish and because I'm Catholic. As William tries to intervene and make sense of the situation, I find my voice. I stand quietly and amazingly cool, determined not to lose my dignity in front of this woman. 'Reg, I would like to leave immediately.' What if she knew I was illegitimate as well? I walk from the room with Reg following behind.

The drive home to my flat is the most difficult situation Reg and I have ever faced. With that one statement by his mother, it is as if this fantasy life with Reg has shattered in an instant. He is extremely upset by his mother's behaviour and cannot apologise enough. She is a simple woman, he pleads, a very simple woman who has no idea what she's talking about. I honestly feel sorry for him because of how terribly ashamed he is about the whole incident. But I can only stare out of the window, reliving the scene and her words. It is obvious the power she has over him. If he chooses to marry me, the price will be her acceptance of him, and God knows what else lurks in a head like that. I know then as I glance at the diamond ring on my finger that it is over between me and Reg and that our relationship will not survive what has happened this Christmas Day.

The New Year comes, and I continue to date Reg, but things aren't the same. Nothing is said openly about the engagement, but the incident at Christmas has forced me to rethink the idea of marriage. I don't need these kinds of problems in my life, and if marrying Reg will bring only more, then I can't see it working. I am still very innocent and had no idea how some English people felt about the Irish living in England. I'd never run into anything like this in my life or had any experience with it, to be looked down upon for being Irish and Catholic. However, I have seen 'For Rent' signs in houses with 'No Irish need apply' written underneath. I just assumed it was because of their drinking, not their religion. Living in a hostel for the past three and a half years and hanging around with the Irish crowd who were all Catholic like myself kept me isolated from such knowledge. I work every day with English girls, and not one of them has made me feel less than them or looked down upon. I've never felt any different from them. How my eyes have suddenly been opened and in such a terribly destructive way for me and Reg.

By the middle of the summer, we both agree to break off the engagement. I give Reg back his ring, telling him that it's the best thing if we both go our own way. We part good friends, and I thank him for his kindness in helping me find my family. I will be for ever grateful to him for that, more than he will ever know. He's made me promise in that sincere grateful way he's always had that if I ever need his help for any reason at all, I'm to call him without hesitation. I promise him that I will.

It feels terribly lonely to be leaving Reg, but I feel deep down that it's the right thing to do. I've grown used to the good times with him, and in a way he's been a kind of father figure to me. When I said I would marry him, I honestly felt deeply for him. He swept me off my feet with the diamond ring, and no one has ever treated me as well as Reg has. I will always remember him as a kind and funny person, and I'm thankful over and over again for having known him.

The night we break everything off and say goodbye for the last time, Reg drops me off right outside the entrance to my flat as he's always done. Each time he did this in the past, he would sit in his shiny Aston Martin and wait until I went in, and we'd wave goodnight a final time at the door. Tonight, though, I just stand there and watch him drive off until he's out of sight. Upstairs, the flat is quiet with Madeleine out somewhere. So what now, Maureen Harte?

I sit down and ponder the past years with Reg. I almost let the glamorous lifestyle take over when I agreed to Reg's marriage proposal. Regardless, it is over, and a new phase in my life has begun. I feel more than anything the same old restlessness, and I'm growing tired of the whole London scene. I will, with God's help, pull through whatever lies ahead of me.

❖ FORTY-NINE ❖

B oth Madeleine and I are feeling the same way about staying in London these past few months. There are thousands of young people spreading out all over the world these days. Many are Irish. The world has had almost ten years to rebuild after the war, and there is a lot happening in far away places. We are young, and it's exciting to think like this, planning new adventures in new places and starting all over again.

So when Madeleine mentions one evening about going to New Zealand, we both discuss it for a few minutes and agree that it sounds like a wonderful idea. And just like that it is settled. Madeleine and I will emigrate to New Zealand. The next day, we begin the legal proceedings with New Zealand House, the embassy in London, for our visas. We know it will take at least three or four months to process our applications, and in the meantime we carry on as usual. We continue on with our social lives, our jobs, our attempts at cooking and our clowning around. At the weekends, we still love to play 'The Blue Tango' or some other hit all day on a Sunday until we're told off.

However, just before we expect to receive our papers, love gets in the way. Madeleine meets a young man named Roy O'Connor and falls madly in love with him. A week hasn't passed after this declaration of love when another announcement follows: Madeleine might want to delay taking off to New Zealand for a little bit. She is apologetic and contrite, but I know how truly smitten she is with Roy, and I'm pleased to see her so happy. I can only laugh affectionately at her lovesickness, asking her who does she think she's fooling. She's going nowhere, and it's written all over her face. I am happy for them both despite my own loss. Madeleine has finally met someone she likes a great deal, and that is the most important thing.

I decide that there is no way I'm going to venture off to New Zealand alone, and I cancel my plans. It is too far and exotic a destination for me, and I'm not going to go without the wise and worldly Madeleine. She would have made it an adventure. But this Roy O'Connor has stolen her heart, and fate, it seems, is again pushing me another way.

With the plans for New Zealand aborted, Madeleine and I decide to try living on our own. The room I choose is near Charing Cross station, close to where I work and right opposite Big Ben and the Houses of Parliament. It's small and affordable, a little furnished bed-sitter on the top floor of a four-storey house. The main room has a pullout couch to sleep on, and from my window I can look out at the parliament buildings below. I often stand there watching the people come and go – that old habit of mine. I share a bathroom and kitchen with other lodgers. In the bathroom outside my door is another meter, like the one in the flat I shared with Madeleine. It robs me of a shilling every time I use the tub to bathe. As if that weren't bad enough, my room is heated by a little gas heater that loves to eat all my money, too. By November, the unusually bitter winter gives the thing a huge appetite – it feeds on sixpence at a time. On cold days, it gluts itself on five of my hard-earned shillings.

On many a cold winter night, as I huddle over the hungry little heater, I think of my future and what might lie ahead. Almost making it to New Zealand has left me with the bug to do something, to go somewhere, to surrender in a big way to my burning restlessness. Whatever that future is, it will take me away from London, that much I know. Never once in my wildest imagination have I considered returning to Ireland to live. There is nothing whatsoever there to lure me back, and, besides, I want to try an entirely new country and start again. America has often been an option for young Irish people seeking their fortune, but it's difficult to get a visa, especially when I've no relative to sponsor me.

Canada comes to mind. Many young Irish people have gone there, and it has all the benefits of America but without the strict entry regulations. The idea of moving to Canada grows on me, and not long after my twenty-fourth birthday I formally apply to Canada House for an entry visa. I complete the necessary forms relatively easily, and it will take six to seven months to process my application.

To save extra money, I pick up a part-time job as an usherette at the Odeon cinema on Tottenham Court Road, close to my day job. I work there three nights a week and most weekends. The one pound an hour I earn as an usherette will help me save the sixty pounds needed for my passage to Canada. I love being an usherette. It feels like a glamorous job, and we have great fun with the courting couples who come to the shows! With a quick flick of the torch beam, we try to time our spotlight on them just as they're about to kiss in the darkness!

After three months of working two jobs, I'm steadily getting my money together for Canada. But the pace of trying to keep up the two jobs begins to wear me down. How long can I keep this up?

I stand before the Odeon manager for our pre-shift uniform inspection. My eyes go blurry for a moment from fatigue. Just as Mr Case is passing, my eyes go blurry again. Then I hear his words dimly, sounding far away. 'Miss Harte, are you quite well? Miss Harte . . .' The room spins around me, then the manager spins, then two of him spin and I fall to the floor and into complete blackness.

When I come to in Mr Case's office, he suggests I take time off to see a doctor. I'm full of apologies and promises that I won't faint any more on the job. He looks at me closely and says, 'Miss Harte, you just blacked out. You fainted! This isn't normal. You should see a doctor! I could arrange to reduce your schedule a little and . . .'

'Oh, I'll be fine, Mr Case. I'm sure of it. I'll be fine.'

'No, Miss Harte, I don't agree that you're fine, and I can't have you collapsing in the aisles.' He decides to send me home and insists that I take my weekend shift off and see a doctor.

I wobble out of the Odeon on Tottenham Court Road and wearily find my way back to my place at Charing Cross. I weep alone in my room, the deep musical tones of Big Ben sounding nine times outside my window as I wallow in my misery. Normally so soothing for me, the chimes do nothing to ease the terrible worry about my passage money. And the way I felt when I came to in Mr Case's office seemed to bring back every hurt, sickness and sore I ever had in the orphanage. Feeling ill like that has terrified me. I can't escape the illogical fear that illness will lead to being taken away and locked up.

Despite my promises to the contrary, the fainting spells continue: I'm carried out of mass twice. I become very worried about fainting while on my own in my room and maybe hitting my head or worse, so I eventually decide to go see a doctor.

'Well, Miss Harte,' he says. 'You are experiencing these spells of fainting because you're anaemic.'

'What does that mean?' I ask, fearful of having to take time off work and having no other means of paying my rent and bills.

'It means that you must stop working the second job and begin to take iron pills immediately. It's a special formula that I'll prescribe – not the brands off the shelf.'

'But I can't stop my job at the Odeon, doctor!' I cry. 'I'm trying to get to Canada. I need to save the passage, and I . . .'

'Miss Harte, listen to me. I understand your concerns, but if you do not take care of your health, you will get rapidly worse and you won't make it to Canada at all. Take care of this problem first, and then see how you are. But I'm afraid I cannot allow you to return to both jobs.'

As a result, I vow to curb my social life as much as possible. I am going to Canada, and nothing is going to stop me.

Seven months after applying, I receive written confirmation from Canada House that I've been accepted, as well as the special visa required to land and travel temporarily through the USA to Canada. The only thing left to do is choose a date of departure and book my ticket. I decide on the nineteenth of January, 1955, only two months from now. I place a deposit to secure a spot in a berth on the RMS *Queen Mary*, a true luxury liner. The voyage across the Atlantic will take at least six days, and I'm booked in to share a berth with three other persons: two going to America and the other heading all the way to Toronto, Canada. This is great news, and I'm pleased I won't be lonely during the Atlantic crossing. The agent assured me that there is great entertainment each evening, including cabaret shows and even ballroom dancing. We will set sail from Southampton and stop in Cherbourg to pick up more passengers before crossing the Atlantic to New York. Imagine, being able to see even a little of France! I'll get a glimpse of New York City, too. I'm so thrilled and excited about this big adventure ahead of me, but nervous and anxious as well.

During my final weeks in London, I receive very sad news in a letter from Mrs Burke. Mrs Hughes has passed away at the age of eighty-five. She died a month ago, although Mrs Burke doesn't say exactly how. What a remarkable lady to have lasted all these years. It is a bit strange to receive this news now, just when I'm about to leave England. It almost seems as though Mrs Hughes is telling me that this is a good time to move on. I do have ties here, it's true – my two uncles and my first cousin – but they're not enough to stop the restlessness in me. Both my mother and my foster mother are gone, and it's time for me to move forward into my own future.

In many ways, Mrs Hughes was the most present connection I had to my birth thanks to those three years of my life when I had a family and was loved. I have no memories of those early years, but I feel them in every cell of my body. The love that I was given by people who would have raised me had tragedy not struck is in every fibre of my being. I feel it in the faith I never lost in the orphanage and in the faith I've kept since. Though it is true that I was never able to truly connect with Mrs Hughes later in my life, when the deep damage of the orphanage had been done, I shall never forget her.

I sit down right away and write two final letters to Ireland: one to Mrs Burke, with some words about Mrs Hughes' passing, and the other to Reverend Mother Brendan. I tell the reverend mother of my plans to go to Canada, adding simply that things haven't worked out between me and Reg. I don't want her to ask questions in any return correspondence.

The evening before I'm to leave for Southampton and the waiting *Queen Mary*, my friends take me out to dinner for a going-away celebration at the good old Lyon's Corner House restaurant. Abby and Margo have arranged it all. Madeleine, Izzy, two girls from my job at Boots and, to my delight, Maggie have come to see me off. Our get-together is both a sad and joyful occasion, and our reminiscing about the old days in Warwickshire House and Bourne & Hollingsworth is loud and hilarious. All the funny stories come up and are relived, tall tales about wild nights out and about the many silly things that we got up to in the hostel. We relive each one with laughter and much fondness.

While the others carry on telling their endless tales and stories, I chat quietly with Maggie. She proudly shows me a picture of her sailor boyfriend Robert, explaining that he's away at sea at present. He is short and kind-looking, with light-blond hair, and by the way she gazes at his photo it seems she's quite in love with him. I know Maggie feels a little out of place here tonight, as I'm the only one she really knows. She has come for my sake, and I'm very touched by this. For many reasons, there isn't a lot left for us to say to one another. Through necessity, we bonded over a shared history, but now that we're both grown up we have little left in common.

However, we will always be connected because of what we endured. There's something in that, something sad. Maggie, like Katy and Lucy, and even poor Colleen, was there with me in that terrible place for those long years, and without her and the rest of them I know I would not be who I am today. All of us will carry the indescribable experience of the industrial school far into the future with us, no matter where we go and no matter how much we change.

Maggie leaves early, and as I move forward to hug her she stiffens at the open display of affection and parting emotion. 'Maureen, I hope you'll be happy in Canada, and maybe one day we'll see each other again,' she says, fighting to get the words out.

'Thank you so much for coming to see me off. I will think of you, and I hope you and Robert get along great and that he's good to you. I'll never forget you, Maggie, never.' With a shy wave to the others, she leaves the restaurant. I watch her move away into the night, feeling very strongly at this moment that I will never see her again.

At the end of the night, when everyone is quiet and my goodbyes have yet to be said, my friends present me with a silver boot for good luck. It's a heavy old-fashioned elf's boot, with a square toe bent up slightly. 'Ye Old Lucky Boot' is engraved on it, and I laugh when I notice a huge bunion. 'This will bring you good luck,' Abby promises.

I tell them I will cherish it, and then my tears fall uncontrollably as I look around at my dear friends. I might never see them again, and the reality becomes too much to bear. When the time comes for our final goodbyes, I cry even harder, struggling to find the words to thank them all for dinner and my gift. I try to tell them how much their friendship has meant to me. Margo pulls me out of it with her wit, telling me that I'll spoil my good looks if I keep crying like this. 'You must look good for this big trip ahead of you, Maureen. Come on now, stop it.'

There are more tight hugs and final goodbyes in the chill outside the Corner House, the place where we've all gathered so many times, talking the hours away and laughing until our sides ached. 'Go!' I tell them all finally. 'Just go. You'll only make me worse.' They walk away voicing 'good luck' and 'we'll be sure to stay in touch' and all the usual heartfelt human promises that pertain to somewhere in the future and the unknown.

Every step back to my room through the damp night feels like a slow dream as my thoughts drift from the happy to the sad, from excitement about a new beginning to deep feelings of loss over all that I must leave behind. I have planned and worked hard to get my passage money together, and I have done my best to face those things that haven't worked out for me in London. Even finding my family is not enough to kill the terrible restlessness inside me. But I will always keep in touch with them, as I have promised.

The ride home on the tube is quiet. The train is mostly empty, and the familiar stations seem desolate, with few people about. I think of my friends, and wish that I could be like them: content and settled and able to stay still and set down roots. Almost everyone I know in London is going steady with someone, easily moving forward and thinking of settling down. And here I am off again, this time to Canada and to yet another new start.

As the train moves beneath the streets of London, I know I am taking away with me memories of some of the best times that I will likely ever have. I think of the glamorous nights at the Lyceum, the laughs and the lavish lifestyle I shared with Reg. I think of Margo, Abby, Madeleine and Izzy, and all those dear friends with whom I shared a life so far removed from where I came from. I have a precious treasure trove of memories to cherish.

From Charing Cross station, I walk slowly home to my little room for one final night in London. Upstairs, the room will be cold, and the hungry little gas heater will clamour greedily for sixpence when I get in.

My luggage lies on the floor beside my couch, packed and ready to go. I undress for bed and get into my flannel nightdress. Then I check a final time that all my paperwork is in order, that my money is safely packed and that I'm not leaving anything behind in the room. The train from Euston Station is an early one, and I'll need to give myself some extra time in the morning. The *Queen Mary* is not going to sail without me on board.

I put sixpence in the gas heater, and pull out the couch, although I'm not at all tired. I walk about the room for a little before wandering over to stand at my window, restlessness filling me as I look out over the parliament buildings and Big Ben. It is late now, much later than I would normally be awake. I watch the famous tower dreamily, as Big Ben chimes twelve times to mark the midnight hour. How can I do anything other than reflect tonight on all that has happened to me since the morning of my leaving day when I stood at my window in the dormitory?

As the last toll fades in the still night, I stay there at the window looking out. I feel removed and distant from this place now, as if it is very far away from me, as if I've already left. Can a person's life be planned or fated ahead of time, I wonder as I recall the Christmas parcel from Mrs Hughes when I was thirteen. So many miracles have happened to and for me, and so much of it has been beyond anything I could've controlled. Mrs Hughes' parcel changed my life for ever, and it led to me solving the riddle of my early years before the orphanage. I think of Sister Brendan's prayers for me and for all the orphans gone out into the world. I think of Mrs Burke, who always encouraged me to hold my head up and walk with pride when I knew nothing but shame. Mrs O'Neill and Julia; Mrs Davies and Reg: all these people have come and gone, and yet how very deeply they've affected me.

In my nightdress pocket, I hold the little photo Mrs Hughes gave me just before I left for England. I take it out, far from sleepy as I continue to pace the little room. I look at the photo. It's me but in what had been another life, and what might have been another life but wasn't. The tears fall as I look at the little girl with her hand up to her mouth, so soon to be taken to the orphanage. That other world will always remain with me. It is who I was and who I am, and it will be part of who I become. I let the tears fall freely now, not bothering to wipe them away. They are not bitter tears; they are just tears of life, of joy and suffering, of regret and hope and things that only God understands.

I finally get into bed as Big Ben booms out a single chime at one in the morning. I pull the covers over me and close my eyes. I try to sleep, but my thoughts race on, spinning through the years. I've always believed that someone or something was guiding me, showing me the way and protecting me. Was it the nuns? Was it my mother, Annie Harte, long dead now and only a face frozen for ever in old photos? When your mother dies, the one who brought you into this world, some part of her stays to watch over you in times of trouble or when you want to give up. Yes, I believe that very much.

No matter what a person is or where they come from, his or her life is lived with people and for people. Life has no real meaning unless it is shared. This is what I have learned, and this is what I will cherish and take with me. So many people have helped me make it to this little room in London, hours before I'm set to move across the world and begin another life. In my short years, I have seen terrible suffering. I have seen it in the eyes of Colleen Carey, who was beaten to madness and forgotten. Colleen never lived to waltz at the Lyceum or to date a young man or to know love or to open a parcel or wear make-up or to experience what it feels like to be cared about. This was because Colleen was labelled illegitimate and in this way made illegitimate. What I saw, in the dormitory the night before they took her away, was very real and very legitimate.

Katy Fallon was beautiful and bright, and because she was labelled illegitimate she became illegitimate and had the flame in her soul snuffed out. Katy will never dance joyously under a swirling ball of light. She will never run through the streets with friends laughing and shouting with the sheer joy of being alive.

If I could have, I would have saved them all, given them some of the life that was so freely given to me by others. I can't do that, but I can remember them. Yes, I will remember them, and I will go back to the orphanage again one day. I will never forget those grey buildings so hidden from the world, just beyond the bend in the road outside the little village of Newtownforbes. I will remember, and perhaps one day the world will know.

As Big Ben strikes two, my weary eyes finally close. How I will miss that soothing sound outside my window when I leave in the morning.